Christ's Humanity in Current and Ancient Controversy: Fallen or Not?

Christ's Humanity in Current and Ancient Controversy: Fallen or Not?

E. Jerome Van Kuiken

LONDON • NEW YORK • OXFORD • NEW DELHI • SYDNEY

T&T CLARK
Bloomsbury Publishing Plc
50 Bedford Square, London, WC1B 3DP, UK
1385 Broadway, New York, NY 10018, USA

BLOOMSBURY, T&T CLARK and the T&T Clark logo are
trademarks of Bloomsbury Publishing Plc

First published in 2017
Paperback edition first published in 2019

© E. Jerome Van Kuiken, 2017

A catalogue record for this book is available from the British Library.

A catalog record for this book is available from the Library of Congress.

ISBN: HB: 978-0-5676-7555-2
PB: 978-0-5676-8643-5
ePDF: 978-0-5676-7557-6
ePub: 978-0-5676-7556-9

Typeset by Deanta Global Publishing Services, Chennai, India

To find out more about our authors and books visit
www.bloomsbury.com and sign up for our newsletters.

Contents

Abbreviations

Agon.	*De agone christiano*
AMOECT	*Adv. Marcionem* (Oxford Early Christian Texts)
An.	*De anima*
ANF	*The Ante-Nicene Fathers*
Antirrh. adv. Apol.	*Antirrheticus adversus Apolinarium*
CD	*Church Dogmatics*
C. Apoll.	*Contra Apollinarem*
C. Ar.	*Contra Arianos*
C. Eunom.	*Contra Eunomium* by Nyssen
C. Gent.	*Contra gentes*
C. Jul.	*Contra Julianum*
C. Jul. op. imp.	*Contra secundam Juliani responsionem imperfectum opus*
Carn. Chr.	*De carne Christi*
Coll. Max.	*Collatio cum Maximino Arianorum*
CW	*The Collected Works of Edward Irving*
Dial.	*Dialogus cum Tryphone*
DSCHT	*Dictionary of Scottish Church History & Theology*
Enchir.	*Enchiridion*
Ep.	*Epistula*
Ep. Adelph.	*Epistula ad Adelphium*
Ep. Epict.	*Epistula ad Epictetum*
Ep. Eust.	*Epistula ad Eustathiam*
Ep. Max.	*Epistula ad Maximum*
Ep. Serap.	*Epistula ad Serapionem*
Ep. Theoph.	*Epistula ad Theophilum*

Epid.	*Epideixis tou apostolikou kērygmatos*
ET	English Translation
Expl. XII cap.	*Explicatio Duodecim Capitum*
Fid.	*De fide*
Fid. symb.	*De fide et symbolo*
FC	The Fathers of the Church: A New Translation
Fund.	*Contra epistulam Manichaei quam vocant Fundamenti*
Haer.	*Adv. haereses*
Hom. Eccl.	*Homiliae in Ecclesiastes*
Hom. op.	*De hominis opificio*
HTR	*Harvard Theological Review*
IJST	*International Journal of Systematic Theology*
In Jo. Ev.	*In Johannis Evangelium*
Inc.	*De incarnatione*
Inc. unigen.	*De incarnatione unigeniti*
Incarn.	*De incarnationis dominicae sacramento*
JECS	*Journal of Early Christian Studies*
JTS (NS)	*Journal of Theological Studies* New Series
KD	*Die Kirchliche Dogmatik*
LFC	A Library of Fathers of the Holy Catholic Church: Anterior to the Division of the East and West
Marc.	*Adversus Marcionem*
Nat. bon.	*De natura boni contra Manichaeos*
NICNT	New International Commentary on the New Testament
NPNF¹	*The Nicene and Post-Nicene Fathers* Series 1
NPNF²	*The Nicene and Post-Nicene Fathers* Series 2
ODCC	*The Oxford Dictionary of the Christian Church*
Or.	*Oratio*
Or. cat.	*Catechetical Oration*
Paen.	*De paenitentia*

Participatio	Participatio: *The Journal of the Thomas F. Torrance Theological Fellowship*
Pecc. merit.	*De peccatorum meritis et remissione*
PG	Patrologia graeca
PGL	*Patristic Greek Lexicon*
PL	Patrologia latina
SC	Sources chrétiennes
Serm.	*Sermones*
SJT	*Scottish Journal of Theology*
Spir.	*De Spiritu Sancto*
StPatr	Studia Patristica
Tom.	*Tomus ad Antiochenos*
Tr.	*Tractatus*
Tract. Ev. Jo.	*In Evangelium Johannis tractatus*
Trin.	*De Trinitate*
TS	*Theological Studies*
VC	*Vigiliae christianae*
Ver. rel.	*De vera religione*
Vit. Moys.	*Vita Moysis*
WSA	The Works of St. Augustine: A Translation for the twenty-first century

Unless otherwise noted, all dates are A.D., all scripture quotations are from the English Standard Version, and all references to Torrance are to Thomas F. Torrance.

Acknowledgements

The inception of this project dates to a spring 1998 course in systematic theology at Wesley Biblical Seminary. My professor and later mentor William Ury assigned as a textbook T. F. Torrance's *The Mediation of Christ*. There I encountered for the first time Torrance's claim that God's Son had assumed a fallen human nature. In his preface, Torrance mentioned his book's genesis as a lecture series given at British Isles Nazarene College and thanked its dean, his former student T. A. Noble. Little did I know in 1998 that those prefatory remarks would hint at my own future. A decade later, I began doctoral research on the relation of the Fall to Christ's humanity at the now-named Nazarene Theological College under Dr Noble's supervision. I owe much gratitude to him, as well as to my examiners, David Fergusson of New College, Edinburgh and David Law of the University of Manchester, for their stimulating questions and encouragement to publish my work.

Research frequently both feels and appears like a solitary endeavour. In reality, however, it relies upon a relational network. Special thanks go to indefatigable Oklahoma Wesleyan University librarian Stephanie Leupp; to Alan Linfield, Donald Macleod, Kevin Chiarot, and the St Louis University and Oral Roberts University libraries, for sharing resources; to students Billy Lopez, Giancarlo Sironi-Paris, and Philipp Jahn, for reviewing my work in modern European languages; to Oklahoma Wesleyan University and The Wesleyan Church, for financial support; and, supremely, to my parents, wife, and Saviour.

Introduction: The Falling Out
Over Fallenness

From the Apostle Paul onward, Christians have expressed the universal saving significance of Jesus Christ by portraying him as reversing a primeval fall of humankind into sin and death (e.g. Rom. 5.12-22). However literally or figuratively theologians have interpreted the Fall, the question, What are its implications for the status of Christ's own humanity?, has persisted for them. Contemporary thinkers who debate this question delineate two broad perspectives: one asserts, while the other denies, that Christ's human nature was in some sense 'fallen', perhaps even 'sinful'. Each perspective's advocates claim support from notable earlier theologians, such as the church fathers.[1]

---

[1] For a sampling of the current debate, see the following: R. L. Sturch, *The Word and the Christ: An Essay in Analytic Christology* (Oxford: Clarendon, 1991), pp. 261–4; G. W. Bromiley, 'The Reformers and the Humanity of Christ', in *Perspectives on Christology: Essays in Honor of Paul K. Jewett* (eds M. Shuster and R. Muller; Grand Rapids: Zondervan, 1991), pp. 79–104; M. Shuster, 'The Temptation, Sinlessness, and Sympathy of Jesus: Another Look at the Dilemma of Hebrews 4:15', in Shuster and Muller, *Perspectives on Christology*, pp. 197–209; T. A. Hart, 'Sinlessness and Moral Responsibility: A Problem in Christology', *SJT* 48.1 (1995), pp. 37–54; M. M. Adams, *What Sort of Human Nature?Medieval Philosophy and the Systematics of Christology* (Milwaukee: Marquette University Press, 1999); S. Machida, 'Jesus, Man of Sin: Toward a New Christology in the Global Era', *Buddhist-Christian Studies* 19 (1999), pp. 81–91; K. M. Kapic, 'The Son's Assumption of a Human Nature: A Call for Clarity', *IJST* 3.2 (2001), pp. 154–66; C. Gschwandtner, 'Threads of Fallenness according to the Fathers of the First Four Centuries', and J. Paton, 'Human Nature in the Light of the Incarnation', *European Explorations in Christian Holiness* 2 (2001), pp. 19–40 and 151–65, respectively; O. Crisp, 'Did Christ Have a *Fallen* Human Nature?', *IJST* 6.3 (2004), pp. 270–88; repr. in idem, *Divinity and Humanity: The Incarnation Reconsidered* (Cambridge: Cambridge University Press, 2007), pp. 90–117; W. R. Hastings, '"Honouring the Spirit": Analysis and Evaluation of Jonathan Edwards' Pneumatological Doctrine of the Incarnation', *IJST* 7.3 (2005), pp. 279–99; D. Bathrellos, 'The Sinlessness of Jesus: A Theological Exploration in the Light of Trinitarian Theology', *Trinitarian Soundings in Systematic Theology* (ed. P. L. Metzger; London: T&T Clark, 2005), pp. 113–26; R. M. Allen, 'Calvin's Christ: A Dogmatic Matrix for Discussion of Christ's Human Nature', *IJST* 9.4 (2007), pp. 382–97; K. M. Kapic, *Communion with God: The Divine and the Human in the Theology of John Owen* (Grand Rapids: Baker, 2007), pp. 93–104; I. J. Davidson, 'Pondering the Sinlessness of Jesus Christ: Moral Christologies and the Witness of Scripture' and I. A. McFarland, 'Fallen or Unfallen? Christ's Human Nature and the Ontology of Human Sinfulness', *IJST* 10.4 (2008), pp. 372–98 and 399–415, respectively; the latter repr. in idem, *In Adam's Fall: A Meditation on the Christian Doctrine of Original Sin* (Chichester: Wiley-Blackwell, 2010); R. M. Allen, *The Christ's Faith: A Dogmatic Account* (London: T&T Clark, 2009), pp. 126–35; K. Chiarot, 'The Non-Assumptus and the Virgin Birth in T. F. Torrance', *Scottish Bulletin of Evangelical Theology* 29.2 (2011), pp. 229–44; H.-J. Ahn, 'The Humanity of Christ: John Calvin's Understanding of Christ's Vicarious Humanity', *SJT* 65.2 (2012), pp. 145–58; T. A. Noble, *Holy Trinity: Holy People. The Theology of Christian Perfecting*

0.1 Rationale, structure, and subjects of this study

Kelly Kapic has described well the significance of the debate over the language and concepts used of the relationship of the Fall to Christ's humanity:

> Why do the least excitable Christians turn instantly into the most passionate debaters when the discussion of whether or not the Son assumed a *fallen* or *unfallen* human nature arises? Professional theologians, pastors and lay people quickly become impassioned because of what they believe is at stake. ... On the one hand, those who seek to affirm that the Son assumed a *fallen* human nature (or sinful flesh) are often interpreted as sacrificing the sinlessness of Jesus and thus leaving believers still in need of a Savior. On the other hand, those who affirm that the Son assumes an *unfallen* human nature (cf., Adam *prior* to the fall) are often charged with presenting a generic Jesus who is not truly man, thus losing the soteriological significance of his life, death, resurrection and ascension. Both parties think nothing less than the very heart of the gospel is in jeopardy.[2]

By examining the claims of both sides in the modern debate in relation to those of the fathers of orthodox Christian theology, the present work aims to move this crucial debate a step closer towards resolution. The structure of this study is to present the views of representatives of both camps of modern debaters, noting particularly their interaction with patristic sources, and then to examine the most important of these sources so as to allow patristic theology to arbitrate the historical claims being made in the modern debate. This structuring is not intended to insinuate that patristic theology is an unimprovable standard of theological truth. Rather, the purpose is twofold: first, to determine the degree of accuracy in modern debaters' handling of Christian tradition; and secondly, to exploit any patristic insights which may contribute towards resolving the current debate.

(Eugene, OR: Cascade, 2013), ch. 7; M. Habets, *Theology in Transposition: A Constructive Appraisal of T. F. Torrance* (Minneapolis: Fortress, 2013), ch. 7; J. R. Radcliff, *Thomas F. Torrance and the Church Fathers: A Reformed, Evangelical, and Ecumenical Reconstruction of the Patristic Tradition* (Eugene, OR: Pickwick, 2014), pp.105–9; D. O. Sumner, 'Fallenness and *anhypostasis*: A way forward in the debate over Christ's humanity', *SJT* 67 (2014), pp. 195–212. Cited 19 June 2014. Online: http:// dx.doi.org/10.1017/S0036930614000064; J. C. Clark and M. P. Johnson, *The Incarnation of God: The Mystery of the Gospel as the Foundation of Evangelical Theology* (Wheaton: Crossway, 2015), chs 4–5; M. Habets, 'The Fallen Humanity of Christ: A Pneumatological Clarification of the Theology of Thomas F. Torrance', *Participatio* 5 (2015), pp. 18–44.

[2] Kapic, 'Assumption', p. 154 (italics his).

Representatives of the modern fallenness and unfallenness views[3] were selected for their contributions to the anglophone, mostly Reformed, version of the debate;[4] for their patristic treatments; and for their interactions with one another, both with members of their own camp and with those on the opposite side. Additionally, each camp has an equal number of representatives. Those chosen to present the fallenness view are Edward Irving, Karl Barth, T. F. Torrance, Colin Gunton, and Thomas Weinandy. The selected unfallenness proponents are Marcus Dods the Elder, A. B. Bruce, H. R. Mackintosh, Philip Hughes, and Donald Macleod.

Representatives from the church fathers were determined by the breadth of reference to them made by both sides in the modern debate. The aim was to select fathers whom both fallenness and unfallenness advocates agreed were significant for the debate. In the interest of balance, five Greek and five Latin fathers were chosen: Irenaeus, Athanasius, Gregory Nazianzen, Gregory Nyssen, and Cyril of Alexandria for the Greeks; Tertullian, Hilary of Poitiers, Ambrose, Augustine, and Leo the Great for the Latins.

0.2 Scholarly antecedents and contributions of this study

Due to brevity and differing foci, the literature cited above does not attempt anything like the burden of this study.[5] Five larger works, all but the last one originating as doctoral studies, do contain significant overlaps with the

---

[3] In *Divinity and Humanity*, p. 91, Crisp denominates the two sides as the 'fallenness' view and the 'sinlessness' view, which rather begs the question. In general, fallenness advocates affirm Christ's sinlessness (Kapic, 'Assumption', pp. 160–6). Following Kapic, Davidson, and McFarland, this study uses the terms 'fallenness' and 'unfallenness' for the two camps. The diverse meanings attached by theologians to these terms will be evaluated in ch. 5.

[4] Among other versions of the debate are those noted in Kapic, 'Assumption', within Eastern Orthodox (157–9, nn. 11, 16) and Dutch Reformed milieux (166, n. 42). Roman Catholics who embrace the fallenness view include Thomas Weinandy (one subject of this study) and H. U. von Balthasar, *Mysterium Paschale: The Mystery of Easter* (trans. with an introduction by A. Nichols; Edinburgh: T&T Clark, 1990; 1st American edn. San Francisco: Ignatius, 2000), p. 22. *Pace* Allen, 'Calvin's Christ', p. 392, n. 50 and *The Christ's Faith*, pp. 126–7, various Lutherans subscribe to the fallenness view, including M. H. Scharlemann, '"In the Likeness of Sinful Flesh"', *Concordia Theological Monthly* 32.3 (March 1961), pp. 133–8; W. Pannenberg, *Jesus – God and Man* (London: SCM, 1968, 2002), pp. 407–18; and Luther himself, according to D. W. Dorries, *Edward Irving's Incarnational Christology* (Fairfax, VA: Xulon, 2002), p. 229; Clark and Johnson, *The Incarnation of God*, pp. 116, 122.

[5] Davidson, 'Pondering', pp. 397–8, urges further research of the sort embodied in the present study.

present study. We will examine each of these works in turn so as to indicate this study's setting.

Harry Johnson's 1962 publication of his London University doctoral thesis asks whether Christ assumed a fallen human nature.[6] Johnson surveys the biblical and historical precedents for an affirmative answer, then concludes with a constructive articulation of this view's soteriological value. Particular points of contact with the present study include Johnson's brief challenge to A. B. Bruce's unfallenness exegesis of Heb. 4.15; the examination of two church fathers, Gregories Nazianzen and Nyssen, which finds Nazianzen implicitly and Nyssen explicitly supportive of a fallenness view; and profiles of eighteen modern fallenness advocates, including Edward Irving, Karl Barth, and T. F. Torrance. Johnson also tries to trace the lines of influence among the modern advocates. He claims that while Barth is aware of many of the earlier advocates, including Irving, whether he is influenced by them is unclear; Barth himself, though, seems to have influenced Torrance. Johnson also devotes nine pages to the question of why the fallenness view historically has endured neglect among theologians. He concludes that the church has overemphasized Christ's divinity to the detriment of his true humanity.[7]

In the 1980s, two doctoral studies from the University of Aberdeen sought to demonstrate the consonance of Edward Irving's fallenness view with Greek patristic Christology.[8] Jacob Nantomah appeals to Irenaeus, Athanasius, and Nyssen; David Dorries, too, examines these fathers in addition to Nazianzen, Basil of Caesarea, and Cyril of Alexandria, as well as the reformers Luther and Calvin. Both Nantomah and Dorries also discuss the objections of Irving's opponents, including Marcus Dods the Elder, and both conclude that the

[6] H. Johnson, *The Humanity of the Saviour: A Biblical and Historical Study of the Human Nature of Christ in Relation to Original Sin, with Special Reference to its Soteriological Significance* (London: Epworth, 1962).
[7] Johnson, *Humanity*, pp. 120 (Bruce), 129–32 (the Gregories), 151–5 (Irving), 167–70 (Barth, using only *CD* I/2), 170–3 (Torrance), 178–85 (lines of influence), 193–202 (neglect of the fallenness view).
[8] J. J. Nantomah, 'Jesus the God-Man: The Doctrine of the Incarnation in Edward Irving in the Light of the Teaching of the Church Fathers and Its Relevance for a Twentieth Century African Context' (unpublished PhD thesis, University of Aberdeen, 1982); D. W. Dorries, 'Nineteenth Century British Christological Controversy, Centring upon Edward Irving's Doctrine of Christ's Human Nature' (unpublished PhD thesis, University of Aberdeen, 1987), published as *Incarnational Christology*.

objectors were mistaken and that Irving's Christology is orthodox in light of the fathers and reformers studied.[9]

In 1997, Duncan Rankin completed a genetic-historical study at the University of Edinburgh on T. F. Torrance's view of Christ's unity with humanity.[10] In addition to Torrance's publications, Rankin uses personal interviews with Torrance; library records of books borrowed by Torrance during his New College, Edinburgh student days; private correspondence between Torrance and Karl Barth; and Torrance's then-unpublished lectures at Auburn Theological Seminary, USA, and New College.[11] Rankin discusses Torrance's fallenness view at length, including his interactions on the subject with Irving, Mackintosh, and Barth. Rankin then compares Torrance's view with Athanasius' and Calvin's unfallenness views (according to Rankin) and Barth's fallenness view.[12] Regarding Torrance's appeal to patristic precedents for his Christology, Rankin notes various scholars' claims that Torrance has distorted the evidence, then concludes that 'the way ahead for Torrance and those influenced by him is through, not around, modern patristics and historical studies'.[13] Rankin also questions the adequacy of Torrance's account of original sin in relation to Christ. Finally, Rankin uncovers the potential influence on Torrance of a hitherto unacknowledged source, fallenness proponent Melville Scott's *Athanasius on the Atonement*.[14]

Lastly, Greek Orthodox priest Emmanuel Hatzidakis published his *Jesus: Fallen?* in 2013.[15] Concerned by the inroads of Protestant postlapsarian

---

[9] Nantomah, 'Jesus the God-Man', chs 4 (objections) and 5 (patristics); Dorries, *Incarnational Christology*, sections 3 (patristics) and 5 (objections). Nantomah's and Dorries' claims of Irving's orthodoxy are repeated uncritically by D. Y. T. Lee, 'The Humanity of Christ and the Church in the Teaching of Edward Irving' (unpublished PhD thesis, Brunel University and London Bible College, 2002), pp. 5, 49, as well as by P. Elliott, 'Edward Irving: Romantic Theology in Crisis' (unpublished Ph.D. thesis, Murdoch University, 2010), p. 233. Cited 23 September 2011. Online: http://researchrepository.murdoch.edu.au/2996/(Elliott cites Dorries but not Nantomah).

[10] W. D. Rankin, 'Carnal Union with Christ in the Theology of T.F. Torrance' (unpublished PhD thesis, University of Edinburgh, 1997).

[11] Among the Auburn lectures, those covering Christology now have been published as T. F. Torrance, *The Doctrine of Jesus Christ* (Eugene, OR: Wipf & Stock, 2002); the complete set of New College lectures has been published as T. F. Torrance, *Incarnation: The Person and Life of Christ* and *Atonement: The Person and Work of Christ* (ed. R. T. Walker; Downers Grove, IL: InterVarsity, 2008 and 2009, respectively). Rankin's study makes use of Torrance's annotations to his lectures, which do not appear in the published version.

[12] Rankin, 'Carnal Union', pp. 99–119 (Torrance's fallenness view); chs 2–4 (Athanasius, Calvin, and Barth, respectively).

[13] Rankin, 'Carnal Union', pp. 268–70 (quotation from 269–70).

[14] Rankin, 'Carnal Union', pp. 276–9, 294 (original sin); Appendix 13 (Melville Scott).

[15] E. Hatzidakis, *Jesus: Fallen? The Human Nature of Christ Examined from an Eastern Orthodox Perspective* (Clearwater, FL: Orthodox Witness, 2013).

Christology among some Orthodox theologians, Hatzidakis attempts a massive refutation based on Orthodox tradition. His central convictions are twofold: first, Christ's humanity was so deified by union with the Logos that it possessed attributes like impeccability, untemptability, immutability, impassibility, and perfect knowledge and beauty. Secondly, any experiences of mutability and passibility (maturation, sorrow, suffering, death) in Jesus' life came only by the express permission of not only his eternal divine will but also his temporal human will (e.g. Jesus consciously chose to feel hunger in the desert).[16] Hatzidakis refers to a number of modern fallenness proponents and opponents and church fathers – including all the moderns and fathers examined in this study – but only superficially.

The above works' overlaps with the present study do not diminish its contributions. First, this study gives balanced coverage to both sides of the modern fallenness debate. Like Johnson, Rankin, and Hatzidakis and unlike Nantomah and Dorries, this study scrutinizes several modern representatives of the fallenness view. Like Rankin but unlike the other works, the fallenness proponents are matched with an equal number of unfallenness advocates. Furthermore, each side is given a fair hearing. By contrast, Nantomah, despite stating that he has striven for objectivity, repeatedly argues by impugning Irving's critics' motives.[17] Dorries dismisses Marcus Dods the Elder's extensive compilation of patristic testimony by appealing to a single alleged factual error and arguing fallaciously that therefore the whole of Dods's research must be suspect.[18] Although Dorries examines some of the same fathers as Dods, Dorries refuses to interact with the details of Dods's anti-Irving patristic

---

[16] For example, Hatzidakis, *Jesus: Fallen?*, pp. 4–6, 25–6, 96–102, 106–7, 131–3, 159, 162–6, 186–7, 278, 283–93, 313, 364–92, 442.

[17] Nantomah, 'Jesus the God-Man', pp. xi–xii (commitment to objectivity), 15, 17–18, 203, 214, 255–6 (*ad hominem* attacks).

[18] '[Dods's] liberal use of ancient church authorities gave the appearance of knowledgeable critique. Yet careful readers should have been warned by telling examples such as the following reference that indicated that he possessed only a superficial grasp of the issues of doctrine. Here, Dods seemed to think that the Monothelite heresy originated from a person named Monothelus!' Dorries proceeds to quote from M. Dods, 'Review of New Publications', *Edinburgh Christian Instructor* (January 1830), pp. 1–96 (32), in which Dods writes, 'Monothelus himself – who in this wide world was he? Never you mind good reader, whoever he was we defy him to have been a more thorough going Monothelite than [Irving]' (*Incarnational Christology*, pp. 369–70). The alleged factual error upon which Dorries has seized is – in all likelihood – a jest. Dods's biographer describes him as 'a man of deep theological scholarship, and at the same time of irrepressible wit' (W. G. Blaikie, 'Dods, Marcus', in *Dictionary of National Biography, 1885–900*, 15; n.p. [cited 28 September 2011]. Online: http://en.wikisource.org/wiki/Dods,_Marcus_(DNB00).) Sadly, Dods's humour was lost on Dorries!

interpretation, which contradicts Dorries's own pro-Irving argument.[19] Hatzidakis argues by means of decontextualized, selective proof texting and handles his sources monolithically, imposing later Orthodox views (especially Maximus the Confessor's, John Damascene's, and Gregory Palamas's) onto earlier church fathers.[20] He also errs blatantly and repeatedly in fact and interpretation.[21]

Secondly, this study provides more expansive patristic coverage than all the above works but Hatzidakis's. Rankin measures the fallenness view against one father (Athanasius), Johnson against two (the Cappadocian Gregories), Nantomah, three (Irenaeus, Athanasius, Nyssen), and Dorries, six (Irenaeus, Athanasius, the Cappadocians, Cyril of Alexandria).[22] This study examines ten fathers. These ten are balanced between five Greek and five Latin fathers, unlike the previous studies, in which only Greek fathers figured. The Latin lacuna in Nantomah's and Dorries's works is peculiar, in that their intent is to demonstrate Irving's orthodoxy via patristic appeal, yet when Irving himself followed the same strategy, he referred predominantly to the Latin

---

[19] Nantomah's and Dorries' fallacies are perpetuated by Lee, 'Humanity of Christ', p. 49.

[20] For example, he responds to Torrance's and Weinandy's pro-fallenness patristic citations simply by countering with his own citations from the same church fathers and appealing to (later) tradition to settle the question. Hatzidakis makes little attempt to show how Torrance's and Weinandy's citations may be reconciled with his own so as to render consistent the fathers' statements (213–15; 346, 353–5, 404, n. 83). Elsewhere, Hatzidakis appeals to Damascene to fix the meaning of Gregory Nazianzen's *Epistle 101* (360, 362) and misrepresents Tertullian as concurring with later fathers on Mary's perpetual virginity (424).

[21] Among Hatzidakis's obvious errors: Karl Barth died in 2007 (11); Colin Gunton and J. B. Torrance 'rebutted Irving' (30, n. 35, citing no sources; cf. the present volume's first chapter to the contrary); the Reformed doctrine of total depravity means that humans have lost the *imago Dei* completely (61); the Nicene Creed attributes 'unbegottedness' to Christ (80); Barth taught kenoticism (394–5) and rejected the Virgin Birth (420); the Catholic dogma of the Immaculate Conception denies Mary's need of salvation (416–18); and twentieth-century biblical scholar John Knox was the homonymous sixteenth-century reformer (429). Hatzidakis's critics include fellow Orthodox priest A. Kimel, 'The Prelapsarian Christ', *Eclectic Orthodoxy* (19 July 2016); 'The God-Man Who Freely Wills His Passions', *Eclectic Orthodoxy* (21 July 2016); 'Would Christ have Died of Natural Causes?', *Eclectic Orthodoxy* (25 July 2016); 'The God-Man Who Could Not Die', *Eclectic Orthodoxy* (31 July 2016); and 'When Did Jesus Decide to Die?', *Eclectic Orthodoxy* (15 August 2016); n.p. Cited 11 October 2016. Online: https://afkimel.wordpress.com and M. A. Nagasawa, 'Penal Substitution vs. Medical-Ontological Substitution: A Historical Comparison', *Nagasawa Family News Pages* (26 August 2016), pp. 1–90 (21–7, 35, 47, 73–86). Cited 27 September 2016. Online: http://nagasawafamily.org/article-penal-substitution-vs-ontological-substitution-historical-comparison.pdf. Because Hatzidakis's work and these responses came to my attention after this study was largely complete, I shall not engage with them directly in the following chapters. Suffice it to say that the evidence compiled by this study significantly challenges Hatzidakis's readings of both ancient and modern figures in the fallenness debate.

[22] Nantomah, 'Jesus the God-Man', does touch briefly on Tertullian (225–6, 259) and Cyril of Alexandria (312).

fathers.[23] Athanasius alone among the Greek fathers studied by Nantomah and Dorries is referenced also by Irving.[24] In the present study, the fathers selected for examination are those to whom appeal is made by both fallenness and unfallenness theologians.

Thirdly, this study updates Johnson's, Nantomah's, Dorries's, and Rankin's efforts. It includes recent contributors to the fallenness debate, such as Colin Gunton, Thomas Weinandy, Philip Hughes, and Donald Macleod.[25] It also goes, in Rankin's words, 'through, not around, modern patristics and historical studies'. The field of patristics is blooming with specialized studies in multiple languages, which this present study harvests.

Finally, while Johnson's, Nantomah's, Dorries's, and Hatzidakis's concern to advocate a particular view produces a certain levelling of the differences among the subjects of their studies, the present study follows Rankin's lead by documenting diversity of opinion and relationship, even within the same camp. This study traces the complex web of relationships among fallenness proponents, among unfallenness proponents, between fallenness and unfallenness proponents, among Greek fathers, among Latin fathers, between Greek and Latin fathers, and between modern proponents of both persuasions and the fathers.

0.3 Overview of this study

Chapter 1 examines the views of the five selected fallenness advocates. Similarities, differences, and lines of influence among them are noted, as

---

[23] As noted above, Nantomah glances at Tertullian, to whom Irving also appeals.

[24] Irving's patristic appeal will be documented in Chapter 1 and Appendix. Nantomah's bibliography, pp. 379–80, indicates that he did not read the article in which Irving adduces patristic support. Dorries, though, did: see 'Nineteenth Century Christological Controversy', pp. 381–5. Thus Nantomah was ignorant of, and Dorries ignored, Irving's appeals to the fathers (both Latin and Greek). In *Edward Irving's Incarnational Christology*, p. 141, n. 47, Dorries does note that Irving uses Irenaeus' signature term, 'recapitulate', in *CW* 5, p. 74. Irving, though, may simply be alluding to the ἀνακεφαλαιώσασθαι of Eph. 1.10 (Greek), from which text Irenaeus drew the term. In the absence of any clearer references to Irenaeus in Irving's corpus, it seems prudent not to presume that Irving used Irenaeus.

[25] After noting Irving's influence upon Barth, Torrance, Gunton, and Macleod, B.-S. Lee, '*Christ's Sinful Flesh': Edward Irving's Christological Theology within the Context of his Life and Times* (Newcastle upon Tyne, UK: Cambridge Scholars Publishing, 2013), p. 245, suggests that 'Irving's influence on later theologians would be a valuable subject for a future study'. The present work honours that suggestion.

are their appeals to or against the fathers. Chapter 2 treats similarly the five selected unfallenness theologians. Chapter 3 moves to the five selected Greek fathers, while Chapter 4 takes up their Latin counterparts. Each of these patristic chapters considers the similarities, differences, and lines of influence in patristic views regarding the relationship of the Fall to Christ's humanity. Chapter 5 evaluates the data generated by the first four chapters, including the confusingly divergent uses of key terms like 'assumed', 'unfallen', 'fallen', 'sinful', and 'sinless', and offers recommendations regarding terminology and further theological inquiry.

0.4 Historical setting of the current debate

Before turning our focus to specific modern fallenness proponents and their opponents, a word regarding the general historical setting of the modern debate is in order. In his historical survey of the fallenness view, Johnson finds that the seventeenth through nineteenth centuries witnessed the increasing emergence of fallenness advocacy in Europe, including, in the lattermost century, Scottish minister Edward Irving and several continental advocates listed by Barth in *Church Dogmatics* I/2. Johnson tracks the modern fallenness view as far back as Flemish mystic Antoinette Bourignon (1616–80) and notes a few lines of influence among the various fallenness proponents listed by Barth.[26] Regarding this list, Rankin states that its members 'appear to have been influenced through a number of mediating figures by the original insights of … Bourignon'.[27] These insights were well known in Scotland, for they were condemned as heretical by the Church of Scotland and Irving specifically sought to distance himself from the charge of Bourginonism.[28] The source or sources of Irving's own fallenness view remain uncertain.[29] The fact that he

---

[26] Johnson, *Humanity*, pp. 137–67. Barth's list is found in *CD* I/2, pp. 154–5.

[27] *Carnal Union*, pp. 249–50, n. 50.

[28] E. Irving, *The Orthodox and Catholic Doctrine of Our Lord's Human Nature* (London: Baldwin & Cradock, 1830), pp. 66–7.

[29] B.-S. Lee, '*Christ's Sinful Flesh*' notes that previous writers have failed to offer a satisfactory account of the sources of Irving's Christology (83) and devotes chapter 3 to the subject, focusing on Samuel Taylor Coleridge and Richard Hooker. Since, however, neither Coleridge nor Hooker attribute sinfulness to Christ's flesh, the enigma of Irving's source for that aspect of his Christology lingers. One of the earlier writers whose accounts B.-S. Lee adjudges unsatisfactory is D. Lee's 'Humanity of Christ', which argues that the place of the Logos as the conciliatory principle in Coleridge's

and his compatriots and friends John McLeod Campbell and Thomas Erskine all three advanced a similar doctrine strongly suggests either lines of influence among them or a common source for their views, although the matter is much debated.[30] Some evidence suggests the later works of Anglican mystic William Law as the source of Erskine's fallenness doctrine, and it may be that these works also influenced Irving and McLeod Campbell.[31] Law, in turn, had studied the writings of German Lutheran mystic and fallenness pioneer Jakob Boehme (1575–1624),[32] whose speculations also influenced other fallenness

philosophical dialectics influenced Irving's view of sinful flesh and sinless personhood within Christ (ii, 26, 33–9, 46–7). This argument is not compelling for three reasons. First, Coleridge sees the dialectical relationship as a symbiosis, not a strife, of opposites (35). Lee, 'Humanity of Christ', p. 38, claims that Irving likewise saw the relationship between Christ's sinful flesh and sinlessness as a 'harmony … not a discord', citing E. Irving, *Christ's Holiness in Flesh, the Form, Fountain Head, and Assurance to Us of Holiness in Flesh* (Edinburgh: John Lindsay, 1831), p. 93. But Irving himself always asserts a discord, not a harmony, between sinfulness and sinlessness in Christ's constitution. To cite evidence strictly from *Christ's Holiness in Flesh*: Christ hated and constantly crucified the Adamic life which he found in his flesh (p. 12); he had to subdue his flesh (23, 38–9, 60); 'all the evil powers inherent in flesh' gathered against him, dismaying him (28). Besides, Irving was a Romantic, not least in Christology: his Jesus is a hallowed Childe Harold, alienated, exiled, and striving against inner and outer opposition (Elliott, 'Edward Irving', pp. 256–64; cf. Lee, '*Christ's Sinful Flesh*', pp. 11, 50). Secondly, Coleridge disagreed with Irving's Christology (Graham McFarlane, *Christ and the Spirit: The Doctrine of the Incarnation according to Edward Irving* [Carlisle: Paternoster, 1996], p. 167; Elliott, 'Edward Irving', pp. 121, 152–3, 160; Lee, 'Humanity of Christ', p. 104). Thirdly, there is evidence that Irving held to a fallenness Christology prior to meeting Coleridge (see below for further details).

30 Cf. P. K. Stevenson, *God in Our Nature: The Incarnational Theology of John McLeod Campbell* (Bletchley, UK: Paternoster, 2004), pp. 183–5; D. Horrocks, *Laws of the Spiritual Order: Innovation and Reconstruction in the Soteriology of Thomas Erskine of Linlathen* (Bletchley, UK: Paternoster, 2004), pp. 187–93; T. F. Torrance, *Scottish Theology: From John Knox to John McLeod Campbell* (Edinburgh: T&T Clark, 1996), p. 287; McFarlane, *Christ and the Spirit*, p. 169; N. R. Needham, 'Erskine, Thomas', in *DSCHT* (eds D. F. Wright, N. M. de S. Cameron, and D. C. Lachman; Edinburgh: T&T Clark, 1993), pp. 302–3; idem, *Thomas Erskine of Linlathen: His Life and Theology 1788–1837* (Edinburgh: Rutherford House, 1990), pp. 126, 474–7; G. M. Tuttle, *John McLeod Campbell on Christian Atonement: So Rich a Soil* (Edinburgh: Handsel, 1986), pp. 39, 67–8, 147, n. 18.

31 Horrocks, *Laws*, pp. 180–90, notes that Law's later books, *The Spirit of Prayer* (London: M. Richardson, 1749/1750) and *The Spirit of Love* (London: G. Robinson & J. Roberts, 1752/1754) taught a Boehme-inspired fallenness view and that Erskine read these books. Horrocks hypothesizes that Coleridge, who mentored Irving and who thought highly of Law's writings, may have recommended them to Irving, thus potentially exposing Irving to Law's fallenness view. Irving first met Coleridge between 7 and 23 July 1823 (Elliott, 'Edward Irving', p. 121), but Irving's first recorded reference to Christ's having 'sinful flesh' appears in a sermon on John the Baptist (*CW* 2, p. 98; Lee, '*Christ's Sinful Flesh*', p. 156) dating to the winter months at the beginning of 1823 (*CW* 2, pp. 191–2; W. Wilks, *Edward Irving: An Ecclesiastical and Literary Biography* [London: William Freeman, 1854], pp. 33, 35, 44. Cited 20 April 2014. Online: http://books.google.com), thus eliminating Coleridge (though not Law) as a source of Irving's fallenness Christology. For Coleridge's relationship with Irving and suggestions of specific Coleridgean influences upon Irving, see Wilks, *Edward Irving*, pp. 149–52, 218; Elliott, 'Edward Irving', ch. 4; Lee, '*Christ's Sinful Flesh*', ch. 3.

32 Horrocks, *Laws*, pp. 180–90; E. W. Baker, *A Herald of the Evangelical Revival: A Critical Inquiry into the Relation of William Law to John Wesley and the Beginnings of Methodism* (New-World Library; London: Epworth, 1948), pp. 36–7, 109–16, 128–39. According to H. J. Martenson, *Jacob Boehme (1575–1624): Studies in His Life and Teaching by Hans J. Martenson (1808–1884) Primate Bishop of Denmark* (trans. T. Rhys Evans; Salisbury Square, UK: Rockliff, 1949), Boehme taught an eternal tension within God of a light principle of love and a dark principle of desire which, in God, is not

proponents and the whole of nineteenth-century Germany.[33] This fact may help to account for the interest in the fallenness view among the nineteenth-century German and Dutch theologians listed by Barth. This, then, is the milieu in which our detailed study begins.

evil but is continually suppressed. This dark principle, however, becomes rebellious and is actualized as Satan (57, 59). In the Incarnation, Christ embodies both the light and the dark principles, as well as the world-principle with its worldly cravings, but he rightly subjects the latter two principles to the light principle (159–60; cf. 164). To accomplish God's plan to subordinate the human self to the divine Spirit, Christ had to die 'that He might vanquish [the self] from within. His outward body, which was in the likeness of sinful flesh, must die' (160).

[33] Boehme influenced Bourignon's disciple, Peter Poiret (57), and the theosophist Oetinger, who in turn had contact with J. K. Dippel (17, 157–8), according to W. R. Ward, *Early Evangelicalism: A Global Intellectual History, 1670–1789* (Cambridge: Cambridge University Press, 2006). Johnson, *Humanity*, includes Poiret (139–42) and Dippel (145–8) in his list of fallenness proponents. Ward, *Early Evangelicalism*, p. 17, notes that early nineteenth-century Germany was much influenced by Boehme (on Boehme himself see pp. 21–2).

The Rise and Progress of the Fallenness View among Select Modern Theologians

University of Edinburgh theologian Hugh Ross Mackintosh famously (if ethnocentrically) declared, 'Theology is created in Germany, corrupted in America and corrected in Scotland.'[1] The modern fallenness Christology, however, is raised in Great Britain, revived in Germany (and Switzerland), returned to Britain, and received in America. As we trace the course of this doctrine, we shall note the biblical and historical (particularly patristic) sources to which its selected proponents appeal, as well as their theological rationales. The object of this chapter is to present the selected theologians' views sympathetically; therefore, critique will be limited.

1.1 Heather and 'heresy': Edward Irving

In the 1820s and 1830s, the Church of Scotland faced claims by one of its sons that Christ's human nature was 'fallen', indeed 'sinful'. The advocate was Annan native and controversial celebrity minister Edward Irving (1792–1834), whose famed rhetorical prowess drew large crowds each week to the National Scotch Church in London.[2] For that doctrine, Irving was found guilty of heresy by

---

[1] D. Graves, 'Hugh Ross Mackintosh's Scottish Theology', n.p. Cited 25 March 2011. Online: http://www.christianity.com/ChurchHistory/11630761/.

[2] Biographical data on Irving may be found in the following sources: T. Grass, *The Lord's Watchman* (Milton Keynes, UK: Paternoster, 2011); N. R. Needham, 'Irving, Edward', *DSCHT* (eds D. F. Wright, N. M. de S. Cameron, and D. C. Lachman; Edinburgh: T&T Clark, 1993), pp. 436–7; A. Dallimore, *The Life of Edward Irving: Fore-runner of the Charismatic Movement* (Edinburgh: Banner of Truth, 1983); A. L. Drummond, *Edward Irving and His Circle* (London: James Clarke, 1936); Wilks, *Edward Irving*. On Irving's popularity as an orator, see C. G. Strachan, *The Pentecostal Theology of Edward Irving* (London: Darton, Longman & Todd, 1973), pp. 25, 209, n. 8; Needham, 'Irving', p. 436; Wilks, *Edward Irving*, ch. 3.

the London Presbytery in 1830[3] and again by the Annan Presbytery in 1833, at which time he was deposed from the ministry.[4] Irving himself returned the charge of heresy upon his opponents, accusing them of implying Gnosticism, Manichaeism, Eutychianism, and Monothelitism by claiming that Christ's humanity was immortal, incorruptible, and sinless.[5] In the years leading up to his defrocking, he published prolifically in defence of his doctrine,[6] to an exposition of which we now turn.

1.1.1 Irving on Christ's fallen flesh: Distinctions and definitions

Misinterpreting Irving is easy unless one heeds certain distinctions and definitions.[7] The first crucial distinction is between the Trinitarian persons of the Son and the Spirit. Irving rejects as Eutychian and apotheosizing any notion that Christ's humanity was sanctified by its union with the divine Son.[8] Rather, the Son's role in the Incarnation was to supply personhood for the human nature (the doctrine of *anhypostasia*) and to accommodate his divine will to direct his human will faithfully within the constraints of the latter's finitude (the doctrines of *kenosis* and Dyothelitism).[9] By contrast, it was the

---

[3]   Dallimore, *Life of Edward Irving*, p. 96; Strachan, *Pentecostal Theology*, pp. 43–5.

[4]   Dallimore, *Life of Edward Irving*, pp. 148–9; Strachan, *Pentecostal Theology*, pp. 193–9.

[5]   *CW* 5, pp. 215–16; cf. 4, 126–7; *CW* 1, pp. 624, 644.

[6]   E. Irving, *The Doctrine of the Incarnation Opened in Six Sermons* (first published in 1828, now in *CW* 5); 'On the Human Nature of Christ', and 'On the True Humanity of Christ', *Morning Watch* 1 (1829), pp. 75–99, 421–45, respectively; *Orthodox and Catholic Doctrine* (1830); *The Opinions Circulating Concerning Our Lord's Human Nature, Tried by the Westminster Confession of Faith* (Edinburgh: John Lindsay, 1830); with T. Carlyle, *The Doctrine Held by the Church of Scotland Concerning the Human Nature of Our Lord, As Stated in Her Standards* (Edinburgh: John Lindsay, 1830); and *Christ's Holiness in Flesh* (1831).

[7]   Lee, 'Humanity of Christ', pp. 48–9. Dods, 'Review', pp. 43, 45, complains about how Irving redefines terms and uses the same terms with different meanings at different points.

[8]   *CW* 5, pp. 123–4. Indeed, on p. 150, Irving insists that God the Son was *incapable* of doing what God the Spirit did to Christ's flesh:

> Was ever the weakness of flesh so proved as by this, that the personality of the Son joined to it could not strengthen it, without the continual energising of the Holy Ghost? Was ever the sinfulness and mortality of the flesh so proved as by this, that the Holy One could not keep it from sin and from corruption but by the operation of the Holy Ghost?

[9]   *CW* 5, pp. 3–5, 87, 155, 159–60, 164–8, 439–40; 'On the True Humanity of Christ', pp. 427–8, 439–40; *Orthodox and Catholic Doctrine*, pp. vii–1. Irving has a kenotic view of the Incarnation (Dorries, *Edward Irving's Incarnational Christology*, pp. 88–97). Nevertheless, Christ remains fully God as well as fully human according to Irving, *The Day of Pentecost, Or, The Baptism with the Holy Ghost* (London: Baldwin & Cradock, 1831), pp. 37, 76. Cf. *CW* 2, pp. 194–5.

Spirit who, under the Son's direction, empowered, sanctified, and sustained Christ's humanity so that his human will harmonized with his divine will.[10]

That the Spirit's constant working was required indicates the nature of Christ's humanity as 'flesh'. Under this term are included all the effects of the Fall: the necessity of suffering, death, and corruption;[11] 'evil propensities',[12] also described as the law of, lust of, or will of the flesh;[13] and liability to temptation by means of all the above.[14] Irving uses the word 'flesh' with two referents: first, as synonymous with 'body'. Thus one of his early sermons portrays the human souls of Christ and of Christians as holy while their flesh is rebellious until resurrection.[15] Likewise, in a March 1829 journal article, Irving denies that 'the Holy Ghost in the conception did impenetrate every particle of his [Jesus'] body, so as that, from being under the condition and law of sin, it should be under the condition and law of holiness …. For if in his conception the particles of his flesh were changed from unholy to holy, from mortal to immortal, then what was left to be done at the resurrection?'[16] Secondly, Irving applies the term 'flesh' to the totality of fallen human nature, both body and soul. He admits that some of his earlier writings give the impression that only Christ's body was subject to the law of sin and death, but in fact 'we can assert the sinfulness of the whole, the complete, the perfect human nature, which He took, without in the least implicating Him with sin'.[17]

[10] *CW* 5, pp. 3–4, 134, 160–2; *Orthodox and Catholic Doctrine*, pp. vii–1; *Day of Pentecost*, pp. 16–17, 26–7, 64–5, 74–8; cf. *CW* 4, pp. 537–9; J. Purves, 'The Interaction of Christology and Pneumatology in the Soteriology of Edward Irving', *Pneuma* 14.1 (1992), pp. 81–90.

[11] *CW* 5, p. 136; 'On the True Humanity of Christ', p. 424; *Orthodox and Catholic Doctrine*, p. 151.

[12] *CW* 5, pp. 169–70 (Irving is here describing *Christ's* 'fallen manhood'); cf. 'On the True Humanity of Christ', pp. 424–5. As Dorries puts it, there is in Christ's flesh an 'inherent movement towards sin' (*Edward Irving's Incarnational Christology*, p. 98; cf. 403).

[13] *CW* 5, p. 320; 'On the True Humanity of Christ', pp. 424–6, 432; *Orthodox and Catholic Doctrine*, pp. 22, 25; *Christ's Holiness in Flesh*, p. 23. Christ had 'a law of sin and death to overcome, a will of the flesh to keep obedient to the will of the Spirit in his mind' (*Christ's Holiness in Flesh*, 60). Irving allows that before the Fall, Adam imaged God in the flesh. Since the Fall, though, flesh is under the law of sin and death (*Christ's Holiness in Flesh*, 44–5).

[14] 'On the True Humanity of Christ', pp. 424–7; *Orthodox and Catholic Doctrine*, p. 20.

[15] *CW* 5, pp. 126–8, 161–3, 320, 330–1, 335 (Christ); 145–6, 335 (Christians).

[16] 'On the Human Nature of Christ', p. 97.

[17] *CW* 5, p. 565; cf. 265. Here 'perfect' means ontological completeness (lacking neither body nor soul), not moral perfection. Thus Irving can write of Christ's choice both 'through the faculties of the human *soul*, to commune with every impious, ungodly, and blasphemous chamber of the fallen intellect and feeling of men' and also to 'endure such a pressure of iniquity as His human nature, His sin-bearing *body*, brought Him into the sense, feeling, bondage, and suffering of' (*CW* 5, 269–70, emphases mine).

Irving's last statement above may seem self-contradictory,[18] unless one recognizes that he carefully distinguishes *substance* ('nature' in the quote above) from *person* (as indicated by the pronoun 'Him'). Irving explains in the preface to one of his books, 'Whenever I attribute sinful properties and dispositions and inclinations to our Lord's human nature, I am speaking of it considered as apart from Him, in itself.'[19] More than once, Irving applies to Christ the 'Yet not I, but sin that dwelleth in me' of Rom. 7.17 to express this distinction.[20] Although Christ's flesh, like ours, willed to commit every kind of sin, and 'did carry up to the mind every form of seduction', yet in Christ's *person* were 'no concupiscence, no thought or meditation of evil, no indwelling of lust, no abiding of anger or malice or hatred'; rather, he disciplined his body to obey God.[21]

To preserve Christ's personal sinlessness despite his sinful human substance, Irving idiosyncratically differentiates three kinds of sin: original sin, constitutional sin, and actual sin.[22] *Original sin* is Adam's wilful forfeiting of his created state, the guilt for which is shared by all naturally generated human persons, whom God holds responsible for not being the persons he created them to be. The divine Son, being uncreated, is not under this responsibility, nor does he assume it in the Incarnation, for no human person is generated in the virginal conception, but rather the Son unites with

---

[18] As Dallimore, *Life of Edward Irving*, p. 79, claims.
[19] *Orthodox and Catholic Doctrine*, p. vii. In *CW* 5, pp. 564–5, Irving repudiates the equation of 'soul' with 'person'. Rather, 'person' is what links the psychosomatic unity of one's nature to God.
[20] *CW* 5, p. 320; 'On the True Humanity of Christ', p. 426; *Christ's Holiness in Flesh*, p. xxx; cf. Strachan, *Pentecostal Theology*, p. 28. In *Christ's Holiness in Flesh*, pp. 42–4 (cf. vii–viii), Irving clarifies his past use of this verse (emphases his):

> I think it is not proper to apply these words [from the verses surrounding Rom. 7.17] unto Christ, in whom the law of the flesh, though ever present, was ever present in the condition of impotence and death, and never arose into the state of warfare there described, being kept down by the power of the Holy Ghost, in the hands of the Son of Man …. [By using Rom. 7.17,] I did not mean, that sin had any activity or potency, that the *I* ever sinned, or any thing which the *I* covers, – any member of the flesh or of the mind, no, not one hair of his head …. We say, that it was flesh sinful in its own properties, converted into holy flesh by its union with his person. … If it be applied to Christ, it is only as a temptation, and not an experience; as a consciousness, but not a consenting; as a liability, but not as a thing admitted or permitted ever to possess him.

[21] 'On the True Humanity of Christ', pp. 426–7; cf. *Orthodox and Catholic Doctrine*, p. 7: Christ assumed our nature 'without meditation of evil, without indulgence of concupiscence'. The evil and concupiscence were ever present in his human nature but were restrained, not entertained, by his person.
[22] *Christ's Holiness in Flesh*, p. 10 (cf. Dorries, *Incarnational Christology*, 83).

anhypostatic human nature by the Spirit's power. Thus Christ is shielded from the guilt of original sin.[23]

The consequence of Adam's sin, however, is *constitutional sin* – the law of sin and death at work in the flesh. By taking flesh from a mother who herself shares humanity's fallen, sinful substance, Christ apportions to himself a part of the common mass of sinful human nature, thereby sharing in the collective sins and carnal temptations of the whole race,[24] as well as in the guilt of having a fallen nature.[25] Yet the divine will in Christ, being immutably immune from temptation, ever wills the will of his Father, while the Holy Spirit continuously neutralizes the sinful impulses of Christ's flesh, converting them into holy thinking, willing, and doing. By these means, Christ never falls into *actual sin*, which is voluntary transgression of God's law.[26] The distinction between constitutional and actual sin appears when Irving writes: 'Sin, in a nature, is its disposition to lead the person away from God; sin in a person, is the yielding thereto.'[27]

Although Irving's doctrine of the Incarnation demands these fine hamartiological distinctions, his doctrine of the Atonement requires him to

---

[23] *CW* 5, pp. 159–60; *Orthodox and Catholic Doctrine*, pp. 23, 80–7; *Opinions Circulating*, p. 58; *Christ's Holiness in Flesh*, pp. 3–4. McFarlane, *Christ and the Spirit*, p. 150, claims that, for Irving, Christ shares in original guilt but not original sin. Given Irving's categories, it is more accurate to say that Christ's humanity (not Christ) shared in constitutional guilt (not original guilt) – that is, his human nature is guilty but his person is not.

[24] *CW* 4, pp. 340–1; *CW* 5, pp. 115, 153–4, 174.

[25] In *Day of Pentecost*, Irving claims that the 'natural life' of Christ's humanity was 'a thing doomed for having once sinned in Adam'. God's justice 'required death for sin; not the death of that person only who had sinned, but the death of that form of being, of that form of life, in what persons soever it may appear'. Therefore Christ died in order to satisfy God's just verdict on the guilty human nature which he bore sinlessly (8–9). This claim will appear to contradict Irving's denial that Christ shared in original sin unless one keeps in mind Irving's distinction between person and nature: original sin and guilt, in Irving's usage, applies only to persons; constitutional sin and guilt apply to fallen human nature. Thus Christ's virginal conception did not remove original sin and guilt either from his anhypostatic humanity (*pace* Dorries, *Incarnational Christology*, 98) or from his divine person (*pace* Lee, 'Humanity of Christ', 39, n. 213), neither of which had original sin and guilt from which to be purified. Rather, the virginal conception removed any possibility for original sin in the man Jesus by uniting his humanity with an impeccable divine person, although his humanity retained constitutional sin and guilt until death. Cf. M. Paget, 'Christology and Original Sin: Charles Hodge and Edward Irving Compared', *Churchman* 121.3 (2007), pp. 229–48 (242): 'Irving establishes Christ's identity with humanity in guilt via an Augustinian realist model of guilt. Christ [better: Christ's humanity] is guilty, without being implicated in original sin' (cf. 246, n. 67's critique of McFarlane, *Christ and the Spirit*).

[26] 'On the True Humanity of Christ', pp. 425–7; *Doctrine Held by the Church of Scotland*, p. 44; cf. *CW* 5, pp. 126–7, 171–4. The claim in Crisp, *Divinity and Humanity*, p. 91, that fallenness proponents like Irving deny Christ's impeccability is false.

[27] *CW* 5, p. 565. Nantomah, 'Jesus the God-Man', quotes this line (125), but inaccurately claims that Irving sees fallen human nature as guiltless (241) and merely sin-prone rather than truly sinful (100–1, 257).

integrate the three forms of sin. On Irving's account, the presence of sin in one of its forms in one member of humanity, namely Christ, enables him to atone for sin in all its forms in all of humanity,[28] for sin is fundamentally a 'simple, single, common power … diffused throughout, and present in, the substance of flesh of fallen human nature'.[29] By ontologically bearing constitutional sin, Christ thus embodies the totality of human sinfulness.[30]

Thus Christ's fallen human nature embodies a paradox:

> Whether Christ's flesh is to be called *sinful* or *sinless*, … both words are necessary to express its true character; sinful as he took it and had it to deal with until the resurrection, sinless as he made it to become by taking it and holding it; sinful inasmuch as it is consubstantial with our flesh; sinless as it is his, in his person and by his person retained.[31]

Much of Irving's protestation against his critics concerns their failure to distinguish among the three kinds of sin, as well as between person and substance and between Christ's human nature as assumed and as sanctified.[32]

One final definition requires consideration. When Irving describes the sanctification or holiness of Christ or Christians, he makes clear that he does *not* mean the annihilation of the law of sin in the flesh.[33] To him, this would be to change human nature itself physically,[34] and he asserts that such change only happens at resurrection.[35] Rather, to be holy in this life means the law of sin is so suppressed that it no longer distorts one's obedience to God.[36] Irving insists that it is possible for human thoughts and acts, by the Spirit's power, to be free from actual sin. This empowerment or sanctification by the Spirit

---

[28] Irving denied both limited atonement and universal salvation (*CW* 5, pp. 151–3, cf. 164).
[29] *CW* 5, p. 217.
[30] Ibid., pp. 174, 217–18. Cf. *Christ's Holiness in Flesh*, p. xxviii; Dorries, *Incarnational Christology*, p. 331.
[31] *Christ's Holiness in Flesh*, p. 93. Cf. p. 10: 'Constitutional sin cannot be attributed to him, who, though constituted flesh and blood as we are, was so under the generation of the Holy Ghost, which, in all scripture, is denominated a holy, and not an unholy state.' Note well Irving's pronoun: 'Constitutional sin cannot be attributed to *him*.' Constitutional sin can, however, be attributed to Christ's human nature.
[32] Ibid., pp. vii–xxx; note especially xxvi, where Irving protests a critic who, when quoting a passage from Irving on the sinfulness of Christ's flesh, 'has had the effrontery too of putting the personal pronoun *he* instead of *it*' (thus transgressing Irving's substance–person distinction).
[33] Ibid., p. 43. Cf. *CW* 5, pp. 145–6. Nantomah, 'Jesus the God-Man', p. 125, n. 1, and Lee, 'Humanity of Christ', pp. 42–3, apparently miss this point; Dorries, *Incarnational Christology*, pp. 369, 403, does not.
[34] *Christ's Holiness in Flesh*, pp. 79–81.
[35] *CW* 5, pp. 151, 162–3, 563–4.
[36] *Christ's Holiness in Flesh*, pp. 38–9. Cf. *CW* 1, pp. 623, 644.

first came to Jesus upon his conception,[37] and it first comes to Christians at the moment of their regeneration.[38] Christ is thus the prototype for the holy, sinless life in sinful flesh that Christians ought to and can lead from the start of their regenerate lives.[39] Irving denies that Christ ever experienced the state of the unregenerate.[40]

1.1.2 Irving's support for his doctrine

In articulating and defending his doctrine, Irving appeals to scripture, church tradition, and theological reasoning. He argues that scripture and tradition teach, and soteriology demands, Christ's full consubstantiality with humanity. Therefore, since humanity exists in a mortal, passible, corruptible, concupiscent state, Christ must, as well, between his conception and resurrection.[41]

Applying this presupposition to scripture, Irving asserts that the biblical term 'flesh' has a consistent connotation of fallenness that must apply even when Christ's flesh is in view.[42] When Rom. 8.3 speaks of the Son's coming 'in the likeness of sinful flesh', the word 'likeness' means *just like* sinful flesh, not *somewhat like* it.[43] We must also read realistically, not symbolically or forensically, apostolic statements that Christ became sin (2 Cor. 5.21)[44] and bore our sins in his body (1 Pet. 2.24),[45] as well as the confessions of sin in the Psalms, which Irving interprets as prophecies of Christ's own subjective experience, 'the only record of his inward man'.[46] His being subject to the Mosaic Law and to temptation 'in all points like as we are' (Heb. 4.15)[47] implies postlapsarian inclinations to idolatry, pride, and other sins which the Law

---

[37] *CW* 5, pp. 121, 124; *Christ's Holiness in Flesh*, pp. xiii, 8–10, 39, 78.

[38] *Christ's Holiness in Flesh*, p. 39; cf. *Day of Pentecost*, pp. 19–20.

[39] *CW* 1, pp. 623–4, 644; *Orthodox and Catholic Doctrine*, pp. 3–4; *Christ's Holiness in Flesh*, pp. 76–82; *Day of Pentecost*, p. 41.

[40] 'On the True Humanity of Christ', pp. 441–2; *Orthodox and Catholic Doctrine*, pp. vii, 3.

[41] This presupposition is explored in T. W. Martindale, 'Edward Irving's Incarnational Christology: A Theological Examination of Irving's Notion of Christ's Sinful Flesh as it relates to the Fullness of the Incarnation', n.p. Cited 15 June 2010. Online: http://www.pneumafoundation.org/resources/articles/ TMartindale-EdwardIrvingIncarnationalChristology.pdf.

[42] *Orthodox and Catholic Doctrine*, p. 20; cf. *Christ's Holiness in Flesh*, p. 45.

[43] *Orthodox and Catholic Doctrine*, pp. 12–13; *Christ's Holiness in Flesh*, p. 1.

[44] *CW* 5, pp. 174, 319–20; *Christ's Holiness in Flesh*, pp. 1, 55–8.

[45] *Christ's Holiness in Flesh*, pp. xxx, 2; cf. *CW* 5, p. 218.

[46] *Christ's Holiness in Flesh*, p. 28; cf. pp. viii, 63; *CW* 5, p. 320. Note that in *CW* 1, pp. 420–4, Irving rejected the application to Christ of the psalmist's confessions of sin. Clearly Irving later changed his mind.

[47] 'Certainly "he was tempted in all points like as we are," which Adam verily was not' (*Orthodox and Catholic Doctrine*, p. 22). Cf. 'On the True Humanity of Christ', pp. 425–6.

must rebuke and the devil may entice.[48] Jesus' 'Not my will' in Gethsemane refers to the God-contradictory 'will of the flesh' within him,[49] and his cry of dereliction shows its presence.[50]

Turning from scripture to tradition, Irving culls passages from Reformed sources, medieval authorities, the creeds, and both Latin and Greek fathers.[51] Because Irving's orthodoxy would be tested primarily by the Scots Confession of Faith and the Westminster Confession of Faith, these documents receive the lion's share of his attention.[52] Where these authorities speak of Christological consubstantiality with humanity in its infirmities, Irving interprets such passages in light of his view of constitutional sin. He reads creedal and confessional references to the Spirit's work in the virginal conception in line with his own definition of sanctification. As noted earlier, he also uses tradition against his critics, linking them to a variety of historic heresies.[53]

Irving uses theological reasoning to affirm on several grounds that the Incarnation requires union with fallenness. First, following the Fall, sinful flesh is the only sort that exists;[54] if God wished to assume flesh rather than create new flesh, he must take it in its current state. Secondly, unfallen human nature is not subject to suffering, death, corruption, or concupiscence and its attendant temptations, so the presence of any of these evils both indicates fallenness and assures that all the rest are present (e.g. if Jesus suffers, then his human nature is fallen and so of necessity cannot but suffer and concomitantly must have sinful inclinations).[55] Thirdly, Christ's taking fallen flesh is necessary in order to fully reveal the strength of sin,[56] the greater power and compassion

---

48 *Orthodox and Catholic Doctrine*, pp. 8–10 (Law), 17, 24 (temptation). Cf. *CW* 2, pp. 216–18, 220–9.
49 *Orthodox and Catholic Doctrine*, p. 22. Cf. *CW* 5, pp. 171–2, 217, 320.
50 *CW* 5, p. 217.
51 'On the Human Nature of Christ', pp. 76–94. The patristic sources cited are the Council of Chalcedon; Hippolytus; Gelasius; Tertullian, *Carn. Chr.*; Cyprian; Athanasius's *C. Ar.*; Chrysostom's *Homiliae in epistulam i ad Timotheum* 6; Ambrose on Jesus' Gethsemane prayer and Heb. 2.14; Augustine; Jerome on Romans 8; Hilary; Justin Martyr; and Leo the Great (Irving often quotes from authors without citing exact written sources; the appendix to this study partially remedies this defect). *Orthodox and Catholic Doctrine*, pp. 32–7, consults the Apostles', Nicene, and 'Athanasian' Creeds.
52 *Orthodox and Catholic Doctrine*, pp. 38–80; *Opinions Circulating*; *Doctrine Held by the Church of Scotland*; *CW* 1, pp. 597–645.
53 See Section 1.1 above; also *Orthodox and Catholic Doctrine*, pp. 44 (Nestorianism, for treating a sinful nature as though it were a sinful person), 71 (Marcionism, for denying Christ could be tempted as we are).
54 *CW* 5, pp. 115–16, 135–6.
55 *Orthodox and Catholic Doctrine*, pp. 22–3, 148, 151; cf. *CW* 5, pp. 213–14, in which Irving produces a nine-link logical chain. His fourth premise is, 'No unfallen creature can suffer' (214). McFarlane, *Christ and the Spirit*, p. 146, admits, 'Here we undoubtedly meet the most tortuous part of Irving's argument'.
56 *CW* 5, pp. 150, 218.

of God,[57] and the deity of Christ.[58] Fourthly, only by the union of Christ's divine nature with sinful human nature can atonement in the true sense of the word (at-one-ment) be forged, producing not mere legal fictions of imputed righteousness but the genuine reconciliation of God and humanity.[59] Fifthly, for God to defeat evil by sheer omnipotence would be dishonourable and give a measure of victory to Satan.[60] Lastly, if the Incarnation involves an unfallen human nature or one cleansed once and for all at conception, as Irving's opponents posited,[61] so that Christ was only '*capable* of death' and corruption rather than '*liable* to death' and corruption,[62] then all that is revealed is that God loves, redeems, empowers, and resurrects *some other kind* of humanity, not our kind. In such a case, Christ cannot be our sympathetic high priest or imitable exemplar.[63]

Despite all his arguments, Irving was found guilty of heresy and deposed. In a year's time, he was dead. Throughout the next hundred years, his name was associated with an aberrant Christology until being rehabilitated by Karl Barth.[64]

1.2 Revolutionizing Christology: Karl Barth

Karl Barth (1886–1968) hardly requires introduction. From Germany and Switzerland, this 'colossus of European Protestant thinkers'[65] revolutionized

---

[57] *CW* 4, pp. 529–31; 5:124–5.

[58] *CW* 5, pp. 116–17, 417–21; *Orthodox and Catholic Doctrine*, p. viii. Irving's claim is that the Fall underscores the Creator–creature distinction and thus readies sinners to recognize the Godhead at work in the fallen manhood of Christ. Dallimore, *Life of Edward Irving*, pp. 77, 81, 97 errs in charging Irving with a denial of Christ's deity. Cf. rebuttals in Martindale, 'Incarnational Christology', p. 24, and Elliott, 'Edward Irving', pp. 152–3.

[59] *CW* 4, pp. 340–1; *CW* 5, p. 5; *Orthodox and Catholic Doctrine*, pp. 88–107, 160.

[60] *CW* 4, pp. 536–7; cf. *Christ's Holiness in Flesh*, p. 66.

[61] The views of Irving's first opponent, Henry Cole, and his initial exchange with Irving are discussed in Martindale, 'Incarnational Christology', pp. 113–14. For Irving's contrasts between his own and his opponents' views, see *CW* 1, p. 589; *CW* 5, p. 4; letters from Irving dated from 1830 and 1831 in [M.] Oliphant, *The Life of Edward Irving* (2 vols; London: Hurst & Blackett, 2nd edn., rev., 1862), vol. 2, pp. 123–4, 171; Irving, 'On the Human Nature of Christ', pp. 75, 97; *Opinions Circulating*, p. 7; *Orthodox and Catholic Doctrine*, pp. vii, 26–8; *Christ's Holiness in Flesh*, pp. 37–8. Dorries, *Incarnational Christology*, pp. 297–448, claims to survey every contribution of Irving's opponents to the debate.

[62] *Christ's Holiness in Flesh*, p. 37 (emphases Irving's).

[63] *CW* 4, pp. 526–8; *CW* 5, pp. 128, 132–3, 438; *Orthodox and Catholic Doctrine*, pp. 27–8, 108–42; *Opinions Circulating*, pp. 1–7, 31–3; and throughout *Christ's Holiness in Flesh* and *Day of Pentecost*.

[64] D. Macleod, 'Christology', *DSCHT*, pp. 172–7 (172); Martindale, 'Incarnational Christology', p. 9.

[65] J. Webster, *Barth* (London: Continuum, 2000), p. 113.

the modern theological landscape, rethinking the entire Christian doctrinal tradition. His revolution links directly to this study.

1.2.1 Tradition, scripture, and theological reasoning

Regarding the relationship of the Fall to Christ's humanity, Barth sets himself against 'all earlier theology, up to and including the Reformers and their successors', as well as modern theology in general, for promoting Christ's sinlessness at the expense of his full participation in our fallenness, our '*natura vitiata*'. Barth singles out a Greek, Gregory Nyssen, and a Latin, Pope Honorius I, to represent this tendency in the early church.[66] As precursors of his own position, Barth quotes six nineteenth-century sources, all continental but one: Edward Irving.[67] Yet Irving seems not to have influenced Barth, who cites him only once and from a secondary source, H. R. Mackintosh's *Doctrine of the Person of Jesus Christ*. Irving simply provides a precedent; more immediate sources influence Barth.[68]

For Barth, that the Incarnation meant the assumption of fallen human nature is required both biblically and soteriologically. Biblically, Barth asserts that *basar* in the Old Testament and *sarx* in the New Testament always refer to corrupt nature, not to prelapsarian human nature.[69] Thus when quoting Jn 1.14's 'the Word became flesh', Barth often recalls that this means the Word assumed

---

[66] *CD* I/2, p. 153. For Nyssen, Barth cites *Or. cat.* 15–16, which defends divine incarnation as appropriate due to, Barth says, 'the intrinsic goodness of human nature' and 'the fact that birth and death in themselves do not involve suffering [Ger.: *das Leiden*] in the strict and proper sense'. (German from *KD* I/2, p. 167. Cited 10 September 2013. Online: *The Digital Karl Barth Library*). As Chapter 3.4 below shows, Nyssen uses the term πάθος in *Or. cat.* with a broader range of meaning than *das Leiden*/'suffering' captures. It would have been more fitting for Barth to have used *die Leidenschaft*/'passion' (in the sense of lust or desire). See the entries for the two German terms in W. P. Kunze, *The German-English Dictionary of Religion and Theology*. Cited 19 April 2014. Online: http://dictionary-theologicalgerman.org. For Honorius, Barth quotes a pronouncement made during the Monothelite Controversy: 'Our nature was assumed by the divinity, not our guilt; it was that nature which was created before sin, not that which was corrupted after the fall' (ET K. Barth, *Church Dogmatics Study Edition* vol 3 [London: T&T Clark, 2010], 157, n. EN152.). Barth later confirms Christ's sinlessness with appeals to Augustine, *Enchir.* 41, and Tertullian, *Carn. Chr.* 16 (*CD* I/2, 156). By pp. 195–6, he appeals to Gregory Nazianzen's *Or.* 30.21 to support the claim that Christ assumed a condemned human nature from his mother.

[67] *CD* I/2, pp. 154–5.

[68] Rankin, 'Carnal Union', pp. 249–53.

[69] *CD* I/2, pp. 151–3, 156; IV/1, pp. 165. In IV/2, pp. 489–90, Barth acknowledges that *basar* and *sarx* 'can simply mean man as a temporal, physical being', but then insists that this meaning is never independent of another meaning, that of 'pathological … anthropology'. Barth allows, however, that 'there will one day be a resurrection of the flesh apart from the sin which now taints it' (*CD* III/2, 28).

a fallen humanity.[70] He understands Rom. 8.3 to mean not that the Son merely resembled humanity in its sin-marked existence but that he actually instantiated such humanity.[71] Additionally, Barth appeals to the Pauline statements that Christ became sin (2 Cor. 5.21), a curse (Gal. 3.13), and a slave (Phil. 2.7, interpreted as slavery to sin).[72]

Soteriologically, Barth insists that God's becoming an unfallen human being would be both unseemly and ineffective for salvation. It is only as Christ wears our fallen flesh that we can be confident and comforted in his salvific solidarity with us, rather than finding him an alien and annoying presence. It is only thus that he can truly represent us as we are, not humanity in abstraction or in Eden but in the sin which besets us. And it is only thus that Christ can create a new humanity within the carcass of the old and so reconcile us to God.[73]

1.2.2 Sinful flesh and salvation

For Barth, fallen existence as 'flesh' is a state of sin, perverted and corrupted away from, and in contradiction against, our true humanity as intended by God.[74] It is to be liable for (negatively) failing to know and love God,[75] and for (positively) hating both God and neighbour.[76] Consequently, it is to live beneath God's condemnation as a creature lacking justification for its existence.[77] This condemnation characterizes the human experience of suffering and mortality.[78]

---

[70] Karl Barth, *The Epistle to the Romans* (trans. E. C. Hoskyns; London: Oxford University Press, 1933), p. 277; *CD* I/2, pp. 152, 159; II/1, p. 151; II/2, p. 122; III/3, pp. 303–4; IV/1, pp. 165, 174–5, 215–16, 480–81; IV/2, pp. 92, 384 (cf. 381).

[71] *Romans*, pp. 278–82; *CD* I/2, p. 152; II/1, p. 397; IV/1, p. 165.

[72] *CD* I/2, pp. 154–5; II/1, p. 397; IV/1, pp. 165, 478. In his commentary on Philippians, Barth simply contrasts 'the form of a servant' in Phil. 2.7 with the confession of Jesus' Lordship in v. 11 and so interprets the phrase as describing 'the appearance and the credit (or rather lack of credit) of a being that is not God, that is not the Lord'. When Barth comes to the next phrase of 2.7, though, he deploys familiar themes of fallenness: the Son 'comes to "exist in the image of man" (we recall by way of explanation the *sarx egeneto*, "and the Word became flesh", of John 1:14, and the still sharper Pauline parallel in Rom. 8:3: *en homoiōmati sarkos hamartias*, "in the form of *sin-dominated flesh*"!)'. – *Epistle to the Philippians* (trans. J. W. Leitch; Louisville: Westminster John Knox, 40th anniversary edn, 2002), p. 63, emphasis his.

[73] *Romans*, pp. 281–2; *CD* I/2, pp. 151–5, 189; III/2, p. 48; IV/1, pp. 157, 223, 481, 552–3; IV/2, pp. 92, 452.

[74] *Romans*, p. 281; *CD* I/2, pp. 188–9; II/1, p. 398; III/2, pp. 28, 35, 40–2, 48; IV/1, pp. 131–2, 158, 216, 481, 484–510; IV/2, pp. 92–3, 96, 379, 384; IV/3/1, pp. 369, 371–3, 434–61.

[75] *Romans*, pp. 278–9; *CD* I/2, p. 151; IV/2, pp. 379, 405.

[76] *CD* I/2, p. 151; II/1, p. 397; IV/1, p. 496.

[77] *CD* I/2, pp. 40, 151, 153, 155; II/1, p. 398; III/2, p. 92; IV/1, pp. 166, 174, 484–92; IV/2, p. 25; IV/3/1, pp. 461–78.

[78] *CD* I/2, p. 151; IV/1, pp. 131–2, 165, 175, 215. Barth sees human pain and death as parts of the good creation apart from the Fall (*CD* III/1, 366–75). Postlapsarian humanity, however, experiences this pain and death as 'serious tokens' of God's wrath against sin (*CD* II/1, 396).

Barth, however, qualifies his analysis. First, 'The commission of sin as such is not an attribute of true human existence as such, whether from the standpoint of its creation by God or from that of the fact that it is flesh on account of the Fall.'[79] To be flesh, then, means to be held accountable for sin but not necessarily to commit sin. (How this may be will be shown in Christ's case below.) Secondly, Barth denies that sin is hereditary or exists at a sub-volitional level.[80] He breaks with the traditional understanding of 'original sin' as a spiritual disease transmitted from a historical Adam. No causal connection obtains between Adam's sinning and our own. 'Adam' typifies all humanity, and 'original sin' designates that, individually and collectively, we freely choose to sin from the beginning of our existence.[81] As John Webster comments, 'In effect, Barth identifies original sin with total depravity.'[82] Every actual sin is an expression of the totality of the rebellious life-act which is original sin.[83]

Inasmuch as Barth teaches that original sin is the totality of human sinfulness and that Christ assumed a humanity identical with ours, the implication is clear: Christ assumed a humanity subject to original sin. This conclusion appears at first to contradict Barth's statement, 'And the Son of God did not assume original sin, but our sinful nature.' This statement, though, must be interpreted in context: Barth, in dialogue with the Lutheran theologian Flacius, is denying that human nature is entirely reducible to original sin. Just as what is baptized is not sin but sinners, so what is assumed is not simply original sin but the nature bearing original sin.[84] Elsewhere, Barth interprets Christ's virginal conception not as quarantining his humanity from

---

[79] *CD* I/2, p. 156.

[80] E. Jüngel, *Karl Barth, a Theological Legacy* (trans. G. E. Paul; Philadelphia: Westminster, 1986), comments, 'Barth thought it wise to "abandon" the concept of hereditary sin, which he viewed as a contradiction in terms, and to replace it with the concept of "primal sin" [*Ursünde*] (*peccatum originale*)' (50, citing *CD* IV/1, p. 501; brackets original). Cf. *CD* I/2, p. 189; III/3, pp. 320, 325.

[81] *CD* I/2, pp. 155, 190–1; IV/1, pp. 499–511; IV/2, pp. 490–1; cf. *Romans*, pp. 171–2. As W. Krötke explains in his 'The humanity of the human person in Karl Barth's anthropology', *The Cambridge Companion to Karl Barth* (ed. J. Webster; trans. P. G. Ziegler; Cambridge: Cambridge University Press, 2000), pp. 159–76 (165): 'Sin is only an actual, ontic human pattern of action that can be justified neither by appeal to God nor to a "predisposition" of the human.' Note, though, that when Barth claims that we sin freely, he distinguishes between two kinds of freedom. The freedom to obey God is *liberum arbitrium*, while the freedom to sin is *servum arbitrium*. We contradict the former by using the latter (*CD* I/2, p. 189; IV/2, p. 93).

[82] J. Webster, *Barth's Moral Theology: Human Action in Barth's Thought* (Grand Rapids: Eerdmans, 1998), p. 72. The whole of ch. 4 concerns Barth's doctrine of original sin.

[83] *CD* I/2, p. 189; IV/2, pp. 490–1; Cf. *CD* IV/1, p. 499.

[84] *CD* III/2, p. 28; cf. pp. 27–9; *pace* Rankin, 'Carnal Union', p. 247.

original sin but as signalling its overcoming in his theanthropic constitution: the Virgin Birth

> indicates the existence of a Man who as a man like all of us in this sinful nature of ours, in the flesh, bears with us the way and the curse of sin, but who as God does not live out the sin [i.e., commit actual sin], because even now He does not live it [i.e., abide in original sin] .... But then His existence in our old human nature posits and signifies a penetration and a new beginning.[85]

The Incarnation is a divine claiming and sanctifying of sinful flesh which excludes sin (whether actual or original), exalting our humanity to a position of perfect alignment with God's will.[86] Barth writes,

> In Him is the human nature created by God without the self-contradiction which afflicts us and without the self-deception by which we seek to escape from this our shame. In Him is human nature without human sin. For as He the Son of God becomes man, and therefore our nature becomes His, the rent is healed, the impure becomes pure and the enslaved is freed. For although He becomes what we are, He does not do what we do, and so He is not what we are.[87]

Due to its union with his deity, Christ's flesh is made capable of knowing God[88] and resisting temptations[89] by the Holy Spirit's power.[90] These temptations are not merely outward but inward, for Christ's very soul endured sorrow and the sense of godforsakenness.[91] Nevertheless, his utter sinlessness is a foregone conclusion – 'The Son of God could not sin – how could God be untrue to Himself?',[92] while retaining the character of a moral achievement.[93]

---

[85] *CD* I/2, p. 189; cf. pp. 188–92. K. Zathureczky, 'Jesus' Impeccability: Beyond Ontological Sinlessness', *Science et Esprit* 60.1 (2008), pp. 55–71 (68), explains, 'The sinlessness of Jesus was not an ontological condition of his being, secured by his virginal conception. The Virgin Birth was not what constituted the sinlessness of Jesus. It was only the indicator of His particular origin.'

[86] *CD* I/2, pp. 152, 155–6, 159; IV/1, pp. 208, 216, 236–7, 258–9, 308, 512; IV/2, pp. 92–3, 96, 379, 452.

[87] *CD* III/2, p. 48; cf. I/2, p. 189. This quote establishes that Barth, like T. F. Torrance after him, can use the language of ontological healing and purification. Cf. the distancing of Barth from and the faulting of Torrance for such language in Rankin, 'Carnal Union', pp. 255–7, 278–9.

[88] *CD* II/1, p. 151.

[89] *CD* I/2, pp. 155–9; III/2, p. 51; IV/1, pp. 215–16, 258–73.

[90] *CD* IV/2, pp. 93–6; indeed, the whole life-course of the theanthropic Christ is the work of the Holy Spirit: *CD* I/2, pp. 197–200; IV/1, pp. 147–8, 308–9; IV/2, pp. 94, 323–5, 347.

[91] *CD* I/2, p. 158; IV/1, pp. 264–8.

[92] *CD* I/2, p. 40; cf. 155. In IV/1's exegesis of Christ's Gethsemane prayers, Barth insists that the Son's will was never resistant to his Father's (269–71).

[93] Karl Barth, *Karl Barth's Table Talk* (ed. J. D. Godsey, *SJT Occasional Papers No. 10*, Edinburgh: Oliver & Boyd), pp. 68–9, quoted in McFarlane, *Christ and the Spirit*, p. 186, n. 56. Cf. *CD* I/2, pp. 158–9;

Christ's sinlessness does not, however, make him an exemplar of general or abstract morality.[94] Rather, it consists solely in the fact that, throughout his life in the flesh, he willingly accepts his divine vocation to identify with and be judged in place of sinful human beings.[95] He confesses that God is in the right against the sinful humanity which he concretely represents instead of attempting to justify or save himself.[96] By thus doing the opposite of what all other humans do, Christ reverses the Fall.[97]

Throughout his earthly sojourn, Christ bears in his humanity the corruption, sin, guilt, and mortality that characterize life in the flesh.[98] Yet if he never sins and so bears no personal guilt, and if there is no inherited Adamic sin or guilt for him to bear, then how can Christ be said to have, in Barth's words, a 'sinful nature' 'with the guilt lying upon it of which it has to repent'?[99] By what means does Christ's humanity acquire sin and guilt?

Barth's answer is that, although God's Son did not and could not *fall* into a state of corruption, sin, guilt, and mortality, he could *humble* himself to our fallen state.[100] In the Incarnation, Christ's being is conditioned by our corruption, sin, and guilt, which are 'alien' to him,[101] as well as by our liability to temptation and death. As Robert Jenson puts Barth's view, 'Of *this* chosen man it can well be said that He was sinful without sinning, rescued from the fall without falling.'[102]

The conditioning of Christ's being by sin includes his association with sinners and his enduring accusation and punishment as a sinner.[103] It is in these senses that Christ is 'sinful'. Barth writes in his exposition of the Apostles' Creed,

---

IV/1, p. 216; IV/2, pp. 92–3. P. D. Jones, *The Humanity of Christ: Christology in Karl Barth's* Church Dogmatics (London: T&T Clark, 2008), pp. 170–6, has an excellent discussion of Christ's sinlessness in *CD* IV/2 as not being a case of divine overriding of the human. Crisp, *Divinity and Humanity*, pp. 90–1, singles out Barth as a chief proponent of the fallenness view, then claims that its proponents deny Christ's impeccability. In Barth's case, this claim is false.

[94] *Romans*, p. 279; *CD* I/2, pp. 152, 156–7; IV/1, pp. 165, 239, 258; IV/2, p. 92.
[95] *Romans*, p. 97; *CD* III/2, pp. 47–8; IV/1, pp. 94–6, 166, 175, 216–24, 237, 258, 552–3; IV/2, p. 92.
[96] *CD* I/2, pp. 157–8; IV/1, pp. 172, 175, 258–60, 445, 554; IV/2, p. 92.
[97] *CD* IV/1, pp. 258–9.
[98] *Romans*, p. 281; *CD* I/2, p. 40; II/1, pp. 397–8; II/2, p. 143; III/2, p. 48; III/3, p. 303; IV/1, p. 481; IV/2, pp. 92–3, 96, 452; K. Barth, *Credo* (trans. J. S. McNab; London: Hodder & Stoughton, 1936, 1964), 73.
[99] *CD* III/2, p. 28 and I/2, p. 40, respectively.
[100] *CD* I/2, pp. 51, 151–9; III/2, p. 51; IV/1, pp. 92, 478; IV/2, pp. 92–3.
[101] *CD* III/2, p. 48; *CD* IV/1, p. 92. In Christ, human nature is free from corruption (III/2, p. 51; cf. 43) because 'He made our human essence His own even in its corruption, but He did not repeat or affirm its inward contradiction' (IV/2, p. 92). Cf. *CD* IV/1, p. 237.
[102] R. W. Jenson, *Alpha and Omega: A Study in the Theology of Karl Barth* (New York: Thomas Nelson & Sons, 1963), p. 60 (emphasis original).
[103] *Romans*, p. 282; *CD* I/2, pp. 152, 172; IV/1, pp. 165, 239; IV/2, p. 92.

'The Son of God as true Son of Man must *suffer*, …. He must have everything *against* Him, success and fortune, wicked men and good, State and Church, His own human nature – which is indeed "flesh" – yes, and God Himself.'[104] In the *Church Dogmatics*, Barth explains how Christ's flesh is '*against* Him':

> He stepped into the heart of the inevitable conflict between the faithfulness of God and the unfaithfulness of man. He took this conflict into His own being. He bore it in Himself to the bitter end. He took part in it from both sides. He endured it from both sides. He took upon Himself, in likeness to us … the 'flesh of sin' (Rom. 8:3). He shared in the status, constitution and situation of man in which man resists God and cannot stand before Him but must die. How could God resist Himself? How could God sin? The Son of God knew no sin (2 Cor. 5:21, Jn. 8:46, Heb. 4:15). But He could enter into man's mode of being, being in the flesh, in which there is absolutely no justification before God (Rom. 3:20), but only sin.[105]

Here Barth denies that Christ perpetuates fallen human resistance towards God, but affirms that Christ stands as, with, and for fallen humanity under the divine judgement upon that resistance. Yet Christ also stands as, with, and for the holy God who judges human sin. Thus his flesh is against him as God in the sense of being judged, while God is against him as flesh in the sense of being the Judge.

1.2.3 The ontology of the incarnation

Barth's view on the fallenness of Christ's flesh as part of the drama of divine–human reconciliation remains steadfast throughout his writings.[106]

---

[104] *Credo*, p. 81 (emphases original). Cf. *CD* II/1, p. 152.

[105] *CD* II/1, pp. 397–8.

[106] But K. S. Kantzer, 'The Christology of Karl Barth', *Bulletin of the Evangelical Theological Society* 1.20 (1958), pp. 25–7, presents Barth's view of Christ's sinlessness as shifting in the following three phases: Christ as a sinner in *Romans*; Christ as possessing a sinful nature but not sinning in *CD* I/2; and Christ as merely afflicted with human weakness in *CD* IV. *Pace* Kantzer, Barth's view is consistent from *Romans* through *CD* IV. The passage in *Romans* to which Kantzer appeals is, 'Jesus stands among sinners as a sinner' (97). The immediate context, however, clarifies the intent of this line: 'The life of Jesus is perfected obedience to the will of the faithful God. Jesus stands among sinners as a sinner; He sets Himself wholly under the judgement under which the world is set' (97). Barth means that Christ's 'perfected obedience' consists in his identifying himself with sinners. Likewise, Barth later affirms both that Christ was sinless (279) and that he was crucified as a sinner (282). Barth uses the same language in *CD* IV/1, where he asserts, 'Jesus Christ was obedient in that He willed to take our place as sinners and did, in fact, take our place. When we speak of the sinlessness of Jesus we must always think concretely of this' (258). In light thereof, Barth can immediately move on to call Christ the 'one great sinner' (259). Nor does Barth in *CD* IV back away from a strong understanding of the sinfulness of the flesh that the Word assumed, an understanding already present in *Romans*'

The doctrine's ontological underpinnings, however, develop during Barth's career and even during the writing of the *Church Dogmatics*.[107] Space forbids describing this development in detail, but the result is that Barth's Christology becomes more thoroughly actualized and eternalized.

By 'actualism' is meant, 'Being is always an event and often an act (always an act whenever an agent capable of decision is concerned)'.[108] On this view, Christ's divine history of condescension to assume damned flesh concurs with his human history in which that very flesh is exalted to perfect alignment with God's will and act.[109] This coordination of humbling and uplifting is not a settled state flowing from a single event; it is a continuous double movement in which Jesus is ever rejecting the seduction of evil in his fleshly condition while simultaneously embracing his divine vocation to exist in that very condition. By his choices, he constantly constitutes himself as both sinful flesh (i.e. flesh under divine judgement) and sinless.[110] Jones captures this paradox well when he writes that Christ 'affirm[s] the death of sinful humanity by constituting himself *wholeheartedly as sin*, in order that God may draw sin into Godself'.[111]

description of the Word's becoming '*sin-controlled flesh*' (277, emphasis original): in IV/1 Barth writes of Christ, 'He took our flesh, the nature of man as he comes from the fall. … His sinlessness was not therefore His condition. It was the act of His being in which He defeated temptation in His condition which is ours, in the flesh' (258–9). A hundred pages earlier, Barth had penned, 'In the fact that God is gracious to man, all the limitations of man are God's limitations, all his weaknesses, and more, all his perversities are His' (158). Likewise, IV/2 claims that Christ was 'a participant in our sinful essence' (92–3). Contrary to Kantzer, Bromiley, 'Reformers', p. 85, detects a shift in Barth on the extent not of Christ's fallenness but of humanity's: in *CD* I/2, Barth denies that, by virtue of creation, human nature remains essentially good though fallen; by *CD* III/2, however, he approximates this very view when 'present[ing] Christ as him in whom alone we see *real* humanity, as distinct from the falsified humanity that we find in ourselves. The humanity that Christ assumed is the true humanity that is sinful in us' (emphasis Bromiley's).

[107] The currently crucial work on Barth's theological development is B. L. McCormack, *Karl Barth's Critically Realistic Dialectical Theology: Its Genesis and Development 1909–1936* (Oxford: Clarendon, 1995). Pages 20–3 give a summary of McCormack's proposed paradigm. His *Orthodox and Modern: Studies in the Theology of Karl Barth* (Grand Rapids: Baker Academic, 2008), pp. 262–5, offers a 'modest correction' to his proposal. Cf. Jones, *Humanity of Christ*, p. 100, n. 80.

[108] G. Hunsinger, *How to Read Karl Barth: The Shape of His Theology* (New York: Oxford University Press, 1991), p. 4; cf. 30–2.

[109] Jüngel, *Karl Barth*, p. 133; A. Neder, 'History in Harmony: Karl Barth on the Hypostatic Union', *Karl Barth and American Evangelicalism* (eds. B. L. McCormack and C. B. Anderson; Grand Rapids: Eerdmans, 2011), pp. 148–76.

[110] Jones, *Humanity of Christ*, pp. 109, 113–14, 175, 231–2; Rankin, 'Carnal Union', pp. 254–7, citing B. L. McCormack, *For Us and Our Salvation: Incarnation and Atonement in the Reformed Tradition* (n.p.: Princeton Theological Seminary, 1993), pp. 20–2. For critiques of Barth's actualism as mediated through McCormack, see M. S. Horton, 'Covenant, Election, and Incarnation: Evaluating Barth's Actualist Christology', *Karl Barth and American Evangelicalism*, pp. 112–47; J. Wynne, 'The Livingness of God; or, the Place of Substance and Dynamism in a Theology of the Divine Perfections', *IJST* 13.2 (2011), pp. 190–203.

[111] Jones, *Humanity of Christ*, p. 224 (emphasis mine). Cf. Zathureczky, 'Jesus' Impeccability', pp. 65–8. Habets, *Theology in Transposition*, p. 175, overlooks Barth's actualism and thus his 'distinctive contribution' to the fallenness debate.

The Son's assumption of fallen flesh is eternalized as a supratemporal act within the being of God which is prototypical of our own being in the flesh. Here Barth's doctrine of election is crucial. The primary object of God's election is none other than God. God eternally wills to be oriented towards humanity.[112]

Furthermore, God wills to demonstrate his sovereignty, holiness, and love by delivering humanity from evil, sin, and death, and so God instrumentally and negatively wills the existence of evil and of fallen humanity.[113] God's will takes the form of Christ, who eternally wills himself to exist as united to fallen flesh in order to reconcile sinners to God. Only by looking to the Incarnate One– not to the largely unknowable qualities of as-yet-unfallen Adam[114] – do we see God's intent for humanity.[115] Our humanity is but a copy of Christ's; he is the 'prototype' of humanity,[116] not only as created but also as fallen. Even before Barth formulated his mature doctrine of election, he could write, 'We are not saying too much when we say that really and originally only Jesus Christ is man who is flesh.'[117] In sum, he

> does not exist as God's Son from eternity to eternity except in our flesh .... At this point we are keeping intentionally and emphatically to the word 'flesh' as used in Jn. [1.14], because in the Bible this word means man as such, man as the enemy of the grace of God. ... He, the pure, holy Son of God, obedient to the Father from eternity to eternity, has Himself become a man like this.[118]

---

[112] *CD* II/1, pp. 271–2, 297; II/2, pp. 76–7, 103–43, 141, 175–6; III/1, pp. 50–1; IV/1, p. 66. Cf. K. Barth, *The Humanity of God* (trans. J. N. Thomas; Richmond, VA: John Knox, 1960), pp. 37–65; Jenson, *Alpha and Omega*, pp. 63–70, 93–5, 145; Jüngel, *Karl Barth*, pp. 127–38; McCormack, *Orthodox and Modern*, chs 7–10. On the debate between McCormack and his interlocutors on the question of which is logically prior, the Trinity or God's self-election, cf., for example, M. T. Dempsey (ed.), *Trinity and Election in Contemporary Theology* (Grand Rapids: Eerdmans, 2011); K. Diller, 'Is God Necessarily Who God Is? Alternatives for the Trinity and Election Debate', *SJT* 66.2 (2013), pp. 209–20; G. Hunsinger, *Reading Barth with Charity: A Hermeneutical Proposal* (Grand Rapids: Baker, 2015); P. D. Molnar, *Faith, Freedom and the Spirit: The Economic Trinity in Barth, Torrance and Contemporary Theology* (Downers Grove, IL: InterVarsity, 2015).

[113] *CD* II/2, pp. 122–4, 141–2, 169–71; III/1, pp. 50–1, 102, 108–9; III/3, pp. 351–2, 361–2. Barth says that God does *not* will evil or the fall into sin, but that God's non-willing as well as God's willing grants reality to its object. (Jones, *Humanity of Christ*, pp. 218–19, finds Barth's logic strained at this juncture.) This is equivalent to what is termed above as God's negative willing.

[114] *CD* II/2, pp. 163–4.

[115] *CD* III/2, *passim*; e.g., pp. 3, 41, 43, 48.

[116] *CD* III/2, p. 50. Cf. *CD* II/2, p. 740; *idem, Christ and Adam: Man and Humanity in Romans 5* (trans. T. A. Smail; New York: Harper Bros., 1956, 1957).

[117] *CD* I/2, p. 44. In the immediate context, Barth is discussing the flesh's knowledge of God, but the wider context (40) indicates that the flesh's sinfulness is also on Barth's mind. Likewise, in II/1, p. 151, the epistemological and hamartiological aspects of flesh intertwine. Cf. Jenson, *Alpha and Omega*, p. 103.

[118] *CD* II/1, p. 151. Cf. Jenson, *Alpha and Omega*, p. 20.

Do these comments posit a pre-existent humanity of Christ? Do they imply an everlasting dualism of flesh versus Spirit within the life of God? We will consider each of these questions in turn.

Barth affirms the existence of the eternal Son prior to his union with human flesh,[119] but opposes any tendency to define or interpret the pre-incarnate Son as undetermined by the incarnate Son.[120] There are three ways that 'the man Jesus already was even before He was'.[121] First, the theanthropic union has been God's purpose from all eternity past, and so may be spoken of as already accomplished.[122] Secondly, the Incarnation was 'objectively prefigured' in the Old Testament.[123] Thirdly, Christ's earthly lifespan partakes of God's own time, in which past, present, and future exist simultaneously in an 'eternal now'.[124]

Time also plays an important role in Barth's denial of 'eternal dualism'[125] between God and fallen flesh. The anti-creation chaos that breaks into the present as evil (e.g. sin, demons); the misery and death which are natural to God's nonetheless-good creation; and God's own incarnate sharing in all these are merely temporary, provisional moments in God's past. They have no future with God; therefore, to Barth's mind, an eternal dualism is avoided.[126] Thus Christ's flesh eternally *was* fallen, but *is not* and *will not be* fallen. Exaltation 'is the true, definitive and eternal form of the incarnate Son of God'.[127]

1.2.4 A glance backward and forward

As we transition to the next section of this chapter, an orientating remark is in order. Whereas Irving appeals to church tradition, both Eastern and Western, in support of the fallen humanity of Christ, Barth chastises the same tradition, both Eastern and Western, for not upholding this view. It

---

[119] *CD* III/1, pp. 54–6; III/2, p. 483; IV/3/1, p. 397. Cf. McCormack, *Orthodox and Modern*, pp. 187, 191.

[120] McCormack, *Orthodox and Modern*, pp. 185–6.

[121] *CD* III/2, p. 464.

[122] *CD* III/2, pp. 484–5; cf. 476–7; II/1, pp. 622; II/2, pp. 104–22, 140–3, 153–62, 175–6; III/1, p. 51; IV/1, p. 66.

[123] *CD* III/2, p. 475; cf. 476, 480–3.

[124] *CD* I/2, p. 52; II/1, pp. 608–40; III/2, pp. 440–54, 464–77, 536–7. Cf. Hunsinger, *How to Read Karl Barth*, p. 241.

[125] *CD* III/1, p. 384.

[126] *CD* III/1, pp. 383–4; III/3, pp. 361–2. (On chaos as essentially past, see III/1, pp. 101–2, 109; III/3, p. 356.) Yet if God's eternity includes a 'past [that] is not left behind, nor does it fade' (*CD* III/2, p. 536), is eternal dualism truly avoided?

[127] *CD* III/1, p. 384; cf. 110, where Barth makes clear that Christ's exaltation is the pledge of the exaltation of the whole cosmos.

has been left to Barth's student, T. F. Torrance, to mediate between these two interpretations of tradition: Torrance grounds the doctrine of Christ's fallen flesh in Eastern patristic theology, while critiquing much of the Western tradition for rejecting it.

1.3 Theologian of mediation: Thomas F. Torrance

Thomas F. Torrance (1913–2007) has been considered a premiere anglophone Reformed theologian of the twentieth century – virtually the Barth of Britain.[128] His association with Barth is apt not only due to the comparative quantity and quality of Torrance's work, but also due to its significant overlap of content with Barth's.[129] During Torrance's student days at New College, Edinburgh, his professor H. R. Mackintosh introduced him to Barth's thought.[130] Torrance later wrote his doctoral dissertation under Barth, and still later supervised the English translation of the *Kirchliche Dogmatik*.[131] Although able to critique Barth's thought,[132] nevertheless Torrance openly confesses its influence upon him.[133]

Torrance presents Barth as teaching that Christ bore a fallen yet sinless human nature,[134] the very view which Torrance himself holds. He claims that Mackintosh first taught him this truth,[135] but that he afterwards received it as an epiphany while reading *KD* I/2.[136] He stakes orthodoxy itself on this view, for 'we have ultimately taken the line of Arians or the Liberals' rather than 'the

---

[128] A. E. McGrath, *T. F. Torrance: An Intellectual Biography* (Edinburgh: T&T Clark, 1999), p. xi; E. M. Colyer, *How to Read T. F. Torrance: Understanding His Trinitarian & Scientific Theology* (Downers Grove, IL: InterVarsity, 2001), pp. 11, 15, 20, n. 14. G. Hunsinger has called him 'arguably the greatest Reformed theologian since Karl Barth' in 'Thomas F. Torrance: A Eulogy', *Participatio* 1 (2009), p. 11. Cited 18 January 2011. Online: http://www.tftorrance. org/journal/participatio_vol_1_2009.pdf.

[129] Colyer, *How to Read*, p. 20, n. 12.

[130] T. F. Torrance, *Karl Barth, Biblical and Evangelical Theologian* (Edinburgh: T&T Clark, 1990), pp. 83, 121.

[131] Colyer, *How to Read*, pp. 39–40, 44. For a historically contextualized tracking of Torrance's mediation of Barth to the English-speaking world, see D. D. Morgan, *Barth Reception in Britain* (London: T&T Clark, 2010), pp. 1–3, 49, 183–4, 193, 220–8, 242–60.

[132] *Karl Barth*, pp. 132–5; cf. McGrath, *T. F. Torrance*, pp. 166–7.

[133] T. F. Torrance, *Theology in Reconstruction* (Grand Rapids: Eerdmans, 1965), p. 128, n. 1; *Karl Barth*, p. xii; T. F. Torrance, *The Christian Doctrine of God: One Being Three Persons* (Edinburgh: T&T Clark, 1996), p. ix.

[134] *Karl Barth*, pp. 103–4, 177–9, 202–5; cf. 161, 229–32.

[135] We will examine this claim in Chapter 2.3.

[136] *Atonement*, pp. 441–2 (Torrance refers to *CD* I/2 but actually read the German original: see McGrath, *T. F. Torrance*, p. 45).

line of the Nicene Creed' unless we can affirm that 'the Son of God became incarnate within our fallen, guilt-laden humanity'.[137]

Yet scholars who concur on the doctrine's importance for Torrance diverge in their understandings of it. P. S. Kang identifies Torrance's view with Irving's and interprets it as Christ's experiencing sorrow, physical weakness, and solidarity with others' conflict with God while himself remaining at peace with God.[138] Duncan Rankin detects a shift in Torrance from an early, 'Apollinarian' abridgement of the fallenness view in his Auburn lectures to a later, more robust affirmation which may imply concupiscence in Christ.[139] Peter Cass hears Torrance teaching that Christ carried original sin and an 'evil inclination' in his flesh throughout his earthly life until it was condemned and slain with Christ himself at Calvary.[140] Kevin Chiarot seconds Rankin's claim of a shift and finds the mature Torrance incoherently holding to Christ's humanity as simultaneously fully sanctified, fallen, progressively sanctified, and progressively hardened.[141] Myk Habets takes seriously the critical reception of Irving in Torrance's Auburn lectures and contends that Torrance sees Christ's assumed humanity as fallen yet hallowed and guiltless of original sin due to union with the all-holy Logos.[142]

1.3.1 Torrance's early Christology

To weigh these competing interpretations, we turn first to Torrance's 1938–9 Auburn Seminary lectures, delivered during a hiatus in his doctoral studies[143] and much influenced by Mackintosh's *Doctrine of the Person of Jesus Christ*

---

[137] T. F. Torrance, *The Mediation of Christ* (Colorado Springs, CO: Helmers & Howard, 2nd edn, 1992), 63.

[138] P. S. Kang, 'The Concept of the Vicarious Humanity of Christ in the Theology of Thomas Forsyth Torrance' (unpublished PhD thesis, University of Aberdeen, 1983), pp. 261–2, 273 (Torrance and Irving), 264–5 (fallenness as sorrow and weakness), 272 (solidarity with hostile humanity yet peace with God). Kang's doctoral supervisor was Torrance's brother James; T. F. himself read part of the thesis and dialogued with Kang (iv).

[139] Rankin, 'Carnal Union', pp. 104–19 (transition from 'Apollinarian eggshells' [quote from p. 109]), 294, A-93 through A-95 (concupiscence). Like Kang, Rankin had personal contact with T. F. Torrance while writing his thesis (ix).

[140] P. Cass, *Christ Condemned Sin in the Flesh: Thomas F. Torrance's Doctrine of Soteriology and Its Ecumenical Significance* (Saarbrücken, Germany: Dr Müller, 2009), pp. 28, 168–9, 206–10, 217.

[141] K. Chiarot, *The Unassumed is the Unhealed: The Humanity of Christ in the Theology of T. F. Torrance* (Cascade, OR: Pickwick, 2013), chs 3–6.

[142] Habets, *Theology in Transposition*, pp. 188–95; *idem*, 'Fallen Humanity', pp. 27–8, n. 41, 30–1.

[143] Torrance, *Doctrine of Jesus Christ*, pp. i–ii; McGrath, *T. F. Torrance*, ch. 3.

and Barth's *KD* I/1–2.[144] Here we find the lush language of fallenness which Torrance will employ over the rest of his career: '[Christ] was made in the concrete likeness of sinful flesh, though without sin, … slaying in his death the sinful humanity'; 'All through his incarnate life God the Son identified himself with us in our fallen humanity, took our sin and our guilt vicariously upon himself'; 'he has actually stooped to enter our frail mortal flesh, the flesh of sin under the judgment of God's holy law and its curse'; 'It is in this fallen and twisted humanity that God's Creator Word … became incarnate and in and through his Incarnate being and life penetrated and endured the contradiction of sinners …. He the Mediator must descend into the blackness of man's alienation from God to save him'; 'We are not to think of this identification of Christ with us in our sin as a legal fiction … but as an actual fact.'[145] Here too we find Irving quoted favourably against bibliolatry.[146]

On the other hand, here with unparalleled clarity, young Torrance, in dialogue with his teachers Mackintosh and Barth, distinguishes his view from Irving's. Torrance's lecture on 'The Humiliation of Christ' has four parts: '1) Jesus The Incarnate Servant'; '2) The Virgin Birth of Jesus'; '3) The Vicarious Humanity of Christ'; and '4) The Sinlessness of the Lord Jesus'.[147] Torrance draws heavily from *KD* I/2 §15 in much of Part One, throughout Part Two, and in Part Three's introductory definition of flesh as fallen and condemned humanity, with the attendant denial that Christ was a 'sinful man' and affirmation of Christ's identification with our sinful, accursed state.[148] Then Torrance breaks with his *Doktorvater's* exposition. *KD* I/2's next two paragraphs contain Barth's critique of patristic through post-Reformation tradition and commendation of Irving and other innovators on the subject

---

[144] Rankin, 'Carnal Union', pp. 75–6, A-19 and A-20; although Rankin's references are to *CD* I/1–2, in fact Torrance had read *CD* I/1 in 1935 (Colyer, *How to Read*, pp. 23, 38), *KD* I/1-2 thereafter (McGrath, *T. F. Torrance*, p. 134), and was reading *KD* I/2 in 1938–9 while at Auburn (Torrance, *Doctrine of Jesus Christ*, p. ii).

[145] *Doctrine of Jesus Christ*, pp. 57, 94, 112, 163–4, 171, respectively.

[146] *Doctrine of Jesus Christ*, p. 100, quoting *CW* 2, p. 392. This quotation is absent from Mackintosh's *Doctrine of the Person of Jesus Christ*, thus indicating that Torrance had read Irving for himself.

[147] *Doctrine of Jesus Christ*, p. v, gives the outline; the lecture itself appears as ch. 8.

[148] Torrance's order differs from Barth's, but the content is often verbatim (in translation) or virtually so. Cf. *Doctrine of Jesus Christ*, ch. 8 part 1, pp. 113–15 with *CD* I/2, pp. 126, 129–33, 136, 149–51, 155, 159–61, 163, 168; part 2, pp. 115–21 with *CD* I/2, pp. 172–202; and part 3, p. 121 with *CD* I/2, pp. 151-2 (quote above from *Doctrine of Jesus Christ*, p. 121//*CD* I/2, p. 152). Note: *Doctrine of Jesus Christ*, p. 113 incorrectly cites *KD* I/2, p. 166. The true citation is *KD* I/2, p. 170. Cited 10 September 2013. Online: *The Digital Karl Barth Library*.

of Christ's fallenness before turning to discuss Christ's sinlessness.[149] Precisely at this point, and before his own treatment of Christ's sinlessness, Torrance inserts a critique of Irving which owes much to Mackintosh.[150]

In *Doctrine of the Person of Jesus Christ*, Mackintosh charges Irving with confusing 'corruptible' (subject to physical death) with 'corrupt' (morally depraved) and illicitly applying the latter to Christ's humanity; describes Irving's teaching that only the Holy Spirit restrained this morally corrupt nature; and equates Irving's language of 'fallen human nature' and teaching of 'the existence in Christ of ... a strong efficacious germ of evil' with the term 'original sin' and the dilution of Christ's sinlessness.[151] Torrance himself honours Mackintosh's distinction between 'corruptible' and 'corrupt': 'We cannot think of [Christ's] flesh as corrupt in the sense of Irving. ... Now we cannot think of the humanity of this Jesus in whom divine nature and human nature are indissolubly united as in any sense corrupt, but in the most supreme sense as Holy'; yet 'We must think of the humanity he assumed as thus coming under the conditions of fallen and corruptible humanity – for he was able to suffer, was weak with weariness, hungered and thirsted; his humanity as such was not immortal.' Torrance also asserts that, due to the theanthropic union, 'we are to think of Christ's flesh as perfectly and completely sinless in his own nature, and not simply in virtue of the Spirit as Irving puts it. We must think of him nevertheless as really one with us, as really a member of our fallen race.'[152] While accepting the language of fallenness, Torrance answers Mackintosh's final concerns by denying original sin in Christ and affirming his 'absolute sinlessness' (using *Doctrine of the Person of Jesus Christ* itself and Emil Brunner's *The Mediator*),[153] concluding with a defence of *non posse peccare* in Christ's case.[154]

---

[149] *KD* I/2, pp. 167–9. Cited 10 September 2013. Online: *The Digital Karl Barth Library*.

[150] Rankin, 'Carnal Union', pp. 99–103. Playing on European geography, Rankin quips, 'Torrance is clearly caught in mid-channel between his late Scottish professor and his new Continental mentor' (101).

[151] H. R. Mackintosh, *The Doctrine of the Person of Jesus Christ* (Edinburgh: T&T Clark, 2nd edn, 1913, 1920), pp. 277–8 (quotes from latter page).

[152] *Doctrine of Jesus Christ*, p. 122. Torrance classes Irving's view as quasi-Ebionite, while also rejecting the opposite, 'almost ... Docetic' error that 'holds [Christ] rather aloof from human struggles and temptations and weaknesses; an emphasis is placed on his human nature as such that it becomes "vergottert" or deified in its own perfection' (121–2). Here he echoes the charge made against Schleiermacher's Christology by Mackintosh in *Doctrine of the Person of Jesus Christ*, p. 255, and his 1933 Croall Lectures, later revised, expanded, and published as *Types of Modern Theology: From Schleiermacher to Barth* (New York: Charles Scribner's Sons, [1937]), pp. 88–90.

[153] *Doctrine of Jesus Christ*, pp. 122–5 (quote from p. 123).

[154] *Doctrine of Jesus Christ*, pp. 126–30.

Torrance's above-sampled language of fallenness begs for interpretation in light of this rejection of Irving. Torrance's pronominal choices are significant: it is always 'our' sin, guilt, and corruption which Christ bears, never 'his'.[155] To Christ's own humanity Torrance attributes the fallen state's physical effects (e.g. mortality) and moral temptations, but never inward sin. In the Incarnation, Christ assumes 'sinful flesh', that is, the same flesh which in all others – including his mother – is an accessory to their sin, and sanctifies it at the moment of assumption so that, in union with his sinless divine person, it too is sinless. Yet it is still 'fallen' insofar as it suffers infirmities and temptations. Additionally, by becoming a member of the human race, Christ enters into ontological solidarity with sinners under the curse of God's wrath.[156] Thus Christ's flesh, while holy, is 'fallen' in the sense of suffering divine judgement upon the sin of which Christ himself is innocent. The strife, agony, and enmity which Christ endures throughout his life and which climaxes in his crucifixion come not from an inward struggle with unholy desires but from two sources: the enmity of God against sin, which Christ increasingly experiences as he progressively identifies himself with sinners and takes responsibility for their guilt, particularly from his baptism to his death; and the enmity of Satan and sinners against him, demonstrated in tempting and persecuting him increasingly even unto death. Therefore, Christ's humanity is 'vicarious': in his holy humanity, he represents God to the world, suffers all its hostility against God, yet offers divine mercy instead of retribution; simultaneously, he represents sinful humanity to God, suffers God's wrath against sin, yet offers human confession and obedience instead of rebellion. In this way atonement is worked out over the whole course of Jesus' earthly life. In his resurrection, the last vestiges of fallenness (subjection to infirmity, mortality, temptation, and divine wrath) fall away and the new humanity which he embodies is perfected.[157]

Before comparing the Auburn lectures to Torrance's later work, we must address Rankin's claim that an early Apollinarianism lurks in their lines that Christ's flesh 'was created out of fallen humanity, but without the will of fallen humanity' and that Christ's 'Person' and 'personality' were divine, not human

---

[155] For this crucial insight, thanks to T. A. Noble, personal communication (12 April 2013).
[156] *Doctrine of Jesus Christ*, pp. 112, 122–3.
[157] *Doctrine of Jesus Christ*, pp. 59, 94–5, 112, 122–3, 161–76.

(Torrance draws this latter point from Brunner). Rankin interprets these lines as denials of any human will or personality in Christ.[158] Regarding the first line, Matthew Baker has argued that Torrance denies not a human will but only a fallen will to Christ.[159] Both Rankin and Baker, though, neglect the immediate context of this line, which concerns the Virgin Birth and recalls points made in Torrance's discussion of it on the previous four pages. In them he repeatedly applies Jn 1.13 ('born, not ... of the will of the flesh nor of the will of man') to Christ. Torrance's line that Christ's flesh 'was created ... without the will of fallen humanity' refers to Christ's conception in the absence of initiative of a fallen will *external* to him.[160] Christ's own human will is not in view here. Regarding the lack of human 'personality' in Christ, Torrance's quotation of Brunner clearly distinguishes the meaning from a psychological conception of the term.[161] What Brunner and Torrance mean by 'personality' is 'personhood', and the doctrine that Christ's humanity is *anhypostatic*, lacking its own person, is orthodox, not Apollinarian.[162]

1.3.2 Christology after Auburn

We now turn to Torrance's later works to test Rankin's and Chiarot's claims of a shift in his fallenness view. First the continuity must be underscored. In his 1952–78 lectures as professor at New College, Edinburgh, Torrance sounds familiar notes:[163] God's Son assumed fallen, sinful flesh, yet in so doing fully sanctified it;[164] and throughout his earthly life, he experienced the progressive outworking of that sanctification through costly obedience and identification with sinners, coupled with increasing opposition not only from sinners and Satan against his holiness but also from God against his vicarious

---

[158] *Carnal Union*, pp. 104–9, using *Doctrine of Jesus Christ*, pp. 122 (no fallen will or human person), 124–5 (no human person or personality).

[159] 'The Place of St. Irenaeus of Lyons in Historical and Dogmatic Theology According to Thomas F. Torrance', *Participatio* 2 (2010), pp. 23–4. Cited 21 January 2011. Online: http://www.tftorrance.org/journal/participatio_vol_ 2_2010.pdf. Radcliff, *Thomas F. Torrance and the Church Fathers*, pp. 97, 107, repeats Baker's claim.

[160] *Doctrine of Jesus Christ*, pp. 118–21 (Jn 1.13 is alluded to on each page). Chiarot, 'Non-Assumptus', p. 230, n. 6, concurs with my interpretation.

[161] *Doctrine of Jesus Christ*, p. 124.

[162] Rankin's misunderstanding of *Doctrine of Jesus Christ* on this point is puzzling, given that he devotes pp. 128–45 of *Carnal Union* to interpreting Torrance's later use of the concept of *anhypostasia*.

[163] McGrath, *T. F. Torrance*, pp. 92–4, evaluates the relationship between the Auburn and Edinburgh lectures as one of development within essential continuity. Cf. Torrance, *Incarnation*, p. vii.

[164] *Incarnation*, pp. 61–4, 82, 98, 100, 204, 232.

sinfulness.[165] Torrance's writings after retiring from New College maintain these themes.[166]

Perhaps the clearest, most concise indicator of his continuity with the Auburn lectures on the subject of fallenness is a 1984 letter to the editor of *The Monthly Record of the Free Church of Scotland*. What provoked Torrance's letter was an article by the editor, Donald Macleod, which challenged Irving's and Barth's ascriptions of fallenness to Christ's humanity as necessarily implying Christ's sinfulness, despite both Irving's and Barth's denials of this implication.[167] Torrance's letter concurs with Macleod that Christ 'was altogether sinless, having neither actual nor inherent sin of any kind. … [Macleod] is again very right in stating that "fallenness" does not characterize true human nature, and that Christ Himself had true human nature.' The problem lies in Macleod's asking, 'Did Christ HAVE a fallen human nature?' Rather than this static conception of Christ's constitution, we must see that 'in the very act of taking our fallen Adamic nature the Son of God redeemed, renewed and sanctified it AT THE SAME TIME. … The only human nature which our Lord HAD, therefore, was utterly pure and sinless.'[168]

Yet there are changes from the Auburn lectures. Perhaps most obvious is the dearth of further reference to Irving.[169] Even Torrance's above-quoted letter to the editor, written in response to attacks on Irving and Barth, names neither man, instead appealing to the Greek fathers and Calvin. Torrance's later volume on Scottish theological history, in which he positively reviews the

[165] *Incarnation*, pp. 61–2, chs 4 and 7 *passim*, 204–6 (111–12 repeat almost verbatim the block quote from *CD* II/1, pp. 397–8 given in 1.2.2 above); *Atonement*, pp. 149–53, 161–2.

[166] T. F. Torrance, 'The Atonement. The Singularity of Christ and the Finality of the Cross: The Atonement and the Moral Order', *Universalism and the Doctrine of Hell* (ed. N. M. de S. Cameron; Carlisle: Paternoster, 1992), pp. 223–56 (236–9); *idem, Preaching Christ Today: The Gospel and Scientific Thinking* (Grand Rapids: Eerdmans, 1994), pp. 58–9; *Mediation*, pp. 63–71, 78–80, 84–5; *Christian Doctrine of God*, pp. 250–2. K. W. Lee, *Living in Union with Christ: The Practical Theology of Thomas F. Torrance* (New York: Peter Lang, 2003), p. 2, claims that Torrance's 'work is remarkably consistent' in content.

[167] D. Macleod, 'Did Christ Have a Fallen Human Nature?', *The Monthly Record of the Free Church of Scotland* (March 1984), pp. 51–3.

[168] T. F. Torrance, 'Christ's Human Nature', *The Monthly Record of the Free Church of Scotland* (May 1984), p. 114 (capitalization his). Rankin, 'Carnal Union', p. 112, n. 264, alerted me to this letter's existence.

[169] T. F.'s brother James, however, mentions Irving favourably alongside Barth in J. B. Torrance, 'The Vicarious Humanity of Christ', *The Incarnation: Ecumenical Studies in the Nicene-Constantinopolitan Creed A.D. 381* (ed. T. F. Torrance; Edinburgh: Handsel, 1981), pp. 127–47 (141). James also supervised Nantomah's and Dorries' theses on Irving (Nantomah, 'Jesus the God-Man', p. vii; Dorries, *Incarnational Christology*, p. xi) and served as general editor for The Devotional Library Series, which included G. McFarlane, *Edward Irving: The Trinitarian Face of God* (Edinburgh: St. Andrews Press, 1996). Perhaps James' openness to Irving was due to his not having studied under Mackintosh, as Thomas did.

fallenness teachings of Irving's confreres Thomas Erskine and John McLeod Campbell, ignores Irving himself.[170]

Another change is in Torrance's view of original sin. At Auburn he had followed Brunner in locating original sin in one's personhood and so denied original sin to Christ on the basis that the Logos had assumed human nature but not a human person – the person of Christ was the divine Logos.[171] In his later writings, however, Torrance relocates original sin to human nature. This move allows him to affirm that in assuming fallen human nature, Christ assumed original sin, only to annihilate it upon assumption.

Coupled with this relocation of original sin is a rising emphasis on Christ's assumption and conversion of the sinful human mind and will.[172] Concerning the mind, Torrance writes that

> the holy Son of God assumed our ... twisted, distorted, bent mind, *but* that in assuming it right from the very beginning, our Lord converted it ... in himself. In taking from us our fallen human nature upon himself, instead of sinning in it as we all do, Jesus condemned sin in our carnal mind, and was himself wholly without sin. And so by living out a life of perfect holiness and purity in his mind, he sanctified and healed our human mind in the whole course of his incarnate and redemptive life from his birth to his crucifixion. He carried our mind into the very depths of his agonising and atoning struggle on the cross – he descended into the hell of the utmost wickedness and dereliction of the human mind under the judgment of God, in order to lay hold upon the very root of our sin and to redeem us from its stranglehold upon us. Yes, it was not only our actual sins, but it was original sin and original guilt that the Son of God took upon himself in incarnation and atonement, in order to heal, convert, and sanctify the human mind in himself and reconcile it to God.[173]

Note well the pronouns: *our* mind is perverse; *his* is pure. The sinlessness of his mind condemns the sinfulness of ours. Yet his mind is still 'our mind' in

---

[170] Torrance, *Scottish Theology*, pp. 263–77 (Erskine), 287–317 (Campbell); cf. Rankin, 'Carnal Union', p. 103, n. 235.

[171] *Doctrine of Jesus Christ*, pp. 124–5.

[172] T. F. Torrance, *The Christian Frame of Mind* (Edinburgh: Handsel, 1985), pp. 8–9; *Mediation*, pp. 39, 79–80; *Preaching Christ Today*, p. 59; *Incarnation*, pp. 117–18; *Atonement*, pp. 70, 163, 437–47. Already in *Doctrine of Jesus Christ*, p. 94, he had spoken of how 'our very minds have been warped and our souls characterized by a radical self-sufficiency and selfishness'.

[173] *Atonement*, p. 440 (emphasis his). Cf. Habets, 'Fallen Humanity', pp. 27–8, n. 41, 30–1, who denies that Torrance's Christ assumed original sin and guilt. Habets misses Torrance's relocation of original sin after Auburn.

its ontological solidarity with ours – it is a human mind derived from a fallen source. Despite being continuously converted and cleansed so as to be free from the sin, including original sin,[174] which Christ has assumed, it retains certain marks of fallenness: first, in birth it is ignorant and requires the labour of learning truth in a sin-darkened world; secondly, it must master obedience amid temptation;[175] and thirdly, although innocent, it takes responsibility for others' sin and so feels the 'dereliction of the human mind under the judgment of God'. Additionally, it endures the enmity and ignorance of its fellow humans' minds.[176] The progress of learning, obeying, and enduring requires that the process of conversion continue apace, for every new situation and stage of life requires to be reclaimed from the power of evil.[177] Lastly, because of his solidarity with us, the conversion of Christ's human mind is the conversion of 'our mind', a reality in which we are called to share.[178]

Much the same may be said concerning the will:

> It is in our place that Jesus prays, standing where we stand in our rebellion and alienation, existing where we exist in our refusal of divine grace and in our will to be independent, to live our own life in self-reliance. In that condition, Jesus prays against the whole trend of our existence and against all the self-willed movement of our life, for when Jesus prays it means that he casts himself in utter reliance upon God the Father. … In this way, Jesus prays … from within our alienation and in battle against our self-will. That is the prayer we are given to overhear: 'Not my will (that is, not the will of the alienated humanity which Jesus has made his own), but thy will be done.' Thus he offers from out of our disobedience, a prayer of obedience.[179]

Again, the shift in pronouns signals the mystery of the Incarnation: in making our will, the will of alienated humanity, his own, Christ stands alongside us in our alienated status but is free of self-will. His will thus combats and condemns

---

[174] *Incarnation*, p. 232. According to T. F. Torrance (ed. and trans.), *The School of Faith: The Catechisms of the Reformed Church* (New York: Harper & Bros., 1959), pp. lxxiv–lxxxvii, xciii, and *Incarnation*, pp. 79–82, Christ overcomes our actual sins through obedience and our original sin through the hypostatic union.

[175] On these first two points, see *Theology in Reconstruction*, p. 132; T. F. Torrance, *The Trinitarian Faith: The Evangelical Theology of the Ancient Catholic Church* (Edinburgh: T&T Clark, 1988), pp. 166–7, 186–8. In *Incarnation*, p. 212, Torrance claims that if Christ had a 'neutral or perfect human nature', then the significance of his temptations is diminished.

[176] *Incarnation*, pp. 142–6, 151–4.

[177] *Trinitarian Faith*, pp. 166–7.

[178] *School of Faith*, pp. xxxv–xxxviii; *Atonement*, pp. 69–70, 442–7; *Mediation*, pp. 84–6.

[179] *Incarnation*, pp. 117–18.

the self-will present in the rest of us.[180] Where we disobey, there he instead prays. The effect is our conversion: Christ 'bend[s] the will of man back into oneness with the divine will'.[181]

We now are prepared to evaluate the Torrance scholars' positions presented at the start of 1.3 above. Kang's identification of Torrance's view with Irving's runs afoul of Torrance's own handling of Irving. Kang is right, however, to see Torrance as teaching that Christ's fallenness was his subjection to sorrow, infirmities, and others' conflict with God while himself remaining at peace with God. Rankin's evidence for the early Torrance's Apollinarianism is misinterpreted; yet the later Torrance does discuss Christ's mind and will to a degree missing from the Auburn lectures. Rankin, Cass, and Chiarot wrongly suggest or assert concupiscence in Torrance's Christ. All three scholars misapply what Torrance says of corporate humanity (i.e. that it is genuinely rebellious and sinful) to Christ's own humanity.[182] For this reason too Chiarot's charge of incoherence fails: Christ is not progressively hardened; others are, as God's gracious initiative in Christ arouses their sinful resistance. Christ's progressive sanctification does not negate his full sanctification at conception, for he does not become holier; rather, his full holiness extends itself into ever-new situations. Nor is this holiness incompatible with Christ's fallenness, which is a bearing of the infirmities, temptations, and condemnation consequent upon the Fall. Our analysis largely supports and supplements Habets' interpretation.[183]

1.3.3 Appeal to scripture

Having described Torrance's view in some detail, we turn to key biblical sources, followed by patristic sources, by which he supports it. Torrance frequently appeals to certain now-familiar Pauline pronouncements. He quotes Rom. 8.3, God's sending of his Son 'in the likeness [Greek: *homoiōma*]

---

[180] Chiarot, *The Unassumed is the Unhealed*, chs 4–5, misses this italicized point and sees Torrance's Christ as battling his own rebellious self-will throughout his earthly life.

[181] Quote taken from *Incarnation*, p. 212; the thought is present in 119–20.

[182] Another Torrance scholar who conjures up the spectre of concupiscence in Christ is G. S. Dawson, 'Far as the Curse is Found: The Significance of Christ's Assuming a *Fallen* Human Nature in the Torrance Theology', in *An Introduction to Torrance Theology: Discovering the Incarnate Saviour* (ed. G. S. Dawson; London: T&T Clark, 2007), pp. 55–74 (63). For more accurate interpretations, cf. Lee, *Living in Union with Christ*, pp. 158–9; M. Habets, *Theosis in the Theology of Thomas Torrance* (Farnham, UK: Ashgate, 2009), pp. 72–5. On the difficulty of interpreting Torrance, see Lee, *Living in Union with Christ*, pp. 6–7.

[183] My main difference from Habets concerns Torrance's shift after Auburn regarding original sin.

of the flesh of sin', claiming that *homoiōma* means 'concrete likeness'. Likewise he cites Paul's statements that Christ became sin (2 Cor. 5.21) and a curse (Gal. 3.13).[184] In addition to these Pauline texts, Torrance often references the Gospel accounts of Christ's cry of dereliction (Mt. 27.46; Mk 15.34), which express the extremity of his identification with our alienation, only to convert it by his prayer of committal (Lk. 23.46).[185]

Occasionally, Torrance uses Hebrews' claims of Christ's identification with us (2.17), sympathy with our weaknesses (4.15),[186] distressed prayers, and painful education in obedience (5.7, 8)[187] as evidence of fellow-fallenness. Concerning Jesus' childhood in Lk. 2.52, Torrance 'leans on the etymology of the word for "grow" in that passage, as the old image of beating out metal with blows. Effort is required to shape something the right way which has a tendency to stay in the wrong shape.'[188]

Torrance also appeals to the Old Testament. Israel's covenant history discloses God's ever-more-intimate relationship to Israel, simultaneous with Israel's ever-intensifying resistance to God. The Incarnation climactically recapitulates this double dynamic as Jesus, like Isaiah's Suffering Servant, absorbs both his own people's rejection of God and God's wrath upon Israel's sin.[189]

1.3.4 Critical retrieval of tradition

Torrance credits Barth, along with Mackintosh, with recovering the Greek fathers' teaching on Christ's fallen flesh,[190] but acknowledges that Barth

---

[184] *Doctrine of Jesus Christ*, pp. 121, 123, 164; T. F. Torrance, *Theology in Reconciliation: Essays towards Evangelical and Catholic Unity in East and West* (London: Geoffrey Chapman, 1975), pp. 153–4, 168, 170; 'Atonement', p. 237; 'Christ's Human Nature', p. 114; *Karl Barth*, p. 202, n. 45; *Theology in Reconstruction*, p. 161; *Mediation*, p. 40; *Preaching Christ Today*, p. 58; *Incarnation*, p. 61, 63, 199, 255, 256; *Christian Doctrine of God*, p. 226. (All these references use Rom. 8.3; some also use the other Pauline passages.) In *Doctrine of Jesus Christ*, p. 109, Torrance discusses Paul's use of *homoiōma* in Phil. 2.7, claiming that *homoiōma* means 'concrete likeness' (italics his) as opposed to mere 'appearance or superficial likeness', which would have been represented by the word *homoiōsis*.
[185] *Doctrine of Jesus Christ*, pp. 122–3, 164, 174–6; *Trinitarian Faith*, pp. 185–6; *Mediation*, p. 43; cf. 79–80; *Incarnation*, pp. 61, 256; *Atonement*, pp. 150, 163, 212, 441; *Christian Doctrine of God*, p. 251.
[186] *Incarnation*, pp. 112, 133–4, 146, 184.
[187] *Theology in Reconstruction*, p. 132; *Incarnation*, p. 64.
[188] Dawson, 'Far as the Curse is Found', pp. 66–7. See Torrance, *Theology in Reconstruction*, p. 132; *Incarnation*, pp. 64, 106. The Greek word for 'grow' is *prokoptō*. Cf. *CD* I/2, p. 158.
[189] *Incarnation*, pp. 37–56; *Mediation*, ch. 2. Cf. *CD* IV/1, pp. 171–5; Chiarot, *The Unassumed is the Unhealed*, ch. 2. Chiarot misinterprets Christ's absorption of this double dynamic as implying enmity between Christ's own human will and God, as does Rankin, 'Carnal Union', p. A-95, more tentatively.
[190] *Karl Barth*, pp. 103–4, 161–2, 177, 179, 202–3 (Barth), 232; *Atonement*, p. 441 (Mackintosh).

himself makes 'strangely few references' to patristic precedent.[191] Torrance amply redresses this lack. His most-used supporting patristic slogans are Gregory Nazianzen's 'The unassumed is the unhealed'[192] (hereafter referred to as the *non-assumptus*)[193] and Cyril of Alexandria's 'What Christ has not assumed, he has not saved.'[194] He also cites Melito of Sardis, Irenaeus, Origen, Marius Victorinus, Damasus, Hilary of Poitiers, Athanasius, Basil of Caesarea, Gregory Nyssen, and Ambrose.[195]

In opposition to these early, mostly Eastern, theologians, Torrance ranges Apollinarianism and the 'Latin heresy'. He asserts that Apollinaris devised

---

[191] *Karl Barth*, p. 202. As 1.2 above has shown, this statement downplays the truth, and Hastings' claim that 'Karl Barth … [has] made a strong case that patristic literature favours the view of the assumption of a fallen human nature' ('"Honouring the Spirit"', p. 287, citing *CD* I/2, pp. 147–59; II/1, pp. 397–8) is flatly false.

[192] Nazianzen's *Ep.* 101, quoted in *Karl Barth*, pp. 103–4, 161, 179, 202, 231–2; 'Atonement', p. 237; 'Christ's Human Nature', p. 114; *Christian Frame of Mind*, p. 9; *Mediation*, p. 39; *Preaching Christ Today*, p. 58; *Incarnation*, pp. 62, 201; *Atonement*, p. 441; *Christian Doctrine of God*, pp. 250–1.

[193] See Rankin, 'Carnal Union', p. 99, n. 226, and Chiarot, 'Non-Assumptus', for precedents for this shorthand reference.

[194] Cyril's *In Ioannis Evangelium* (J.-P. Migne [ed.], Patrologia graeca [162 vols; repr., Turnholti, Belgium: Typographi Brepols Editores Pontificii, 1966] 74, p. 89c), quoted in 'Atonement', p. 237; 'Christ's Human Nature', p. 114; *Karl Barth*, pp. 104, 202; *Preaching Christ Today*, p. 58; *Atonement*, p. 441.

[195] T. F. Torrance, *Divine Meaning: Studies in Patristic Hermeneutics* (Edinburgh: T&T Clark, 1995), pp. 84–91 (Melito), 68–9 (Irenaeus), 191–5 (Athanasius); *Reconciliation*, pp. 143–71 (Athanasius, the Cappadocians, and Cyril), 228–31 (Athanasius); *Christian Frame of Mind*, pp. 8–9 (Nazianzen); *Trinitarian Faith*, pp. 101–2, 142, n. 111 (Athanasius), 153 (Nyssen and Basil), 156–7 (Irenaeus), 159–67 (Origen, Victorinus, Damasus, Hilary, Athanasius, Nazianzen, Nyssen, Ambrose), 267, 299 (Athanasius); *Karl Barth*, p. 202 (Irenaeus, Athanasius, Nazianzen, Nyssen, Cyril); 'Christ's Human Nature', p. 114 (Irenaeus, Athanasius, Nazianzen, Cyril); *Atonement*, pp. 440–1 (Irenaeus). Torrance cites the following sources: Melito, *Peri Pascha*; Irenaeus, *Epid.* 5, 10, 24, 29–39, 53, 99; *Haer.* 2.33; 3.18.1-3; 3.19.5-6; 3.21.2 [These citations are, except for 3.18.1-3, incorrect; they should be 2.22; 3.19; 3.20.2]; 5.9.1; an unnamed, unnumbered Irenaean fragment; Origen, *Dialogus cum Heraclide* 7; Victorinus, *Adv. Arium* 3.3; Damasus, *Ep.* 2; Hilary, *Trin.* 1.13; 11.18-20 ('However, Hilary had a habit of qualifying what he said in this connection which appears to leave his conception of God's self-identification with sinful humanity somewhat ambiguous – see *De Trin.*, 10.47-48; 11:16-7' [*Trinitarian Faith*, p. 162, n. 54]); Athanasius, *Ep. Adelph.* 4–5; *Tom.* 7; *Ep. Epict.* 7; *Ep. Serap.* 1.6, 9; 2.9; *C. Apoll.* 1, 2; *C. Ar.* 1.37-64; 2.1-12, 14, 18, 47-48, 53-56, 65-72, 74-77; 3.19, 22-24, 27-28, 30-35, 38-40, 43-44, 52-57; 4.6-7, 33, 35-36; *C. Gent.* 40-42; *Inc.* 2–4, 9, 14–15, 44–45; *In Psalmos* 21.31; 50.12; Basil, *Ep.* 261.2-3; Nyssen, *Adv. Apollinarem* 26; *Antirrh. adv. Apol.* 26; *C. Eunom.* 2.13; *Ep. adv. Apollinarem* (no further citation given); *Or. cat.* 14; Ambrose, *Ep.* 261.2 (This citation also is incorrect; Torrance has reduplicated his citation of Basil. The correct citation remains unidentified); Nazianzen, *Ep.* 101; *Or.* 1.23; 2.23-25; 4.5-6; 22.13; 30.5-6, 21; Cyril, *In Jo. Ev.* (PG 74, pp. 89c, 157d-160a, 273b-76d, 535c-52b, 576c-85d, 753b-56c); *Ad Nestorium* 3 (PG 77, p. 117a); *Adv. anthropomorphitas* (PG 76, p. 1120bc); *Adv. Nestorium* 1, 3 (PG 76, pp. 21c, 132c, 164a-68b); *C. Orientales* (PG 76, pp. 321c-24a); *Inc. unigen.* (PG 75, pp. 1213a-17a); *De recta fide ad reginas* 2 (PG 76, pp. 1364c-68c); *De recta fide ad Theodosium* (PG 76, pp. 1161b-d; 1164a); *Dialogus de Trinitate* (PG 75, pp. 681d-84a); *Glaphyra in Leviticum* (PG 69, pp. 510ab, 548d-49d, 553a-80a); *Homilia paschalis* 10 (PG 77, pp. 617b-d); *In epist. ad Corinthos* (PG 74, pp. 936c, 944a); *In epist. ad Hebraeos* (PG 74, pp. 968b-d); *In epist. ad Romanos* (PG 74, pp. 817d-20b); *Quod unus sit Christus* (PG 75, pp. 1208bc, 1268bc, 1275c, 1304d-05a, 1305c, 1320d, 1337b-40a, 1352b-56c, 1360a-61c); *Scholia* (PG 75, pp. 1383a, 1390c-91a, 1373d-74d, 1382c-83d); *Thesaurus* (PG 75, pp. 272d-73a, 392d-401b, 468d-69a). Radcliff, *Thomas F. Torrance and the Church Fathers*, constructively evaluates Torrance's handling of patristic sources. Unfortunately, Radcliff's appendix (201–14) repeats Torrance's incorrect patristic references.

his view that Christ lacked a human mind not only for ontological reasons (How can one person have two minds, that is, two control-centres?) but also for soteriological reasons (If sin is rooted in the human mind, then how could Christ be sinless if he had a human mind?).[196] Against this background, the anti-Apollinarian writings of Athanasius, the Cappadocians, and Cyril affirm Christ's assumption not only of a human mind, but also of a *sinful* human mind which he heals.

The 'Latin heresy' is Torrance's term for Western Christianity's historic tendency to think only in terms of external relations, one manifestation of which is to attribute to Christ an unfallen humanity.[197] Leo's *Tome* is a prime example,[198] although Tertullian and Augustine share the blame for the West's bifurcation of Christ's humanity from ours.[199] Torrance also faults the Chalcedonian Definition's failure clearly to indicate that Christ's humanity was fallen, not neutral.[200] The 'Latin heresy' has infected most Western theology from the fifth century forward. Among those who have escaped its influence, Torrance lists Peter Lombard, Martin Luther, John McLeod Campbell, H. R. Mackintosh, and Karl Barth.[201]

Torrance thus agrees with Barth's fallenness view but disagrees with his evaluations of the fathers and Irving. If the Swiss divine's brief endorsement gave Irving a reprieve from the verdict of heresy, Barth's Scots successor cast its shadow back over his compatriot. It remained for another Barth scholar – an Englishman – to promote Irving's Christology enthusiastically.

1.4 The world, the flesh, and the Spirit: Colin Gunton

Colin E. Gunton (1941–2003) taught at King's College, University of London, from 1969 until his unexpected death in 2003.[202] Through his lectures, writings,

---

[196] *Theology in Reconciliation,* pp. 143–6; *Atonement,* p. 439.
[197] *Karl Barth,* pp. 215–16, 229–32; cf. 202–3; 'Atonement', p. 238; *Preaching Christ Today,* pp. 58–9; cf. *Mediation,* pp. 39–40.
[198] *Christian Frame of Mind,* pp. 9, 10; *Karl Barth,* pp. 203, 232.
[199] *Theology in Reconciliation,* p. 230; *Christian Frame of Mind,* p. 10; *Divine Meaning,* pp. 193–4.
[200] *Incarnation,* pp. 200–2.
[201] *Karl Barth,* p. 232; *Preaching Christ Today,* p. 59.
[202] S. R. Holmes, 'Obituary: The Rev Prof Colin Gunton', *The Guardian* (3 June 2003), n.p. Cited 13 September 2010. Online: www.guardian.co.uk/news/2003/jun/03/guardianobituaries. highereducation.

founding of the Research Institute in Systematic Theology, and co-founding and co-editing of the *International Journal of Systematic Theology*, Gunton significantly influenced anglophone theology.[203] As his former doctoral supervisor, Robert Jenson, claimed in his obituary for Gunton, 'It is not too much to say that, through his books and the people he influenced, he has been the leading agent of a transformation of the British theological landscape.'[204]

From the days of his doctoral thesis until his death, Gunton spent his theological career in critically constructive appropriation of Barth's theology.[205] Yet whenever Gunton discusses Christ's fallen flesh, he appeals not to Barth (whom he critiques as not taking this point seriously enough)[206] but to Irving. Gunton became aware of Irving through reading *CD* I/2. Unlike Barth, though, he went on to read Irving's writings for himself and unearthed in them much material for his own theological agenda.[207] As an indication of both men's influence upon him, Gunton included an engraving of Irving, as well as a photograph of Barth, in his office-wall gallery of mentors.[208]

1.4.1 A fallen network

Gunton's appropriation of Irving must be understood in light of Gunton's theme of relationality. All things exist only within networks of relationships

---

[203] Holmes, 'Obituary'; G. McFarlane, 'Profile: Colin E. Gunton', *Catalyst* 27 (2001), p. 2. Cited 13 September 2010. Online: http://catalystresources.org/issues/272mcfarlane.html; 'King's announces the 2003 Fellows'. Cited 13 September 2010. Online: www.kcl.ac.uk/news/wmprint.php?news_id=225&year=2003; L. Harvey, introduction, *The Theology of Colin Gunton* (ed. L. Harvey; London: T&T Clark, 2010), pp. 1–7 (1).

[204] R. W. Jenson, 'Colin Gunton (1940–2003)', *Theology Today* 61.1 (April 2004), p. 85. Note: According to Holmes, 'Obituary', Gunton was born in 1941.

[205] As attested by Gunton's colleagues C. Schwöbel, foreword, and S. R. Holmes, introduction to C. E. Gunton, *The Barth Lectures* (ed. P. H. Brazier; London: Continuum, 2007), pp. xx–xxi and 1, respectively. On Gunton's debts to and disputes with Barth's theology, see J. Webster, 'Gunton and Barth', *Theology of Colin Gunton*, pp. 17–31. On Gunton's significant contributions to British Barth reception, see Morgan, *Barth Reception*, p. 283, and D. Knight, 'From Metaphor to Mediation: Colin Gunton and the Concept of Mediation', *Neue Zeitschrift für Systematische Theologie und Religionsphilosophie* 43.1 (2001), pp. 118–36 (120).

[206] C. Gunton, foreword to T. Weinandy, *In the Likeness of Sinful Flesh: An Essay on the Humanity of Christ* (Edinburgh: T&T Clark, 1993), pp. ix–xi (x). For a book-length rebuttal on Barth's behalf, cf. Jones, *Humanity of Christ*.

[207] C. E. Gunton, *The Promise of Trinitarian Theology* (Edinburgh: T&T Clark, 2nd edn, 1997), pp. 34, 69; *Barth Lectures*, p. 193; D. A. Höhne, *Spirit and Sonship: Colin Gunton's Theology of Particularity and the Holy Spirit* (Farnham, UK: Ashgate, 2010), p. 36. The first fruit of Gunton's reading of Irving was what Höhne terms a 'watershed essay on Irving's Christology' (36), C. Gunton, 'Two Dogmas Revisited: Edward Irving's Christology', *SJT* 41.3 (1988), pp. 359–76, repr. in C. E. Gunton, *Theology through the Theologians: Selected Essays 1972–1995* (Edinburgh: T&T Clark, 1996), pp. 151–68.

[208] Holmes, introduction to *Barth Lectures*, p. 1.

which constitute them as the particular things that they are.[209] God is three particular persons who are who they are only in relation to one another, and God makes the world and humans in such a way that they reflect finitely the divine reciprocal reality.[210] Thus humans are of a piece with the rest of the created order,[211] yet the universe cannot achieve its God-ordained destiny apart from the perfecting, priestly role of humankind.[212]

Humans are constituted not only by their relation to God and the world, but also by their relation to one another. Heredity and social environment both act as conditioners of individual human persons, who in turn condition others. This does not mean that humans lack free will, however: one freely chooses what to do with one's inheritance and social location.[213] The doctrine of the Fall explains the alienation and strife within these relational networks. Whether or not there was a literal Adam or a historical moment at which the Fall occurred,[214] the doctrine is true to reality: the intergenerational cycle of abuse is one instance of the 'essentially social form' of human depravity traditionally named original sin, whose fatal legacy individuals act upon 'inevitably but voluntarily'.[215] Humanity's collective wrongdoing takes on a life of its own, corrupting the social structures which shape human existence – the 'principalities and powers' – so they become demonic.[216]

For Gunton, 'The essence of sin is to attempt to be like God in ways other than that laid down for those who, because they are finite in time and space, are also limited in their capacity for knowledge and achievement.' Sin is thus

---

[209] C. E. Gunton, *Christ and Creation* (Bletchley, UK: Paternoster, 2005), pp. 36–44.

[210] *Promise*, pp. 83–117, 137–57; *Christ and Creation*, pp. 43–6, 101; C. E. Gunton, *Father, Son and Holy Spirit: Essays toward a Fully Trinitarian Theology* (London: T&T Clark, 2003), pp. 3–18; cf. C. E. Gunton, *The One, the Three and the Many: God, Creation and the Culture of Modernity* (Cambridge: Cambridge University Press, 1993). For two accounts of Gunton's development to his mature Trinitarian philosophy of personhood and relationality, see S. R. Holmes, 'Towards the *Analogia Personae et Relationis*' and Christoph Schwöbel, 'The Shape of Colin Gunton's Theology. On the Way towards a Fully Trinitarian Theology', *Theology of Colin Gunton*, pp. 32–48 and 182–208, respectively.

[211] C. E. Gunton, *The Triune Creator: A Historical and Systematic Study* (Grand Rapids: Eerdmans, 1998), 186–7; *idem*, *The Christian Faith: An Introduction to Christian Doctrine* (Oxford: Blackwell, 2002), pp. 38–9.

[212] *Christ and Creation*, pp. 102–3, 119–22.

[213] Ibid., pp. 38–40.

[214] C. E. Gunton, *Yesterday and Today: A Study of Continuities in Christology* (Grand Rapids: Eerdmans, 1983), pp. 174–5; *Christ and Creation*, p. 45; *Christian Faith*, pp. 61–2.

[215] *Christian Faith*, pp. 61–2 (quotes from p. 61).

[216] C. E. Gunton, *The Actuality of Atonement: A Study of Metaphor, Rationality and the Christian Tradition* (Grand Rapids: Eerdmans, 1989), pp. 65–73; *Christian Faith*, pp. 137, 167–70. Cf. 'Two Dogmas', p. 368; *Triune Creator*, p. 189; *Christian Faith*, p. 60, n. 1.

the reverse image of the Incarnation, in which the eternal Son displays God's true likeness by taking upon himself human finitude in order to reconcile the world to God.[217] Yet not only does the Word become finite flesh, but *fallen* flesh.

Following Irving, Gunton supplies ontological and soteriological justifications for the claim that Christ assumed a fallen humanity.[218] Ontologically, the whole creational network lies subjected to evil and death. Barring an *ex nihilo* event, the Son must take flesh from the mass of fallen creation.[219] This he did by drawing his humanity from his mother, who was herself thoroughly fallen.[220] Furthermore, Christ was born and lived in the midst of a fallen society. Thus through both heredity and social setting, Christ was conditioned by fallenness.[221]

The ontological rationale serves the soteriological: if Christ had not entered creation's web of fallen relations, he could not have brought salvation to it. As we shall explore in detail later, the fallen flesh which he assumes becomes the medium through which he works healing into the fabric of the universe. Important as Christ's participation in fallenness is for Gunton, however, it is equally vital to him to insist that Christ never committed sin. Uniquely among human beings, Christ's fallen nature never issued forth in sinful behaviour,[222] even though he 'exacerbated as much as healed' the social conditions under which he lived, thus contributing to their fallenness.[223]

Nevertheless, Gunton notes the ambiguity bound up in the language of fallenness. Thus he critiques Irving:

> Edward Irving, using language too subject to misunderstanding, spoke of Christ's 'sinful' or 'fallen' flesh. Because it is people, not flesh, who sin and are fallen perhaps it would make the point more adequately if we were to say that the matter from which the Spirit builds a body for the Son is that same corrupt matter as that which constitutes persons of other human beings.[224]

---

[217] *Christian Faith*, p. 60; cf. C. E. Gunton, *Enlightenment and Alienation: An Essay towards a Trinitarian Theology* (Grand Rapids: Eerdmans, 1985), p. 154.

[218] 'Two Dogmas', pp. 366–8.

[219] *Christ and Creation*, p. 53, n. 13; *Triune Creator*, pp. 223–4.

[220] *Actuality*, pp. 130–1; *Christ and Creation*, pp. 50–2; *Christian Faith*, p. 99; C. E. Gunton, *Theology through Preaching: Sermons for Brentwood* (Edinburgh: T&T Clark, 2001), pp. 70–1.

[221] *Christian Faith*, pp. 101–2.

[222] 'Two Dogmas', p. 369; *Atonement*, p. 132; *Christian Faith*, pp. 101–2, 108; *Father, Son and Holy Spirit*, p. 152; *Theology through Preaching*, pp. 174–6.

[223] *Christian Faith*, p. 101.

[224] Ibid., p. 102.

This ambiguity is especially pronounced when Gunton considers Christ's inner experience:

> Did Jesus have 'sinful impulses', as is often asked? That depends upon what is meant. If entertaining the suggestion that he might worship the devil ... is a sinful impulse, then he did. What is at stake is not what was entertained, but whether what is entertained involves already the broken relation to God in which sin consists. The point of the confession 'like us in all things sin apart' is that the one who brings redemption is not himself in need of redemption, but lives victoriously in the realm of death as its conqueror.[225]

In these two passages, Gunton associates the terms 'sinful' and 'fallen' with moral culpability and suggests that such culpability should not be ascribed to physical human nature ('flesh') apart from the person to whom it belongs. Human *physicality* is 'corrupt matter' in the sense of being prone to decay; human *persons* fall into sin. The term 'sinful' is best reserved for persons, not their physical natures;[226] yet the term remains elastic, meaning either *being drawn towards potential sin* or *actually partaking of sin*. Regarding the term 'fallen', Gunton is even vaguer, affirming nebulously that Christ 'in some way shares our fallen condition'.[227]

How, though, does Christ keep from sinning despite sharing our fallenness? How does a single sinless-though-fallen life effect universal redemption? In order to answer these questions, we must bring in Gunton's pneumatology.

1.4.2 Flesh and Spirit

Gunton denies that Jesus was directed or empowered by his own divine nature as the eternal Word. In the Incarnation, 'God the Son self-emptied into the condition of the flesh, the while remaining fully himself.'[228] To be 'flesh' means to be frail and dependent.[229] As God in the flesh, then, Christ's kenotic ignorance and weakness paradoxically demonstrate the divine

---

[225] Ibid., p. 108.
[226] In *Christ and Creation*, p. 51, Gunton transgresses this rule by speaking of 'the soil of sinful earth' whence Christ takes his humanity.
[227] *Christian Faith*, p. 101; cf. *Theology through Preaching*, pp. 174–6.
[228] *Christian Faith*, p. 103.
[229] Ibid., pp. 39, 102–3.

omniscience and omnipotence.[230] His every act is simultaneously fully divine (for he remains the eternal Word) and fully human (for he is the Word made flesh).[231]

But if God the Son exercises no superhuman control over his humanity, finite and fallen as it is, whence are his miraculous powers and perfect alignment with his Father's will? Here Gunton draws from Irving's pneumatology[232] while faulting Barth for following Irving's Christology regarding the flesh but not the Spirit.[233] By the Spirit, Christ faithfully performs God's will and works. The Spirit's role is always to perfect, whether by completing the life of the Trinity or by moving the world towards its eschatological fulfilment. The Spirit shapes the course of Christ's earthly life, perfecting him through resistance to temptation and resilience in his mission, until on the Cross he offers his perfected humanity as a blameless sacrifice to God.[234]

Gunton's pneumatology resolves for him the ancient dilemma of Christ's impeccability. If Christ was unable to sin, says Gunton, then his life's outcome was so 'preprogrammed' as to make all his trials and temptations – indeed, his humanity – meaningless. If, though, Christ was able not to sin, this falsifies his fallenness: postlapsarian human nature requires grace to avoid sinning. Gunton's solution is that Christ was enabled by the Holy Spirit not to sin.[235] The Spirit does not 'preprogram' but bestows liberty to live up to the Father's calling, and Jesus uses this gift to stay true to his mission.[236]

---

[230] *Yesterday and Today*, pp. 161–2, 172; *Christ and Creation*, pp. 79–89; *Christian Faith*, pp. 92–5, 114, 189; *Theology through Preaching*, pp. 81–3, 198–9; *Barth Lectures*, pp. 166–7.

[231] *Christ and Creation*, p. 81; *Christian Faith*, pp. 79, 95. A. Spence, 'The Person as Willing Agent: Classifying Gunton's Christology', *Theology of Colin Gunton*, pp. 49–64, maps Gunton's Christology in relation to Nicene–Chalcedonian orthodoxy and the ancient Christological heresies. Spence finds in Gunton an Irenaean Christology insufficient to avoid Arianism.

[232] *Promise*, pp. 34, 68–9; *Theology through the Theologians*, p. 115. For what follows on Gunton's nexus of Christology and pneumatology, see further in P. Cumin, 'The Taste of Cake: Relation and Otherness with Colin Gunton and the Strong Second Hand of God', *Theology of Colin Gunton*, pp. 69–72.

[233] C. E. Gunton, 'The triune God and the Freedom of the Creature', *Karl Barth: Centenary Essays* (ed. S. W. Sykes; Cambridge: Cambridge University Press, 1989), pp. 46–68 (63–4). For a Barthian response, see Webster, 'Gunton and Barth', p. 28.

[234] *Christ and Creation*, pp. 46–63; *Father, Son and Holy Spirit*, pp. 144–63; cf. *The One, the Three and the Many*, pp. 180–209.

[235] *Christian Faith*, pp. 105–6; cf. *Christ and Creation*, pp. 11, 54; *Barth Lectures*, p. 194.

[236] *Promise*, pp. 37, 66–7. Knight, 'From Metaphor to Mediation', critiques Gunton's critique of Robert Jenson's unconcern regarding Jesus' sinlessness, but Knight's conclusion (133) sounds Guntonian.

1.4.3 Renewing the world

The Son's mission is to restore and perfect the trajectory of lapsed creation by uniting himself in the Virgin's womb with a sample taken from the fallen whole, then purifying and reorienting that sample through a lifetime of obediently reversing Adam's failure. In Christ's crucifixion, his obedience is perfected by his summative self-offering to God – the very destiny for which God created humanity and the cosmos, albeit realized under the conditions of evil. God responds by raising Christ from the dead by the Spirit, thus liberating this sample of creation fully from the Fall and actualizing a prototype of all things' destiny. Because of the interrelatedness of the cosmos, one part's perfection reverberates throughout the whole. The ascended Christ pours out upon humanity the Spirit who perfected him. Within human endeavours, the Spirit inspires present anticipations of the future universal perfection in the general resurrection and the new heavens and new earth.[237]

1.4.4 A second glance backward and forward

Gunton's advocacy has been welcomed by this chapter's concluding theologian. While never grounding the doctrine of Christ's fallen flesh in extensive engagement with scripture or pre-Reformation Christian tradition,[238] Gunton wrote a commendatory foreword to our final theologian's treatise on biblical and historical precedents for this doctrine. To this book and its author we now turn.

1.5 Broadening consensus: Thomas Weinandy

In Thomas G. Weinandy, OFM Cap. (b. 1946), the doctrine of an Incarnation in fallen flesh has crossed continental and confessional boundaries. The proponents examined thus far have been European and Reformed. Weinandy

---

[237] *Actuality*, pp. 130–40, 170, 202; *Promise*, pp. 180–92; *Triune Creator*, pp. 228–36; *Christ and Creation*, pp. 19, 29, 60–3, 80–1, 90–2, 100–3, 110–16; *Father, Son and Holy Spirit*, pp. 153–63, 192–9. Gunton favours universalism but allows for annihilationism (*Christian Faith*, pp. 164–6).

[238] In *Father, Son and Holy Spirit*, p. 192, he does mention in passing and without citation 'the anti-Apollinarian theologians' who affirmed Christ's fallen human nature (quoted in Cumin, 'Taste', p. 69). In 'Two Dogmas', p. 366, he twice paraphrases Nazianzen's *non-assumptus*.

is an American Catholic theologian.[239] His 1993 monograph *In the Likeness of Sinful Flesh: An Essay on the Humanity of Christ* presents a sustained case from scripture and tradition for the fallenness of Christ's humanity. Weinandy obtained a foreword from Gunton and, in the book, acknowledges his debt to Gunton's pivotal article on Irving's Christology.[240] Within the book's compass, Weinandy also surveys the contributions of Irving and Barth.[241]

1.5.1 Conceiving sinful flesh aright

As a faithful Catholic, Weinandy insists that there are *two* examples of a human being who bears sinful flesh but does not sin in it: Jesus and, due to the Immaculate Conception, his mother.[242] Catholic doctrine teaches that Jesus and Mary were both free from concupiscence, the inward proclivity towards sin. Weinandy affirms this teaching[243] and so must define what it means to bear 'sinful flesh' without concupiscence. For him, it means to inherit one's humanity from a lineage of sinners stretching back to Adam.[244] It dooms one to suffer both bodily and psychologically from 'hunger and thirst, sickness and sorrow, temptation and harassment by Satan, being hated and despised, fear and loneliness, even death and separation from God'.[245] Lack of concupiscence preserved Jesus and Mary from moral defect[246] and thus from inward temptation, yet their sanctity only made their experience of temptation greater than our own.[247] Weinandy does seem to allow for sin to have affected Christ's

---

[239] 'Curriculum Vitae: Revd. Dr. Thomas G. Weinandy, O.F.M. Cap.', n.p. Cited 22 March 2011. Online: http://thomasweinandy.com/cv.html.

[240] *Likeness*, p. 57, n. 6.

[241] Ibid., pp. 56–61 (Irving), 61–4 (Barth), 64–70. Weinandy relies on a single primary source each for Irving (*CW* 5) and Barth (*CD* I/2) and misinterprets Irving in the following line: 'Irving believed that to rely *solely* on the Son's divinity as the *solitary* source of holiness within the humanity of Jesus bordered on Docetism or Monophysitism' (59, italics mine). This phraseology implies that the holiness of Christ's humanity was a joint product of the Son's divinity and the Spirit's activity. Section 1.1.1 above has shown that Irving repudiated any ascription of the holiness of Christ's humanity to his divinity; for Irving, the Holy Spirit was 'the solitary source of holiness within the humanity of Jesus'.

[242] Gunton's foreword to *Likeness* (x) asks after the Mariological implication of Weinandy's attribution of sinful flesh to Jesus. Weinandy responds in a postscript (153–6). Inasmuch as Irving (*CW* 1, 589) and Torrance (*Mediation*, 40) expressly link belief in the Immaculate Conception with rejection of Christ's sinful flesh, it is noteworthy that a Catholic theologian affirms both.

[243] *Likeness*, pp. 18, 98–100 (Jesus), 155–6 (Mary).

[244] Ibid., pp. xiii, 17–18, 25, 27, 128, 153, 155.

[245] Ibid., p. 18.

[246] Ibid., pp. 42–3, 155.

[247] Ibid., pp. 100, 155. Weinandy's rationale is that concupiscence entails an inner weakness that saps one's strength to resist before temptation peaks. Lack of concupiscence meant that Jesus and Mary

inner self at a sub-moral level, for he writes, 'By fending off temptation, Jesus was reversing, in his own human mind, will, and emotions, the condition in which we, in our human psyche, have been bound by Satan since the Fall.'[248]

Does 'sinful flesh' of this sort include original sin?[249] Weinandy carefully qualifies his answer. From the moment of conception, both Mary and Jesus were shielded from the *moral* pollution of original sin but not from its *amoral* effects of passibility, temptability, and mortality.[250] Despite this qualifier, Weinandy claims that it is Christ's death in 'sinful flesh' on the Cross that exposes the reality of original sin.[251]

1.5.2 The testimony of the New Testament

Weinandy devotes a division of his monograph to an examination of the New Testament materials which support his contention. He begins with the Pauline passages. Romans 8.3, which provides the title of his book, describes 'Jesus' radical conformity to and solidarity with our sinful flesh (*sarx*). He too knew the dominion of sinful flesh made visible on the Cross where that flesh was condemned (cf. Rom. 8.3-4). Our sinful condition was made manifest and fully exposed in and through Jesus' humanity.'[252] For Paul, *sarx* generally means 'the whole person absorbed in complete self-centeredness and engrossed in the desires and passions of this earthly life.'[253] Likewise, Rom. 6.6-7 describes how the 'sinful body' that Christ shares with us died when it was crucified on Calvary. This 'sinful body' refers to 'the whole person mastered by the disposition of sin.'[254] Thus Christ became a sin offering for us by becoming sin (2 Cor. 5.21), assuming the poverty (2 Cor. 8.9) and slavery (Phil. 2.7) of our

were able to withstand to the point of enduring maximal temptation. Weinandy notes, 'According to our principle, the holier one becomes, the more intense will be one's temptations. The lives of the saints seem to bear this out' (100, n. 11).

[248] Ibid., p. 102.

[249] While the magisterial reformers, following one strand of earlier tradition, identified concupiscence with original sin, the Council of Trent officially distinguished the two. Concupiscence was seen as inclining one towards sin but not as being sin in itself. See 'Original Sin', *ODCC* (2005), n.p. Cited 18 May 2012. Online: http://www.oxford-christianchurch.com/entry?entry=t257.e5017. Weinandy follows the Tridentine distinction.

[250] *Likeness*, pp. 42–3, 98–9, 155–6. Weinandy explains that Mary's preservation from the moral damage of original sin includes her freedom from estrangement from God, original guilt, and concupiscence (155).

[251] Ibid., p. 84, n. 12.

[252] Ibid., p. 80.

[253] Ibid., p. 76.

[254] Ibid., p. 75; cf. 82–90.

subjugation to sin. He entered into this state by being 'born of a woman' and 'born under the law' (Gal. 4.4-5) – both of which phrases Weinandy takes as implying participation in sin.[255]

Turning to the Gospels, Weinandy detects in Jesus' genealogy a stress on the marked sinfulness of the messianic line. His baptism of repentance, temptations, healing of the ill and leprous, thirst by the Samaritan well, and fellowship with sinners at table and on Golgotha all signal his ontological identification with our sinful state.[256] His cry of dereliction does so as well, although Weinandy denies that it was a cry of despair. Instead, he reads it as a prayer of faith and hope from out of the midst of Christ's estrangement from his Father.[257] John's Gospel makes clear that the Word became not merely *sōma* (humanity *per se*) but *sarx* (sinful humanity), a divine sanctuary stained by sin just as the former Israelite sanctuaries had been. He is lifted up on the Cross like the bronze serpent in the wilderness to display to the world the sinfulness of the *sarx* which he shares with all humankind.[258]

Lastly, Weinandy looks to the Letter to the Hebrews. Rather than interpreting it as contrasting sinful Aaronic priests with a sinless messianic priest, he takes the reverse view: Hebrews opposes the earthly priests' ceremonial purity and physical perfection with the heavenly priest's full self-identification with human sin. Jesus' sympathy with our weakness in the face of temptation is only possible because he himself has shared that weakness, which is due to his and our shared sinful condition.[259]

In reflecting upon the biblical data that Weinandy has gathered, it bears noting that his definitions of 'flesh' and 'sinful body' appear to stand in tension with his denials that Christ possessed original sin and concupiscence. For if

---

[255] *Likeness*, pp. 78–82. On p. 78, Weinandy glosses 'born of a woman' as follows:

> Paul accentuated that the Son was born of a woman, thus sharing a common humanity with all who are born of women. However, within the biblical tradition, 'to be born of a woman' also carried with it negative implications. For example: 'How then can man be righteous before God? How can he who is born of woman be clean?' (Job 25.4; cf. 14.1; 15.14-16; Eccl. 5.15-17). For Jesus to be born of a woman then meant that he too shared in our uncleanliness. He bore the trials and endless toil associated with sin and evil.

With regard to 'born under the law', Weinandy notes that the Law of Moses was given to restrain evil impulses but that it had the effect of exposing human sinfulness, thus becoming a curse to us. It was under this curse that Christ was born (79). Cf. Weinandy's coverage of 1 Pet. 2.23-24 on p. 90.

[256] Ibid., pp. 93–104, 116, 127–8.
[257] Ibid., pp. 122–3.
[258] Ibid., pp. 112, 130.
[259] Ibid., pp. 98, 132, n. 7.

'the whole person' is 'absorbed in complete self-centeredness and engrossed in the desires and passions of this earthly life', having been 'mastered by the disposition of sin', how can the Saviour have had flesh and a sinful body without such concupiscent characteristics? If, on the other hand, self-centredness and a sinful disposition were lacking from Christ's humanity, then how can the crucifixion of such a humanity become 'the hermeneutical foundation for the doctrine of original sin', revealing 'that the inherited humanity in which we were born (as too was Jesus) is so contaminated by sin and so deprived of righteousness that it must die and be re-created in the risen Christ'?[260]

1.5.3 The testimony of tradition

As with scripture, so with ecclesiastical tradition: Weinandy uses a division of his monograph to explore the doctrine of Christ's fallen flesh in earlier theologians' thought. Yet Weinandy offers an important *caveat* at the outset:

> Since no patristic treatises specifically address the question of whether or not Jesus possessed a humanity tainted by the sin of Adam, we cannot obtain an exact picture of what the various Fathers believed about this, if they indeed had an opinion. ... Nonetheless, relevant testimony is available which allows us to determine, if not always precisely, the Fathers' fundamental posture and the direction in which their Christological thought was advancing.[261]

This remarkable cautionary note stands in contrast with Torrance's retrievals of the tradition, which can give the impression that the fathers and Barth teach precisely the same doctrine as he does.[262] Weinandy does, however, appeal to Torrance's *Trinitarian Faith* for patristic support.[263]

In order to trace the trajectory of the fathers' thought, Weinandy compiles testimonies to Christ's salvific identification with the fallen human race through his sinful human lineage, birth, inner feelings, temptations, needs, ignorance, suffering, and death, yet without any concupiscence or

---

[260] Ibid., p. 84, n. 12.
[261] Ibid., p. 23.
[262] As noted by Lee, *Living in Union with Christ*, pp. 6–7, and D. Fergusson, 'Torrance as a Scottish Theologian', *Participatio* 2 (2010), pp. 86–7. Cited 21 January 2011. Online: http://www.tftorrance. org/journal/participatio_vol_2_2010.pdf. Cf. Radcliff, *Thomas F. Torrance and the Church Fathers*, pp. 116 n. 9, 147–55, 193.
[263] *Likeness*, p. 30, n. 25.

commission of sin. Such testimonies come from Ignatius, Irenaeus, Origen, Cyril of Jerusalem, Tertullian, Athanasius, Ambrose, Augustine, Ambrosiaster, Gregory Nazianzen, Basil, John Chrysostom, the Council of Chalcedon, and Cyril of Alexandria.[264] Among those who, according to Weinandy, deny such a thorough identification are Clement of Alexandria, Hilary of Poitiers, Nestorius, and Julian of Halicarnassus.[265]

Weinandy takes special pains with two papal writings, Leo I's *Tome* and Honorius I's pronouncement during the Monothelite Controversy. Leo states that the Logos assumed our nature as it was created originally, along with its infirmities, but that he did not assume the sin introduced by the Fall. Reading this statement in light of Leo's preaching elsewhere that God's Son assumed both our human substance and our sinful condition, Weinandy understands Leo to affirm Christ's bearing of the postlapsarian condition of sin-consequent infirmities but not of the sin from whence these infirmities proceed. On the other hand, Honorius declared that, in the Incarnation, '[T]hat nature was assumed which was created before sin, and not that which was defiled after the prevarication. ... For another law is in our members; however the Savior did not have a contrary or diverse will.' Weinandy acknowledges the authority of the pope's statement but urges that 'Honorius' primary intention [was] to uphold the harmony of wills within Christ and not to make a definitive statement on the nature of Jesus' humanity'; therefore Weinandy may safely

[264] Ibid., pp. 25–36. Weinandy cites the following sources: Ignatius, *Trallians* 9 (cf. *Smyrnaeans* 1-4); Irenaeus, *Haer.* 2.12.4; 3.12.3 [These first two references are irrelevant to Weinandy's argument]; 3.18.1, 7; 3.19.3; 3.21.10; 5.praef.; Origen, *Commentarium in evangelium Matthaei* and *Homiliae in Lucam*; Cyril of Jerusalem, *Catecheses* 4.9, 12.15; Tertullian, *Marc.* 2.27; *Carn. Chr.* 4–6, 16, 10–25; Athanasius, *Inc.* 54; *C. Ar.* 1.43, 51, 60; 2.14, 47, 55, 66, 69-70; 3.31, 33, 38, 43, 57; Ambrose, *Incarn.* 76; *Expositio Psalmi CXVIII* 6, 22; Augustine, *Agon.* 12; *Trin.* 13.18; *Enchir.* 41; *Tract. Ev. Jo.* 3.12; 4.10; 10.11; 15.6; 41, 5; *Serm.* 185; Ambrosiaster, *In ad Corinthios Secunda*, 5, 21; Nazianzen, *Ep.* 101.7; *Or.* 38.13; Basil, *Ep.* 261.3; Chrysostom, *Homiliae in epistulam ii ad Corinthianos* 11.5, 21; Chalcedon on Christ's human consubstantiality, 'for to be *homoousios* with us demands more than a generic, ahistorical sameness of species, but a communion with us as we are in reality – brothers and sisters defiled by the sin of Adam' (35); Cyril of Alexandria, *Adv. Nestorii blasphemias* 1.1, 3.2; *De adoratione in spiritus et veritate*, 3; *Ep. ad Nestorium* 2; *Inc. unigen.* 2, 12; and *Quod unus sit Christus*. In his 'Cyril and the Mystery of the Incarnation', *The Theology of St. Cyril of Alexandria: A Critical Appreciation* (ed. T. G. Weinandy and D. A. Keating; London: T&T Clark, 2003), pp. 23–54, Weinandy cites further support from Cyril's *In Jo. Ev.* 1.14a; 3.5; 12.27; 14.20; 17.18-19; *C. Nestorium*, 1.1, 3, and *Explicatio Duodecim Capitum*, 2 and 10. In his *Athanasius: A Theological Introduction* (Farnham, UK: Ashgate, 2007), pp. 32–4, 42, 96–8, he also cites Athanasius' *Inc.* 8–9, 44; *C. Ar.* 1.46-48, 59; 2.10, 56, 61, 64, 67; *Ep. Adelph.* 4; *Epistulae festales* 6.4; 10.8; 11.14.

[265] *Likeness*, pp. 23–5 (Clement and Hilary), 33 (Nestorius), 35, n. 39 (Julian). Weinandy cites Clement's *Stromata* 6.9 and Hilary's *Trin.* 10.23-25. Weinandy's inclusion of Nestorius is ironic, given that Cyril of Alexandria accused him of compromising Christ's sinlessness (see ch. 3.5 below).

disagree with Honorius' assertion of Christ's unfallen humanity[266] without denying papal infallibility.

Moving beyond the patristic period, Weinandy lauds Bernard of Clairvaux and Thomas Aquinas as upholders of Christ's sin-damaged humanity. Anselm, however, and Catholic tradition after Thomas stand reproved for losing sight of this truth.[267] Weinandy also notes that three ecumenical councils have defined that Christ was without sin (including concupiscence).[268]

1.5.4 Weinandy's contributions

Weinandy's monograph brings together in a summary fashion the insights of the four fallenness theologians previously canvassed in this chapter. His retrieval of church tradition supplies Gunton's lacuna in this regard and receives Gunton's qualified approval.[269] More significantly, this retrieval goes beyond Torrance's by rehabilitating Western theologians whom Torrance holds as complicit in the 'Latin heresy'. Weinandy thereby has broadened the consensus historically as well as confessionally and geographically.

Conclusion

Through a survey of selected proponents, this chapter has traced the modern development of the doctrine that Christ's humanity was fallen, even sinful. Edward Irving pioneered advocacy of this doctrine. His view was considered heretical until Karl Barth endorsed him in the context of propounding his own rather different fallenness view. Barth influenced T. F. Torrance (who likewise engaged briefly with Irving); Barth and Irving influenced Colin Gunton; and Gunton mediated Irving's influence to Thomas Weinandy (who also interacted with Barth and Torrance).

All five proponents agree that the terms 'fallen' and 'sinful' are appropriate to describe the humanity assumed by Christ. They further agree that in the

---

[266] Ibid., pp. 35–6 (Leo, citing *Tome* 2–4; *Serm.* 71.2 [misprinted as 7:2]), 36–7, n. 41 (Honorius). It is Honorius' pronouncement which Barth rejects in *CD* I/2, p. 153.

[267] *Likeness*, pp. 40–52. Weinandy's claiming of Aquinas for the fallenness side is challenged by Allen, *The Christ's Faith*, p. 128, n. 97; McFarland, *In Adam's Fall*, p. 134, n. 14.

[268] Those councils are Second Constantinople (AD 553), Lateran (AD 649), and Eleventh Toledo (AD 675) (*Likeness*, p. 52).

[269] Gunton, foreword to *Likeness*, pp. ix–x.

nature which he assumed, he was subject to Fall-consequent infirmities (e.g. temptation, suffering, mortality) yet never sinned. Beyond these points of agreement lie substantive differences.

Regarding Christ's conception, Irving describes it as preventing original sin in his person and suppressing constitutional sin (specifically, the 'law of the flesh' or guilty concupiscence) in his human nature. Barth and the mature Torrance teach that Christ assumed human nature in its state of original sin but healed it at the moment of conception, while taking responsibility before God for the guilt of the rest of humanity. Gunton sees Christ as assuming a physically corruptible body amid a sinful relational network but not guilt thereby. Weinandy accepts the Immaculate Conception of Mary, whereby the moral taint of original sin (including concupiscence and guilt) is denied both to her and to Christ, although leaving them marked by its amoral effects. Occasionally, Weinandy's descriptions of the sinful human condition entered by God's Son strain against the denial of original sin and concupiscence to him.

Regarding Christ's inner experience while on earth, Irving affirms a lifelong mastering of already-guilty evil desires. Barth speaks of Christ's inward temptations but simply means that he felt sorrow and godforsakenness. Torrance's view concurs with Barth's: neither of them attributes concupiscence or self-will to Christ; both see the enmity under which he agonizes across his lifetime as coming from sinners against God and God against sinners, not as coming from Christ's own heart. Gunton allows for Christ to have inclinations towards sin without thereby sinning. Weinandy denies any inward, concupiscent source of the temptations suffered by Christ but sees his resistance to them as reversing the Fall's psychological effects on his mind.

A final arena of contention among this chapter's theologians concerns the harmony of their doctrine with Christian tradition. Does the historic church, both Greek and Latin, affirm the fallenness of Christ's flesh (Irving) or not (Barth)? Or is it the case that the Greeks are supportive while the Latin fathers are not (Torrance)? Or is there a trajectory of both Greek and Latin validation of this doctrine among the early fathers, with a consequent falling away from the truth of Christ's human fallenness during the Middle Ages, at least in the Latin West (Weinandy)?[270]

---

[270] Note that Weinandy's medieval survey in *Likeness* only deals with Western theologians.

Chapter 2 will survey the appeals to the fathers and scripture by unfallenness champions. Chapters 3 and 4 will focus on resolving the disputed appeals to patristic sources by studying the fathers' doctrinal writings and exegesis of key biblical passages. Based on the findings, Chapter 5 will evaluate the modern debate and offer final conclusions. To return to Mackintosh's epigram with which this chapter began, theology, wherever created and however corrupted, may and must be corrected for the sake of the Lord and the church which it serves.

2

The Defence of the Unfallenness View among Select Modern Theologians

Chapter 1 has chronicled the development of the modern fallenness view from its emergence in the ministry of Edward Irving to its advocacy by Karl Barth, T. F. Torrance, Colin Gunton, and, most recently, Thomas Weinandy. In Chapter 2, we trace the history of the opposing view from early reactions to Irving through to its contemporary expression. Four of the five unfallenness proponents surveyed are Scots, a fact indicative of the depth of Irving's impact upon his compatriots. The other proponent, a resident in turn of four continents, redresses the otherwise Caledonian concentration of this chapter. In examining these scholars' positions, we shall follow the same course as in Chapter 1, recording their biblical, patristic, and theological appeals in a generally sympathetic manner.

2.1 Exposing Irving's errings: Marcus Dods

When controversy first ensued regarding Irving's Christological opinions, perhaps his most significant opponent[1] was a fellow Scots minister in England, the elder Marcus Dods (1786–1838)[2] of Belford, Northumberland. Dods, a major contributor to the periodical *The Edinburgh Christian Instructor*, used its pages to critique Irving's view in 1830. The following year Dods published a much-expanded rebuttal as a book, *On the Incarnation of the Eternal Word*.[3]

---

[1] Nantomah, 'Jesus the God-Man', p. 214; Dorries, 'Christological Controversy', p. 424.

[2] Not to be confused with his homonymous youngest son (1834–1909) who became a New Testament professor at New College, Edinburgh. See 'Marcus Dods – Definition', in *Encyclopædia Britannica* (1911); n.p. Cited 21 November 2011. Online: www.wordiq.com/definition/Marcus_ Dods.

[3] Biographical information taken from Blaikie, 'Dods, Marcus'; S. Isbell, 'Dods, Marcus', *DSCHT*, pp. 249–50. Two versions of Dods' book exist under the same title: a longer version prepared by Dods himself and published in London in 1831; and an anonymous, posthumous shorter version in which, according to its front matter, Dods' original *Edinburgh Christian Instructor* reviews were combined, edited, and published in Newburgh, New York by David L. Proudfit in 1842. All further references will be to the London version.

Dods finds Irving erring in theological reasoning and in claims of support from scripture and patristic theologians.

2.1.1 Dods's doctrinal logic

In the arena of theological reasoning, Dods claims that it is terminologically inappropriate to take 'sinful' as synonymous with 'peccable'[4] or to speak of a 'fallen human nature'. Regarding the latter, 'human nature' per se is immutably good, having been created by God; to say otherwise is Manichaeism. Human *nature* did not fall; if it had, then Adam would have lost his *humanitas* when first he sinned. Rather, the Fall negatively impacted human nature's functionality. Christ assumed a human nature unchanged since Adam's creation but without its postlapsarian dysfunction: 'In Christ the human nature was not obstructed and perverted in its operations, by that law of the flesh which dwells in fallen man.' Furthermore, inasmuch as human nature only exists as the nature of a particular person, to speak of a fallen nature in abstraction from the particular person who bears it is absurd. If Christ's flesh is fallen, then either Christ himself is fallen or else his humanity is a distinct person along Nestorian lines.[5]

Using the same logic, Dods excoriates Irving's belief in Christ's quiescent Godhead. Just as belief in an unfallen person with a fallen nature is metaphysical folly, so also is belief in a divine person without a divine nature's attributes. A limited deity is a self-contradiction, an entity akin to the Christ of Arius or the Baal of Elijah's taunts atop Mount Carmel. Christ's miracles prove that, while enduring infirmity, he was yet the Almighty.[6]

Turning to the *munus triplex*, Dods ties his rejection of Christ's human fallenness and divine quiescence to pastoral theology. Christ as prophet perfectly reveals to Fall-fooled sinners God's attributes, such as holiness, justice, immutability, and love. Christ as priest perfectly satisfies the demands of these attributes as confronted by humankind's rebellion. Christ as king possesses perfect authority over his own life, having ceded none to Satan through personal sinfulness, and thus may voluntarily give his life and assume

---

[4] M. Dods, *On the Incarnation of the Eternal Word* (London: R. B. Seeley & W. Burnside, 1831), p. viii.

[5] *Incarnation*, ch. 7 (quotation from p. 372); Dods quotes Augustine, *Fund.* 33; *Nat. bon.* 3. Nantomah, 'Jesus the God-Man', pp. 223–4, cannot follow Dods' philosophical argumentation.

[6] *Incarnation*, pp. 151–3; 233, n. 1; 243–4; 319–20.

it again for our salvation rather than being under any necessity of dying. A sinful human nature in Christ would obscure his revelation, defile his atoning sacrifice, and subject him to death's and the devil's mastery forever. An ordinary infant, fallen in nature but as yet lacking any actual sins, would reveal God or atone for sin just as well as such a Christ. The death of any common sinner would display God's moral character to just the same extent as a sin-stained Jesus' crucifixion would. His intercession would be neither more nor less effectual than that which any fallen being may offer for another. Indeed, if we are saved through the self-redemption of a sinful Saviour, why may we sinful ones not do likewise and redeem ourselves? In short, all confidence in the singular value of Christ as our Mediator is lost.[7]

Fundamental to Dods's argument above is his belief that perfect holiness requires that sinful impulses be absent, not merely suppressed. Any propensity to sin is itself utterly sinful and renders its bearer guilty *in nuce* of all wickedness, making perfect holiness impossible.[8] Although Christ took flesh from a fallen mother, the Holy Spirit generated him as holy so that he inherited no sinful proclivities. Otherwise, what end would the Virgin Birth serve?[9]

If, though, Christ never experienced inclinations towards sin, how can he be a moral exemplar? Dods denies that the Incarnation was meant for this purpose, although he traces back to Lactantius the contrary opinion. Dods believes Lactantius' logic undermines Christ's deity and sinlessness: for Christ to set a usable example, he must be exactly like us, with no advantages of divinity or of freedom from either original or actual sin.[10]

Although for Dods, a fully divine and sinless Saviour cannot be a moral model for strugglers with sin, still he can sympathize with them. Dods appends to Part I of his book an anonymous preacher's sermon on Heb. 4.15 to demonstrate this contention.[11] According to the sermon, God himself both tempts (Gen. 22.1) and is tempted (Ps. 95.9), but in neither case is it with

---

[7] *Incarnation*, chs 1–4. Chapter 2 studies Christ's prophetic office, ch. 3 his sacerdotal, and ch. 4 his regal.

[8] *Incarnation*, pp. 62–4, 135, 138.

[9] Ibid., pp. 46–53.

[10] Ibid., pp. 380–2; Dods quotes Lactantius, *Divinarum institutionum* 4.24.

[11] *Incarnation*, pp. 390–413. D. Macleod, *The Person of Christ* (Downers Grove, IL: InterVarsity, 1998), p. 285, n. 42, identifies the sermon's author as, reputedly, James M'Lagan, to whom Dods dedicates his volume (*Incarnation*, p. vi). Dods' inclusion of this sermon effectively answers Nantomah, 'Jesus the God-Man', p. 221, n. 2, who charges that the unfallenness view is unpreachable.

evil desires, only holy ones.[12] Thus in demanding the sacrifice of Isaac, God tempted Abraham's rightful fatherly affection and righteous trust in God's promise of many descendants through Isaac. This biblical example shows that temptation involving a holy desire is worse than temptation involving a sinful desire. Jesus, then, being tempted solely by holy desires, has tasted temptation's worst and can sympathize with us however severe our temptations. Moreover, his suffering from others' sins sensitizes him to our feeling when suffering from our own sins, and his bearing of imputed guilt initiates him into the guilt-consciousness that burdens us. True, Christ had divine powers and promises to sustain him, but these did not shelter him from a full sharing in infirmity and temptation (e.g. in Gethsemane), and we too have God's Spirit and promises to uphold us amid our trials. Thus Christ is a sinless yet sympathetic Mediator.

2.1.2 Dods's scriptural support

In addition to Heb. 4.15, Dods appeals against Irving to multiple scriptures. Among these are the Mosaic sacerdotal regulations, designed to make the high priest as ceremonially holy as possible. These laws underscored the imperfect holiness of even the Levitical high priests while foreshadowing Christ's sacrosanctity.[13]

Turning to Johannine assertions that the Word came in the flesh (Jn 1.14; 1 Jn 1.1; 5.20), Dods finds no kenotic diminution of the Word's divinity; rather, it is precisely in the flesh that the divine attributes manifest themselves. Furthermore, John stresses the *reality* of that flesh, never its fallenness or sinfulness.[14] The Fourth Gospel also quotes Jesus' assertion that Satan 'hath nothing in me' (Jn 14.30 KJV). Dods hears this statement as implying the absence in Christ of anything relating to sin or its derivative, death.[15] Jesus' invulnerability to involuntary death further appears in his claim that none can take his life but that he has power to discard and retrieve it (Jn 10.17-18), as

---

[12] The preacher claims that this is how Jas 1.13 must be interpreted, rather than in an absolute sense (396–8).

[13] *Incarnation*, pp. 134–5.

[14] Ibid., pp. 312–21 (on Jn 1.14); 337–41 (on 1 John).

[15] Ibid., pp. 222–3, 535–6 (on these latter pages citing Nyssen's *Hom. Eccles.* 7 in support).

also in his authoritative behaviour at his arrest and on the Cross, culminating in dismissing his spirit.[16]

Dods recognizes Rom. 8.3 as a *crux interpretum*. Long before Irving fastened on it, the Gnostics used this verse to deny that Christ was truly incarnate, since flesh is inherently sinful; he had only its similitude ('likeness of ... flesh'). Tertullian replied that 'likeness' qualifies 'sinful', not 'flesh': Christ's flesh was real, but missing the sin that marks our flesh. Later, the Pelagians reversed the Gnostic logic: Rom. 8.3 teaches the exact identity of Christ's flesh with ours, and therefore both his humanity and ours lack original sin. Augustine thundered back that this passage envisages the sinfulness of all flesh save Christ's. Irving, then, combines a Pelagian construal of 'likeness' with a Gnostic construction on 'sinful flesh'. Dods himself affirms that Rom. 8.3 rules out *both* a complete unlikeness *and* a complete identification between Christ and sinful flesh.[17]

2.1.3 Dods's patristic support

Surveying the first four Christian centuries, Dods concludes that neither the orthodox nor heretics ever claimed the sinfulness of Christ's flesh – with two exceptions, noted below. The heretics, however, were condemned for dividing Christ's person from his human nature in like manner to Irving, who resurrects Gnosticism and Manichaeism and out-Nestorianizes Nestorius.[18] The two exceptions to early Christians' concord regarding the sinlessness of Christ's humanity were a book of unknown authorship, *Pauli Praedicatio*, and a Donatist, Parmenianus. Both held that Christ received baptism to cleanse his flesh from sin. Parmenianus' Catholic opponent, Optatus, claimed rather that Christ's holiness sanctified the baptismal waters.[19]

---

[16] Ibid., pp. 131–2, 154, 215–27 (citing Nyssen, *On the Resurrection*; Augustine, *Tr. Ev. Jo.* 47.6), 232, 527 (citing Cyril of Jerusalem, *Catechesis*, 13.13, 13.16).

[17] *Incarnation*, pp. 322–3, quoting Tertullian's *Marc.* 5.14 and Augustine's *C. Jul.* 5.15 and *C. Jul. op. imp.* 6.33 (which quotes Hilary of Poitiers in support of Augustine's interpretation). Dods also cites Hilary of Rome's commentary on the Pauline epistles (525–6; hereafter in this section, all page numbers in parentheses refer to Dods, *Incarnation*); Ambrose's *Paen.* 1.3.12 (543); and Augustine's *Ep.* 164.19 (563–5).

[18] *Incarnation*, pp. viii–xi, 234–6, 285–8, 316–17, 326, 420–45, 452–9 (citing Cyril of Alexandria's *Twelve Chapters* 4, 11), 569–70, 73.

[19] *Incarnation*, pp. 522–5, citing Optatus' treatise against Parmenianus and, for reference to *Pauli Praedicatio*, an anonymous treatise inserted among Cyprian's writings. Cyril of Jerusalem takes the same view as Optatus (526–7, citing *Catechesis* 14.6). The view of *Apostolic Constitutions* 7.22 is similar (469).

Dods marshals an army of ancient testimonies against Irving's tenets: Christ's divine attributes remained fully operational in the Incarnation;[20] his human traits are attributed to his person, not simply to his humanity;[21] he was born without the stain of sin introduced by the Fall;[22] he was free from all peccability, passions, and, on some accounts, even infirmities;[23] his body was under no necessity of death or corruption;[24] in no sense did he save or atone for himself.[25] Some of the fathers even believed Jesus' mother to be free from fallenness – how much more her Son![26] Dods does not concur with the most extreme patristic statements regarding Mariology or Christ's lack of infirmity, but cites them to show how far the early theologians were from attributing sinfulness to Christ's flesh. He especially commends the Christologies of Irenaeus' *Adversus haereses*, Tertullian's *De carne Christi*, Ambrose's *De incarnationis dominicae sacramento*, and the works of Athanasius and Augustine in general.[27]

Dods acknowledges no common ground with Irving's view. To him it is a congeries of heresies based on a poor grasp of reason, scripture, and tradition. Our next subject, who, like Dods, denies fallenness to Christ's humanity, will display greater affinity than Dods does for aspects of Irving's doctrine.

---

[20] Eusebius of Caesarea, *Demonstratio evangelica* 4.13 (513); Nyssen, *Or. cat.* 10 (536); Basil, *Hom.* 25 (527–30).

[21] *1 Clement* 2.1 (467–8); Ignatius, *Ephesians* 1.1 (472–3); Ambrose, *Spir.* 3.11.76, 79; *Incarn.* 7.75 (540–2). Dods' point is that, if sinfulness is attributable to Christ's humanity, then, *contra* Irving, it must be attributed to his person, too.

[22] In addition to the works of Augustine, Ambrose, Hilary of Rome, Optatus, and Cyril of Jerusalem cited above: Augustine, *Pecc. merit.* 2.24; *C. Jul. op. imp.* 4.57 (47–50); *Trin.* 4.14 (139–40); Leo's *Tome* and Christmas sermons (460–2); Tertullian, *Carn. Chr.* 16 (492–3); Gregory Thaumaturgus' creed (503); Chrysostom, *Sermon on the Nativity* (546–7). Indeed, Irenaeus, *Haer.* 4.75-76; 5.16, affirms that unfallen Adam's humanity was but a reflection of Christ's (484–6).

[23] Gregory Nazianzen, *Ors.* 37, 42 (531–2), 51 (45–6); Justinian's confession and anathemas (462–3); Clement of Alexandria, *Paedagogus* 1.2; *Stromata* 4.9 (489–91); Hippolytus, *Eranistes of Theodoret*, 1, 3 (493–4); Origen, *C. Celsum* 1, 3 (495–8); Hilary of Poitiers, *Trin.* 10 (519–21); Macarius, *Hom.* 11 (520–2); Basil, *Hom.* 25; *C. Eunom.* 4 (527–31); Nyssen, *Hom. Eccles.* 7; *Homily on the Resurrection* 1 (535–9); Ambrose in *Incarn.* 7.75 allows that Christ's human mind truly grew in wisdom, but in *Fid.* 5.18 claims that Christ only feigned ignorance (542–3).

[24] In addition to Augustine's, Nyssen's, and Cyril of Jerusalem's comments on John's Gospel cited above: Augustine, *Trin.* 4.16 (214); Anselm, *Cur Deus Homo?* 2.11 (247–8); *Apostolic Constitutions* 5.14 (469); Cyprian, *De idolorum vanitate* (498–9); Gregory Thaumaturgus' ninth anathema (502); Eusebius of Caesarea, *Demonstratio evangelica* 3.4; 10 *passim* (513–14); Athanasius, *De decretis* 14; *C. Ar.* 3; *Inc.* 32–33; 21–24, 44 (515-18); Nazianzen, *Or.* 38 (532); Amphilocius, *Dogmatic Epistle to Pancharius* (540); Basil of Seleucia, *Hom.* 32 (561–2).

[25] Gregory Thaumaturgus' seventh anathema; the Council of Ephesus' tenth anathema (502).

[26] Methodius of Tyre's discourse on the Presentation (504); Amphilocius, *Sermon on the Mother of God* (540); Chrysostom, *Sermon on the Annunciation* (546–7).

[27] *Incarnation*, pp. 333 (Augustine), 487 (Irenaeus), 492 (Tertullian), 515 (Athanasius), 542, n. 2 (Ambrose).

2.2 Descent and development: A. B. Bruce

In the same year in which Dods published his *Incarnation of the Eternal Word*, Alexander Balmain Bruce (1831–99) was born. Raised in the Free Kirk, Bruce served as one of its ministers and, from 1875 until his death, as a professor of New Testament exegesis and apologetics at Free Church College in Glasgow. His most enduring contribution to Christology was *The Humiliation of Christ*, originally delivered as the 1874 Cunningham Lectures[28] and thereafter published.[29] It is this work that will chiefly occupy our attention, although passages from others of Bruce's writings will be adduced where relevant.[30]

2.2.1 Bruce's agenda and axioms

Delivered as a flurry of kenotic Christological theorizing was blowing towards Britain from Germany,[31] Bruce's *Humiliation of Christ* proposes to examine the doctrine of Christ from a professedly novel perspective: that of his humiliation.[32] Bruce considers in turn Christ's 'physical' (i.e. ontological) humiliation in assuming a human nature, his ethical humiliation in undergoing temptation and moral development, and his 'official' humiliation in carrying out the office of Saviour.[33] Throughout, Bruce presents his constructive biblical

---

[28] Incorrectly dated by two otherwise helpful sources as the 1876 Cunningham Lectures in T. R. Thompson, 'Nineteenth-Century Kenotic Christology: The Waxing, Waning, and Weighing of a Quest for a Coherent Orthodoxy', in *Exploring Kenotic Christology: The Self-Emptying of God* (ed. C. S. Evans; Oxford: Oxford University Press, 2006), pp. 74–111 (86, n. 16), and as the 1879 Cunningham Lectures in R. R. Redman Jr., *Reformulating Reformed Theology: Jesus Christ in the Theology of Hugh Ross Mackintosh* (Lanham, MD: University Press of America, 1997), p. 124. The first edition of *The Humiliation of Christ* was published in 1876, two years after Bruce gave his Cunningham Lectures.

[29] Biographical data on Bruce may be found in the following sources: '1911 Encyclopædia Britannica/ Bruce, Alexander Balmain', *Wikisource, The Free Library*; n.d.; n.p. Cited 28 September 2011. Online://en.wikisource.org/w/index.php?title=1911_Encyclop%C3%A6dia_Britannica/Bruce,_ Alexander_Balmain& oldid=662873; 'Bruce, Alexander Balmain', in ODCC (2005), n.p. Cited 28 September 2011. Online: http://www.oxford-christianchurch.com/entry?entry=t257.e1019.

[30] The following works of Bruce will be examined in this section: *The Humiliation of Christ in its Physical, Ethical, and Official Aspects* (New York: A. C. Armstrong & Son, 2nd edn, 1889; repr., n.p.: Forgotten Books AG, 2010); *Apologetics; or, Christianity Defensively Stated* (Edinburgh: T&T Clark, 2nd edn, 1893); *St. Paul's Conception of Christianity* (Edinburgh: T&T Clark, 1894); and *The Epistle to the Hebrews: The First Apology for Christianity. An Exegetical Study* (Edinburgh: T&T Clark, 1899).

[31] Thompson, 'Nineteenth-Century Kenotic Christology', pp. 74–86; Redman, *Reformulating*, pp. 124–5, notes how influential Bruce's *Humiliation* was in both introducing Britons to kenoticism and cautioning against its more radical formulations.

[32] *Humiliation*, pp. 1–3.

[33] Bruce devotes four lectures to the ontology of Christ's humiliation, while assigning one lecture each to its ethical and soteriological aspects.

and theological interpretations in dialogue with theologians ranging from the church fathers to such modern divines as Irving and Dods.

Bruce begins his exposition by drawing from the Christ-hymn of Philippians 2 and from the epistle to the Hebrews a series of axioms regarding Christ's humiliation. Philippians presents a pre-existent person who voluntarily replaces a status of divine majesty with a status of human finitude and servitude, yet retains the same personhood, self-consciousness (the 'mind of Christ'), and divine essence as before the Incarnation.[34] Hebrews adds that the Saviour must be as fully one with humanity – both in nature and in experience of temptation, accursedness, and death – as if he were merely human, personal sinfulness only but absolutely excepted. It is in this utmost identification with human lowliness that Christ is exalted.[35]

2.2.2 Christ's humiliation in historical theology

In applying these axioms to the ancient church's Christological disputes, Bruce first evaluates Apollinarianism. Apollinaris denied to Christ a human mind for the sake of three *desiderata*: the unity of Christ's personhood under the direction of a single, divine mind; the virtue of Christ's sufferings inasmuch as they afflicted his divine soul, not an ordinary human soul in him; and the pledge of his moral infallibility due to the substitution of the impeccable Logos for a human rationality and volition that, in Apollinaris' opinion, not only *may* but *must* lead their possessor into sin. Bruce protests along moralistic lines: such a view rules out the sanctification of our own human souls save 'by the mutilation of [our] nature, or by a magical overbearing of [our] nature by divine power'.[36] Furthermore, while Apollinaris asserts divine passibility (a doctrine with which Bruce is sympathetic),[37] God-in-Christ's experience of suffering is truncated:

---

[34] *Humiliation*, pp. 22–3.
[35] Ibid., pp. 26–36. Heb. 2.10, 11, 14-18; 4.15; and 5.7 are, for Bruce, key passages on the question of Christ's humanity both here and in *Hebrews*, pp. 101–2, 114, 118, 124–6, 171, n. 1, 181–9.
[36] *Humiliation*, p. 45. Bruce repeatedly contrasts two types of power: the moral and the metaphysical ('magical' or 'physical' in his terminology). True religion operates by the former, while superstitious evils like sacramentalism and sacerdotalism vainly rely upon the latter. See pp. 271–2, 437; *Apologetics*, p. 409; *Conception*, pp. 285–92; *Hebrews*, p. 438.
[37] In *Humiliation*, pp. 123–4, Bruce appeals to the Bible's theopathetic language and again applies his moral concern to doctrine: though God and humanity may be dissimilar metaphysically, they are similar morally; therefore God is capable of moral anguish – indeed, he is capable of infinite moral anguish due to his metaphysical status.

Place is found for the physical fact of death, but no place is found for the *moral* suffering connected with temptation. Christ is so carefully guarded from sin, that He is not even allowed to know what it is to be tempted to sin. The author of the theory ... solves the problem of Christ's sinlessness by annihilating the conditions under which the problem has to be worked out. There is no human *nous*, no freedom, no struggle. ...[38]

The fathers' own record is only relatively better. Hilary of Poitiers equates all infirmity with sin and so excludes Christ from even bodily weaknesses.[39] Cyril of Alexandria grants him frailty of flesh but not of mind: Jesus only *appeared* to grow in wisdom or to lack knowledge of the Parousia.[40] Leo and the Definition of Chalcedon fail to discuss whether Christ possessed human personality or infirmities such as ignorance, and if so, how these related to his divinity. The indefiniteness of Chalcedon on such issues brought on 'the dreary period of Christology' in which metaphysical debates produced 'an *anatomical figure* in place of the Christ of the Gospel history'.[41]

By contrast with Apollinarianism, the fathers promoted the doctrine of 'redemption by sample'[42]: Christ takes a human nature complete in both body and soul in order to renew it. Gregory Nazianzen's *non-assumptus* dictum must be understood in this light. Bruce gives Cyril of Alexandria's explanation of the matter:

Christ must take flesh that He might deliver us from death; and He must take a human soul to deliver us from sin, destroying sin in humanity by living a human life free from all sin, – rendering the soul He assumed superior to sin by dyeing it, and tinging it with the moral firmness and immutability of His own divine nature.[43]

Cyril affirms that Christ bore humanity's every limitation save sin alone.[44] Likewise, Gregory Nyssen combats Apollinaris' claim that a human mind

---

[38] Ibid., p. 46.

[39] Ibid., pp. 238–43, citing *Trin.* 10.23, 25, 35, 44, 47.

[40] Ibid., pp. 55–7, 368–74, citing *Adv. anthropomorphitas* 14; *C. Orientales*, Anathema 4; *Quod unus sit Christus* (PG 75, p. 1332); *Adv. Nestorium* (PG 76, p. 154); *Ad reginas de recti fide oratio altera* 16; *Thesaurus*, Assertiones 22, 28; *C. Theodoretum*, Anathema 4.

[41] Ibid., pp. 65–8 (quotations from the lattermost page; italics original).

[42] Ibid., p. 254, n. 2 (all capitals in the original).

[43] Ibid., p. 47. The quotation is from *Inc. unigen.* 8. On the same page, Bruce also quotes Athanasius, *De salvatori adventu Jesu Christi* (= *C. Apoll.* 2), 'about the middle'.

[44] Ibid., p. 55, quoting *Adv. anthropomorphitas* 14 (Cyril makes this exception twice in the passage quoted).

in Christ would necessarily involve him in sinfulness, asserting instead that 'mind is not sin'.[45] In contradistinction from a later version of the doctrine of redemption by sample, the fathers never taught that 'Christ took a portion of *sinful* humanity and made it holy, and through it sanctified the whole lump; but only that He took a portion of humanity in a sinless state, and kept it sinless through a life of temptation, and presented it to His Father as the firstfruits of a renewed humanity'.[46]

That later version of the doctrine arose first among the eighth-century Spanish Adoptionists and again in Bruce's own day through Edward Irving's preaching. Bruce sees their view as rendering superfluous both the Virgin Birth (since it claims that Christ inherited original sin just as Adam's natural offspring do)[47] and the Cross (for how does the killing of Christ's merely latently sinful flesh either satisfy God's justice or help us in our struggles with the flesh?).[48] In addition, Irving, in particular, equates all mortality, corruptibility, liability to temptation and disease, and all other infirmities with fallenness. Bruce contends instead that an unfallen being like Christ may be capable of dying without coming under the necessity of dying, may be truly tempted without suffering concupiscence, and may bear infirmities without their being sinful.[49]

2.2.3 Christ's unfallen mortality, temptations, and infirmities

Bruce moderates Dods's claim that special divine action was necessary in order for Christ to die. Like unfallen Adam, his body was naturally liable to death by such means as deprivation of food, accidental or premeditated injury, or disease. Adam's failure left him no escape from this mortal condition, thus

---

[45] Ibid., 45, claiming to quote *Antirrh. adv. Apol.* 5 (this line actually appears in *Antirrh. adv. Apol.* 11.)
[46] Ibid., p. 254, n. 2 (italics original); cf. 311–12.
[47] Bruce remarks,

> Irving speaks of the manner of Christ's conception as having the effect of taking away original sin. But this is simply a quibble; for he explains his meaning by remarking that Christ was not a human *person*, never had personal subsistence as a mere man. Beyond a doubt the theory requires that original sin should be ascribed to Christ; for original sin is a vice of fallen human *nature*. (255; italics original)

[48] Ibid., p. 437. Bruce critiques two methods of applying to believers Christ's self-mortification: the wishful thinking of 'faith-mysticism' and the '*sacramental magic*' of the transubstantiation of our bodies by Christ's resurrection body in the Eucharist (italics original).
[49] Ibid., pp. 238–43, 255–8. Bruce notes that Irving concurs with Hilary of Poitiers in seeing all infirmities as marks of sin, but whereas Hilary denied to Christ both infirmity and sin (*Trin.* 10.23, 25, 35, 44, 47), Irving assigns both to Christ.

condemning him to die; Jesus, by contrast, freely chose not to evade his foes' plots and the natural processes of death.[50]

Bruce seconds Dods, though, regarding Christ's temptations: his impeccability assures the outcome without annulling real moral struggle, and temptations due to sinless infirmities may equal or outpace those from sinful inclinations. Thus Abraham was tempted to slay his son out of holy love for God. Thus Jesus was tempted to seek a worldly kingdom, not from pride but from desire to avoid the pain involved with his Father's will.[51]

According to Bruce's reading of Hebrews (2.10; 5.7-9; 7.28; 12.2),[52] Christ's conflicts with temptation formed an essential part of the real moral development which he underwent in his humanity while remaining sinless. Opposing Cyril's claim that anything short of perfection implies sin, Bruce distinguishes moral integrity from moral perfection. Adam before the Fall had the first but not the second, else he would never have fallen. A child, too, may attain the former while lacking the latter[53] – and the juvenile Jesus was such a child par excellence.

How are Christ's human infirmities and development to be reconciled with his divine powers and perfections? Bruce surveys the traditional *extra Calvinisticum* doctrine and the modern kenotic theories,[54] finds them all problematic, and resolves to hold to the biblical evidence for both the undiluted deity and the thoroughgoing humanity of Christ apart from a comprehensive explanation.[55] Bruce does, though, explain how omnipotence is made available to Christ's tempted humanity without overwhelming its infirmities. Drawing upon the sixteenth-century Reformed theologian Ursinus, Bruce proposes that the Logos channels wisdom and virtue to his humanity not directly or of metaphysical necessity, but morally (i.e. voluntarily) through the Spirit who proceeds from him. This mediated omnipotence is itself not metaphysical power to defeat temptation but rather moral power to do so.[56]

---

[50] *Humiliation*, pp. 260-1. On the latter page, Bruce comments that Dods' claim that Christ could choose to die by his divine power (*Incarnation*, pp. 99, 165) is misunderstood if interpreted to mean that Christ had to perform a miracle in order to die.

[51] *Humiliation*, pp. 265-70. On p. 270, n. 2, Bruce commends the sermon appended to Dods' *Incarnation*, part I.

[52] Bruce sees Heb. 12.2 as describing Jesus as perfecting his own faith (*Humiliation*, p. 274).

[53] Ibid., pp. 274-88.

[54] Ibid., pp. 126-9, 134-92. Bruce titles the *extra Calvinisticum* the 'double life' view: the Logos lives a life of cosmic governance concurrently with his earthly life in Jesus of Nazareth.

[55] Ibid., pp. 58, 171, 191-2.

[56] Ibid, pp. 124-6, 271-2. Note the underlying assumption of the *filioque* in this model.

Having been perfected through temptation, Christ offers himself to his Father on Calvary as both a sample of and a substitute for humanity. As a sample, he is the Holy One who dies to *maintain* the absolute absence of sin from his life – not to *attain* it, as in Irving's view – through obedience even unto death. As a substitute, he is 'made sin for us' in the sense of bearing the punishment for our transgressions by his bodily death.[57]

2.2.4 Bruce's evolving explanation of flesh and sin

Bruce is aware that a pillar of the theory of redemption by sinful sample is the New Testament's (and particularly Paul's) negative use of the term *sarx*, especially in Rom. 8.3, in which God's Son is said to be *en homoiōmati sarkos hamartias*. Bruce notes that this phrase raises two exegetical questions: Does *homoiōma* here emphasize similarity or dissimilarity between the Son and sinful flesh? Does *hamartias* bespeak an essential, hence inseparable, attribute of *sarx* or an accidental, separable attribute? He allows that various combinations of answers are exegetically permissible and, in *Humiliation*, offers no personal interpretation beyond denying that Paul held a Manichaean view of the flesh.[58]

In his later writings, Bruce clarifies his views. Pauline *sarx* is basically synonymous with *sōma*. It refers to the material half of the human constitution, the remaining half being the human spirit, mind, or soul. Paul sees *sarx* as the 'seat of sin' not because of a metaphysical philosophy that flesh is inherently evil, but because of the moral experience that it is the source of desires – especially libido – that distract from religious devotion and tempt towards sin.[59] Yet exegeting Rom. 8.3, Bruce comments, 'Properly speaking, what the apostle calls "flesh of sin" is not sinful. Sin and sinlessness belong to the person

---

[57] Ibid., pp. 309–21. Bruce sees redemption by sample taught in 2 Cor. 5.14 and redemption by penal substitution in 2 Cor. 5.21 (317–18). Regarding the latter doctrine, he approves of Calvin's view that Christ suffered only the *effects* of God's wrath; the Father was never displeased with the Son (337, 341). Furthermore, Christ never suffered the torments of the damned; rather, the infliction of God's wrath upon a perfectly holy, divine person was sufficient to counterbalance the sin-debt of the whole world (341–51).
[58] Ibid., pp. 431–6.
[59] *Conception*, pp. 140, 144–5, 262–78. Cf. Jesus' own view, according to Bruce, in *Apologetics*, pp. 57–60.

and not to the nature. The flesh as such is in no case bad. It is the inversion of the right relationship between flesh and spirit that is sin.'[60]

Bruce notes that orthodox tradition views Rom. 8.3 as teaching the *unlikeness* of Christ's flesh to ours, but sides with modern scholars who reverse that judgement. For Christ to share our 'sinful flesh' means that his humanity is enough like ours that he can be tempted through physical appetites. Yet Christ lived victoriously within our common flesh by the Spirit's power, setting Christians an example. That power is moral, not metaphysical: for the Spirit to produce flesh metaphysically different than ours would not ensure sinlessness, which is a moral quality resulting from the Spirit's influence on Christ's will, not on his body.[61] Thus the biological fact of the Virgin Birth *signifies* rather than *effects* Jesus' sinlessness.[62]

Bruce denies traditional understandings of total depravity and original righteousness. Romans 7's first-person confession, which describes humanity as a whole, distinguishes sin in the flesh from God's law in the mind because humanity is not generally totally depraved, but possesses a feeble goodness of soul.[63] The Gospels' Jesus thinks likewise, sympathizing with the masses whose 'moral nature [was] not so much depraved as undeveloped' and who, being guilty only of fleshly sins, needed but 'to rouse the man against the brute'. Christ reserves his ire for the Pharisees, whose very spirits were perverse.[64]

This depiction of the Galilean crowds anticipates Bruce's description of Adam in light of the then-new Darwinian theory. Evolution resulted in 'a being who was not merely an animal, but in rudimentary form *human*'. This development marked the 'possibility of moral life' – but only the possibility. The first man possessed original innocence but not original righteousness in the sense of moral perfection. He was morally childlike and full of animal impulses through which evil might master him if he did not learn to master them. This new creature had the potential to move downwards as well as upwards towards moral perfection. The Fall was a *fall back* towards the inferior bestial state whence he had come, a refusal to advance morally.[65] This course

---

[60] *Conception*, p. 285.
[61] Ibid., pp. 172–4, 279–92, 332; cf. *Apologetics*, pp. 400–10.
[62] *Apologetics*, p. 409.
[63] *Conception*, pp. 139, 144–5.
[64] *Apologetics*, pp. 57–8 (quotations from p. 57).
[65] *Apologetics*, pp. 62–3; cf. *Conception*, pp. 42, 274.

of moral advancement, Hebrews indicates, Christ has passed through sinlessly despite sharing our nature, in order to sanctify us.[66]

Bruce's mature hamartiological discussions allow Jesus to share with fallen humankind the same 'sinful flesh' (i.e. a physical nature with natural appetites vulnerable to sin's allurements) and to overcome by the Spirit – themes dear to fallenness advocates like Irving and Gunton. Yet Bruce's Christ had a sinless, unfallen humanity during his earthly life, for inclinations towards evil characterized *prelapsarian* human nature and are not in themselves sin, and Christ always disciplined his flesh so as never to exist in the state of moral retardation which constitutes fallenness. In his later writings, Bruce rebukes Irving's doctrine as forcefully as at first.[67] Yet Irving's fortunes would soon improve, thanks to the theologian to be considered next.

2.3 Catalyst for fallenness: H. R. Mackintosh

Edinburgh's New College theologian Hugh Ross Mackintosh (1870–1936)[68] represents the hub at which meet all the figures studied thus far. One of his professors had been the elder Marcus Dods's homonymous son,[69] to whose memory Mackintosh dedicated his first important work, *The Doctrine of the Person of Jesus Christ*. In that book, Mackintosh uses A. B. Bruce's writings and perpetuates their interest in kenoticism and rejection of Irving's fallenness view. Mackintosh became a strong voice in anglophone Reformed theology during his lifetime, exercising great influence as a teacher and writer.[70] One significant aspect of that influence involved exposing English speakers to trendsetters in German-language theology such as the early Karl Barth, for whose work Mackintosh expressed critical appreciation, culminating in his posthumously

---

[66] *Hebrews*, pp. 101–2, 114, 118, 124–6, 171, n. 1.

[67] *Apologetics*, p. 61; *Conception*, pp. 286–92; *Hebrews*, p. 118.

[68] Biographical information taken from 'Mackintosh, Hugh Ross', ODCC (2005), n.p. Cited 28 September 2011. Online: http://www.oxford-christianchurch.com/entry?entry=t257.e4242.

[69] Redman, *Reformulating*, p. 11.

[70] 'Mackintosh, Hugh Ross'; Redman, *Reformulating*, pp. 1, 7. These sources identify Mackintosh's three major works as *The Doctrine of the Person of Jesus Christ* (1912); *The Christian Experience of Forgiveness* (1927); and *Types of Modern Theology* (1937). For a recollection of Mackintosh's impact on his students, see T. F. Torrance, 'Appreciation: Hugh Ross Mackintosh Theologian of the Cross', in H. R. Mackintosh, *The Person of Jesus Christ* (ed. T. F. Torrance; Edinburgh: T&T Clark, new edn, 2000), pp. 71–94 (75). This book is a distillation of the Christology of *Doctrine of the Person of Jesus Christ* and should not be confused with the larger work.

published *Types of Modern Theology*.[71] He directed his students, including T. F. Torrance, to Barth's *CD* I/1.[72] In the second half-volume of the *Dogmatics*, though, Barth himself displays Mackintosh's influence: Barth quotes Irving's precedent for his own view that Christ assumed fallen flesh, yet the quotations come not directly from Irving but from Mackintosh's quotations of him while critiquing him in *Doctrine of the Person of Jesus Christ*.[73] As narrated in Chapter 1, Barth's solitary reference to Irving rehabilitates him, bringing him to the attention of Colin Gunton and, through Gunton, to Thomas Weinandy. Ironically, Mackintosh's rejection of Irving leads to Irving's acceptance. In this light, and in light of Mackintosh's promotion of Barth to Torrance and others, one must give Mackintosh his due for the anglophone world's interest in the fallenness view.

Did Mackintosh himself hold that view? Torrance affirms so, crediting his mentor[74] with first introducing him to it prior to Torrance's reading of Barth.[75] As evidence, Torrance points to Mackintosh's frequent appeal to the patristic *non-assumptus*;[76] his version of kenoticism, according to which Christ condescended to 'our estranged condition under the condemnation of his eternal truth and righteousness'; and his doctrine of the Atonement.[77] We will test Torrance's claim against the two major works which he references: *Doctrine of the Person of Jesus Christ* and *The Christian Experience of Forgiveness*.[78]

2.3.1 *The Doctrine of the Person of Jesus Christ*

Mackintosh intended *Doctrine of the Person of Jesus Christ* as a students' textbook in Christology.[79] The book comprises a section on the doctrine's New

---

[71] 'Mackintosh, Hugh Ross'; *Reformulating*, pp. xiii, 16, 21–2; Morgan, *Barth Reception*, pp. 26–9, 34–5, 48–9, 160–1.
[72] Torrance, 'Appreciation', p. 73.
[73] *CD* I/2, p. 154, citing Mackintosh, *Doctrine of the Person of Jesus Christ*, p. 277. On Mackintosh's correspondence with Barth and their single personal meeting, see Redman, *Reformulating*, pp. 21–2.
[74] For Mackintosh's influence on Torrance, see McGrath, *T. F. Torrance*, pp. 51–3, 163–4; R. Redman, 'Mackintosh, Torrance and Reformulation of Reformed Theology in Scotland', *Participatio* 2 (2010), pp. 64–76. Cited 9 December 2011. Online: www.tftorrance. org/journal/participatio_vol_2_2010.pdf.
[75] Torrance, *Atonement*, p. 441. Cf. *Karl Barth*, p. 232.
[76] Torrance, 'Appreciation', p. 86; *Atonement*, p. 441.
[77] Torrance, 'Appreciation', pp. 80–1, 86 (quotation from p. 81; the words are Torrance's, not Mackintosh's).
[78] Ibid., p. 75. In his foreword to *The Person of Jesus Christ*, pp. vii–ix, Torrance praises *Doctrine of the Person of Jesus Christ* as 'one of the really great works in Christian Dogmatics' (vii).
[79] *Doctrine of the Person of Jesus Christ*, p. vii.

Testament sources, one on its historical development, and a final section on Mackintosh's own kenotic reconstruction of it. He uses Bruce's writings when covering the synoptic Gospels, Hebrews, German kenoticism, and Irving.[80]

Within the New Testament, Mackintosh underscores the Gospels' and Hebrews' depictions of Christ's genuine human development, limited knowledge, dependence upon his Father for guidance and miraculous power, and real battles with temptation – yet without any taint of even inward sin, for 'no corrupt stain existed in His nature to which temptation could appeal.'[81] As for the Pauline ascription to Christ of 'the likeness of sinful flesh', Mackintosh explains that 'the meaning is simply that while Christ's flesh is as real as ours, and as human, it was not like ours sinful. The flesh of man, with this one exception, was the pattern of His flesh, but in Him alone it may be seen in a perfected relation to the Spirit.'[82]

In keeping with his kenotic concern, Mackintosh's historical survey focuses on the church's overall tendency, prior to the nineteenth century, to obscure the robust humanity in the New Testament's portrait of Jesus of Nazareth. The issue of Christ's relationship to sinful humankind arises occasionally.[83] Irenaeus receives applause for holding together Christ's person and work through a soteriology of 'personal identification': 'In His infinite love He was made as we are in order that He might make us to be as He is. Our fleshly and corruptible nature is, as it were, fused or inoculated with Deity, and so made immortal.'[84] Similarly, Gregory Nazianzen rightly insisted against Apollinaris that in order to make humanity whole, Christ must take a whole humanity – hence 'the unassumed is the unhealed'.[85]

The above could appear to support Torrance's claim that Mackintosh taught the fallenness view. What, though, does Mackintosh mean by salvific 'personal identification'? And how does he understand Nazianzen's dictum? In his coverage of the Synoptics, Mackintosh had commented that Jesus' baptism

---

[80] Synoptics: A. B. Bruce, *The Kingdom of God* (Edinburgh: T&T Clark, 2nd edn, 1890); Hebrews: *Hebrews*; kenoticism and Irving: *Humiliation*.

[81] *Doctrine of the Person of Jesus Christ*, pp. 11–14, 26, 35–8, 79–80, 100–2, 104–7 (quotation from p. 79).

[82] Ibid., p. 63.

[83] Mackintosh discusses the Spanish Adoptionists (225) but never mentions their teaching that Christ had sinful flesh or makes use of Bruce's analysis of them.

[84] Ibid., pp. 145–6 (quotations from 146). Mackintosh generally cites secondary rather than primary sources for his historical survey. Nevertheless, the second quotation above begins with a line from Irenaeus' *Haer.* 5.praef.

[85] Ibid., p. 200 (quoting Nazianzen, *Ep.* 101).

was not a confession of sin but a self-identification with sinners 'in which He numbered Himself with the transgressors and took all their burdens as His own'.[86] Later, Mackintosh writes of the Atonement as 'Jesus' self-identification with the sinful' and quotes Nazianzen's dictum again – just after a passage on the necessity of Christ's thorough sinlessness to his perfect humanity![87] For Mackintosh, then, 'personal identification' and the *non-assumptus* mean that God's Son becomes *really* human and *sympathetically reckons* himself sinful. Mackintosh will develop the latter theme in *The Christian Experience of Forgiveness*.

Turning to the modern period, Mackintosh critiques two opposing thinkers on the subject of Christ's relation to sin. Schleiermacher's insistence on Christ's sinlessness verges on Docetism, for Schleiermacher excludes moral struggle from Christ's life.[88] Irving veers to the other extreme, associating Christ's moral struggle and physical corruptibility with moral corruption. The result is a diluted doctrine of Christ's sinlessness, for he possesses a 'strong efficacious germ of evil', which the terms 'original sin' and 'fallen human nature' commonly connote.[89] As we saw in Chapter 1.3.1, young Torrance is influenced by this critique to reject Irving. In claiming Mackintosh for the fallenness view, though, Torrance overlooks Mackintosh's equation of fallenness with original sin in this passage. For Mackintosh, to attribute fallenness to Christ would be to attribute original sin to him.

The full significance of Christ's full sinlessness appears in Mackintosh's reconstruction of Christology. He rejects, on the one hand, the merely human 'good teacher' of liberalism and, on the other, the two-natured Christ of Chalcedon. Both traditions are blind to the fact that self-conscious, ethical Will is the ultimate metaphysical category. Liberals grant Jesus' union of will with God but miss the implication: Jesus therefore *is* God. Chalcedonian

---

[86] Ibid., pp. 36–7 (quotation from latter page).
[87] Ibid., pp. 404–5 (quotation from latter page). It is p. 404's quotation of Nazianzen which Torrance cites in a handwritten note in his Auburn lectures – the first of Torrance's many appeals to the dictum (Rankin, 'Carnal Union', pp. 107–8).
[88] *Doctrine of the Person of Jesus Christ*, p. 255; repeated in *Types of Modern Theology*, pp. 88–90 (see 2.3.3 below).
[89] *Doctrine of the Person of Jesus Christ*, pp. 276–8 (quotation from lattermost page). Mackintosh suggests that Irving may have been confused by the Fathers' tendency to make 'flesh' synonymous with 'humanity', and so misconstrued their meaning of 'corrupt'. In *Reformulating*, Redman misinterprets Mackintosh's term 'corruptible' as meaning 'open to the possibility of sin' (97–8). In fact, Mackintosh immediately defines the term himself: 'liable to corruption or decay ... liable to decay and death, as being capable of dying' (278).

and post-Chalcedonian orthodoxy postulates substance as greater than will, thereby dividing Christ's unity of life between two autonomously existent, amoral, quasi-material entities called 'divine nature' and 'human nature', each with its own will. For Mackintosh, by contrast, in Christ divinity and humanity are 'two *aspects* of a single concrete life'.[90] Since no human nature exists apart from a personal will, and since there is only one divine-human, sinless will in Christ, an Irving-like formula such as 'sinful in humanity but not in divinity' or 'sinful in nature but sinless in person' becomes impossible.

Sinlessness is, as previously mentioned, crucial for Christ's perfect humanity. Mackintosh critiques traditional orthodoxy for doing injustice to Christ's full humanity. Yet against those who claim that Christ cannot be one with us in nature or sympathy without himself having a sinful humanity, Mackintosh argues the reverse. Sin diminishes one's humanity; therefore a sinless Christ is the most fully human Christ. Indeed, any sin within Christ would dull his experience of temptation and his sympathy. Beset by sinless infirmities and temptations, he has known the fullest extent of agony in choosing God's path over natural human desires, and his hard-won victories attract us to him for aid with our struggles.[91]

Not only is sinlessness evidence of Christ's perfect humanity, but also of his deity, which enables his human moral perfection.[92] His sinlessness is a miracle, of which the absence of a human father in his conception is a sign but not a source: Christ could have inherited already-sinful proclivities through Mary[93] or been conditioned towards sin by his environment, but instead, he developed from infancy to adulthood 'with a nature untainted, immaculate, nowise handicapped from the very outset by seeds of evil germinating in the soil of character'. Indeed, 'From outset to end no desire, motion, conception, or resolve existed in the soul of Jesus which was not the affirmation and execution

---

[90] *Doctrine of the Person of Jesus Christ*, pp. 213–15, 288–303 (quotation from 295; italics original), 415–18; cf. 113–14. On Mackintosh's concrete Christocentric theological method and abhorrence of abstractions, see A. Purves, *Exploring Christology and Atonement: Conversations with John McLeod Campbell, H. R. Mackintosh and T. F. Torrance* (Downers Grove, IL: InterVarsity, 2015), pp. 87–90.

[91] *Doctrine of the Person of Jesus Christ*, pp. 386–7, 393–5, 401–6; on p. 404, in the midst of this argument, Mackintosh quotes the *non-assumptus*.

[92] Ibid., pp. 403–4, 412. Mackintosh holds that Jesus knew he was impeccable but 'not in advance how or how soon the final triumph [over each temptation] would be vouchsafed' (481; cf. 412–13).

[93] Ibid., pp. 532–3.

of the will of God.'[94] As we have seen, this unbroken continuity of will between Christ and God constitutes the deity of Christ for Mackintosh.[95]

The importance of sinlessness as evidence for Christ's deity is heightened by Mackintosh's kenoticism. In the Incarnation, the Son transposes his attributes of omniscience, omnipotence, and omnipresence from actuality into potentiality, rendering them incompletely usable until his resurrection.[96] Accordingly, we may not point to these attributes in the earthly Christ's life as evidence of his divinity. Rather, our appeal must be to such attributes as his sinlessness, which reveals divine holiness; his forgiveness, which demonstrates divine pardon; and his self-sacrifice, which manifests divine love.[97] To these three attributes Mackintosh will return in his second major work.

2.3.2 *The Christian Experience of Forgiveness*

Doctrine of the Person of Jesus Christ examined the Incarnation. Fifteen years later, Mackintosh published *The Christian Experience of Forgiveness*, which emphasized the Atonement. Here Mackintosh repeats that Christ reveals divine love and forgiveness, especially on the Cross, and in doing so reveals his own deity.[98] Christ also reveals the true character of sin: it is unchristlikeness, the contradiction in heart or act to his trusting love of God.[99] Given this definition of sin and Mackintosh's stress on human congenital evil,[100] the implication is that Christ's humanity is, in very nature, the antithesis of our depravity.

This contrast between our sinfulness and Christ's sinlessness is transcended by Christ's reconciling movement. Developing the concept of personal

---

[94] Ibid., pp. 413–14.
[95] R. R. Redman Jr., 'H. R. Mackintosh's Contribution to Christology and Soteriology in the Twentieth Century', *SJT* 41.4 (1988), pp. 517–34 (520), quotes Mackintosh's *Lecture Synopses* (unpublished and undated summaries of his class lectures), sheet 50, which asserts that the ethical relationship between Jesus and God, far from diminishing Christ's divinity, is the profoundest metaphysical reality.
[96] *Doctrine of the Person of Jesus Christ*, pp. 465–86; cf. 106–7. For historical context and theological analysis, see Thompson, 'Nineteenth-Century Kenotic Christology', pp. 87–95; cf. Purves, *Exploring*, pp. 92–5. The kenoticism of Reformed theologians like Irving and Mackintosh belies the claim by Allen, *The Christ's Faith*, p. 126, that kenoticism is a peculiarly Lutheran interest.
[97] *Doctrine of the Person of Jesus Christ*, pp. 13–14, 326–43, 397, 401, 412, 466–7, 486. Redman, 'Contribution', p. 525, notes that Mackintosh's later lectures and writings do not explicitly discuss kenoticism.
[98] H. R. Mackintosh, *The Christian Experience of Forgiveness* (New York: Harper & Bros., 1927), pp. 83–102, 210–12.
[99] Ibid., pp. 54–5, 61.
[100] Ibid., pp. 41, 53–4, 63–9, 234. Mackintosh denies total depravity as overstating the case, but affirms Kant's concept of radical evil.

identification first articulated in *Doctrine of the Person of Jesus Christ*, Mackintosh analyses the Atonement via the analogy of human forgiveness. For forgiveness to occur, the forgiver must sympathize with the offender and bear the cost of forgiving. God in Christ sympathizes with sinners by self-identifying with them and bears the cost of forgiving them. This self-identification increases throughout Christ's lifetime and culminates on the Cross in his acceptance on our behalf of God's judgement upon sin.[101] As in *Doctrine of the Person of Jesus Christ*, Mackintosh has in mind that Christ took on sinners' responsibility, not their warped nature.[102] Yet their very nature is changed through their mystical union with him.[103]

Thus far, Torrance's claim that his Edinburgh teacher schooled him in the fallenness view stands unsubstantiated.[104] Whether quoting Nazianzen's *non-assumptus*, advocating kenoticism, or explicating Christ's atoning identification with sinners, Mackintosh never speaks of the Incarnation as including a fallen or sinful humanity.[105] Indeed, he specifically critiques Irving for doing so. One possibility remains: perhaps reading Barth changed Mackintosh's mind.

2.3.3 *Types of Modern Theology*

To test this hypothesis, we examine the coverage of the Swiss theologian in the Scot's last major work. What we find is, first, that although Mackintosh

---

[101] Ibid., pp. 188–93, 198, 207–8, 215–19, 224–9. Purves, *Exploring*, p. 177, frets that Mackintosh overloads the analogy between human and divine forgiving, which assumes a 'shared moral order between God and humankind'.

[102] *Christian Experience*, p. 198, echoes *Doctrine of the Person of Jesus Christ* on Christ's baptism: 'It was not for Him a baptism of repentance; yet it was an act or experience in which He refused to be reckoned apart from the other members of God's family and stood at their side before the Divine holiness.'

[103] *Christian Experience*, pp. 122–4, 157, 226–9. Cf. Redman, *Reformulating*, pp. 183–200. In *Doctrine of the Person of Jesus Christ*, Mackintosh clarifies that this is a personal union, not a substantial union (334).

[104] Pace Radcliff, *Thomas F. Torrance and the Church Fathers*, p. 109 (n. 339 confuses Mackintosh's *Doctrine of the Person of Jesus Christ* with his similarly titled *Person of Jesus Christ*), p. 195. Influenced by Torrance (*Reformulating*, pp. xvi, 5), Redman likewise makes the unsupported claim in 'Contribution' that Mackintosh taught that 'God took our sinful human nature upon himself in the incarnation' (532).

[105] Cf. G. D. Dragas, 'T.F. Torrance as a Theologian For Our Times: An Eastern Orthodox Assessment' (lecture presented at the annual meeting of the Thomas F. Torrance Theological Society, Chicago, 16 November 2012. Cited 3 August 2015. Online: http://www.youtube.com/watch?v=Frhvk-MY3dg), 00:49:17–00:54:15. Dragas, Torrance's one-time Greek Orthodox student, recounts how he and Torrance disagreed on whether Christ had assumed a fallen human nature. Dragas silenced Torrance by reading aloud the treatment of Christ's sinlessness and unfallen humanity in Mackintosh's *Doctrine of the Person of Jesus Christ* and identifying Mackintosh's view with the Orthodox view.

delineates both what he appreciates about Barth (the seriousness of his project and his assault on humanism) and where he demurs (aspects of Barth's doctrine of revelation; his 'excessive *actualism*'),[106] a doctrine of Christ's fallen flesh appears on neither list. Secondly, Mackintosh only refers to Barth's early works, culminating in the newly translated *CD* I/1. Mackintosh died two years before Barth published his second half-volume, in which he openly affirms his solidarity with Irving (using as a source Mackintosh's *Doctrine of the Person of Jesus Christ!*) and other fallenness proponents.[107] Finally, Mackintosh notes that Barth's thought is protean and prone to exaggerated expression and apparent self-contradiction;[108] it is perilous, therefore, to presume that Mackintosh concurred or would have concurred with Barth on any specific theological point absent an explicit statement to that effect. Whatever he may have communicated to students like Torrance in a classroom lecture or private conversation, Mackintosh's publications support his inclusion in the unfallenness camp. The evidence indicates that he served the fallenness view as a catalyst, an agent of change in its favour who himself remained unchanged by it.[109]

2.3.4 Taking stock of transition

Barth's massive influence triggered a turning of the tide of opinion regarding a fallen humanity of Christ.[110] The unfallenness theologian whose view we next examine lived through and well beyond this shift, yet does not explicitly engage with fallenness proponents on that issue. Barth is the only one of them singled out for criticism, and then for other reasons (as we shall see below). Nor does he refer to other modern unfallenness advocates. Like his native continent, he is an island unto himself. Nonetheless, he does bridge the period between

---

[106] *Types*, pp. 281–2, 314–19 (quotation from p. 314; italics original).

[107] Barth's avowal of fallenness in *KD* I/2, which inspired Torrance, bewildered another of Mackintosh's former students. In *God Was in Christ* (New York: Charles Scribner's Sons, 1948), pp. 16–17, D. M. Baillie asks if Barth means simply to affirm Christ's passibility and mortality or to ascribe to him original sin. Citing Bruce's *Humiliation*, Baillie notes the precedents for Barth's view in the Spanish Adoptionists, Gottfried Menken, and Edward Irving and claims that the fallenness position has always been considered heretical. *Pace* Clark and Johnson, *The Incarnation of God*, p. 118, n. 29, Baillie was hardly pro-fallenness.

[108] *Types*, pp. 264–5, 313–14.

[109] This claim applies only to the fallenness view. Mackintosh was affected by other aspects of Barth's theology, according to Redman, *Reformulating*, pp. 22–5, although Morgan, *Barth Reception*, p. 160, may overstate the case; cf. McGrath, *T. F. Torrance*, p. 124.

[110] In 1912/13, Mackintosh could write, 'No modern thinker with whom I am acquainted could be said to hold Irving's position' (*Doctrine of the Person of Jesus Christ*, p. 277, n. 1).

Mackintosh and the twenty-first century with an unfallenness perspective grounded in biblical scholarship, informed by the church fathers (especially Athanasius), and representative of theology beyond Scottish Presbyterianism.

2.4 The importance of image: Philip E. Hughes

The life of Anglican cleric Philip Edgcumbe Hughes (1915–90) encompassed the globe: born in Australia, he received his education in South Africa, England, and his homeland. He taught for six years at Tyndale Hall, Bristol, served for three years as secretary of the Church Society, and edited its periodical, *The Churchman*, for several years. In 1964 he immigrated to the United States, where he taught in seminaries until his death. His academic interests, like his life, were wide-ranging: his many writings include New Testament commentaries, Reformation studies, and forays into apologetics, ethics, and dogmatics.[111] His magnum opus, published a year before his death, synthesizes these interests in a Christologically controlled study of theological anthropology, *The True Image: The Origin and Destiny of Man in Christ*.[112]

Hughes structures *True Image* under three headings: the creation of humanity in the image of God; the Fall's damage to that image; and its renewal and perfection in the reconciliation wrought by Christ, the incarnate image of God. This tripartite structure is not original to *True Image*; although it is developed most fully there, it appears in Hughes' writings from up to twenty-seven years prior,[113] indicating an enduring theological framework for his thought. We therefore shall follow the order of this framework in our comments below.

---

[111] Biographical and bibliographical information may be found at 'History – Secretaries – Philip Edgcumbe Hughes', n.p. Cited 3 December 2011. Online: www.churchsociety.org/aboutus/History/Secretaries-Hughes.asp; P. E. Hughes, 'The Sovereignty of God – Has God Lost Control', n.p. Cited 3 December 2011. Online: www.the-highway.com/articleMay99.html; and W. R. Godfrey and J. L. Boyd III (eds), *Through Christ's Word: A Festschrift for Dr. Philip E. Hughes* (Phillipsburg, NJ: Presbyterian & Reformed Publishing, 1985), pp. vii, 247–52.

[112] P. E. Hughes, *The True Image: The Origin and Destiny of Man in Christ* (Grand Rapids: Eerdmans, 1989).

[113] P. E. Hughes, *Paul's Second Epistle to the Corinthians: The English Text with Introduction, Exposition and Notes* (NICNT; Grand Rapids: Eerdmans, 1962; repr. 1986), p. 130; idem, 'The Creative Task of Theology', in *Creative Minds in Contemporary Theology: A guidebook to the principal teachings of Karl Barth, G. C. Berkouwer, Emil Brunner, Rudolf Bultmann, Oscar Cullmann, James Denney, C. H. Dodd, Herman Dooyeweerd, P. T. Forsyth, Charles Gore, Reinhold Niebuhr, Pierre Teilhard de Chardin, and Paul Tillich* (ed. P. E. Hughes; Grand Rapids: Eerdmans, 1966), pp. 9–25 (9–12); idem, *Hope for a Despairing World: The Christian Answer to the Problem of Evil* (Grand Rapids: Baker, 1977), chs 2–3.

2.4.1 Humanity made and marred in God's image

Of vital importance to Hughes is humanity's creation *in*, not *as*, the image of God. The second person of the Trinity is himself the image of God; humankind, then, is created in the divine Son. This reality means that there is an 'affinity', grounded in creation, between the one who is God's image and the ones who are in that image. This creational congruity provides a basis for the Incarnation, for the Son is not so utterly other than humanity as to render theanthropic union unfitting.[114] Beyond affirming this affinity, Hughes itemizes six attributes by which humans show that they are in God's image: personality, spirituality or religiosity, rationality, morality, authority, and creativity.[115]

The Fall occurred when humanity overreached its created bounds by preferring to be God rather than be in God's image.[116] The effect was the distortion (but not destruction) of the image's imprint in humanity by total depravity, as evidenced by the degradation of the six attributes listed above,[117] and by the ultimate ungodlikeness of death.[118] Because all human nature was 'concentrated' in Adam, the whole race shared in his transgression.[119] For Hughes, it is critical that the Genesis accounts of Creation and Fall be taken as reliable historiography, lest the historicity of the Christ-event itself come to be dismissed or Pelagianism's 'each his own Adam, each her own Saviour' be revived. Thus he rejects Barth's, Brunner's, and Reinhold Niebuhr's symbolic interpretations, as well as the evolutionary explanation that 'original sin' is the holdover of humanity's animal heritage, to be overcome through racial self-effort and the immanent emergence of Christ as the first of a new, higher species.[120]

---

[114] *Hope*, pp. 67–70, 72; *True Image*, pp. ix, 15–50, 213–14.

[115] *Hope*, pp. 50–5; *True Image*, ch. 5; cf. 'Creative Task', p. 10.

[116] *Corinthians*, p. 205; 'Creative Task', pp. 10–11; *True Image*, pp. 116–17.

[117] *Hope*, pp. 57–64; *True Image*, chs 5–6, 14.

[118] *True Image*, ch. 10.

[119] *True Image*, pp. 131–3. Hughes claims that the aorist tense of Paul's 'all sinned' (Rom. 3.23; 5.12) indicates 'a single definite act in the past – the sin of Adam in which all participated' (130). Cf. *Corinthians*, p. 195. But cf. D. A. Carson, *Exegetical Fallacies* (Grand Rapids: Baker, 2nd edn, 1996), 69: 'There may be contextual reasons for thinking that all persons did in fact die when Adam committed his first sin …; it is just that the aorist verb ἥμαρτον … does not prove it.'

[120] *True Image*, pp. 68–9, 99–101, 113, 121, 129, 224–31. Hughes also rejects Barth's concept of *das Nichtige* as the origin of evil, finding it unsupported in scripture, unrequired by God's creative work, and impinging on metaphysical dualism (101–7). Cf. P. E. Hughes, *A Commentary on the Epistle to the Hebrews* (Grand Rapids: Eerdmans, 1977), p. 445.

2.4.2 Humanity restored by God's image

Rather than being an evolutionary breakthrough, the Incarnation is the salvific descent of the original image of God. Because humanity was created in God's image, that is, in the Son, his entrance into human nature restores and fulfils in his own theanthropic life the design for which humankind was made. The Son assumes our common human nature from his mother, but his conception by the Holy Spirit preserves him from inheriting our common fallenness, which would have left him in need of a Saviour himself. He begins his earthly career with a humanity 'unfallen as was Adam's at first', yet needing to maintain integrity despite testing.[121] This he does *as a human being*: while Hughes rejects all kenotic theories,[122] he also denies Christ's impeccability (*non posse peccare*) as implying an Apollinarian overruling of the human by the divine in Christ, as devaluing his temptations and sinlessness for us in our struggle against sin, and as logically leading to additional divine attributes, such as impassibility and immortality, being predicated of his earthly humanity, rendering Calvary impossible.[123]

Christ's sinless perfection, then, is not static but an achievement – not that he ever was sinful or imperfect, but that he preserved his purity in the teeth of temptation. This victory prepared him for the object of his coming, the offering up of his spotless life to make atonement for sin.[124] Hughes emphasizes that the manner of Christ's death matters. He died not from age, accident, disease, or secret assassination, but willingly, as a condemned evildoer between two other evildoers and as the substitute for a third (Barabbas), yet all the while manifestly innocent. The manner marks the meaning of Christ's death as a penal substitution by which he satisfied divine justice.[125] His subsequent exaltation from the tomb to God's throne establishes the originally intended perfecting of human nature. Through their union with Christ, believers already taste that perfection. One day it will overtake the whole cosmos[126] and the wicked will be destroyed.[127]

---

[121] *True Image*, pp. 134 (quotation from this page), 214–18; cf. *Hebrews*, p. 188.

[122] *True Image*, ch. 17. 'Even in his death-throes on the cross and when his lifeless body is laid in the tomb he is upholding the universe by his word of power (Heb. 1:3)' (233).

[123] *True Image*, pp. 331–4.

[124] *Corinthians*, pp. 212–13; *Hope*, pp. 77–9; *True Image*, pp. 328, 331.

[125] *Hebrews*, pp. 185–6; *Hope*, pp. 80–2; cf. 113–14; *True Image*, pp. 335–7, 340–1; in chs 31–32, Hughes surveys the history of Atonement theories and urges that the Atonement is objective and also inspires a subjective response.

[126] *True Image*, pp. 381–5, 408–14; cf. *Hope*, p. 73.

[127] *True Image*, ch. 37 advocates annihilationism.

2.4.3 Patristic and biblical support

In describing God's plan of redemption, Hughes' writings draw repeatedly upon Athanasius for a number of points: God will not allow corruption and futility to frustrate his purpose for creation, and so, in order to save those made in his image, he sends the image itself, his Son. The immortal, incorruptible, impassible Logos took mortal, corruptible, passible flesh like our own – yet unblemished by sin and thus qualified for sacrifice – so that he might suffer and die for us, overcome death and corruption in himself by his divine power, and transmit that victory to us through the process of deification, thus fulfilling our divinely intended destiny.[128] *True Image* also surveys the other Christological formulations of the patristic period from the Docetists through Chalcedon.[129] Throughout this section, Hughes works with primary sources and interprets them in a manner consistent with the unfallenness position. Thus, for instance, he understands Gregory Nazianzen's *non-assumptus* simply as affirming the Son's assumption of human nature in its psychosomatic fullness, not its sinfulness, for our salvation.[130] Likewise, in examining Leo's *Tome*, Hughes notes not only that the two natures of Christ each retain their ontological integrity in the hypostatic union, but also that their union excludes 'any moral shortfall in the person of the Mediator: "He did not participate in our faults because he shared in human weaknesses. He took the form of a slave without stain of sin, increasing the human, not diminishing the divine."'[131] In a later section, Hughes quotes Augustine's insistence on Christ's oneness with our humanity yet difference from our sin as the prerequisites for his efficacious atonement.[132]

Turning to scripture, Hughes carefully discusses both halves of 2 Cor. 5.21. That Christ 'knew no sin' refers to his incarnate experience, for it is on the basis of his sinless humanity that he could atone for the world's sin.

---

[128] *Corinthians*, pp. 194–6, citing *Inc.* 8, 10, 20; *Hope*, pp. 45–6, 73, 76, citing *Inc.* 6, 10, 13; *True Image*, pp. 219, 276–9, 281–2, 343, 382, citing *Inc.* 4, 6–10, 13; *C. Gent.* 1; *Ep. Epict.* 6–9; *Ep. Adelph.* 3–4, 8; *Ep. Max.*; *De decretis* 3.14; *C. Ar.* 1.39, 42; 2.47, 67, 69-70; 3.39; *Syn.* 51. *True Image*, ch. 23 covers Athanasius' Christology, while ch. 24 argues that Athanasius, like Hughes, saw deification in terms of soteriological, not ontological, change.

[129] *True Image*, chs 19–27. Hughes' sole critique of Chalcedon is that it did not incorporate Athanasius' (and Hughes') theology of the divine image (327).

[130] Ibid., p. 289, citing Nazianzen's *Ep.* 101. On p. 277, Hughes had noted Athanasius' similar position, citing *Ep. Epict.* 7–8.

[131] Ibid., pp. 312–13 (quotation from latter page; internal quotation is from *Tome* §§2–4).

[132] Ibid., p. 343, citing Augustine, *Trin.* 4.14.

Hughes links this Corinthian clause to 1 Pet. 3.18 and a series of verses from the Gospels which attest Christ's sinlessness.[133] That Christ was 'made sin' means not that God made Christ a sinner or sinful, which would immediately invalidate his sacrifice, but that God judged the world's sin in Christ by punishing him for it. Here Hughes cites Isa. 53.5-6 as explanatory of Paul's meaning.[134]

Hughes' interpretation of Heb. 2.18 and 4.15 denies impeccability's opposite extreme, the notion that Christ must have possessed sin in order to sympathize fully with us in the experience of temptation. The presence of temptation, Hughes notes, does not require sinfulness in the one tempted. Moreover, Jesus' perseverance through the greatest temptations produced in him sympathy beyond that of anyone who has succumbed to temptation's lesser degrees.[135] His character, as Heb. 7.26 describes it, is utterly free from the very root of sin, so that his motives as well as his actions are void of all evil.[136]

Hughes offers exegetical, historical, and dogmatic support for the unfallenness view without ever frontally assaulting the opposing position. This chapter's final theologian is scarcely so demure. With him, we return to the succession of Scots explicitly against the fallenness view.

2.5 Fallacious fallenness: Donald Macleod

The final unfallenness theologian to be considered is Donald Macleod (b. 1940). As professor of systematic theology from 1978 to 2011 at Free Church College,[137] Macleod shared Edinburgh's Mound with New College, where T. F. Torrance taught theology until retiring in 1979.[138] Macleod's physical proximity to Torrance's school belies the doctrinal distance between the two men. In his

---

[133] Mt. 3.17; 17.5; Lk. 23.4, 14, 22, 41, 47-48; Jn 8.46; 10.30; 14.10-11; 17.11, 21-22.
[134] *Corinthians*, pp. 212–15.
[135] *Hebrews*, pp. 123–4, 172–3.
[136] Ibid., pp. 272–5.
[137] Biographical information taken from 'Biography', n.p. Cited 27 May 2013. Online: http://www. donaldmacleod.org/?page_id=7. Macleod still teaches part-time at Free Church College (now Edinburgh Theological Seminary), according to 'Donald Macleod', n.p. Cited 13 September 2016. Online: http://www.ets.ac.uk/teaching-faculty/part-time-faculty.
[138] Colyer, *How to Read*, p. 43.

writings, Macleod has rejected Torrance's, Barth's, and Irving's affirmation of Christ's fallen humanity.[139]

Macleod sees Christ's sinlessness as guaranteed by his deity. Through incarnation, God may suffer and be tempted, but cannot sin.[140] This sinlessness extends beyond Christ's actions to the core of his unfallen humanity[141] and to its conception in Mary's womb.[142] The church's consensus that Christ was free even from a sinful disposition held sway from ancient times until challenged by first Irving, then Barth, and finally those like Torrance whom, Macleod alleges, Irving and Barth profoundly influenced.[143] Against their biblical, patristic, and theological support, Macleod offers an array of counterarguments.[144]

2.5.1 Issues of interpretation

Biblically, Macleod sees the 'flesh' that the Logos became (Jn 1.14) as connoting human existence within the wretchedness of *external* conditions brought on by the Fall.[145] Christ's unfallen nature does not mean that he was untempted or sheltered within 'a sanitised spiritual environment' but that 'there was in Him no propensity to sin nor affinity with sin'[146] as evidenced by Lk. 1.35,[147]

---

[139] In his March 1984 article in *The Monthly Record*, 'Did Christ Have a Fallen Human Nature?', Macleod singled out Irving and Barth for critique. It was this article to which Torrance replied in a letter to the editor published in the May 1984 *Monthly Record*. Subsequently, Macleod included Torrance alongside Irving and Barth as fallenness advocates in 'Christology', *DSCHT*, pp. 172–7, republished in expanded form as ch. 5 in his *Jesus is Lord: Christology Yesterday and Today* (Fearn, UK: Mentor, 2000). Our investigation considers these and the following of Macleod's works: *Person of Christ*; *A Faith to Live By: Studies in Christian Doctrine* (Fearn, UK: Mentor, 1998); 'The Christology of Chalcedon', in *The Only Hope: Jesus Yesterday Today Forever* (ed. M. Elliott and J. L. McPake; Fearn, UK: Mentor, 2001), pp. 77–94; *From Glory to Golgotha: Controversial Issues in the Life of Christ* (Fearn, UK: Christian Focus, 2002); '"Church" Dogmatics: Karl Barth as Ecclesial Theologian', in *Engaging with Barth: Contemporary Evangelical Critiques* (ed. D. Gibson and D. Strange; Nottingham, UK: Apollos, 2008), pp. 323–45.
[140] *Person of Christ*, pp. 229–30.
[141] 'Did Christ Have a Fallen Human Nature?', p. 51; *Person of Christ*, pp. 221–2; *Faith to Live By*, p. 127; *From Glory*, pp. 27–8.
[142] *Person of Christ*, pp. 39–42. Macleod prefers to speak of the Spirit's *creation* of Christ's sinless humanity from Mary's ovum rather than of a *sanctification* of Christ's humanity, which suggests either that the ovum itself was sinful and required purification or else that, until the Spirit hallowed it, a sinful foetus existed apart from union with the Logos.
[143] *Person of Christ*, pp. 222–4; *Jesus is Lord*, pp. 125, 127; *From Glory*, p. 29; '"Church" Dogmatics', p. 335, n. 45. Chapter 1.3 of this study demonstrates the implausibility of Macleod's claim that Irving was a major influence on Torrance.
[144] Lee, 'Humanity of Christ', pp. 39–52, attempts to refute several of these counterarguments but is hampered by misunderstandings of Irving, Macleod, and Kapic.
[145] *Faith to Live By*, pp. 119, 122, 127.
[146] Ibid., p. 127; cf. 'Did Christ Have a Fallen Human Nature?', pp. 51, 53.
[147] *Person of Christ*, p. 225.

Heb. 7.26, and 1 Pet. 1.19.[148] Regarding Rom. 8.3, Macleod quotes Calvin's interpretation that 'likeness' means *similarity to*, not *sameness as* sinful flesh. Macleod also notes that, so far from 'likeness' requiring identity between Christ's flesh and our own, some modern scholars like John Knox argue that the term excludes Christ from sharing even a real humanity.[149]

Moving from scripture to tradition, Macleod complains that Torrance interprets patristic sources through Barth's and Irving's lenses and fails to distinguish clearly his own opinions from those of the fathers whose thought he ostensibly describes. For Macleod, Athanasius teaches Christ's assumption merely of flesh, not of corruption and sin, and (according to some modern scholars) had little interest in Christ's real, historical humanity,[150] while Nazianzen's *non-assumptus* is a response to Apollinaris' denial to Christ of a human mind, not an affirmation of fallenness, as the context clearly indicates. Macleod also rebuffs Irving's appeal to the tradition that Christ took his human substance from Mary as proof that his humanity was fallen, being taken from a fallen mother. This tradition's historical matrix was the church's anti-Docetic polemic for Christ's true humanity, not his fallen humanity. In fact, Cyril of Alexandria, Augustine, and Leo all deny to Christ a fallen nature.[151]

2.5.2 Faults in reasoning

Macleod extensively addresses the fallenness proponents' theological reasoning. He repeats Dods's and Bruce's criticisms[152] and adds his own, some

---

[148] 'Did Christ Have a Fallen Human Nature?', p. 51; *From Glory*, p. 28; '"Church" Dogmatics', p. 339.

[149] *Jesus is Lord*, p. 128, citing Knox's *The Humanity and Divinity of Christ: A Study of Pattern in Christology* (Cambridge: Cambridge University Press, 1967). Cf. 'Did Christ Have a Fallen Human Nature?', p. 51; *From Glory*, p. 28; '"Church" Dogmatics', p. 336. Macleod does not address how Knox's exegesis might be influenced by his presumption that Christ's genuine humanity is incompatible with sinlessness and a divine nature (*Humanity and Divinity*, pp. 46–7, 67–70 [Knox misreferences Rom. 8.3 as Rom. 8.2 on pp. 33, 44, 51]). Cf. Lee, 'Humanity of Christ', p. 43.

[150] *Jesus is Lord*, pp. 125–7. Macleod does not support his claims from the Athanasian corpus. Among the modern scholars whom he cites is R. P. C. Hanson, *The Search for the Christian Doctrine of God* (Edinburgh: T&T Clark, 1988), p. 451. D. O. Eugenio, *Communion with God: The Trinitarian Soteriology of T. F. Torrance* (Eugene, OR: Pickwick, 2014), p. 41, critiques Macleod's 'minimal' patristic coverage with its 'microscopic analysis that disregards the overall picture'. To Macleod's point, one may reply that Athanasius' alleged unconcern with Christ's historical humanity need not exclude great concern with Christ's humanity as a theological concept.

[151] *Person of Christ*, pp. 167–8, 224–5, citing Nazianzen, *Ep.* 101 (cf. *Jesus is Lord*, p. 128); Cyril of Alexandria, *Answers to Tiberius*, 4, 13; Augustine, *Trin.* 13.23; Leo, *Tome*.

[152] 'Did Christ Have a Fallen Human Nature?', pp. 52–3; *Person of Christ*, pp. 225, 228–9, 286, n. 12 (here also referencing critiques from Mackintosh's *Doctrine of the Person of Jesus Christ*); *Jesus is Lord*, pp. 107–10; *From Glory*, pp. 30–1, 36–7. Cf. *Person of Christ*, p. 228; *Jesus is Lord*, pp. 128–9 on Irving's and Torrance's alleged Nestorianism. (*Humiliation* is the work of Bruce's which Macleod uses.)

of which misconstrue his opponents' views. For instance, he charges Irving and Torrance with ignoring the historical understanding of the term 'fallenness' as the sinfulness, total depravity, and corruption of one's nature.[153] Yet as Chapter 1 of this study has demonstrated, they use the term in just this sense. In another case, Macleod claims that Irving denied that Christ's human nature was sanctified at conception.[154] As support for this claim (which contradicts Irving's own clear statement in *Christ's Holiness in Flesh*, p. 78), Macleod cites *CW* 5, pp. 563–4, where Irving says that Christ's flesh was not *changed* at conception. Here Macleod reads his own understanding of sanctification as the eradication of fleshly sinfulness into Irving's words, rather than discerning that Irving defines sanctification differently. Macleod also cites *CW* 5, pp. 123–4, where Irving preaches that the mere union of Christ's divine nature with his human nature *in utero* did not sanctify the latter. But Irving's point is that the *Spirit*, not the *Son*, sanctified Christ's flesh.[155]

Others of Macleod's rebuttals are more germane. To Irving's proposal that Christ assumed a fallen humanity as the only sort available, Macleod responds that this makes fallenness inherent in the definition of humanness, thus rendering prelapsarian Adam and glorified saints alike inhuman.[156] Instead, we must believe that the God who produced a righteous, holy, glorious Adam[157] from dust can produce an unfallen Second Adam from a sinful woman.[158] Yet Christ's earthly state, though unfallen, was not the same as unfallen Adam's. Rather than Adam's original state of paradisiacal perfection or Christ's present state of heavenly glory, his was a state of humiliation, of freely sharing for love's sake the sorrows, godforsakenness, and death due to the fallen.[159]

---

[153] *Person of Christ*, pp. 228–9; *Jesus is Lord*, p. 129. In 'Did Christ Have a Fallen Human Nature?', p. 52 and *From Glory*, pp. 35–6, Macleod reverses the argument in Barth's case: given that fallenness in *CD* IV/1 means hostility and incapacity, how can a fallen Saviour save?

[154] *Jesus is Lord*, pp. 130–1.

[155] *CW* 5, p. 564 (Lee, 'Humanity of Christ', pp. 42–3, in defending Irving against Macleod, also reads sanctification as eradication into Irving). Macleod's other arguments in *Jesus is Lord*, pp. 131–2 (and possibly obliquely in *Faith to Live By*, p. 134) against Irving's and Torrance's 'incarnational redemption' theories equally fail. *Pace* Macleod, Irving and Torrance do not minimize the importance of the cross or of Jesus' lifetime of choices which led him there. See sections 1.1 and 1.3 in Chapter 1 above and G. Pratz, 'The Relationship between Incarnation and Atonement in the Theology of Thomas F. Torrance', *Journal for Christian Theological Research* 3.2 (1998), n.p. Cited 15 March 2011. Online: http://www2.luthersem.edu/ctrf/jctr/Vol03/Pratz.htm.

[156] 'Did Christ Have a Fallen Human Nature?', p. 53; *Person of Christ*, p. 225; *From Glory*, pp. 37–8.

[157] *Faith to Live By*, p. 81, rejects modern theology's portrait of Adam as originally having sinful, animalistic proclivities. Nor was Adam morally neutral. His proclivities were towards the good.

[158] *Person of Christ*, p. 41.

[159] 'Did Christ Have a Fallen Human Nature?', p. 53; *Person of Christ*, pp. 229–30.

Macleod also detects inconsistency in Irving's and Barth's insistence on the importance of fallen humanness in Christ for establishing continuity with the fallen race. Both theologians compromise this insistence by allowing for marked *discontinuities* between him and us, such as his birth from a virgin, his awareness of unique sonship, and his never having sinned. On the latter point, Macleod notes that all Barth's arguments in *CD* I/2 against Christ's unfallenness could be aimed at Christ's actual sinlessness, too, for if one must be fallen to sympathize with the fallen, then how else than by sinning could Christ sympathize with sinners?[160]

Finally, Irving insists that only a fallen being could suffer and be tempted like us: a Christ unfallen is a Christ unfeeling. To the contrary, Macleod replies, Christ's heart was not desensitized by any sin of its own; therefore he was 'uniquely vulnerable' to the pain caused by sin in the world. He suffered not *as* one fallen but *for* ones fallen as their atoning substitute. He suffered greater pain in temptation than we, for he never escaped its full fury by succumbing. Although unable to be tempted through incipiently sinful lusts, Christ encountered satanic appeals to his unfallen, sinless weaknesses, his godly desires, and his very identity as Son. And though impeccable, Christ conquered temptation only through the Spirit's strengthening of his faith, hope, and love.[161] In the Incarnation, Christ humbled himself by adding to his divine nature a lowly human nature and by restraining continually throughout his earthly life the free exercise of his divine powers.[162] In these ways, he entered fully into human experiences, including suffering and temptation, and was fundamentally changed by them: 'We have no right to confine these things to his human nature .... In Christ, divine personality is caught up in the process of learning and becoming.'[163] Having learnt compassion through earthly experience of temptation, the ascended Christ uses his sovereignty to preserve us from being tempted beyond endurance.[164] Moreover, because the

---

[160] *Person of Christ*, p. 225 (Irving); 'Did Christ Have a Fallen Human Nature?', p. 52; *From Glory*, pp. 33–4 (Barth).

[161] *Person of Christ*, pp. 196, 226–9; *From Glory*, pp. 38–52 (quotation from p. 39); cf. 113–14; 'Did Christ Have a Fallen Human Nature?', p. 53. Macleod denies that Christ's divine nature preserved his human nature sinless, for natures cannot act upon, with, or against one another; only persons may do so. To claim otherwise implies Nestorianism (*From Glory*, pp. 51–2; 'Christology of Chalcedon', p. 89; cf. *Person of Christ*, p. 170).

[162] *Person of Christ*, pp. 205–20.

[163] Ibid., p. 69.

[164] *From Glory*, pp. 137–8.

second person of the Trinity is homoousially and perichoretically bound to the Father and the Spirit, what affects him affects them, too.[165] By this means, the whole Godhead has shared in Christ's human experiences – particularly his suffering. Thus the impeccable, unfallen God fully feels our afflictions.[166]

Conclusion

This chapter has surveyed a succession of selected modern scholars in their defence of the doctrine that Christ's humanity was not fallen. Marcus Dods, followed by A. B. Bruce and H. R. Mackintosh, all weighed Edward Irving's fallenness claims and found them wanting. Mackintosh, however, inadvertently encouraged the rehabilitation of the fallenness view under Karl Barth. Since then, this view has encountered opposition implicitly during the twentieth century from Philip Hughes, and explicitly over the turn of the century from Donald Macleod.

These five opponents of Christ's fallenness equate that term with original sin and guilty proclivities towards sin. They deny that Christ assumed a human nature with such properties – indeed, Dods and Bruce teach that sin and fallenness are properties only of *persons*, not *natures* or *physical flesh*[167] – and therefore see his humanity as unfallen. Yet this claim is qualified in significant ways.

First, none of the five argues that Mary was unfallen or that Christ incarnated himself in some 'heavenly flesh' with no relation to his mother. All of them see the Virgin Birth as signalling divine initiative to preserve Christ from fallenness, understood as sinfulness. Therefore it is not the case for these theologians that the Logos found ready to hand, so to speak, a sample of prelapsarian flesh with which to unite; rather, in his incarnation under the Holy Spirit's aegis, flesh fallen in his mother was *restored* in her Son to an unfallen, that is, sinless, state. Secondly, all five insist that Christ entered fully into the temptations, suffering, and sinful milieu of a fallen world and died as the atoning sin-bearer, all the while remaining personally unfallen (i.e. fully

---

[165] *Person of Christ*, p. 263; 'Christology of Chalcedon', pp. 92–4.
[166] *Person of Christ*, pp. 229–30. Cf. *Faith to Live By*, pp. 123, 130–1; *From Glory*, pp. 104–8.
[167] Cf. Gunton's caveat in ch. 1.4.1 above.

sinless). Thirdly, some disagreement exists over the exact moral character of the unfallen state. Here Bruce is more open than Dods, Hughes, or Macleod[168] to seeing in unfallen Adam and Christ the presence of animal desires needing to be tamed through a course of development from mere innocence to mature righteousness. For this reason, Bruce alone of the unfallenness camp allows that Christ bore 'sinful flesh' – that is, *sin-prone* flesh – which yet was unfallen.

Regardless of any difference, however, all five theologians find the contention that Christ's humanity was *real* and *full*, not *fallen*, in scripture and fathers both Greek and Latin. Dods, Bruce, and Mackintosh even critique patristic Christology as moving towards the opposite extreme of the fallenness position by accounting inadequately for Christ's infirmities. Ironically, several of the patristic sources on which unfallenness advocates draw for support are the same as those adduced by their fallenness counterparts! Chapters 3 and 4 seek to arbitrate this clash of interpretations by investigating the patristic writings to which both sides appeal. To the church fathers, then, we now turn.

---

[168] Mackintosh's view is unclear, since he avoids discussing Adam or the Fall in detail. See his *Doctrine of the Person of Jesus Christ*, p. 442 (cf. 62); *Christian Experience of Forgiveness*, p. 52.

3

The Greek Fathers on the Fallenness or Unfallenness of Christ's Humanity

The previous two chapters have documented the debate between modern fallenness and unfallenness theologians. Proponents on either side have referenced the early church, including (and for Gunton, exclusively so) the Greek fathers. This chapter examines the Greek patristic evidence to determine how well grounded is the reading which the modern debaters give to the Greek fathers. The subsequent chapter will investigate the Latin fathers.

Within the limits of this study, we cannot exhaustively canvass every patristic source to which modern debaters have appealed. We will rely upon samples deemed representative due to breadth of citation. The patristic sources cited most widely among the debaters are (in order of descending breadth) Gregory Nazianzen's orations and *Epistola* 101; the works of Augustine and Athanasius;[1] Leo's *Tome*; Tertullian's *De carne Christi* and *Adversus Marcionem*, Hilary of Poitiers' *De Trinitate*, and the writings of Cyril of Alexandria[2] and Gregory Nyssen; and Irenaeus' and Ambrose's works.

Two further preliminary words are in order. First, this and the next chapter will refer to 'original sin' with reference to the hamartiologies of fathers besides Augustine, who coined the term, and Leo, who followed Augustine. This broad use of the term is no more invalid than the application of Tertullian's term 'Trinity' (*trinitas*) to Greek or earlier Latin theology, and is consistent with scholarly practice. The same scholarship, however, cautions that Augustine's particular formulation of the doctrine of original sin not be read into other theologians' versions of the doctrine. Binding these versions together is the

---

[1] Including some works now believed to be pseudonymous. See the section on Athanasius below.
[2] Including, in Bruce's and Torrance's cases, *Adv. anthropomorphitas*, now seen as a pseudonymous compilation and redaction of Cyril's *Answers to Tiberius*, *Doctrinal Questions and Answers*, and another work, together with Nyssen's *Christmas Sermon*, according to L. Wickham in Cyril of Alexandria, *Select Letters* (ed. and trans. L. R. Wickham; Oxford: Clarendon, 1983), pp. xlviii–xlix.

consensus that Adam's fall into sin put humankind under the dominion of Satan, death, and disordered desires which incline towards sin. This consensus holds regardless of individual fathers' conceptions of our culpability for Adam's sin, the mode of its transmission, or its effect on free will.[3]

Secondly, the Greek fathers surveyed in this chapter had an abiding interest in Christ's deliverance of human nature from φθορά, 'corruption'. The patristic ascription of this term to Christ's humanity has led some modern readers to conclude that the fathers saw Christ's humanity as *morally* corrupt. In fact, though, the early church typically used this term to describe *physical* corruption, the 'decay' to which material bodies are prone.[4]

With these points in mind, we turn to the views of five specific Greek fathers: Irenaeus, Athanasius, Gregory Nazianzen, Gregory Nyssen, and Cyril of Alexandria.

3.1 Theology's Trailblazer: Irenaeus

Irenaeus of Lyons (ca. 130–ca. 200) represents an appropriately catholic starting point for our investigation. A native of Asia Minor who became a

---

[3]   H. Rondet, *Original Sin: The Patristic and Theological Background* (trans. C. Finegan; Staten Island, NY: Alba House, 1972); N. P. Williams, *The Ideas of the Fall and of Original Sin: A Historical and Critical Study* (London: Longmans, Green & Co., 1927); F. R. Tennant, *The Sources of the Doctrines of the Fall and Original Sin* (Cambridge: Cambridge University Press, 1903); cf. T. A. Noble, 'Prolegomena for a Conference on Original Sin', *European Explorations in Christian Holiness* 2 (2001), pp. 10–17; R. Greer, 'Sinned We All in Adam's Fall?', in *The Social World of the First Christians* (ed. L. M. White and O. L. Yarbrough; Minneapolis: Fortress, 1995), pp. 382–94. Williams' learned content suffers from a psychological typology (William James' 'once-born' vs. 'twice-born' distinction) imposed upon the data so as to favour the 'sunny genius of Christian Hellenism' over a more fanatical, pessimistic '"African" or "twice-born" mode of feeling' (*Ideas*, p. 257).
[4]   J. J. O'Keefe, 'The Persistence of Decay: Bodily Disintegration and Cyrillian Christology', in *In the Shadow of the Incarnation: Essays on Jesus Christ in the Early Church in Honor of Brian E. Daley, S.J.* (ed. P. W. Martens; Notre Dame: University of Notre Dame Press, 2008), pp. 228–45; O'Keefe examines Irenaeus and Athanasius as well as Cyril. J. Roldanus, *Le Christ et l'Homme dans la Théologie d'Athanase d'Alexandrie: Étude de la Conjonction de sa Conception de l'Homme avec sa Christologie* (Leiden: Brill, corrected edn, 1977), pp. 59–65, appears to concur with Athanasius. Cf. 'φθορά', *A Patristic Greek Lexicon* (ed. G. W. H. Lampe; Oxford: Clarendon, 1961), pp. 1474–5. Misreaders of the fathers on this score include O'Keefe himself in his youth (by his own admission); Irving, according to Mackintosh, *Doctrine of the Person of Jesus Christ*, p. 278; Dorries, *Incarnational Christology*, p. 166; G. Aulén, *Christus Victor: An Historical Study of the Three Main Types of the Idea of the Atonement* (trans. A. G. Hebert; New York: Macmillan, 1960), p. 44; and Tennant, *Sources*, pp. 310, 312, n. 2. W. J. Burghardt, *The Image of God in Man according to Cyril of Alexandria* (Washington, DC: Catholic University of America Press, 1957), pp. 85–100, rightly affirms the primarily physical meaning of φθορά, but attempts to demonstrate that Cyril also uses ἀφθαρσία in a moral sense as synonymous with sanctification. By my lights, Cyril is *correlating* physical incorruption with moral holiness, not *equating* incorruption and holiness.

missionary to Gaul, a writer in Greek whose seminal work, *Against Heresies*, survives in its entirety only in Latin, Irenaeus transcends the later division of Eastern and Western Christianity, and his masterpiece influenced orthodox teachers in both East and West.[5] We will study this work alongside his only other extant complete book, *The Demonstration of the Apostolic Preaching*.[6]

The heresies against which Irenaeus writes *Against Heresies* were primarily Gnostic. As Irenaeus describes them, they shared the perspective that material enfleshment is an evil condition. The body is the inept creation of one or more inferior spiritual beings, and liberation from it is true salvation. Some Gnostics taught that Christ only appeared to have flesh and to suffer, while others claimed that Jesus was a naturally born human whose superior soul won deliverance for himself from the bondage of embodiment. In either case, the Gnostics' blurring together of material createdness with sinfulness led to denials of Christ's incarnation, atoning death, and resurrection, as well as, often, to an ethic of carnal indulgence.[7] Irenaeus combats these aberrations with his own theological system.

3.1.1 Creation and Fall in the divine economy

Contrary to the Gnostics, Irenaeus insists on humankind's creation by no lesser being than the triune God himself, with the Father acting through the agency

---

[5] Biographical and bibliographical information available from the following sources: P. Parvis, 'Who Was Irenaeus? An Introduction to the Man and His Work', J. Secord, 'The Cultural Geography of a Greek Christian: Irenaeus from Smyrna to Lyons', and I. M. C. Steenberg, 'Tracing the Irenaean Legacy', all in *Irenaeus: Life, Scripture, Legacy* (ed. S. Parvis and P. Foster; Minneapolis: Fortress, 2012), pp. 13–24, 25–33, 199–211, respectively; 'Irenaeus, St', *ODCC* (2005), n.p. Cited 13 March 2012. Online: http://www. oxford-christianchurch.com/entry?entry=t257.e3565; D. Minns, 'Irenaeus', in *Early Christian Thinkers: The Lives and Legacies of Twelve Key Figures* (ed. P. Foster; Downers Grove, IL: InterVarsity, 2010), pp. 36–51; R. M. Grant, *Irenaeus of Lyons* (Florence, KY: Routledge, 1996), pp. 1, 7, 39; St Irenaeus of Lyons, *On the Apostolic Preaching* (trans. J. Behr; Crestwood, NY: St Vladimir's Seminary Press, 1997), pp. 1–5. Unless otherwise noted, all citations of *Epid.* are from this source and all citations of *Haer.* are from A. Roberts and J. Donaldson (eds), *The Ante-Nicene Fathers* (10 vols; repr., Peabody, MA: Hendrickson, 1994; electronic version: *AGES Digital Library* version 8, 2000) vol. 1.

[6] Torrance, *Atonement*, pp. 440–1, mentions an Irenaean fragment which may liken the Incarnation to Christ's cleansing of a leper (Mt. 8.2-3 par.), but cites no source. In *Divine Meaning*, p. 67, n. 27, he cites another Irenaean fragment from a collection appended to Irenaeus, *Adversus Haereses* (ed. W. W. Harvey; 2 vols.; Cambridge: Cambridge University Press, 1857). A search of Harvey yielded no exact matches to Torrance's description in *Atonement*, but fragment 33 does compare Naaman's cleansing from leprosy (2 Kgs 5.14) with baptismal regeneration (Harvey vol. 2, p. 497. Cf. *Haer.* 4.8.2. In any case, Torrance's interpretation is tentative, as he indicates.

[7] *Haer.* 1.1-9, 11-31. Not all of the heretics opposed by Irenaeus were Gnostics; he also writes against the Ebionites, who taught that Jesus was a mere man (5.1.3).

of his two 'hands', the Logos and the Spirit. Inasmuch as God formed Adam from the soil and animated him, materiality is literally the very ground of the human constitution, and will remain so forever.[8] Its goodness derives from its Creator's goodness. Yet humanity, though possessing original goodness, required improvement: in the divine plan or 'economy' (Greek οἰκονομία; Lat. *dispositio*[9]) the newly made Adam and Eve were spiritually, morally, intellectually, and sexually infantile,[10] requiring a programme of development to attain the full measure of the Image of God, Jesus Christ, in whose image they were made.[11]

This programme became prolonged by the Fall, which was, ironically, an attempt at foreshortening the developmental process. The primal couple seized at a knowledge for which they had been unready.[12] Their moral unrestraint loosed the animal desires innate to the flesh but formerly leashed by innocence and rationality.[13] Mortality, too, became no longer a possibility inherent to bodily existence[14] but a doom dominating it.[15]

---

[8]   *Haer.* 5 *passim*, esp. 5.6.1. For the sources of the 'two hands' metaphor in scripture and Theophilus of Antioch, see A. Briggman, *Irenaeus of Lyons and the Theology of the Holy Spirit* (Oxford: Oxford University Press, 2012), pp. 104–19; J. Lawson, *The Biblical Theology of Saint Irenaeus* (London: Epworth, 1948), pp. 119–39. On Irenaeus' commitment to materiality, see D. Minns, *Irenaeus: An Introduction* (London: T&T Clark, 2010), pp. 70–1.

[9]   With three exceptions, in which *dispensatio, creatio*, and *ex omnibus factus* are each used once, as noted in a fine chapter on 'economy' by E. Osborn, *Irenaeus of Lyons* (Cambridge: Cambridge University Press, 2001), pp. 74–94. On the rationale for Creation's initial imperfection, cf. *Haer.* 4.38-39; R. F. Brown, 'On the Necessary Imperfection of Creation: Irenaeus's *Adversus Haereses* IV, 38', *SJT* 28 (1975), pp. 17–25; E. P. Meijering, *God Being History: Studies in Patristic Philosophy* (Amsterdam: North-Holland Publishing, 1975), pp. 64, 71; Minns, *Irenaeus*, pp. 88–90.

[10] *Haer.* 2.26.1; 3.22.4, 3.23.5; *Epid.* 12, 14; A. N. S. Lane, 'Irenaeus on the Fall and original sin', in *Darwin, Creation and the Fall: Theological challenges* (ed. R. J. Berry and T. A. Noble; Nottingham, UK: Apollos, 2009), pp. 130–49 (131–3, 136–7).

[11] *Haer.* 4.5.1, 4.11.1. Cf. I. M. Mackenzie, *Irenaeus's* Demonstration of the Apostolic Preaching*: A Theological Commentary and Translation* (Aldershot, UK: Ashgate, 2002), p. 116; A. Orbe, *Espiritualidad de San Ireneo* (Rome: Editrice Pontificia Università Gregoriana, 1989), pp. 1–44; G. Wingren, *Man and the Incarnation: A Study in the Biblical Theology of Irenaeus* (trans. R. Mackenzie; Philadelphia: Muhlenberg Press, 1959), pp. 26–38.

[12] Minns, 'Irenaeus', p. 47; cf. J. Vogel, 'The Haste of Sin, the Slowness of Salvation: An Interpretation of Irenaeus on the Fall and Redemption', *Anglican Theological Review* 89.3 (2007), pp. 443–59. On whether Irenaeus sees the Fall as inevitable, cf. Minns, *Irenaeus*, pp. 82, 91 with Lane, 'Irenaeus', pp. 137–40.

[13] *Haer.* 3.23.5; 4.38.4; 5.8.1-4, 5.9.1.

[14] In passages like *Haer.* 3.20.2 and *Epid.* 15, Irenaeus can speak of humanity's possessing immortality prior to the Fall; however, *Haer.* 5.12.1-3 explains that humanity lost its life in Eden because it had only the ephemeral breath of life, not the eternal Spirit of life available in Christ. Cf. *Haer.* 5.3.1, which says that humans are naturally mortal, and 5.7.1, which interprets Gen. 2.7 as teaching that human nature comprises an immortal soul and a mortal body (i.e. a soul incapable of decomposition and a body capable of it). Cf. Lane, 'Irenaeus', pp. 145–6.

[15] *Haer.* 5.10.2, 5.23.2; *Epid.* 31.

Irenaeus pioneers a doctrine of what later would be termed 'original sin'.[16] Because of the solidarity of the human race, in consequence of Adam's sin, we all have become estranged from God.[17] Irenaeus repeatedly draws on Jesus' parable of the strong man and his houseful of possessions (Mt. 12.29 par): through the Fall, Adam and Eve became captives of the strong man, Satan, and their descendants are born in his house of captivity, fettered from birth by the Edenic transgression.[18]

3.1.2 Salvation through recapitulation

Irenaeus' resolution to humanity's prelapsarian incompletion and postlapsarian incarceration lies in his signature motif of recapitulation (Greek ἀνακεφαλαίωσις; Lat. *recapitulatio*). Recapitulation involves the fulfilment of something earlier in the economy by something later than and parallel to the earlier. Fulfilment may occur through the latter *reflecting, perfecting,* or *correcting* the earlier.[19] Thus, the chiliastic Irenaeus describes the Millennium as a reflection of Eden, not as a perfecting advance beyond it nor as a correcting adjustment to it.[20] The apocalyptic Beast or Antichrist perfects all evil, not by

---

[16] Tennant, *Sources*, pp. 282–91. J. N. D. Kelly, *Early Christian Doctrines* (repr., Peabody, Mass.: Prince Press, rev. edn, 2004), p. 170. Lane, 'Irenaeus', pp. 141–2; Osborn, *Irenaeus*, pp. 216–19; Kelly, *Early Christian Doctrines*, pp. 171–2; and Wingren, *Man and the Incarnation*, p. 63, assert that Irenaeus taught that all humanity shares Adam's guilt. Powell, *Ideas*, pp. 196–7, sees an implicit doctrine of original guilt. M. C. Steenberg, *Of God and Man: Theology as Anthropology from Irenaeus to Athanasius* (London: T&T Clark, 2009), p. 46, disagrees, but his proof texts from *Haer.*, when taken in context, are unconvincing. Lawson, *Biblical Theology*, pp. 216–17, also disagrees, but confuses subjective awareness of guilt with the objective fact of guilt; the latter may be present where the former is limited or absent. G. Bray, 'Original Sin in Patristic Thought', *Churchman* 108.1 (1994), pp. 37–47 (42–3), admits that Irenaeus' comments in *Haer.* 5.16.3 'suggest' a doctrine of original guilt, but claims that Irenaeus' 'probable' position is that humanity inherits death due to Adam's transgression but not responsibility for that transgression. Cf. Greer, 'Sinned We All', pp. 382–94. E. Osborn, 'Irenaeus: Rocks in the Road', *The Expository Times* 114.8 (2003), pp. 255–8 (257), warns against too sharply bifurcating Irenaeus' and Augustine's views of original sin.

[17] *Haer.* 5.17.1, 3.

[18] *Haer.* 3.8.2, 3.18.6, 3.23.1-2, 3.23.7; 4.22.1; 5.21.1, 5.21.3; *Epid.* 37; cf. Wingren, *Man and the Incarnation*, pp. 50–63.

[19] For a thorough discussion of recapitulation, see Osborn, *Irenaeus*, pp. 97–140. The terms *perfection* and *correction* are his; *reflection*, mine. N. V. Harrison, *God's Many-Splendored Image: Theological Anthropology for Christian Formation* (Grand Rapids: Baker, 2010), p. 41, describes three elements of Irenaean recapitulation: repetition of creation, reversal of the Fall, and summation of history (hence, reflection, correction, and perfection, respectively). Cf. T. Holsinger-Friesen, *Irenaeus and Genesis: A Study of Competition in Early Christian Hermeneutics* (Winona Lake, IN: Eisenbrauns, 2009), ch. 1, who cautions against 'recapitulation inflation': the tendency of modern interpreters to treat recapitulation as a theoretical framework governing Irenaeus' theology. Holsinger-Friesen urges that for Irenaeus recapitulation was an exegetical tool and not a conceptual mould.

[20] *Haer.* 5.32.1, 5.33.4.

correcting it, but by summing it up so that all evil may be disposed of by the Beast's damnation.[21] The Virgin Mary reflects Eve's virginal state but corrects her disobedience by accepting the Annunciation.[22]

Irenaeus applies all three forms of fulfilment when speaking of Christ's recapitulative work. His Virgin Birth reflects Adam's formation from virgin soil. The Lukan Christ's reversed genealogy, moving backwards from him through the generations to Adam, indicates that he gives life to them rather than they to him, thereby perfecting them. His development from childhood to seniority sanctifies every stage of human life. He faces temptation, particularly regarding food, just as Adam did, but corrects Adam's transgression by overcoming temptation. On the sixth day of creation week, Adam disobeyed at a tree and died; on the sixth day of the week, Christ obeyed by dying on a tree. His shed blood reflects and perfects all the righteous blood spilt on earth. By his incarnation, death, and resurrection, he sets human nature free to share the divine immortality and incorruptibility, thus perfecting his image in humankind.[23]

3.1.3 Christ's flesh and the Fall

In their appeals to Irenaean theology, representatives of both sides in the modern fallenness debate must grapple with the nuances of his thought. Dods argues that since unfallen Adam's humanity was made in Christ's image, how much more unfallen must Christ himself be?[24] Dods, however, overlooks Irenaeus' doctrines of recapitulation and economy: at creation, Adam was made like Christ, but in redemption, Christ has been made like Adam. On the other hand, fallenness advocates understand Irenaeus to teach that Christ was made like Adam in his fallen estate. Irenaeus, however, sees Christ as recapitulating both Adam's prelapsarian formation and postlapsarian death. In the following analysis, we seek to do justice to both sides of Irenaeus' view.

We begin with Irenaeus' account of the flesh. In opposing the Gnostic notion of the flesh as inherently bad, he sharply contrasts the substance of the flesh with the sinful condition into which it has fallen. All the Pauline

---

[21] *Haer.* 5.28.2, 5.29.2.

[22] *Haer.* 3.22.3-4; 5.19.1. This motif goes back to Justin Martyr, *Dial.* 100. All citations of *Dial.* are from *ANF* 1.

[23] *Haer.* 2.22.4-6; 3.19.1; 3.21.9-10, 3.22.3-4; 5.14.1; 5.19.1, 5.21.2-3, 5.23.2. Cf. Mackenzie, *Irenaeus's Demonstration*, pp. 116–17, 127–9, 136–7, 160–1; Aulén, *Christus Victor*, pp. 28–9.

[24] Dods, *Incarnation*, pp. 484–6.

pronouncements against the flesh and its works refer to the latter, never the former. Thus Irenaeus distinguishes between mortification and suicide: Christians must kill their flesh's sinful lusts and acts, not their flesh itself.[25] Furthermore, Irenaeus is confident that Christians do live in freedom from such lusts and acts.[26] He sees the flesh as capable of being purified in this life from its sinful state and of being maintained in that purity through the Holy Spirit's agency.[27] The flesh remains mortal, but infusions of incorruptibility by the Holy Spirit and the Eucharist[28] presently prepare it for future resurrection and, following the Millennium, complete assimilation into the divine immortality and incorruptibility.[29] This entire process of assimilation is made possible through the person and work of Christ.[30]

Irenaeus emphasizes that, in the Incarnation, Christ assumed the same substance of flesh that Adam and all Adam's offspring share; indeed, if Christ had assumed some heterogeneous body, whether the Gnostics' 'psychical body'[31] or a body formed from soil in exact parallelism to Adam's formation, then he would not have been truly human and so could not have reconciled humanity to God.[32] What, then, was the condition of the flesh assumed by Christ? Irenaeus explains in his *Demonstration*, 'So, "the Word became flesh" that by means of the flesh which sin had mastered and seized and dominated, by this, it might be abolished and no longer be in us.'[33] In a parallel passage in *Against Heresies*, Irenaeus writes,

> Certainly, it behooved him who could put sin to death and redeem humanity who was liable to death, to become what [this latter] was, namely, humanity – humanity which had been drawn into slavery by sin, but was held bound by death. The result would be that sin would be put to death by humanity, and humanity would escape from death.[34]

---

[25] *Haer.* 5.8, 5.12.1-4, 5.14.1, 5.14.4.

[26] *Epid.* 95–6. Cf. 2, 87, 89–90, 93; *Haer.* 5.6.1.

[27] *Haer.* 4.13; 5.8; *Epid.* 41–2; C. T. Bounds, 'Competing Doctrines of Perfection: The Primary Issue in Irenaeus' Refutation of Gnosticism', StPatr 45 (2010), pp. 403–8, esp. 407. For a Lutheran reading of Irenaeus that sees him as teaching an ongoing intrapersonal struggle with sin in the Christian life, cf. Wingren, *Man and the Incarnation*, pp. 170–5.

[28] *Haer.* 4.18.5; 5.2.2-3 (the Eucharist), 5.8, 5.12.1-4, 5.20.2 (the Spirit).

[29] *Haer.* 5.32-33, 5.35.

[30] For example, *Haer.* 3.19-20; cf. Holsinger-Friesen, *Irenaeus and Genesis*, pp. 174–214.

[31] *Haer.* 1.6.1.

[32] *Haer.* 3.21.10.

[33] *Epid.* 31; ET Behr, *Demonstration*, p. 60.

[34] *Haer.* 3.18.7; ET St. Irenaeus of Lyons, *Against the Heresies (Book 3)* (trans. and annotated by D. J. Unger, with an introduction and further revisions by I. M. C. Steenberg; New York: The Newman Press, 2012), p. 92 (brackets translators').

These statements seem to imply that the Logos assumed human nature in its sin-subjected condition. Yet immediately following each of these statements, Irenaeus stresses that Christ received the same formation as Adam by being born of a descendant of Adam and by being born virginally as a parallel to unfallen Adam's formation from virgin soil. Irenaeus' overarching point is that, in the Virgin Birth, humanity has been re-created: it is humanity due to Christ's deriving his substance from Adam; it is a re-creation due to that substance's receiving its formation through a direct act of God using undefiled material, as in Eden.[35] As Irenaeus writes elsewhere, in the Virgin Birth, 'The pure One open[ed] purely that pure womb which regenerates men unto God, and which He Himself made pure.'[36] Here the utmost purity of Christ's birth – and hence his humanity's freedom from the domination of sin – rests on multiple supports: the virginity of his mother, the holy character of her Son, his sanctification of her, and the regenerative effect of his birth. The purity of Christ's birth corresponds to the purity of his infant life. In interpreting Isaiah 7, Irenaeus links together the Virgin Birth with its offspring's instinctual rejection of evil: 'Before the child knows good from evil, He shall reject the evil, to choose good.'[37] In sum, when speaking of Christ's human origin, Irenaeus describes it as the restoration of human nature to a prelapsarian state of innocence – 'paradise regained'.

Irenaeus also sees the Incarnation as recapitulating humanity's battle with Satan.[38] Christ undergoes temptation just as Adam did. Rather than implying that Christ struggles with disordered inclinations, Irenaeus' account of the desert temptations has Christ dispassionately and calculatingly countering

[35]   *Haer.* 5.1.3 contrasts fallen Adam with the work of the Logos and the Holy Spirit in the Incarnation 'in order that Adam might be created [again] after the image and likeness of God' (*ANF* 1, p. 527). Cf. A. Houssiau, *La Christologie de saint Irénée* (Louvain: Publications Universitaires de Louvain & Gembloux, France: J. Duculot, 1955), pp. 237–9, 243; A. Orbe, *Teología de san Ireneo* (4 vols.; Madrid: Biblioteca de Autores Cristianos, 1985, 1987, 1988, 1996) vol. 2, pp. 353–4, 359; Wingren, *Man and the Incarnation*, pp. 79–110, each of whom sees the Incarnation as repristinating human nature's original purity. By contrast, Baker, 'The Place of St. Irenaeus', p. 22, claims that Irenaeus sees the Virgin Birth in terms only of formal parallelism and consubstantiality with Adam, not of the condition of the humanity assumed. Cf. Mackenzie, *Irenaeus's* Demonstration, pp. 135–6, for an attempt at a balanced statement.
[36]   *Haer.* 4.33.11; ET *ANF* 1, p. 509.
[37]   *Epid.* 53 (Isa. 7.16 quoted from Behr, *Demonstration*, p. 75); cf. Osborn, *Irenaeus*, p. 110. In *Haer.* 3.21.4, Irenaeus attributes this instinct to Christ's deity. Since Irenaeus never ascribes a contrary impulse to Christ's flesh, we should understand the Christ-child's humanity as being perfectly submissive to the divine will. Cf. *Haer.* 5.1.3. Holsinger-Friesen, *Irenaeus and Genesis*, pp. 136–7, n. 125, speaks of Irenaeus' 'acute interest in the text of Isaiah 7.10-17' and discusses its possible recapitulatory significance in relation to Gen. 2–3.
[38]   For example, *Epid.* 31.

Satan's stratagems.[39] Likewise, Christ is unburdened by original guilt: to free the strong man's captives, the incarnate Word enters the prison, unfastens the bonds of original guilt and Adamic transgression from the captives, and binds the strong man, Satan, with those same bonds; Christ himself is the liberator, not a prisoner.[40] Irenaeus explicitly contrasts the condition of Christ's flesh with the fettered condition of all other flesh: Christ's 'righteous flesh has reconciled that flesh which was being kept under bondage in sin, and brought it into friendship with God.' Irenaeus continues,

> If, then, any one allege that in this respect the flesh of the Lord was different from ours, because it indeed did not commit sin, neither was deceit found in His soul, while we, on the other hand, are sinners, he says what is the fact. But if he pretends that the Lord possessed another substance of flesh, the sayings respecting reconciliation will not agree with that man. For that thing is reconciled which had formerly been in enmity. Now, if the Lord had taken flesh from another substance, He would not, by so doing, have reconciled that one to God which had become inimical through transgression.[41]

Irenaeus' distinction between the righteous flesh of Christ and the flesh in bondage indicates that, from birth forward, they share simply a common substance rather than a common condition of enmity towards God.[42]

Irenaeus combines the themes of Christ's birth, unbound condition, and victory over Satan in a typological interpretation of the birth of Jacob (Gen. 25.26). Like Jesus, Jacob emerges from the womb as '*the supplanter* – one who holds, but is not held; binding the feet, but not being bound; striving and

---

[39] Minns, *Irenaeus*, pp. 106, 112–4. R. Williams, '"Tempted as we are": Christology and the Analysis of the Passions', StPatr 44 (2010), pp. 391–404, traces how Irenaeus' paralleling of Christ's temptations with Adam's suggested to later commentators that Christ, like Adam, was tempted while in a prelapsarian state of sinlessness.

[40] *Haer.* 3.18.2, 6; 4.33.4; 5.21-24 (cf. *Epid.* 37), note especially 5.21.3's line that 'the Word bound [Satan] securely as a fugitive from Himself, and made spoil of his goods, – namely, *those men whom he held in bondage*' (*ANF* 1, p. 550, emphasis mine). Here Christ clearly is distinguished from those in captivity, *pace* Minns, *Irenaeus*, pp. 116, 130, and Baker, 'The Place of St. Irenaeus', pp. 22–3, but as repeatedly recognized by Orbe, *Teología*, vol. 1, pp. 52, 62, 680–7; vol. 2, pp. 353, 359, and Wingren, *Man and the Incarnation*, pp. 84–7, 98, 102–3, 109, n. 82, 114–15, 119–20, 133–5, 149, n. 3.

[41] *Haer.* 5.14.2-3; ET *ANF* 1, pp. 541–2. Note that Irenaeus paraphrases 1 Pet. 2.22 but changes 'He committed no sin' to 'it committed no sin' ('it' referring to Christ's flesh) and 'neither was deceit found in His mouth' to 'in His soul'. On the significance of these changes as portraying the total sinlessness of Christ's human nature, see Orbe, *Teología* vol. 1, pp. 685–6.

[42] Houssiau, *La Christologie*, p. 246.

conquering; grasping in his hand his adversary's heel, that is, victory'.[43] From nativity forward, Christ exists unshackled by any sin or guilt, whether original or actual, and his freedom enables him to free the captives and to capture their captor.

Regarding Pauline passages which speak of Christ's becoming sin (2 Cor. 5.21), a curse (Gal. 3.13), and the likeness of sinful flesh (Rom. 8.3), Irenaeus does not deal with 2 Cor. 5.21 but does refer to Gal. 3.13 once and Rom. 8.3 twice.[44] The reference to Gal. 3.13 occurs in the midst of a catena of verses quoted to prove Christ's true humanity by his experience of suffering and death, in opposition to Docetism. Irenaeus does not indicate whether he equates being made a curse with being crucified per se or with a spiritual condition superadded to crucifixion (i.e. the pangs of damnation). The former interpretation is preferable, given that Irenaeus describes the Antichrist, not Christ, as bearing in himself the damnation of all evil.[45] Justin Martyr, who influenced Irenaeus,[46] insisted that Christ was cursed not by God but by the Jews.[47]

Since Irenaeus' first quotation of Rom. 8.3 appears amid a lengthy reflection on the Virgin Birth, what has been said above about that event's sanctifying significance bears recalling. The salvific worth of the theanthropic union, Irenaeus explains, is that by it God imparts immortality to humanity. One who receives salvation in the present may anticipate 'making such progress as to become wholly like [*consimilis fiat*/συνεξομοιωθῇ] Him who died for them. For He was made *in the likeness* [*similitudinem*/ὁμοιώματι] *of sinful flesh* that He might condemn sin, and then cast it out of the flesh as condemned; and also, that He might invite humankind to His own likeness [*similitudinem*/ὁμοίωσιν].'[48] In these lines, 'to become wholly like Him' corresponds with 'that He might invite humankind to His own likeness',

[43] *Haer.* 4.21.3; ET *ANF* 1, p. 493 (italics original). Cf. Orbe, *Teología* vol. 4, pp. 326–7, nn. 11–12. As Orbe indicates, Irenaeus interweaves historical, ecclesiological, and Christological interpretations of this text.
[44] *Haer.* 3.18.3 (Gal. 3.13), 20.2; 4.2.7 (Rom. 8.3). Wingren, *Man and the Incarnation*, p. 86, sees an allusion to Rom. 8.3 in *Epid.* 31.
[45] *Haer.* 5.28.2, 29.2. Cf. Wingren, *Man and the Incarnation*, pp. 187–8.
[46] Grant, *Irenaeus*, p. 1.
[47] *Dial.* 93–5.
[48] *Against the Heresies (Book 3)*, p. 96 (italics Unger and Steenberg's; Lat. and Greek: Irénée de Lyon, *Contre les Hérésies Livre III Tome II: Texte et Traduction* (trans. A. Rousseau and L. Doutreleau; SC 211; Paris: Cerf, 1974), pp. 390–1; cf. 185, n. 13.

while 'who died for them' foreshadows the line which quotes Rom. 8.3. Hence the 'likeness of sinful flesh' relates to Christ's sharing our experience of sin's consequence, death, and contrasts with 'His own [present] likeness' as immortal, which we shall experience with him. As demonstrated above, Irenaeus does not understand Christ's own flesh as genuinely 'sinful', but neither does he take 'likeness' in a Docetic sense. We will draw further conclusions after examining the other passage in which Irenaeus quotes Rom. 8.3.

In that passage, Irenaeus appeals to an Old Testament type of the crucified Christ:

> For the law never hindered [Jews] from believing in the Son of God; nay, but it even exhorted them so to do, saying that men can be saved in no other way from the old wound of the serpent than by believing in Him who, in the likeness of sinful flesh, is lifted up from the earth upon the tree of martyrdom [τῷ ξύλῳ τῆς μαρτυρίας], and draws all things to Himself, and vivifies the dead.[49]

Here Irenaeus blends allusions to Genesis 3 ('the old wound of the serpent'; 'the tree'), Numbers 21 (the incident of the bronze serpent), Rom. 8.3, and John's Gospel (3.14; 5.21-40;[50] 12.32). Some of this intertextuality reflects other early Christian literature: Irenaeus' mentor Justin writes that the impaled bronze serpent demonstrates that the serpent which inflicted sin upon humanity is conquered by the Cross.[51] *The Epistle of Barnabas* sees the inanimate yet life-giving serpent on a pole as a type of the crucified, dead Christ who gives life.[52] Irenaeus does not indicate whether he views the bronze serpent as symbolic of the defeated devil, of Christ's likeness to sinful flesh, or of something else. As before, though, he sets Rom 8:3 in the context of Christ's saving death. Orbe comments on Irenaeus' use of Rom 8:3 in this passage, 'The Son of God is lifted on high as a human being. Although innocent, he is consubstantial with sinful human beings. He has the same human nature. And due to being

---

[49] *ANF* 1, p. 465 (Greek: SC 211, p. 391).
[50] John 5.21-40 speaks of Christ's vivifying the dead and of μαρτυρία.
[51] *Dial.* 91, 94, 112.
[52] *Barn.* 12 in M. W. Holmes (ed. and trans.), *The Apostolic Fathers: Greek Texts and English Translations* (Grand Rapids: Baker, 3rd edn, 2007), pp. 418–21.

consubstantial, "innocent flesh" can save "sinful flesh".[53] For Irenaeus, then, Christ's being 'in the likeness of sinful flesh' means that he shares the same fleshly substance which *in all others exists in a sinful condition*.[54] It may also underscore that Christ died, just as sinful persons do, and died in a manner particularly befitting a sinner – as one judged guilty and condemned to a shameful, agonizing death.

Irenaeus' naming of Christ's Cross as 'the tree of martyrdom' draws us into his theology of martyrdom. His teacher Polycarp had died a martyr, as did Christians during Irenaeus' time in Lyons.[55] As noted above, Irenaeus believes that Christians may be free from sinfulness of the flesh in this life. He sees Christian martyrs as the holiest of believers, for they die not due to any sins of their own but due to their slayers' sins. A martyr dies with a heart full of love for enemies and a mouth full of prayer for executioners' pardon. Thus 'the love, goodness, and mercy of martyrs in the midst of their torments are the sign of their perfection. The martyr does nothing other than to imitate the Christ, the perfect martyr.'[56] For Christ, then, to die 'upon the tree of martyrdom' is for him to die without sinfulness in his flesh.

3.1.4 Christ's flesh and death

Yet if Christ's flesh is free from all guilt and sin, how can he experience their consequences, suffering and death? Irenaeus explains:

> Indeed, just as He was man that He might undergo temptation, so He was the Word that He might be glorified. The Word, on the one hand, remained

---

[53] Orbe, *Teología* vol. 4, p. 22 (here Orbe also cites Justin and *Barnabas* on the bronze serpent). Cf. vol. 1, pp. 680–3, particularly the following: 'In his virtue, the Word assumed an innocent, "righteous flesh," of the same substance and nature as the sinful nature of Adam and his children. In Christ, sinful flesh became innocent and holy. ... It would be absurd for the flesh of humanity to remain – *in Christ* –alienated and in enmity toward God' (682; italics original; ET mine).

[54] Houssiau, *La Christologie*, pp. 243–6. Wingren, *Man and the Incarnation*, pp. 86–7, thusly interprets *Epid.* 31 and its allusion (according to him) to Rom. 8.3.

[55] Irenaeus, *Apostolic Preaching*, pp. 1–2; Parvis, 'Who Was Irenaeus?', pp. 14–16. Cf. D. J. Bingham, 'The Apocalypse, Christ, and the Martyrs of Gaul', *Shadow*, pp. 11–28.

[56] Houssiau, *La Christologie*, pp. 188–9 (quote from latter page; ET mine), summarizing *Haer.* 3.18.4-6; cf. Osborn, *Irenaeus*, pp. 241–2. M. A. Donovan, *One Right Reading?: A Guide to Irenaeus* (Collegeville, MN: The Liturgical Press, 1997), p. 83, sees a chiastic structure in 3.18.2-7, which covers Christ's incarnation and suffering, with 18.5's discussion of martyrdom as the x-point. This structure serves to stress the martyrs' *imitatio Christi*. Wingren, *Man and the Incarnation*, p. 155, paradoxically claims that martyrs' deaths show *both* that they are still partially mastered by sin and death *and* that they imitate the crucified Christ, whom Wingren everywhere grants was unmastered by sin and death.

quiescent [*requiescente*/ἡσυχάζοντος], that He could be tempted and dishonored and crucified and die; on the other hand, the man was absorbed [*absorto*], that He might conquer and endure and show Himself kind, and rise again and be taken up [into heaven].[57]

As previously noted, Irenaeus' anthropology allows that human flesh is inherently capable of passion and death. He sees the Logos as passive enough to allow temptation, suffering, and death to touch his human weakness, yet active enough to overcome them and to grant life both to others and to his own human nature. Throughout Jesus' life – whether in his birth, baptism, resistance to temptation, healings, or resurrection[58] – human sin, corruption, and death were being 'absorbed' or 'swallowed up' by the divine victory of incorruption and immortality (1 Cor. 15.54).[59]

Inasmuch as the Logos, through voluntary restraint of his divine influence over his flesh, suffers the physical effects of the Fall, Irenaeus applies the term 'fallen' (πεπτωκυῖαν) to Christ's flesh when speaking of its mortality: 'And He demonstrated the resurrection, becoming Himself "the firstborn from the dead", and raising in Himself fallen ["deiectum (πίπτω)"] man ... as God had promised, by the prophets, saying, "I will raise up the fallen ['deiectum (πίπτω)'] tabernacle of David", [Amos 9:11/Acts 15:16] that is, the flesh [descended] from David.'[60]

In relation to sin, however, Christ maintains an *unfallen* state throughout his life. Irenaeus notes that in tempting Jesus to false worship, Satan urges him to 'fall' (Mt. 4.9). Irenaeus sees this word as an admission that to serve Satan

---

[57] *Haer.* 3.19.3; ET *Against the Heresies (Book 3)*, pp. 93–4 (brackets Unger and Steenberg's); cf. 179–81, n. 25. Note the irony of the *Word* being *quiet* (the primary meaning of ἡσυχάζω). Houssiau, *La Christologie*, pp. 192–5, provides literary and theological analysis of this passage, noting that the absorption of the human spells an end to its *frailty*, not to its *reality* (195).

[58] *Haer.* 3.19.1-2 (birth); 3.17.1-3 (baptism; cf. 3.9.3); 3.19.3 (temptation, works, resurrection). In his comments on Christ's baptism, Irenaeus links the rite with regeneration unto incorruption. The implication is that Christ's humanity, too, received this at baptism. In Irenaeus' dynamic view of the Logos' interaction with his human nature, the making incorrupt of Christ's flesh in the Jordan does not contradict the same occurrence initially in Mary's womb and ultimately in Joseph's tomb – a point missed by Briggman, *Irenaeus*, pp. 59–77. Cf. D. A. Smith, 'Irenaeus and the Baptism of Jesus', *TS* 58 (1997), pp. 618–42.

[59] *Haer.* 3.19.1 alludes to this verse, which is still on Irenaeus' mind in 3.19.3 (as quoted above).

[60] *Epid.* 38; ET Irenaeus, *Apostolic Preaching*, p. 64 (final bracketed insertion translator's); Lat. and Greek: Irénée de Lyon, *Démonstration de la Prédication apostolique* (trans. A. Rousseau; SC 406; Paris: Cerf, 1995), p. 136. *Epid.* 62 also applies Amos 9.11/Acts 15.16 to Christ's resurrection, in which he raises up David's 'fallen' (πεπτωκυῖαν in Acts 15.16; 'dirutum (πίπτω)' in SC 406, p. 174) fleshly tent. Dorries, *Incarnational Christology*, p. 157, n. 26, therefore is incorrect that Irenaeus never used the term 'fallen'.

is to 'fall' from God's glory to the verge of death. Unlike Adam and all other humans, Christ refuses this temptation.[61] Rather than falling into sin, the Son comes 'stooping low [*descendens*/καταβὰς] even to death'[62] as a Saviour from sin and death.

3.2 Defending the incarnate God: Athanasius

In a different century and continent, Bishop Athanasius of Alexandria (ca. 296–373), arch-defender of the Nicene confession of Christ's consubstantiality with God the Father,[63] felt Irenaeus' influence[64] and shared many of his views: humans were created in the image of the Logos, with their natural mortality and passions suspended so long as they remained in paradisiacal fellowship with God. The Fall left the race enslaved by Satan to sinfully disordered passions, condemned for Adam's transgression, and sentenced to death and physical corruption. Salvation has come through the Logos' becoming human in order that, by his birth, earthly life, death, and resurrection, humanity might be renewed in his image.[65] Yet unlike Irenaeus, Athanasius portrays prelapsarian

[61] *Haer.* 5.22.2–23.1. Irenaeus repeatedly uses forms of πίπτω in this passage, according to Irénée de Lyon, *Contre les Hérésies Livre V Tome II: Texte et Traduction* (trans. A. Rousseau, L. Doutreleau and C. Mercier; SC 153; Paris: Cerf, 1969), p. 285. In his *Dial.* 88, Irenaeus' mentor Justin had spoken of 'the race of men, who from Adam had fallen [ἐπεπτώκει] under death and the deceit of the serpent' (Williams, *Ideas*, p. 174). Irenaeus teaches that Christ's humanity fell under death but not under the devil's deceit.
[62] *Haer.* 3.18.2; ET *ANF* 1, p. 446; Lat. and Greek: SC 211, p. 345.
[63] For biographical and bibliographical information, see D. M. Gwynn, *Athanasius of Alexandria: Bishop, Theologian, Ascetic, Father* (Oxford: Oxford University Press, 2012); K. Anatolios, *Athanasius* (London: Routledge, 2004), pp. 1–39; Weinandy, *Athanasius*, pp. 1–10; A. Pettersen, *Athanasius* (Harrisburg, PA: Morehouse, 1995), pp. 1–18.
[64] K. Anatolios, 'The Influence of Irenaeus on Athanasius', StPatr 36, pp. 463–76; *idem*, *Athanasius: The Coherence of His Thought* (New York: Routledge, 2002), p. 206; E. P. Meijering, *Orthodoxy and Platonism in Athanasius: Synthesis or Antithesis?* (Leiden: Brill, 1974), pp. 12, 15–17, 105.
[65] *C. Gent.* 2–3, 32–4; *Inc.* 3–13, 19–21, 44, 54. The condemnation of all humanity for Adam's transgression appears clearly in *Inc.* 20: because all humans must pay their debt by dying, Christ died for all 'in order to make them all guiltless and free from the first transgression [τῆς ἀρχαίας παραβάσεως]' (Athanasius, Contra Gentes *and* De Incarnatione [ed. and trans. R. W. Thomson; Oxford: Clarendon, 1971], pp. 182–3 [Greek on all even-numbered pages and ET on all odd-numbered pages hereafter cited from this source]). Cf. *Inc.* 7–8, which references 'the transgression' (ἡ παράβασις) which dooms all to death and corruption (Contra Gentes *and* De Incarnatione, pp. 150–3). Nevertheless, G. W. H. Lampe, 'Christian Theology in the Patristic Period', in *A History of Christian Doctrine* (ed. H. Cunliffe-Jones; London: T&T Clark, 1978; repr. 2006), pp. 21–180 (157), and Kelly, *Early Christian Doctrines*, p. 347, deny that Athanasius saw Adam's fall as engendering 'actual guilt' in the rest of the race. Cf. Bray, 'Original Sin', p. 43, Tennant, *Sources*, pp. 313–14; Williams, *Ideas*, p. 261; Roldanus, *Le Christ*, pp. 70–1, 132–3.

humans as quasi-Platonic philosophers[66] in a penultimately perfect state,[67] not children requiring maturation, thus increasing their culpability for the Fall.

3.2.1 The Word and his flesh

Fundamental to Athanasius' thought is the distinction between the Logos and his flesh. The former is the divine subject and agent in Christ; the latter is the human object and instrument (ὄργανον)[68] of the Logos' action. Athanasius uses the term 'flesh' in the biblical sense as a synecdoche for the whole of human nature, including the soul, although the latter is underemphasized.[69] Because the Logos has united himself to the flesh, its expressions of passibility and mutability (e.g. birth, growth in wisdom, hunger, ignorance, fear, suffering, and death) are predicable of the Logos. They are not, however, proper to him in an unqualified sense,[70] for he continues impassible and immutable in himself, as befits his divinity, and he progressively transmutes his flesh so that it comes to participate in his divine attributes[71] as a prototype of Christians'

[66] *C. Gent.* 2–3; Meijering, *Orthodoxy*, pp. 5, 8–9; Anatolios, *Athanasius*, pp. 44–6; C. Kannengiesser, 'Athanasius of Alexandria and the Foundation of Traditional Christology', *TS* 34 (1973), pp. 103–13 (108), notes that Athanasius' Platonic Adam only appears once, at the beginning of the Alexandrian's first book.

[67] *C. Gent.* 3 says that God intended humanity to stay in its Edenic state; *Inc.* 3, though, says that in addition to paradise, humanity was to inherit heaven.

[68] Weinandy, *Athanasius*, p. 48, urges that this term not be interpreted as 'an impersonal instrument employed as a tool, but as the vehicle by which and through which the Son himself genuinely and truly experiences and acts in a personal human manner'.

[69] *Ep. Epict.* 8. Cf. *Tom.* 7; *C. Ar.* 3.30. Unless otherwise noted, all citations of these sources are from P. Schaff and H. Wace (eds), *The Nicene and Post-Nicene Fathers* (2 series; 28 vols; repr., Peabody, MA: Hendrickson, 1994; electronic version: *AGES Digital Library* version 8, 2000), series 2, vol. 4. Scholars debate whether Athanasius affirmed a human soul in Christ, whether the bishop changed his mind on this matter, and why he said so little on the subject. For a sampling of views, see C. A. Beeley, *The Unity of Christ: Continuity and Conflict in Patristic Tradition* (New Haven, CT: Yale University Press, 2012), pp. 142, 152, 163, 165, 176–7; G. D. Dragas, 'Athanasius Contra Apollinarem (The Questions of authorship and Christology)', *Church and Theology* 6 (1985), pp. 5–609 (289–99); idem, *Saint Athanasius of Alexandria: Original Research and New Perspectives* (Rollinsford, NH: Orthodox Research Institute, 2005), ch. 1; Anatolios, *Coherence*, pp. 67–78; Pettersen, *Athanasius*, pp. 109, 130–2; Weinandy, *Athanasius*, pp. 91–6; Hanson, *Search*, pp. 446–56; Roldanus, *Le Christ*, pp. 252–76; A. Grillmeier, *Christ in Christian Tradition* (trans. J. Bowden; 2 vols; Atlanta: John Knox, 2nd edn, 1975) vol. 1, pp. 308–28.

[70] P. J. Leithart, *Athanasius* (Grand Rapids: Baker, 2011), pp. 121–9, examines the interplay of predicate and property in *C. Ar.* 3 and urges on the basis of 3.31, 32, 34, 38, 41, 54 that Athanasius sees both the flesh and its passions as proper to the Logos just as the Logos is proper to the flesh – the intrapersonal union in Christ reflects the interpersonal union in the Godhead. Yet 3.31, 34, 41 distinguish the divine attributes proper to the Logos from the creaturely attributes proper to the flesh. Athanasius always qualifies his ascription of the latter to the Logos. Cf. Anatolios, *Athanasius*, pp. 66–74; Roldanus, *Le Christ*, p. 181.

[71] Anatolios, *Coherence*, pp. 142–54. As Anatolios notes, this Athanasian version of *communicatio idiomatum* belies the claim that he saw Christ's humanity as a mere 'tool' or 'space-suit' (the latter metaphor taken from Hanson, *Search*, p. 448).

deification.[72] Armed with this crucial distinction, Athanasius can say that the Logos took accursed flesh without becoming accursed himself,[73] that he sanctified, liberated, and saved his own flesh but that, strictly speaking, he did not sanctify, liberate, or save himself.[74]

This process of redemptive transmutation within Christ's flesh began *in utero.* He not only received from his mother the substance common to humanity,[75] but 'transport[ed] our errant race [πλανηθεῖσαν γέννησιν] into himself';[76] 'took a servant's form, putting on that flesh which was enslaved to sin';[77] and, coming in the likeness of sinful flesh, 'became sin for us and a curse'.[78] While it may be possible to interpret these phrases merely as the imputation of error, slavery, sin, and curse to Christ or as an analogy whereby, for example, his servitude to God contrasts with our servitude to sin, such interpretations are questionable on both formal and material grounds. Formally, Athanasius treats the Son's assumption of creatureliness, flesh, infirmity, sin, and curse in parallel manner and as states illustrative of one another, which may imply that he sees an ontological dimension to them all.[79] Thus the bishop glosses Phil. 2.7-8, interpreting verse 8's 'he humbled [ἐταπείνωσεν] himself' with reference to the assumption of a 'body of humiliation [ταπεινὸν]' (Phil. 3.21) and verse 7's 'taking the form of a slave [δούλου]' with 'putting on the enslavement [δουλωθεῖσαν] of the flesh to sin' (cf. Rom. 6–8).[80] Materially, Athanasius describes sin

[72] For a study of the patristic (particularly Greek patristic) doctrine of deification, see N. Russell, *The Doctrine of Deification in the Greek Patristic Tradition* (Oxford: Oxford University Press, 2004); Russell covers Athanasius' view (166–88) and traces its origin to Irenaeus (105, 169). See also Roldanus, *Le Christ*, pp. 165–7.

[73] *C. Ar.* 2:47, 55-56; *Ep. Epict.* 9. Torrance in *Trinitarian Faith*, p. 161, claims that 'Athanasius could say that "the whole Christ became a curse for us"', quoting *C. Ar.* 2.47, but the original setting of this line is Athanasius' denial that the 'whole Christ' became accursed any more than the whole Logos became flesh: 'We do not conceive the whole Word Himself to be flesh, but to have put on flesh ... we do not simply conceive this, that the whole Christ has become curse and sin, but that He has taken on Him the curse' (*NPNF²* 4, p. 374).

[74] *C. Ar.* 1:46-50; 2:61, 72; *Ep. Epict.* 4, 9.

[75] *Ep. Epict.* 2, 4–5, 7.

[76] *Ep. Adelph.* 4; ET Anatolios, *Athanasius*, p. 238; Greek: *NPNF²* 4, p. 576, n. 8.

[77] *C. Ar.* 1.43; ET *NPNF²* 4, p. 331.

[78] *C. Ar.* 2.55; ET *NPNF²* 4, p. 378. Athanasius quotes Rom. 8.3 both in this passage and in the above-cited *Ep. Adelph.* 4.

[79] *C. Ar.* 2.47, 55; *Ep. Epict.*8; Roldanus, *Le Christ*, pp. 167–70; but cf. Cardinal Newman's note on 2.55 regarding Christ's 'real manhood and imputed sinfulness' and on *C. Ar.* 1.43 that Christ assumed a 'fallen nature' from Mary, yet without original sin (*NPNF²* 4, pp. 378 n. 8 and 331, n. 2, respectively), as well as St Cyril of Alexandria, *On the Unity of Christ* (trans. J. A. McGuckin; Crestwood, NY: St Vladimir's Seminary Press, 2000), pp. 56–7, for a denial by one of Athanasius' successors that Christ became flesh in the same way that he became sin.

[80] *C. Ar.* 1.43; Greek: W. Bright, *The Orations of St. Athanasius Against the Arians* (Ann Arbor, MI: University Microfilms International, 1978), p. 45 (ET mine).

as having become internal to the flesh, so that the Logos could not eliminate sin simply through external ethical instruction, for 'being continually held captive [by Adam's transgression], it admitted not the Divine mind'. Rather, the Logos himself became internal to sinful flesh, indwelling it so as to expel its sin and make it 'capable of the Word' so that 'we might have a free mind'.[81] Likewise, Isaiah and Peter do not say that Christ merely cured our sins and infirmities through an external healing but that he carried them to the Cross in his own body, internalizing them in order to expunge them.[82]

Athanasius insists that the Logos was not polluted by the tainted flesh which he took. His birth from a virgin indicates that his body was pure, a fit temple[83] and priestly garment.[84] Such language indicates a cleansing of Christ's humanity from sin at conception. Athanasius believes that there were precedents for such prenatal purification: Jeremiah and John the Baptist were among those 'made holy and clean from all sin' even in the womb. Yet personal sinlessness did not exempt them from the consequence of Adam's sin, the curse of death and corruption. Liberation could come only through the assumption and transmutation of human nature initiated by the Incarnation.[85] By this means the Logos would do a more thorough work, freeing humanity not only from sin, but also from the mortality and corruptibility,[86] which, while latent within prelapsarian flesh, had become actualized by the Fall.[87]

This transmutation of human nature in Christ that had begun in Mary's womb continued until Joseph's tomb. In his childhood and even during adulthood, Christ carried the infirmity of human ignorance and steadily

---

[81] *C. Ar.* 1.60; 2.56; ET *NPNF*[2] 4, pp. 341, 378. Athanasius' logic demands that Rom 8:3, which he quotes in 1.60 and 2.55, be read as teaching that Christ assumed genuinely sinful flesh. Note also the interplay of noetic concepts: the personal Rational Word (Logos) cannot convert our rational mind by spoken rational words (associated in 1.60 and 2.55 with the Mosaic Law) but only by uniting ontologically our rationality with his own.

[82] *C. Ar.* 2.47; 3.31, both citing Isa. 53.4 and 1 Pet. 2.24. Cf. *C. Ar.* 2.69.

[83] *Inc.* 8. Athanasius speaks of Mary and of the body of Christ which she conceived as 'pure' because 'unalloyed by intercourse with men' (Contra Gentes *and* De Incarnatione, p. 153).

[84] *C. Ar.* 2.7. As Leithart, *Athanasius*, p. 32, notes, Athanasius here parallels the making of Aaron's sacerdotal robe by women with Mary's role in producing flesh for Christ.

[85] *C. Ar.* 3.33; ET *NPNF*[2] 4, p. 411; cf. n. 2, where Newman points out that Athanasius' view of Jeremiah and John was not idiosyncratic. Athanasius quotes Rom. 5.14, indicating that he interprets this verse not as contrasting Adam's transgression with a different class of sin (i.e. sin *extra legem*) but with personal sinlessness. On the necessity of Christ's internalizing our mortality, see *Inc.* 44; Dragas, *Saint Athanasius*, pp. 90–1.

[86] *Inc.* 17, with a quotation from 1 Pet. 2.22 on Christ's sinlessness.

[87] Thus Steenberg, *Of God and Man*, p. 168, distinguishes between 'corruptibility as a natural condition in man' and 'the *actual corruption* of the human being' in Athanasius' thought. (Italics his.) Cf. Dragas, *Saint Athanasius*, pp. 30, 36.

overcame it in his own humanity for the sake of our instruction.[88] His baptism was a moment of sanctification (in the sense of consecration to service) for his flesh.[89] Throughout his earthly life, 'He brought about the complete eradication from the flesh of every bite of the serpent and the repulsion of any evil that had sprung up from the movements of the flesh. ... So the Lord himself says: "The prince of this world is coming and he finds nothing in me"' (John 14:30).[90] For instance, the fear of death is due to our alienation from God and bondage by earthly passions.[91] In his first Gethsemane prayer and his cry of dereliction, Christ's humanity displayed this fear of death, the same minding of merely human things that he had rebuked in Peter (Mt. 16.23). But his succeeding prayers, 'Not my will but yours' and 'Into your hands I commit my spirit', exhibited him overcoming his human will's weakness by his divine will's immutable might.[92] After a lifetime of conquering the flesh's infirmities, he offered up its mortality and corruptibility on the Cross as a holy sacrifice in order to complete their destruction.[93] While the life-giving Logos could have restrained his mortal flesh from dying, he could only uproot mortality from his flesh and ours by passing through death into resurrected life.[94]

Christians benefit from Christ's victory, becoming impassible by present renunciation of sinful passions, becoming immortal and incorruptible by future resurrection. Celibates and martyrs exemplify the freedom which Christ has won. Celibates triumph over erotic passion, anticipating the unmarried state of the eschaton. Martyrs are free from thanatophobic passion and overcome the passion of their sufferings by their hope of immortality.[95]

3.2.2 Pseudo(?)-Athanasian writings

Thus far we have examined writings whose attribution to Athanasius is accepted generally in current scholarship. Both fallenness and unfallenness

[88] *C. Ar.* 3.38-53. Cf. Pettersen, *Athanasius*, pp. 123–9.
[89] *C. Ar.* 1.41, 46-47, 50. Athanasius treats Jesus' sanctification and messianic anointment as synonymous.
[90] *C. Ar.* 2.69; ET Anatolios, *Athanasius*, p. 162.
[91] *C. Gent.* 3; cf. *Ep. Max.* 3's citation of Heb. 2.15 (*NPNF*² 4, p. 579).
[92] *C. Ar.* 3.54-58. Cf. Pettersen, *Athanasius*, pp. 128–9.
[93] *Inc.* 9; *Ep. Epict.* 6.
[94] *Inc.* 21–2, 26, 31; Roldanus, *Le Christ*, pp. 170–1; *pace* Beeley, *Unity*, pp. 136–8, who misreads Athanasius as teaching that Christ's body was incorruptible from conception.
[95] *Inc.* 48–52; *C. Ar.* 2.69.

advocates also appeal to works whose Athanasian authorship modern scholars often deny: the Fourth Oration *Contra Arianos* and the two books *Contra Apollinarium*.[96] The Fourth Oration discusses the dynamic mediation of Christ: in his humanity, he receives from us our passions and infirmities (including those expressed in the cry of dereliction) and offers them to God in order to destroy them. In his humanity, too, he receives from God power and exaltation in order to share them with us. In his divinity, he receives nothing from either party, being immutably impassible and omnipotent.[97] The Fourth Oration thus preserves the Athanasian understanding that salvation is wrought internally within the theanthropic union.

Contra Apollinarium opposes Apollinaris' alleged doctrines that Christ had heavenly flesh rather than flesh of Adamic descent and that, within that flesh, the divine Logos substituted for the human mind (or soul). Both doctrines seek to insulate Christ from becoming sinful in becoming human: flesh descended from Adam has 'become accustomed to sin, and has received the transmission of sin'; but sin is conceived in the mind, which from childhood onward delights in evil (Gen. 8.21) and employs the flesh to commit it, hence human nature *en toto*, both flesh and mind, is captive to sin.[98] Apollinarianism reduces soteriology to simulacra: Christ mimics human nature and we mimic his sinlessness.[99]

In response, *Contra Apollinarium* charges Apollinaris with mimicking the errors of Marcion and Mani by seeing sin as intrinsic to human nature rather than as the dysfunction of it.[100] God created Adam sinless in both flesh and mind. When Adam yielded to temptation, Satan introduced his seed (Mt. 13.25) and law (Rom. 7.23) of sin within human nature, 'and thenceforward sin was active

---

[96] On the Fourth Oration, see A. H. B. Logan, review of M. Vinzent, *Pseudo-Athanasius: Contra Arianos IV*, *JTS* (NS) 49.1 (1998), pp. 382–5; Hanson, *Search*, p. 418. On *Contra Apollinarium* (also spelled *Apollinarem*), see C. E. Raven, *Apollinarianism: An Essay on the Christology of the Early Church* (Cambridge: Cambridge University Press, 1923), pp. 242–53; cf. Dragas, 'Athanasius Contra Apollinarem', for a massive rebuttal, and Hanson, *Search*, pp. 645–51, for a counter-rebuttal. For a time, Charles Kannengiesser denied Athanasian authorship of the Third Oration, but has publicly withdrawn this view (Anatolios, *Athanasius*, p. 246, n. 74). Cf. C. Stead, review of C. Kannengiesser, *Athanase d'Alexandrie évêque et écrivain*, *JTS* (NS) 36.1 (1985), pp. 220–9.
[97] *C. Ar.* 4.6-7.
[98] *C. Apoll.* 1.2, 7; 2.6, 8, 11. Quotation from 2.8: ET *Later Treatises of S. Athanasius, Archbishop of Alexandria, with Notes; and an Appendix on S. Cyril of Alexandria and Theodoret* (trans. members of the English Church; Oxford: James Parker & Co., and London: Rivingtons, 1881), p. 126; Greek: PG 26, p. 1144b. Unless otherwise noted, all citations of *C. Apoll.* are from *Later Treatises*.
[99] *C. Apoll.* 1.2, 20; 2.1, 3, 11.
[100] *C. Apoll.* 1.12, 14, 19; 2.3, 8.

... in the direction of every appetite [ἐπιθυμίαν].[101] Christ restored human nature to its original, unfallen condition by assuming a complete human nature, both flesh and mind. This assumption of a complete human nature does not make Christ sinful, for sin is no part of human nature per se. No seed or law of sin existed in Christ's humanity, as Satan discovered upon tempting him.[102] When scripture attributes 'flesh' to Christ, the definition is 'the orderly form of our whole constitution, but without sin'.[103] Likewise, his human soul (or mind) was 'constituted ... in a sinless state'.[104] Because his humanity was both complete and sinless, he was able to ransom our bodies with his body and our souls with his soul on the Cross.[105]

Against Apollinaris' theory of salvation by imitation, these books argue the insufficiency of Christ's merely avoiding sinning; he must have avoided sinning *in the very nature which had sinned* – that is, one derived from Adam. His sinless life in our common nature reveals that this nature has been renewed in him and may be so in us. This renewal occurred in the 'wondrous "generation" [Isa. 53.8]'[106] of the Virgin Birth, which marks both Christ's continuity with the human race, since he sprang 'from the seed of David and Abraham, and of Adam', and also his discontinuity with its failure, 'having taken from the Virgin all that God originally fashioned and made in order to the constitution of man, yet without sin as also the Apostle says, *In all points like to us, yet without sin* [Heb. 4.15]'.[107] Hence the Christ-child, like Adam in Eden, knew neither good nor evil, but unlike Adam, rejected evil rather than God's command.[108]

All the above appears in *Contra Apollinarium*'s use of key Pauline texts. The Son's likeness to sinful flesh (Rom. 8.3) is an authentic participation in the Adamic substance of flesh, but not in its sinfulness, which Christ condemns by embodying flesh 'unreceptive of sin' (ἀνεπίδεκτον ἁμαρτίας).[109] The 'form of

---

[101] *C. Apoll.* 1.15; ET *Later Treatises*, 106; Greek: PG 26, p. 1120c; cf. 2.6, 8.

[102] *C. Apoll.* 1.15; 2.10. Both passages quote Jn 14.20; 2.10 says that Christ's flesh was 'without carnal desires and human thoughts' because 'the will belonged to the Godhead only' (*Later Treatises*, p. 128). Cf. 1.17 ('And in this consists the marvel – that the Lord became Man, and *yet apart from sin* [Heb. 4.15]: for He became wholly a new Man to exhibit what He could do' [*Later Treatises*, p. 109; cf. 124 n. 'm']).

[103] *C. Apoll.* 2.18; ET *Later Treatises*, p. 141.

[104] *C. Apoll.* 1.19; ET *Later Treatises*, p. 111.

[105] *C. Apoll.* 1.18-19.

[106] *C. Apoll.* 2.6; ET *Later Treatises*, p. 123.

[107] *C. Apoll.* 2.5; ET *Later Treatises*, p. 122 (italics original); cf. 1.13. The author assumes Pauline authorship of Hebrews.

[108] *C. Apoll.* 2.6, combining Isa. 7.16 with Genesis 3.

[109] *C. Apoll.* 1.7 (ET mine; Greek: PG 26, p. 1104c); 2.6. See 'ἀνεπίδεκτος' *PGL*, pp. 135-6.

a servant' (Phil. 2.7) does not describe sinful human nature, as some heretics claim;[110] nor does it suggest an insubstantial appearance, as say other heretics;[111] rather, it refers to Logos' assumption of the original formation of Adam, that is, of both body and soul.[112] That body suffered and died, while that soul experienced sorrow and distress, not as subject to sin, death, and corruption, but as subject to God's plan to condemn sin through Christ's sinlessness and liberate humanity from death and corruption through his descent into hades and resurrection.[113]

Contra Apollinarium's insistence on the assumption of flesh renewed to Edenic purity (and in that sense unfallen) complements the statements in Athanasius' recognized writings regarding the assumption of enslaved, errant flesh. It bears recalling that, prior to nineteenth-century sceptical scholarship, they all were seen as the work of one presumably self-consistent author.[114] Although Athanasius, as we saw above, describes the Incarnation as the assumption of 'flesh which was enslaved to sin' as part of 'our errant race', nowhere does he claim that Christ's flesh was sin-servile or errant following the moment of its assumption. Rather, Athanasius sees Christ's flesh as purified from sin at conception, while he endures throughout his life the consequences introduced by sin into human experience – ignorance, fear of death, corruptibility, the curse of mortality. *Contra Apollinarium* agrees that Christ experienced these consequences, while insisting that they did not spring from any sinful propensity within Christ, but that a re-creation of fallen humanity occurred in the Virgin's womb. Combining Athanasius' acknowledged works with *Contra Apollinarium*, we may say that what the Logos assumed was from 'our errant race' but that, by assuming it, he immediately renewed it in a 'wondrous "generation"'; he took sin-slaved flesh and instantly it became sin-free, God-slaved flesh.[115] Yet like Jeremiah and the Baptist, Christ carried the

---

[110] *C. Apoll.* 2.4.

[111] *C. Apoll.* 2.1.

[112] *C. Apoll.* 1.5, 12; 2.1, 3, 10.

[113] *C. Apoll.* 1.5, 14, 17. The use of μορφή in these passages, as well as context, suggests that the author still has in mind Phil. 2.7's 'form [μορφῆ] of a servant' when writing these comments. See PG 26, pp. 1101–02ab; 1117c–20b.

[114] Dragas, *Saint Athanasius*, pp. 133–4.

[115] *C. Ar.* 2.10, 14 says that humanity, enslaved to corruption and idols, was freed by Christ, and interprets Phil. 2.7's 'form of a servant' with reference to the servitude of created beings to their Creator Logos rather than the servitude of fallen beings to sin, as in *C. Ar.* 1.43. Evidently Athanasius is capable of diverse nuancing of Phil. 2.7.

consequences of humanity's erring and sin throughout his earthly course. In this manner he 'became sin' and bore it.[116] In Christ's case, however, his divinity progressively overcame those consequences, culminating in his resurrection.

On the other hand, *Contra Apollinarium* differs from Athanasius' accepted writings with its emphasis on the soul or mind of Christ. This fact may suggest development beyond the bishop's own thought.[117] It is a development also championed by our next Greek father.

3.3 'The unassumed is the unhealed': Gregory Nazianzen

The theology of Gregory Nazianzen (329/330–389/90),[118] briefly archbishop of Constantinople and even more briefly president of the Second Ecumenical Council held there in 381, intersects with several strands of this study. His thought overlaps with Athanasius'; he influenced Augustine, fellow Cappadocian Gregory Nyssen, and Cyril of Alexandria to varying degrees; his *Epistola* 101 and other writings helped to shape the Christological debate leading up to the Council of Chalcedon;[119] and modern fallenness and unfallenness theologians alike claim support from that epistle and its epigrammatic 'the unassumed is the unhealed' (Τὸ ... ἀπρόσληπτον, ἀθεράπευτον).[120] We shall examine this

---

[116] Cf. Roldanus, *Le Christ*, p. 174.

[117] On this possibility, see the literature cited in notes 69 and 96 above.

[118] These are the consensually accepted dates: cf. C. A. Beeley, *Gregory of Nazianzus on the Trinity and the Knowledge of God: In Your Light We Shall See Light* (Oxford: Oxford University Press, 2008), pp. 5, 61; J. McGuckin, *Saint Gregory of Nazianzus: An Intellectual Biography* (Crestwood, NY: St Vladimir's Seminary Press, 2001), pp. vii, xi; D. F. Winslow, *The Dynamics of Salvation: A Study in Gregory of Nazianzus* (Cambridge, MA: Philadelphia Patristic Foundation, 1979), p. 1. For proposed birthdates as early as 325/326, see F. W. Norris, L. Wickham and F. Williams, *Faith Gives Fullness to Reasoning: The Five Theological Orations of Gregory of Nazianzen* (Leiden: Brill, 1991), p. 1; B. E. Daley, *Gregory of Nazianzus* (London: Routledge, 2006), p. 3. For biographical information, see McGuckin's biography; Beeley, *Gregory of Nazianzus*, pp. 3–62; Daley, *Gregory of Nazianzus*, pp. 1–60; A. Hofer, *Christ in the Life and Teaching of Gregory of Nazianzus* (Oxford: Oxford University Press, 2013).

[119] Beeley, *Gregory of Nazianzus*, pp. 59 (Chalcedon), 277–83 (Athanasius), 303–9 (Nyssen), 321 (Augustine), 322 (Cyril). For his trinitarian doctrine, the Chalcedonian Council awarded Nazianzen the title 'the Theologian', an appellation previously used only of the Apostle John (Beeley, *Gregory of Nazianzus*, p. vii; Norris, Wickham and Williams, *Faith Gives Fullness*, p. 12, n. 56; Hofer, *Life and Teaching*, pp. 2–3).

[120] *Ep.* 101.5; Greek: PG 37:182c. As often noted, this dictum has roots in Origen, *Dialogue with Heracleides* 7 (e.g. Beeley, *Gregory of Nazianzus*, p. 127; Norris, Wickham and Williams, *Faith Gives Fullness*, pp. 155–6). Nazianzen was much indebted to Origenism (Beeley, *Gregory of Nazianzus*, pp. 271–3). M. F. Wiles, 'Soteriological Arguments in the Fathers', StPatr 9 (1966), pp. 321–5 (322), finds the *non-assumptus'* origins not only in Origen but also in Tertullian.

line in its context and in light of Nazianzen's crucial Theological Orations on the Son (*Ors.* 29 and 30) and his Christmas Oration (*Or.* 38).[121]

3.3.1 The mind of Christ

Nazianzen penned *Epistola* 101 in old age against the same Apollinarian errors opposed in *Contra Apollinarium*. Against these errors, Nazianzen insists that Christ derived his flesh from the Virgin, not heaven, and acquired a human rational mind (or soul), too. Thus his human constitution was complete.[122] This insistence by Nazianzen, however, was not new. Earlier in his career, he had confronted the Eunomian denial of a human mind in Christ.[123] Nazianzen echoes Origen and anticipates Augustine by seeing the human mind as the mediator between the divine Mind and its antithesis, the material body and world.[124] To omit a human mind in the Incarnation would result in the indecorous direct union of Godhead with ignoble flesh.[125] Against the Apollinarians' protest that two minds cannot occupy the same person, Nazianzen replies that they have committed a category mistake by treating immaterial realities as though material.[126]

Far more important to Nazianzen than these ontological considerations, though, are soteriological concerns: 'The unassumed is the *unhealed.*' Nazianzen's whole soteriology rests on the correlation between the Incarnation and deification (θέωσις):[127] like Irenaeus, he sees Christ's advent as restoring the developmental trajectory towards God which humanity lost in Eden. This Christ does by uniting to himself not only the various constituents of

---

[121] For the contexts and significance of these orations and *Ep.* 101 as crucial texts for Nazianzen's theology, cf. Beeley, *Gregory of Nazianzus*, pp. 39, 40, 43, 122–43; McGuckin, *Saint Gregory of Nazianzus*, pp. 390–3; Norris, Wickham and Williams, *Faith Gives Fullness*; Saint Gregory of Nazianzus, *On God and Christ: The Five Theological Orations and Two Letters to Cledonius* (trans. F. Williams and L. Wickham; Crestwood, NY: St Vladimir's Seminary Press, 2002). Both Dods, *Incarnation*, p. 532, and Weinandy, *Likeness*, pp. 28–9, appeal to *Or.* 38. Barth, *CD* I/2, pp. 195–6, and Torrance, *Trinitarian Faith*, pp. 162–3, cite *Or.* 30.

[122] *Ep.* 101.4-10. For an extensive analysis of this epistle, see Hofner, *Life and Teaching*, ch. 4.

[123] Norris, Wickham and Williams, *Faith Gives Fullness*, pp. 66, 153 (citing *Ors.* 2.23; 22.13; 38.13).

[124] Daley, *Gregory of Nazianzus*, p. 227, n. 388; cf. *Or.* 38.13.

[125] *Ep.* 101.8, 10-11.

[126] *Ep.* 101.6-7.

[127] Nazianzen himself coined this nominal form from the verb θεόω (Beeley, *Gregory of Nazianzus*, p. 117). On Nazianzen's entire theology as following a kenotic-theotic parabola, see F. W. Norris, *Gregory Nazianzen's Doctrine of Jesus Christ* (New Haven, CT: Yale, 1971).

humanity (mind and body) but also the various experiences (πάθη)[128] of humanity (e.g. birth, temptation, suffering, death), sanctifying them by contact with his divinity.[129]

3.3.2 The epithets of Christ

The New Testament describes the Incarnation by phrases such as 'made sin' (2 Cor. 5.21), 'made a curse' (Gal. 3.13), and 'taking the form of a slave' (Phil. 2.7), as well as by recording Jesus' cries of distress at Gethsemane and Golgotha. In Orations 29–30, Nazianzen explains how he interprets such passages using a theanthropic hermeneutic. As divine, the Son is guiltless and uncursed, the Father's equal, and without any divergence of will from the Father; neither his own divinity nor his Father forsake his humanity in the midst of the Passion[130] – indeed, as God, the Son is impassible.[131] In becoming human, he condescends to the troubling titles and experiences given above. Yet Nazianzen makes clear that sin has no continuance in the totalities of Christ's human nature and experience.[132] The Holy Spirit purified Mary in body and soul to prepare her for Christ's conception, and the very act of uniting divinity with humanity in her womb deified and sanctified the human nature involved,[133] so that his nativity frees us from our birth-bonds.[134] Jesus had no need of baptismal cleansing, but was baptized to hallow the baptismal waters so that they in turn might cleanse us.[135] Nazianzen appeals to the principle that like sanctifies like: Christ's holy mind and flesh restore others' sinful mind and flesh.[136] In all these cases, sinlessness is attributed to Christ's humanity, not merely to his divinity. This sinlessness includes freedom from original, not just

[128] On this term's significance for Nazianzen, see Beeley, *Gregory of Nazianzus*, pp. ix–x. On its range of meaning in patristic discourse, see 'πάθος', *PGL*, pp. 992–5.
[129] Winslow, *Dynamics*, pp. 61, 64–6, 90, 100, 190–2; cf. Beeley, *Gregory of Nazianzus*, pp. 118–21.
[130] *Or.* 30.5-6, 12.
[131] *Ep.* 101.4.
[132] *Ors.* 30.12, 14, 21; 38.13.
[133] *Or.* 38.13; cf. 29.19; *Ep.* 101.8.
[134] *Or.* 38.17. For Nazianzen's negative view of birth as involving slavery and passion, cf. *Ors.* 30.3; 40.2.
[135] *Ors.* 29.20; 30.20; 38.16; 39.15-16 (on Christ's baptism); 40.29 (on Christian baptism). In *Or.* 39.15, Nazianzen says that Christ was baptized 'to bury the whole of the old Adam in the water' (PG 36, p. 352b; ET *NPNF²* 5, p. 357). This line could be misread as describing Christ's humanity as 'the old Adam', were it not for 39.13, which distinguishes between the new Adam, Christ, and the old Adam whom he saves. Thus, in context, Nazianzen is preaching that the baptism of Christ's spotless humanity readies the waters to regenerate our sin-smirched humanity.
[136] τῷ ὁμοίῳ τὸ ὅμοιον ἁγιάσας (*Ep.* 101.9 [PG 37, p. 188b]); cf. *Ors.* 30.20-21; 38.13-14; *Ep.* 101.8-9; Hofner, *Life and Teaching*, pp. 114–17. The principle 'like sanctifies like' could be applied as well to Christ's own humanity by viewing the divine Mind in Christ as sanctifying the human mind in him.

actual, sin, for Nazianzen's dispute with the Apollinarians concerns whether a full humanity in Christ entails original sin. Nazianzen agrees with Apollinaris that original sin plagues humanity[137] and that Christ lacks original sin; their disagreement concerns whether that lack implies a lack in Christ's humanity.

In what sense, then, are Christ's negative titles and experiences applicable to him? Here Nazianzen's comments must be read carefully, as he does not always mean precisely the same thing.[138] Sometimes the application is a verbal counterfactual:

> The one who releases me from the curse was called 'curse' because of me; 'the one who takes away the world's sin' was called 'sin' and is made a new Adam to replace the old. In just this way too, as head of the whole body, he appropriates my want of submission. So long as I am an insubordinate rebel with passions [πάθεσιν] which deny God, my lack of submission will be referred to Christ. But when all things are put in submission under him, when transformed they obediently acknowledge him, then will Christ bring me forward, me who have been saved, and make his subjection complete. ... Thus it is that he effects our submission, makes it his own and presents it to God. 'My God, my God, look upon me, why have you forsaken me?' seems to me to have the same kind of meaning. *He* is not forsaken either by the Father or, as some think, by his own Godhead. ... No, in himself, as I have said, he expresses our condition. *We* had once been the forsaken and disregarded; then we were accepted and now are saved by the sufferings of the impassible [ἀπαθοῦς πάθεσιν]. He made our thoughtlessness and waywardness his own, just as the psalm [Ps. 22], in its subsequent course, says.[139]

The context is an exegesis of Paul's doctrine of Christ's eschatological subordination to his Father (1 Cor. 15.24-28). Nazianzen sees his own

---

[137] On the Apollinarian doctrine of original sin, see Wickham's discussion in *On God and Christ*, p. 150; R. A. Norris Jr., *Manhood and Christ: A Study in the Christology of Theodore of Mopsuestia* (Oxford: Clarendon, 1963), pp. 112–21. For Nazianzen's doctrine and the debate over whether he taught original guilt, cf. Tennant, *Sources*, pp. 318–19; Williams, *Ideas*, pp. 282–92; Bray, 'Original Sin', pp. 43, 46; Lampe, 'Christian Theology', p. 157; Kelly, *Early Christian Doctrines*, pp. 348–52; Winslow, *Dynamics*, p. 69. For Nazianzen's realistic sense of his personal involvement in Adam's sin, see, in addition to the passages cited by Kelly, *Ors.* 19.13-4; 22.13 (PG 35, pp. 1060b–61a; 1145bc; ET St. Gregory of Nazianzus, *Select Orations* [trans. M. Vinson; FC 107; Washington, DC: Catholic University of America Press, 2003], pp. 104–5, 127).

[138] As Hofner, *Life and Teaching*, ch. 3, shows, Nazianzen uses a range of related terms and ideas for the mixtures of differents found in such cases as the Incarnation, psychosomatic union, character traits, his own friendship with Basil of Caesarea, and Christ's relationship to believers. Hofner warns against reducing this varied usage to a single source (i.e. Stoic notions of mixture) or meaning (e.g. ontological blending).

[139] *Or.* 30.5; ET *On God and Christ*, pp. 96–7 (italics original); Greek: PG 36, pp. 108d, 109ab. Cf. *Ep.* 101.12; Winslow, *Dynamics*, p. 101.

insubordination, including the God-denying passions resultant upon Adam's sin, as perpetually being 'referred to Christ' until the eschaton. This is a verbal, counterfactual referral rather than an actual participation by the ascended Christ in our rebellious passions, for later in the same discourse Nazianzen denies the latter possibility.[140] He makes the same point regarding the cry of dereliction: Jesus' humanity is not forsaken even as he humanly 'expresses our condition' of 'thoughtlessness and waywardness'. Christ assumes our estrangement's responsibility and results but not its reality. Likewise, Nazianzen's oration afterward places on Christ's lips the words of a parallel psalm (Ps. 59.3) and explains that its references to 'my iniquity' and 'my sin' mean 'not that he did, but that he did not, have iniquity and sin'.[141] In light of all the above, Nazianzen's language of Christ's being 'called' sin and curse should be taken to mean that these terms are counterfactual: he received our epithets to redefine our reality.[142]

Sometimes, however, Nazianzen has in view a more factual, yet still nuanced, application of terms and experiences to Christ. Of Phil. 2.7, he writes, 'He was actually subject as a slave to flesh, to birth, and to our human experiences [πάθεσι]; for our liberation, held captive as we are by sin, he was subject to all that he saved.'[143] An incautious reading would see the 'all' to which Christ was subject as including our captivity to sin. But Nazianzen specifically lists flesh, birth, and πάθη as those things to which Christ became a slave. The 'all' to which Christ was subject is the 'all that he saved,' and he did not save sin, but πάθη, birth, and flesh *from* sin. Similar is Nazianzen's allusion to Phil. 2.7 amid his discussion of the Epistle to the Hebrews' attributions of learning, obedience, suffering, petition, submission, and temptation to Christ: 'Receiving an alien "form" he bears the whole of me, along with all that is mine, in himself, so that he may consume within himself the meaner element, as fire consumes wax or the Sun ground mist, and so that I may share in what is his through the intermingling.'[144] The 'meaner element' here specifically

---

[140] *Or.* 30.14, on Heb. 7.25.

[141] *Or.* 30.12, on Ps. 59.3; ET *On God and Christ*, p. 103.

[142] Cf. Norris, Wickham and Williams, *Faith Gives Fullness*, pp. 51, 163. Norris' language suggests that he sees sin, curse, rebellion, deviancy, and godless passions as belonging factually, not counterfactually, to Christ's humanity. Norris does not attempt to harmonize this view with Nazianzen's frequent assertions of Christ's sinlessness.

[143] *Or.* 30.3; ET *On God and Christ*, pp. 94–5; Greek: PG 36, p. 105c.

[144] *Or.* 30.6; ET *On God and Christ*, p. 97; Greek: PG 36, p. 109c. As Hofner, *Life and Teaching*, p. 92, n. 4, points out, Nazianzen's metaphors reflect Ps. 67.3 (LXX) and Sir. 43.4.

indicates human flesh as opposed to soul and as created, not merely as fallen:[145] for Nazianzen, the prelapsarian condition of humanity involved 'a "creative struggle"' between flesh and soul. The natural obduracy of the flesh provided the soul with opportunity for self-mastery and with the necessary traction for the soul's theotic marathon. The Fall turned fleshly passions from starting blocks into stumbling blocks, which hindered the soul's progress.[146] In Christ's earthly life, Nazianzen finds fleshly wants and weaknesses restored to their original purpose. Gethsemane witnesses Jesus' human will quite naturally struggling with God's will, yet submitting at last.[147] His submission shows that his passions are sinless: there is infirmity absent iniquity.[148]

In sum, Nazianzen recognizes a process of self-healing or self-sanctification by the divine Logos of his assumed human nature and its experiences. This process of θέωσις aims at overcoming created frailty and finitude along with the Fall's exacerbation of both. What is missing in Christ's humanity, at least after the moment of his conception, is any lingering sinfulness. Nazianzen grants the imputation of sin to Christ, even after the Ascension, but not any instantiation of sinfulness within him.

3.4 Imagining incarnation: Gregory Nyssen

We turn now to Nazianzen's Cappadocian comrade, Gregory Nyssen (ca. 335–394/5).[149] The younger Gregory depicts the Incarnation with several pointed images and phrases. Christ's assumption of human nature is like a shepherd

---

[145] In discussing human psychosomatic constitution, *Ep.* 101.8 equates flesh with 'the meaner element' and clay, as well as equating mind with 'the higher' element and the image of God (*On God and Christ*, 160). For Nazianzen the divine image lies in the soul, not the body (*Ors.* 22.13; 38.11). On Nazianzen's sometimes vague and inconsistent theological anthropology, cf. Norris, *Doctrine*, pp. 70–8, 143–8.

[146] Winslow, *Dynamics*, pp. 55, 68; R. R. Ruether, *Gregory of Nazianzus: Rhetor and Philosopher* (Oxford: Clarendon, 1969), pp. 134–5; cf. Daley, *Gregory of Nazianzus*, p. 227, n. 383 on *Or.* 38.11.

[147] *Or.* 30.12.

[148] The interpretation given above blends elements of Winslow, *Dynamics*, pp. 55, 68, and Norris, Wickham and Williams, *Faith Gives Fullness*, p. 171. Another possible interpretation of *Or.* 30.12 is that Nazianzen treats Christ's 'Let this cup pass' in Gethsemane as parallel to 'Why have you forsaken me?' at Calvary, that is, as a statement which does not reflect his actual human disposition. On this reading, Christ's human will can no more resist the Father's will than can Christ's divine will, but Christ prays as if he were an ordinary man with a contentious will, thereby identifying himself with our situation, before revealing by his 'Not my will, but yours be done' that he has been merely role playing. Cf. the translation in *On God and Christ*, pp. 102–3, with that in E. R. Hardy and C. C. Richardson (eds), *Christology of the Later Fathers* (London: SCM, 1954), p. 185.

[149] For biographical and bibliographical details, see Gregory of Nyssa, *The Letters: Introduction, Translation and Commentary* (trans. A. M. Silvas; Leiden: Brill, 2007), pp. 1–57; A. Meredith, *The Cappadocians* (Crestwood, NY: St Vladimir's Seminary Press, 1995), pp. 52–97.

who shoulders a straying sheep;[150] like the sun descending to occupy a shadowy cave, 'taking up unto himself our filth';[151] like God's presence enflaming but not consuming Horeb's bramble-bush, whose thorns mark its fallen condition; like Moses' hand, which became leprous, and his rod, which became a serpent, the signifier of sin.[152] The Pauline pronouncement that Christ 'became sin' means that he 'unite[d] with himself the sinful human soul'[153] and was 'invested with our sinful nature'.[154] Such language seems unequivocal: the humanity assumed by Christ was sinful.[155]

3.4.1 Srawley's thesis

Was this humanity transformed into a sinless and unfallen state at the moment of the virginal conception? In an important article,[156] J. H. Srawley draws this conclusion after surveying some of the above texts and noting that they may refer to the humanity assumed by Christ *prior to* his assumption of it. In addition, Srawley reviews positive statements from Nyssen regarding the utter sinlessness of Christ's humanity, a sinlessness extending past the mere non-commission of

---

[150] *C. Eunom.* 2.13; 12.1; *Antirrh. adv. Apol.* 16. Unless otherwise noted, all citations of *C. Eunom.* are from *NPNF*² 5 and all citations of *Antirrh. adv. Apol.* are from PG 45.

[151] *Antirrh. adv. Apol.* 26; ET mine. J. Zachhuber, *Human Nature in Gregory of Nyssa: Philosophical Background and Theological Significance* (Leiden: Brill, 2000), pp. 192–3, notes that Nyssen's mentor Origen employed a Christological adaptation of Plato's Allegory of the Cave (*Republic*, 518a). Nyssen follows suit. Cf. F. M. Young, *From Nicaea to Chalcedon: A Guide to the Literature and its Background* (Philadelphia: Fortress, 1983), p. 117.

[152] *Vit. Moys.* 2.26-34. Unless otherwise noted, all citations of *Vit. Moys.* are from Gregory of Nyssa, *The Life of Moses* (trans. A. J. Malherbe and E. Ferguson; New York: Paulist, 1978). On p. 170, n. 118, the translators document Nyssen's use of thorns as types of sins, temptations, demons, and Christ's humanity. If the former three types relate to the Fall, then the latter one likely does as well. Cf. Gen. 3.17–18 for the link between thorns and the Fall.

[153] *Antirrh. adv. Apol.* 23 (ET mine).

[154] *Vit. Moys.* 2.32; ET *Life of Moses*, p. 62.

[155] Torrance, *Trinitarian Faith*, pp. 162, 164; Kelly, *Early Christian Doctrines*, p. 351; Nantomah, 'Jesus the God-Man', pp. 333–4; Dorries, *Incarnational Christology*, p. 184; Johnson, *Humanity*, pp. 130–2; A. Meredith, *Gregory of Nyssa* (London: Routledge, 1999), p. 48. By contrast, L. F. Mateo-Seco, *Estudios Sobre La Cristologia de San Gregorio de Nisa* (Pamplona: Ediciones Universidad de Navarra, 1978), pp. 429–33, holds that Christ assumed immaculate human nature from an immaculate mother, but does not address the above passages. Nyssen does speak of Mary as 'immaculate' (ἀμιάντου) in *Antirrh. adv. Apol.* 6 (PG 45, p. 1136c). This may simply mean that Mary's virginity was unspoilt or that she did not experience the sinful libido that attends fallen human copulation (*Or. cat.* 16); cf. *Estudios*, pp. 124–5; Mateo-Seco, Ὁ εὔκαιρος θάνατος. Consideraciones en torno a la muerte en las *Homilias al Eclesiastes* de Gregorio de Nisa', in Gregory of Nyssa, *Homilies on Ecclesiastes: an English Version with Supporting Studies: Proceedings of the Seventh International Colloquium on Gregory of Nyssa (St. Andrews, 5-10 September 1990)* (ed. S. G. Hall; Berlin: Walter de Gruyter, 1993), pp. 277–97 (291). In *Hom. Eccl.* 7, Nyssen insists that Christ alone never sinned; no additional exception is made for Mary. In her case, Mateo-Seco, *Estudios*, pp. 429–33, conflates commitment to sinlessness with its attainment.

[156] J. H. Srawley, 'St Gregory of Nyssa on the Sinlessness of Christ', *JTS* 7.27 (1906), pp. 434–41.

actual sin,[157] for Nyssen quotes Heb. 4.15 and 1 Pet. 2.22/Isa. 53.9 in support of the claim that Christ had no sinful desires.[158] Srawley finds in Nyssen's *Epistle to Eustathia* a clear statement that Christ's humanity was transformed into a sinless state immediately upon his conception, while the complete deification of his humanity awaits his post-Easter state, as Nyssen elsewhere indicates.[159]

Srawley's analysis is incisive, but his claim that Christ's 'human nature, when once assumed, did not continue in its fallen state'[160] does not account for Nyssen's imagery in *De Vita Moysis*. There the burning bush does not shed its postlapsarian thorns upon being indwelt by God. There too the cleansing of Moses' hand from leprosy and the reversion of his serpent into a rod do not typify Christ's conception but his Resurrection and Ascension. It would seem that in some sense he bears fallenness and remains 'sinful' throughout his earthly career.

3.4.2 A response to Srawley

The interpretative key lies in Nyssen's complex anthropology.[161] For him, essential human nature is that which reflects in us God's attributes. Inasmuch as God is incorporeal, the human body is not essential to human nature; nevertheless, the body is original to the human creation and will endure into eternity in its resurrected form. Beyond these original components of God-reflective soul

---

[157] 'St Gregory', p. 436 (citing *Antirrh. adv. Apol.* 54), 437 (citing *Or. cat.*, 16).

[158] 'St Gregory', pp. 436–7, quoting *C. Eunom.*, 6.3. D. F. Stramara Jr., 'The Sinlessness and Moral Integrity of Jesus according to Gregory of Nyssa', *Patristic and Byzantine Review* 24.1–3 (2006), pp. 67–83 (74–5), takes issue with Srawley but may give English terms like 'tendency' and 'propensity' a weaker sense than Srawley intends.

[159] 'St Gregory', pp. 437–8, 440, quoting *Ep. Eust.* on Christ's conception; 440, citing *C. Eunom.*, 6; *Ep. Theoph.*; and *Antirrh. adv. Apol.* 53 on Christ's glorified state.

[160] 'St Gregory', p. 435. 'Nor have I been able to find a single passage in Gregory's writings which clearly states that he regarded the humanity assumed by Christ as subject, subsequent to His birth, to the consequences of the Fall' (435–6). Yet Srawley grants that Nyssen ascribes 'human weakness' to Christ in the form of dread of death in Gethsemane (436). Consonant with the modern unfallenness view, Srawley equates fallenness with sinfulness.

[161] This paragraph relies on H. Boersma, *Embodiment and Virtue in Gregory of Nyssa: An Anagogical Approach* (Oxford: Oxford University Press, 2013), ch. 3; P. C. Bouteneff, 'Essential or Existential: The Problem of the Body in the Anthropology of St Gregory of Nyssa', in Gregory of Nyssa, *Homilies on the Beatitudes: An English Version with Commentary and Supporting Studies. Proceedings of the Eighth International Colloquium on Gregory of Nyssa (Paderborn, 14–18 September 1998)* (ed. H. R. Drobner and A. Viciano; Leiden: Brill, 2000), pp. 409–19; Hardy and Richardson, *Christology*, pp. 239–40; J. Pelikan, *Christianity and Classical Culture: The Metamorphosis of Natural Theology in the Christian Encounter with Hellenism* (New Haven, CT: Yale University Press, 1993), pp. 88, 191, 277–8, 290–5; G. B. Ladner, 'The Philosophical Anthropology of St. Gregory of Nyssa', *Dumbarton Oaks Papers* 12 (1958), pp. 59–94. Cited 7 June 2013. Online: http://www.jstor.org/stable/1291117; J. Daniélou, *Platonisme et Théologie mystique: doctrine spirituelle de Saint Grégoire de Nysse* (Paris: Aubier, 2nd edn, 1944), pp. 46–64, 72.

and attendant body, Nyssen locates sexuality, which he believes God added to primal human nature due to his foreknowledge of the Fall. Following the Fall, Adam, Eve, and all their descendants were clothed in 'garments of skin', which typify the body's envelopment by the flesh with its πάθη[162] and mortality. Evil, too, became intermingled with human nature.[163] Yet Nyssen is careful to stress that the components of human nature are not intrinsically evil. Against the heretics, he insists that the sinless Christ assumed a human mind, for 'the mind … is not sin'.[164] Likewise, Christ took a passible human body. Nyssen distinguishes between two senses of the term πάθος. In its loose sense, the term refers simply to any natural, morally neutral biological ἔργον[165] such as birth, growth, hunger, weariness, suffering, death, and physical corruption. There is nothing unbecoming about the impassible God passing through such experiences in his incarnate state, en route to overcoming them in his resurrection. The strict sense of πάθος applies solely to a sinful passion such as greed or lust.[166] Nyssen denies that Christ experienced any πάθη of this latter variety.[167] Although tempted in all points as we are, he was without sin

---

[162] Richardson comments, 'No English word can adequately render *pathos*, which has several nuances. Gregory regards its primary sense as moral' (Hardy and Richardson, *Christology*, p. 292, n. 22). Unfortunately, Richardson restricts both the term's nuances and its moral sense by translating it everywhere in *Or. cat.* as 'weakness'. In Grégoire de Nysse, *Discours Catéchétique* (trans. R. Winling; SC 453; Paris: Cerf, 2000), p. 75, Winling notes the difficulty of translating the term into French and leaves it untranslated. In *Estudios*, p. 112, n. 73, Mateo-Seco helpfully observes,

> Nyssen uses this term in a double sense: passion in the philosophical sense corresponding to the action-passion binomial and as passion corresponding to pleasure. [J. H.] Srawley comments [in *The Catechetical Oration of Gregory of Nyssa* (Cambridge, Cambridge University Press, 1956)]: 'As applied to birth the πάθος to which he refers [in *Or. cat.* 13] is properly the πάθος of the parent (ἡδονή) and denotes *passion* [.] As applied to death it implies imperfection, frailty, weakness, exhibited in the submission to φθορά.' (*o.c.*, p. 60, nt. 5) [ET mine]

Stramara, 'Sinlessness', p. 69, sees the term as encompassing 'the experiences which one has, whether resulting from external or internal causes'. Cf. Daniélou, *Platonisme*, pp. 46, 71–2; J. W. Smith, *Passion and Paradise: Human and Divine Emotion in the Thought of Gregory of Nyssa* (New York: Crossroad, 2004), chs 3, 7; K. Corrigan, *Evagrius and Gregory: Mind, Soul and Body in the 4th Century* (Farnham, UK: Ashgate, 2009), pp. 136–45.

[163] *Hom. op.* 16–20; *Or. cat.* 8; *Vit. Moys.* 2.22. On the Origenist origin of Nyssen's interpretation of the 'garments' of skin, see L. R. Hennessey, 'Gregory of Nyssa's Doctrine of the Resurrected Body', StPatr 22, pp. 28–34. Unless otherwise noted, all citations of *Hom. op.* are from NPNF² 5 and all citations of *Or. cat.* are from Hardy and Richardson, *Christology*.

[164] *Antirrh. adv. Apol.* 11. Cf. 'The soul is not sin' (*C. Eunom.*, 2.13). ET mine.

[165] *Or. cat.* 16 (SC 453, p. 222).

[166] *Hom. Eccles.* 7. According to Daniélou, *Platonisme*, p. 46, in the strict sense, 'πάθη designates the collection of human sinful tendencies. They correspond very exactly with what our modern language calls the "deadly sins"' (ET mine). In *Or. cat.* 16, Nyssen uses ὁρμή and ἡδονή as synonyms for sinful πάθος (SC 453, p. 224). On ὁρμή as 'compulsion', see Stramara, 'Sinlessness', pp. 74–5.

[167] *C. Eunom.*, 6.3 (PG 45, pp. 721–4); *Ep. Eust.* (NPNF² 5, pp. 1026–8); *Or. cat.*, 16 (SC 453, pp. 222, 224); cf. 7, 9, 13, 15, 28. Daniélou, *Platonisme*, p. 71, claims that it was the particular case of the Incarnation which required Nyssen to distinguish the two senses of πάθη.

(Heb. 4.15), whether original[168] or actual; the Evil One could find nothing in him (Jn 14.30).[169] Srawley underscores Nyssen's distinction between the loose and strict senses of πάθος[170] but leaves unmentioned the fact that for Gregory, even πάθη, in the loose sense, are due to the Fall. Thus birth, suffering, and such are fallen (and sexuality itself proleptically is fallen), hence sin-consequent although not properly sin.

This distinction illuminates Nyssen's otherwise seemingly contradictory comments in *De Vita Moysis* on the word picture of Christ as a serpent. On the one hand, Gregory links Exod. 4.2-4 with 2 Cor. 5.21: 'By becoming sin he became also a serpent, which is nothing other than sin.'[171] On the other hand, Nyssen writes of the bronze serpent (Num. 21.5-9) as a type of Christ, 'This figure is a likeness [ὁμοίωμα] of a serpent and not a serpent itself, as the great Paul himself says, *in the likeness* [ὁμοίωμα] *of sinful flesh*. Sin is the real serpent, and whoever deserts to sin takes on the nature of the serpent.'[172] In the former case, the context is Christ's 'being invested with our sinful nature';[173] in the latter, the serpentine image of Christ saves believers from venomous serpents, which embody evil desires (πονηρᾶς ἐπιθυμίας).[174] Thus for Nyssen, Christ bears a 'sinful' nature but not sinning πάθη. His humanity is termed 'sinful' because it suffers sin's consequences of biological neediness and mortality, not because it experiences sin itself in the form of depraved desire.

Gregory assures his readers that Christ is not polluted by assuming our filth,[175] nor is Heaven's Physician made ill by treating our disease.[176] His conception is unstained by libidinous πάθος, the conduit of original sin, even though he undergoes the πάθος of birth. His life is undefiled by wrongful πάθη

---

[168] In *Antirrh. adv. Apol.* 11 and *C. Eunom.* 2.13, quoted above, Nyssen's assertion that the mind/soul is not sin follows his quotation of Heb. 4.15 and expounds that verse's χωρὶς ἁμαρτίας, which Nyssen evidently understands to refer to ontological, not merely functional, sinlessness. Note that *Antirrh. adv. Apol.* opposes Apollinaris, who taught the ontological depravity of the human mind. For Nyssen's view of original sin, cf. Tennant, *Sources*, pp. 321–2; Williams, *Ideas*, pp. 278–9; Kelly, *Early Christian Doctrines*, pp. 348–52; Srawley, 'St Gregory', p. 436; E. V. McClear, 'The Fall of Man and Original Sin in the Theology of Gregory of Nyssa', *TS* 9 (1948), pp. 175–212; Mateo-Seco, *Estudios*, pp. 124–5, ch. 3.

[169] *Hom. Eccl.* 7.

[170] Srawley, 'St Gregory', pp. 436–7.

[171] *Vit. Moys.* 2.33; ET *Life of Moses*, p. 62.

[172] *Vit. Moys.* 2.275; ET *Life of Moses*, p. 124; Greek: PG 44, pp. 413d, 416a. Note that Nyssen interprets ὁμοίωμα to mean similiarity, not identity, between the likeness and the likened.

[173] *Vit. Moys.* 2.33; ET *Life of Moses*, p. 62.

[174] *Vit. Moys.* 2.275 (Greek: PG 44, p. 413d); cf. 2.276. On Nyssen's use of animals to typify πάθη, cf. Daniélou, *Platonisme*, pp. 73–9.

[175] *Antirrh. adv. Apol.* 26; cf. *C. Eunom.* 6.2.

[176] *C. Eunom.* 6.3; 10.4; *Or. cat.* 16.

even as he endures the πάθος of temptation. His suffering of the πάθος of death ends not in decomposition but in resurrection and immortality.[177] In all these ways, Nyssen sees divine incorruption and impassibility echoed provisionally in Christ's earthly existence. In the Resurrection and Ascension, the process of deification culminates in his own human nature and becomes available for all other humans to begin to experience. Rather than Christ's becoming contaminated in sharing human nature, his deification of it in himself is the prototype for what he makes available to believers – although the process may take much longer for them than for him.[178]

Nyssen makes explicit that Christ took human nature in its fallen and sinful condition. The very assumption of this nature so purified it as to exclude sinful passions from Christ's human experience. Yet throughout 'the days of his flesh', Christ's humanity was 'sinful' (ἁμαρτικήν) in an imprecise sense due to his enduring the Fall's effects. A related paradoxical paradigm appears in the thought of the final Greek father covered by this study, Cyril of Alexandria.

3.5 'Seal of the Fathers': Cyril of Alexandria

With good reason, future generations awarded Cyril (378–444), patriarch of Alexandria and scourge of Nestorianism,[179] the title, 'Seal of the Fathers'.[180] He drew his Christology from Athanasius, Gregory Nazianzen, and perhaps Irenaeus,[181] and supported it by appeal to various patristic authorities, including Ambrose and Gregory Nyssen.[182] His doctrine found ecumenical vindication

---

[177] *Or. cat.* 13, 15-16, 23, 27-28 (SC 453). Cf. Mateo-Seco, *Estudios*, pp. 112, n. 73, 114, 122–5.

[178] For example, *C. Eunom.* 5.5; *Or. cat.* 24-26, 35. Cf. Srawley, 'St Gregory', pp. 440–1; Meredith, *Gregory of Nyssa*, p. 48; B. Daley, '"Heavenly Man" and "Eternal Christ": Apollinarius and Gregory of Nyssa on the Personal Identity of the Savior', *JECS* 10.4 (2002), pp. 469–88. Like Athanasius, Nyssen is misrepresented by Beeley, *Unity of Christ*, pp. 199–221.

[179] For biographical details, see Cyril of Alexandria, *Select Letters*, pp. xi–xliii; *idem, On the Unity of Christ*, pp. 9–32; N. Russell, *Cyril of Alexandria* (London: Routledge, 2000), pp. 1–58.

[180] L. Koen, *The Saving Passion: Incarnational and Soteriological Thought in Cyril of Alexandria's Commentary on the Gospel according to St. John* (Stockholm: Almqvist & Wiksell, 1991), p. 19.

[181] R. L. Wilken, *Judaism and the Early Christian Mind: A Study of Cyril of Alexandria's Exegesis and Theology* (New Haven, CT: Yale University Press, 1971), pp. 129–30, n. 24; 130–1; S. A. McKinion, *Words, Imagery, and the Mystery of Christ: A Reconstruction of Cyril of Alexandria's Christology* (Leiden: Brill, 2000), pp. 17–18; Russell, *Cyril of Alexandria*, pp. 5; 18; Koen, *Saving Passion*, pp. 18, 25; Beeley, *Gregory of Nazianzus*, p. 322; but cf. D. A. Keating, *The Appropriation of Divine Life in Cyril of Alexandria* (Oxford: Oxford University Press, repr. 2005), p. 199, n. 24, who finds no indication that Cyril read Irenaeus.

[182] Russell, *Cyril of Alexandria*, p. 219, n. 89; Cyril pioneered the practice of appealing to earlier fathers to establish doctrine (Russell, *Cyril of Alexandria*, p. 50; Cyril, *On the Unity of Christ*, p. 11).

at the Council of Ephesus (431), over which he presided, and subsequently at the Council of Chalcedon (451).[183]

3.5.1 Christ's 'fallen body'

According to Cyril, unfallen Adam's flesh had physical desires (e.g. for food) but he was their absolute master. It had the natural potential to disintegrate, but the presence of the Holy Spirit preserved it incorruptible. Adam's transgression inflicted upon himself and his descendants the contagion of death, corruption, and the 'law of sin' – disorderly desires which lure towards wrongdoing.[184]

This is the condition of the human nature which Christ assumed. Cyril writes of 'having the fallen body [τοῦ προσπεσόντος σώματος] united in an ineffable manner with the Word that endows all things with life'.[185] Again, he asserts that 'it was vital for the Word of God … to make human flesh, subject to decay [τῇ φθορᾷ] and infected with sensuality [τὸ φιλήδονον] as it was, his own'.[186] Nor was this 'fallen body', this infected flesh, soulless, but possessed a human soul subject to distress, hence conditioned by the Fall. Christ must have taken a complete, postlapsarian psychosomatic unit, Cyril insists, 'for what is not assumed, neither is saved [ὅ γὰρ μὴ προσείληπται, οὐδὲ σέσωσται]'.[187]

3.5.2 Christ's life-giving flesh

From conception, the union of the life-giving, sinless Logos with fallen human nature wrought the latter's deification: his flesh became life-giving and the 'law

---

[183] Cyril, *Select Letters*, p. xxxix; Russell, *Cyril of Alexandria*, p. 50.

[184] *First Letter to Succensus* 9 (*Select Letters*, pp. 78–9 [Greek on all even-numbered pages and ET on all odd-numbered pages hereafter cited from this source]); *On the Unity of Christ*, p. 64; *In Romanos*, Rom. 5.18-19, quoted in Burghardt, *Image of God*, p. 152; *Doctrinal Questions and Answers* 6 (*Select Letters*, pp. 200–5). In the latter two passages, Cyril explicitly denies that Adam's descendants sinned along with him; rather, all inherit the penalty of death which fell upon Adam. For further on Cyril's doctrine of original sin, cf. Burghardt, *Image of God*, pp. 153–4, esp. n. 69; Koen, *Saving Passion*, p. 43; Bray, 'Original Sin', p. 46; F. Young, 'Theotokos: Mary and the Pattern of Fall and Redemption in the Theology of Cyril of Alexandria', and D. A. Keating, 'Divinization in Cyril: The Appropriation of Divine Life', both in *Theology of St. Cyril*, pp. 55–74 and pp. 149–87 (152–7), respectively.

[185] *In Jo. Ev.*, Jn 1.14; ET Russell, *Cyril of Alexandria*, p. 105; Greek: PG 73, p. 160c. Cf. Young, 'Theotokos', p. 66. PGL, p. 1181, gives a truncated account of προσπίπτω as 'fall before' in supplication' and does not list Cyril's use of this term. More helpful is the same entry in *A Greek-English Lexicon* (ed. H. G. Liddell and R. Scott; Oxford: Clarendon, 9th edn, repr. 1976), p. 1523, which includes the definition 'prostrate oneself' (italics original). Liddell and Scott's definition shows that the verb can be reflexive.

[186] *First Letter to Succensus* 9 (*Select Letters*, pp. 78–9).

[187] *In Jo. Ev.*, Jn 1.14; ET mine; Greek: PG 74, p. 89cd. Cf. *Inc. unigen.* (PG 75, p. 1388bc); *Quod unus sit Christus* (PG 75, p. 1332); McKinion, *Words*, pp. 149–79; L. J. Welch, *Christology and Eucharist in the Early Thought of Cyril of Alexandria* (San Francisco: Catholic Scholars Press, 1994), ch. 2.

of sin' within it was nullified.[188] Cyril follows his predecessors in describing deification as a dynamic, lifelong process:[189] from childhood onward, Christ advanced in human wisdom, stature, and obedience although as deity he was perfect;[190] in his baptism, he humanly received sanctification and divinely sanctified the waters;[191] in his ministry, he hungered as a man but fed multitudes as God;[192] in the Olivet Discourse, he confessed earthly ignorance of the Parousia yet retained heavenly omniscience;[193] in Gethsemane, he allowed his flesh to express its natural fear, then converted it into submission to his Father's will before fear ripened into cowardice;[194] in his crucifixion, he suffered in the flesh even as he remained impassible in Godhead;[195] in the Resurrection, his mortal remains were raised while his immortal power did the raising.[196] Against Nestorius' overemphasis on such distinctions, though, Cyril stresses the interpenetration of human and divine attributes in the one person of Christ. Thus miraculous power came from Jesus' divinity but was displayed through his human touch;[197] conversely, to be born or suffer is proper to human, not divine, nature, yet such creaturely experiences were truly attributable to the impassible Logos.[198]

Within that theanthropic union, there was no sin in Christ's flesh which could be attributed to his divine Person. We all inherit the guilt and death

---

[188] *Adv. Nestorium* 4.5 (ET Cyril of Alexandria, *Five Tomes Against Nestorius* [trans. P. E. Pusey; LFC 47; Oxford: James Parker & Co., 1881], pp. 9–12. Cited 2 September 2012. Online: http://www. elpenor. org/cyril-alexandria/against-nestorius.asp). Unless otherwise noted, all citations of *Adv. Nestorium* are from this source. Cf. *First Letter to Succensus* 9 (*Select Letters*, pp. 78–9); *Quod unus sit Christus* (PG 75, p. 1272).

[189] Keating, 'Divinization', p. 184.

[190] *In Jo. Ev.*, Jn 1.15; *Adv. Nestorium* 3.4; *Inc. unigen.* 13, 34. Unless otherwise noted, all citations of *In Jo. Ev.* are from Russell, *Cyril of Alexandria*, and all citations of *Inc. unigen.* are from Cyril of Alexandria, *Scholia on the Incarnation of the Only-Begotten* (trans. P. E. Pusey; LFC 47). Cited 1 September 2012. Online: http://www.elpenor.org/cyril-alexandria/incarnation-only-begotten.asp.

[191] *Adv. Nestorium* 4.2; *Inc. unigen.* 34; *On the Unity of Christ*, 100. Cf. Wilken, *Judaism*, pp. 127–41; Keating, 'Divinization', pp. 152–7.

[192] *Adv. Nestorium* 5.3.

[193] *Tiberius* 4 (*Select Letters* pp. 150–3; note well 153, n. 29).

[194] *In Jo. Ev.*, Jn 6.38, 39; 12.27; *Adv. Nestorium* 5.3; *On the Unity of Christ*, pp. 102–4.

[195] *Adv. Nestorium* 1.proem; *Expl. XII cap.* on Anathema 12; *Inc. unigen.* 34. Unless otherwise noted, all citations of *Expl. XII cap.* are from Russell, *Cyril of Alexandria*.

[196] *Inc. unigen.* 34.

[197] *In Jo. Ev.*, Jn 6.53.

[198] *On the Unity of Christ*, pp. 107–10. On Cyril's view of the theanthropic union, cf. R. Kearsley, 'The Impact of Greek Concepts of God on the Christology of Cyril of Alexandria', *Tyndale Bulletin* 43.2 (1992), pp. 307–29; J. M. Hallman, 'The Seed of Fire: Divine Suffering in the Christology of Cyril of Alexandria and Nestorius of Constantinople', *JECS* 5 (1997), pp. 369–91; J. J. O'Keefe, 'Impassible Suffering? Divine Passion and Fifth-Century Christology', *TS* 58 (1997), pp. 39–60; D. Fairbairn, *Grace and Christology in the Early Church* (Oxford: Oxford University Press, 2003), chs 3–4. For an overview of Nestorius and the Nestorian controversy, see Young, *From Nicaea*, pp. 213–40.

penalty for Adam's original act of sin, but Christ undid that guilt in himself through his career of flawless obedience. Never was he guilty of Adam's transgression: neither Satan nor the Jews could find sin (including Adamic sin) in him (Jn 8.46; 14.30; 1 Pet. 2.22).[199] Cyril does speak of sensual desires as 'the law of sin,' but he describes Christ as 'curb[ing] the innate, the sensual impulses' within his own flesh so that it 'ceased to be infected with sensuality.'[200] Cyril specifically denies that Christ's fleshly fear, ignorance, hunger, and other infirmities were sinful.[201] One of the Alexandrian's dozen anathemas is directed against Nestorius' claim that Christ offered his sacrifice for himself as well as for others; to Cyril, such a claim blasphemously insinuates that Christ was sinful.[202]

This principle of the separation of Christ from sin echoes in Cyril's exegesis. His relation of Rom. 8.3 and 2 Cor. 5.21 to the prophecy that the Isaianic Servant would be 'numbered among the transgressors' (Isa. 53.12)[203] indicates that 'the likeness of the flesh of sin' and 'became sin' describe the imputation of sin to Christ. Cyril stresses that Christ came in the likeness of sinful flesh, not in sinful flesh itself. The latter would mean that Christ was a sinner, a notion which Cyril repudiates with a Paul-like μὴ γένοιτο![204] The former means that Christ came in the appearance of a sinner due to his becoming a human being, all the rest of whom were sinners. Moses' rod which became a serpent, his hand which turned leprous, and the bronze serpent all typify this same truth.[205] Even Christ's so-called cry of dereliction was really an appeal to

---

[199] *Tiberius* 13; *Adv. Nestorium* 1.1; 3.5.

[200] *First Letter to Succensus* 9 (*Select Letters*, p. 79); cf. *Tiberius* 12 (*Select Letters*, pp. 170–1). As Kearsley, 'Greek Concepts', pp. 320–1, points out, Cyril links passibility with the possibility of sin and so stresses the impassibility of the divine Logos as the ground of the sinlessness of the flesh hypostatically united to it.

[201] *In Jo. Ev.*, Jn 12.27; *Tiberius* 4 (*Select Letters*, 150–3); *Tiberius* 9 rules that Christ endured hunger, weariness, 'sleep, anxiety, pain and other innocent human experiences' (ἀνθρωπίνων καὶ ἀδιαβλήτων παθῶν) (*Select Letters*, pp. 78–9).

[202] *Third Letter to Nestorius* 9 (*Select Letters*, pp. 26–7); *Expl. XII cap.* on Anathema 10; *Adv. Nestorium* 3.5. Cf. Wilken, *Judaism*, pp. 210, 217–18. Nestorius later explained himself in *The Bazaar of Heracleides* (ed. and trans. G. R. Driver and L. Hodgson; repr. New York: AMS Press, 1978), pp. 249–51: Christ sacrificed for himself to increase his merit, not to expiate any demerit. Bathrellos, 'Sinlessness', pp. 115–16, has renewed the charge that Nestorius' Christ was sinful, citing the assertion in *Bazaar*, p. 63, that Christ 'took a nature which had sinned' with its 'anger and concupiscence and thoughts' (cf. 211). The first quotation merely echoes the sentiments of fathers from Irenaeus through Cyril himself, as this chapter has documented. The second quotation recalls Plato's tripartite soul with its irascible, concupiscible, and rational elements. Chapter 4.1.1 of this study shows that Tertullian, like Nestorius, attributes sinless anger, concupiscence, and reasoning to Christ. Nestorius insists on Christ's human sinlessness in nature and act (pp. 32–3, 62–8, 72–5, 172–3, 212–13, 247, 251).

[203] *Inc. unigen.* 16; *Quod unus sit Christus.* ET *On the Unity of Christ*, pp. 56, 61.

[204] *In Romanos* 8:3 (PG 74, p. 820a); *Quod unus sit Christus* (PG 75, p. 1305c).

[205] *Inc. unigen.* 15, 16; *Adv. Nestorium* 4. proem.

God to end his long abandonment of human nature, for now in the Second Adam is found 'the nature of man made clean, its faults corrected, made holy and pure'. On this basis, then, he entreats his Father to grant grace to all whose nature still languishes under sin.[206] Cyril thus rehearses themes found in the earlier Greek fathers.

Conclusion

This chapter has examined the thought of five Greek fathers (or more, if indeed some of Athanasius' works are pseudonymous) to whom modern proponents of both the fallenness and unfallenness views appeal. At the terminological level, the results are complex. Our study has shown that the fallenness camp has patristic precedent for its attribution of the terms 'fallen' (Irenaeus, Cyril)[207] and 'sinful' (Nyssen) to Christ's humanity. Yet unfallenness advocates may find consolation in Irenaeus' denial that Christ's humanity 'fell' into sin; in Irenaeus' and *Contra Apollinarium*'s use of prelapsarian imagery for Christ's human origins and innocence; and in the fathers' general insistence on his sinlessness. Their ability both to apply and to deny the same language to Christ demands that we move to the conceptual level in order to understand their perspective.

The fathers view the Logos as taking a human nature which otherwise exists in a condition of captivity to sin and mortality. In the virginal conception, he heals and hallows it so that it is freed from domination by Satan and death, from sinful passions, and, for those fathers who believe in it, from original guilt. Nevertheless, throughout his earthly life Christ bears the consequences of sin by being reckoned guilty, suffering various infirmities, and dying, then brings human nature in himself into the impassibility, immortality, and incorruptibility of the resurrection.

The status of the sinless πάθη which exist in Christ is variously assessed by the fathers. For Irenaeus, Athanasius, and Cyril, fleshly desires were part of

---

[206] *Quod unus sit Christus*. ET *On the Unity of Christ*, pp. 105–6 (quotation from latter page). Cf. *Adv. Nestorium* 5.4; W. J. Jennings, 'Undoing Our Abandonment: Reading Scripture through the Sinlessness of Jesus. A Meditation on Cyril of Alexandria's *On the Unity of Christ*', *Ex Auditu* 14 (1998), pp. 85–96.

[207] Both use forms of πίπτω. Williams, *Ideas*, pp. 252–3, 275–6, notes that the noun πτῶμα later became the standard Greek designation for the Fall.

humanity's original state but were completely submissive to reason (and, for Cyril, to the Holy Spirit). Nazianzen agrees that they were original to human nature but portrays them as unruly even in Eden. Nyssen, though, denies that they existed before the Fall. For him, even birth is a fallen function. All the fathers, though, see Christ as overcoming temptations related to these fleshly desires, thereby conforming them to the will of God.

Except for their diversity of views regarding sinless πάθη, the Greek fathers concur on the relationship of the Fall to Christ's humanity. Do the Latin fathers? To that question we now turn.

4

The Latin Fathers on the Fallenness or Unfallenness of Christ's Humanity

The preceding chapter explored the Greek fathers' views relative to the fallenness debate. In the present chapter, we shift attention to the Latin fathers to survey their opinions on the same subject. In particular, we look to the five fathers most-often referenced in the modern debate: Tertullian, Hilary of Poitiers, Ambrose, Augustine, and Leo the Great.

4.1 Pioneer in the West: Tertullian

The West's indigenous theology began in Carthage with Tertullian (fl. ca. 195–212), who was himself heavily influenced by Irenaeus. A convert from paganism to Christianity, Tertullian became a pugnacious polemicist for his new faith, deploying a full arsenal of rhetorical techniques against a variety of opponents, whether pagans, Jews, heretics, or fellow Catholics. Although he wrote in both Greek and Latin, only his works in the latter language have survived. In them he pioneered the technical theological terminology used thereafter in the Western church, even when in later years he was adjudged as heretical due to his writings' schismatic tendencies.[1]

---

[1] For biographical information, cf. E. Ferguson, 'Tertullian', in *Early Christian Thinkers: The Lives and Legacies of Twelve Key Figures* (ed. P. Foster; Downers Grove, IL: InterVarsity, 2010), pp. 85–99; G. D. Dunn, *Tertullian* (London: Routledge, 2004), ch. 1; G. L. Bray, *Holiness and the Will of God: Perspectives on the Theology of Tertullian* (Atlanta: John Knox, 1979), ch. 2; T. D. Barnes, *Tertullian: A Historical and Literary Study* (Oxford: Clarendon Press, 1971). I have used Dunn's and Bray's dating of Tertullian's life, following Barnes' revisionist account; Ferguson, 'Tertullian', p. 85, gives more traditional dates of ca. 160–ca. 240. On Tertullian's 'massive debt to Irenaeus', see E. Osborn, *Tertullian, First Theologian of the West* (Cambridge: Cambridge University Press, 1997, 2001), p. 7.

Over a third of Tertullian's extant oeuvre assails Marcionism,[2] and it is to two volumes of this group that fallenness and unfallenness debaters appeal: *Adversus Marcionem* and *De carne Christi*.[3] Both date to the last years of Tertullian's literary output,[4] thus embodying his mature Christology. According to the Carthaginian, Marcion taught that Christ had merely the appearance of a body, not true flesh. *De carne Christi* broadens the scope of Tertullian's assault to include Marcion's former disciple Apelles and the Valentinians. All these heretics agreed that the material world was inherently, irredeemably evil, the product of a bad creator. Only the human soul was worthy of salvation by a Christ who himself was kept as insulated as possible from materiality.[5] Clearly, theological anthropology played a dominant role in these heretics' Christologies, as also in Tertullian's replies. For this reason, we shall include coverage of his important work on the subject, *De anima* (206/7),[6] as supplying context for his view of Christ's humanity.

4.1.1 Tertullian's anthropology

Against the heretics, Tertullian insists that the Creator is the one true and good God, who made the first humans as good, psychosomatically unified beings. Their souls imaged God through the rational ordering of their emotions and physical urges. Despite possessing all the knowledge and power needed to remain obedient to God, they freely chose to heed Satan's seductions and thereby inflicted a double bondage on all their offspring from birth onwards: the external enticements of evil spirits and the internal affliction of a sinful 'second nature (*alia natura*)' with its irrational impulses towards evil. This sinful nature, however, has not superseded the original, divinely created good

---

[2] R. Cantalamessa, *La Cristologia di Tertulliano* ([Fribourg, Switzerland]: Edizioni Universitarie Friburgo Svizzera, 1962), p. 35.

[3] Unless otherwise noted, all citations of *Marc.* and *Carn. Chr.* and all quotations in both Latin (on even-numbered pages) and English (on odd-numbered pages) are taken from Tertullian, *Adversus Marcionem* (ed. and trans. E. Evans; 2 vols.; Oxford Early Christian Texts; London: Clarendon, 1972) and *Tertullian's Treatise on the Incarnation* (ed. and trans. E. Evans; London: SPCK, 1956), respectively.

[4] Dunn, *Tertullian*, p. 6, dates *Marc.* to 207/8 and *Carn. Chr.* to 208–12. Barnes, *Tertullian*, pp. 47–8, 55, concurs on *Marc.* but urges 206 for *Carn. Chr.* Cf. AMOECT 1, pp. xv, xviii.

[5] AMOECT 1, pp. xiii, xv; *Tertullian's Treatise*, pp. xii–xvii, xxiv–xxxii; A. Viciano, *Cristo Salvador y Liberador del Hombre: Estudio sobre la Soteriología de Tertuliano* (Pamplona: Ediciones Universidad de Navarra, 1986), pp. 240–7.

[6] Barnes, *Tertullian*, pp. 47, 55.

nature; it has only shrouded it. Thus all humanity is a mixture of *inherent* goodness and *adherent* evil.[7]

It is this sinful human nature which Christ assumed, but in the act of its assumption he purified it. Against the heretical claim that if Christ took our flesh, then his flesh must have been sinful, Tertullian rejoins, 'By clothing himself with our flesh he made it his own, and by making it his own he made it non-sinful.'[8] The implication is that Mary's flesh, from whence Christ derived his humanity,[9] was sinful. Tertullian repeats Irenaeus' typology whereby the Virgin Mary's vivifying faith in the angel's words remedies the Virgin Eve's fatal faith in the serpent's words.[10] He also, however, accuses Mary of unbelief in her Son during his earthly ministry.[11] The sinlessness of Christ's humanity, then, is due not to his mother but to God's own incarnating action. Again like Irenaeus, Tertullian connects the Virgin Birth with both Adam's prelapsarian formation from virgin soil and Christians' regeneration.[12] The former parallel indicates how Christ may be fully human apart from being procreated sexually, and it identifies him as the new, sinless Adam, the second founder of the human race; it does not, though, imply that Mary's flesh existed in an unfallen state, except in the analogous sense of being virginal. The latter parallel signifies a movement from a postlapsarian condition of sinful flesh (our own, in Christians' case; Mary's, in Christ's case) to a new, sin-free life.

---

[7] *An.* 16, 39–41 (quotation from Kelly, *Early Christian Doctrines*, p. 176, quoting *An.* 41; unless otherwise noted, all citations of *An.* are from ANF 3); *Marc.* 2.2, 5, 8-9, 16. Cf. Viciano, *Cristo Salvador*, pp. 92, 275, 281. Tertullian clearly teaches a doctrine of original sin (Tennant, *Sources*, pp. 328–36; Williams, *Ideas*, pp. 231–45), but does he teach original guilt? Bray thinks so (*Holiness*, pp. 81, 88), as does Evans (*Tertullian's Treatise*, p. 152); gainsaying them are Williams, *Ideas*, pp. 238–41 (but cf. Rondet, *Original Sin*, p. 52); Ferguson, 'Tertullian', p. 91; Kelly, *Early Christian Doctrines*, pp. 175–6; Lampe, 'Christian Theology', pp. 61, 157; Osborn, *Tertullian*, pp. 163–75. Steenberg, *Of God and Man*, pp. 82–4, speaks of the transmission of intergenerational guilt via imitation, not imputation. Tertullian's rhetoric misleads certain interpreters: contrary to Ferguson, 'Tertullian', p. 91, *An.* 38 does not intend that humans are totally innocent until puberty, but only that they are innocent of libido. (Cf. Irenaeus' depiction of the first couple as children.) On the other hand, Steenberg, *Of God and Man*, p. 82, inaccurately appeals to *Carn. Chr.* 4 as proof that Tertullian teaches that sinful libido in procreation is the means of sin's transmission. Here Steenberg's language betrays that he reads as Tertullian's own view the Carthaginian's portrayal of Marcion's position! On the need for care in interpreting Tertullian's rhetoric, see Dunn, *Tertullian*, pp. 19–20; Osborn, *Tertullian*, pp. 8–10.

[8] *Carn. Chr.* 16 in *Tertullian's Treatise*, p. 56.

[9] *Carn. Chr.* 17–23.

[10] *Carn. Chr.* 17. Cf. *Haer.* 3.21.10 (Cantalamessa, *Cristologia*, p. 69).

[11] *Carn. Chr.* 7.

[12] *Carn. Chr.* 17; 20; cf. 4; *An.* 40-1. Cf. Viciano, *Cristo Salvador*, pp. 272, 285–91. For Irenaeus' statement, see *Haer.* 4.33.11.

Tertullian holds in creative tension three crucial propositions: the sinful condition of flesh generally; the sinlessness of Christ's flesh as a victory over the former condition; and the continuing reality of the substance of flesh, which is not abolished in the abolition of its sin. Thus the Carthaginian confesses Christ as the single sinless human, whose soul experienced anger and concupiscence (here simply meaning strong desire) without defilement because they were subject to his rationality,[13] 'neither ... [was his flesh] sinful, when in it there was no guile'.[14] Yet the marvel is that he is sinless in the very same flesh as ours: 'For what would it amount to if it was in a better kind of flesh, of a different (that is, a non-sinful) nature, that he destroyed the birthmark of sin?'[15]

4.1.2 Christ's relation to sin and death

These three propositions interweave in Tertullian's exegesis of Rom. 8.3. Here he combats two heretical interpretations: Marcion's, in which Christ's coming 'in the likeness of sinful flesh' (*in similitudine carnis peccati*) means that Christ has only the appearance of essentially sinful flesh, not its reality; and Alexander the Valentinian's, which takes the same Pauline phrase to mean that Christ's flesh was exactly like ours in its sinfulness, so that to eradicate its sin he had to eradicate the very substance of his flesh.[16] Tertullian replies that Paul does not say simply that Christ came in 'the likeness of flesh', which might imply insubstantiality; rather, 'the likeness of sinful flesh' means that Christ's flesh is consubstantial with ours, but not sinful.[17] The 'sin of the flesh ... was brought to nought[18] in Christ, not the material but its quality, not the substance but its guilt', for Christ's flesh 'is to be equated with Adam in species but not in

---

[13] *An.* 16, reflecting Plato's tripartite division of the soul into the irascible, concupiscible, and rational elements. Tertullian's Old Latin version of the New Testament used *concupiscentia* of Jesus' desire in Lk. 22.15, a usage later rejected in the Vulgate (Williams, *Ideas*, p. 244, nn. 1, 3–4).

[14] *ita nec peccatricem in qua dolus non fuit* (*Carn. Chr.* 16 in *Tertullian's Treatise*, pp. 56–7). Like Irenaeus, Tertullian here adapts 1 Pet. 2.22's 'He committed no sin, neither was deceit found in his mouth', but whereas Irenaeus replaces 'mouth' with 'soul', thus moving from the material instrument to the immaterial source of its speech, Tertullian takes 'mouth' as a synecdoche for 'flesh': the antecedent of the above-quoted '*qua*' is '*carnem*' (*Tertullian's Treatise*, p. 54). For further on Tertullian's doctrine of Christ's sinlessness, see Cantalamessa, *Cristologia*, pp. 90–2.

[15] *Carn. Chr.* 16 in *Tertullian's Treatise*, p. 57.

[16] Cf. Cantalamessa, *Cristologia*, p. 90, on Alexander's interpretation. Note that Marcion and Alexander have exactly opposite understandings of the meaning of *similitudo*/ὁμοίωμα.

[17] *Marc.* 5.14; *Carn. Chr.* 16.

[18] Tertullian substitutes Rom. 6.6's verb '*evacuavit*' for Rom. 8.3's verb '*damnavit*' (Cantalamessa, *Cristologia*, p. 90) or '*condemnavit*,' apparently confusing the underlying Greek's κατέκρινεν for καταργηθῇ (*Tertullian's Treatise*, p. 151).

defect'.[19] Furthermore, even if 'likeness' were to qualify 'flesh', it would suggest not a difference in substance but a difference in origin due to the Virgin Birth.[20]

Although Christ's human nature was free from both original and actual sin from the womb forward, it remained capable of dying; indeed, the reason he was born in the flesh was that he might die in it for our salvation.[21] At one point Tertullian sounds as though he associates present salvation from sin (regeneration) strictly with Christ's birth and future salvation from death (resurrection) exclusively with Christ's death and resurrection: 'Christ alone had the right to become incarnate of human flesh, so that he might reform our nativity by his own nativity, and thus also loose the bands of our death by his own death, by rising again in that flesh in which he was born with intent to be able to die.'[22] Elsewhere, though, Christ's birth and death together establish our regeneration:[23]

> This is the new birth, that man is being born in God, since the day when God was born in man, taking to himself flesh of the ancient seed without the agency of the ancient seed, so that he might reshape it with new (that is, spiritual) seed when he had first by sacrifice expelled its ancient defilements [*antiquitatis sordibus*].[24]

Christ died, Tertullian teaches, as a sacrifice for sin. Yet in so doing, Christ did not become sinful. In Tertullian's interpretation of Numbers 21, like other early exegetes, he typifies the snakebites as sin's effects and the pole on which the bronze serpent is mounted as Christ's curative Cross, but the bronze serpent

---

[19] *evacuatam esse in Christo ... peccatum carnis, non materiam sed naturam, nec substantiam sed culpam ... genere non vitio Adae aequanda* (*Carn. Chr.* 16 in *Tertullian's Treatise*, pp. 56–7; cf. *Marc.* 5.14). On Tertullian's use of *vitium* and *culpa* to refer to Adam's original sin, transmitted to his descendants, see Viciano, *Cristo Salvador*, pp. 91–2.

[20] *Marc.* 5.14; cf. *Carn. Chr.* 16.

[21] *Carn. Chr.* 5.

[22] *Marc.* 3.9 in *AMOECT* 1, p. 197. Lampe, 'Christian Theology', p. 61, comments, 'This "Irenaean" interpretation of Christ's saving work is characteristic of the small amount of exposition which Tertullian devotes to the subject.'

[23] Viciano, *Cristo Salvador*, p. 291, explains that for Tertullian, Christ's birth commences humanity's regeneration, but this renewal is not applied to the rest of the race until after Christ's death.

[24] *Carn. Chr.* 17 in *Tertullian's Treatise*, pp. 58–9. Cantalamessa, *Cristologia*, p. 67, and Viciano, *Cristo Salvador*, pp. 271–2, see '*antiquitatis sordibus*' as original sin. In *Marc.* 3.7, Tertullian uses *sordidis* to describe Christ's humanity. Viciano, *Cristo Salvador*, p. 93, claims that in this case, the term refers simply to the humility of the Incarnation. Context supports this interpretation: Tertullian applies Zech. 3.3-5 to Christ, for 'he is at first clothed in filthy garments [*sordidis indutus*], which means the indignity of passible and mortal flesh, when also the devil stands as his adversary ...: afterwards he is divested of his previous foulness [*despoliatus pristinas sordes*], and arrayed in robe and mitre and shining crown, which means the glory and dignity of his second coming' (*AMOECT* 1, pp. 188–91).

itself depicts not Christ but the defeated devil.[25] Similarly, the Carthaginian rejects Marcion's interpretation of Gal. 3.13 as teaching that the Creator cursed Christ; rather, by being hung on a tree, Christ came under the general curse previously legislated against all who died in that manner.[26] Whether describing Christ's death or incarnation, Tertullian places him amid sin and evil but does not identify him with them; instead, from out of their midst he renders redemption.

In the fires of strife, Tertullian forged the beginnings of the Western theological tradition. That tradition would find its greatest exponent two centuries later in another North African, Augustine of Hippo. Between the two compatriots come a pair of theologians who move in opposite Christological directions: Hilary of Poitiers, who takes great pains to stress the Son's impassibility, and Ambrose of Milan, who affirms Christ's condescension in making our afflictions his own.

4.2 The passionlessness of the Christ: Hilary of Poitiers

The fourth century produced the first systematic theologian to write in Latin, Hilary of Poitiers (ca. 315–367/8), called 'the Athanasius of the West' for his staunchly pro-Nicene stance on Christ's deity. Although native to the West and indebted to Tertullian's thought, Hilary also knew Greek and was introduced to the East's theology during a four-year exile there from his bishopric (ca. 356–360). He synthesized these influences in his *De Trinitate*.[27] This work's Christology is variously assessed in the modern fallenness debate: Irving cites it without qualification in support of his view; Dods, Bruce, and Weinandy pillory Hilary as an unfallenness extremist (thus rehearsing a discomfort

---

[25] *Marc.* 3.18; cf. *De idololatria* 5; *Adversus Judaeos* 10 (*ANF* 3, pp. 63–4, 166, respectively). Cf. Justin, *Dial.* 91, 94, 112.

[26] *Marc.* 5.3.

[27] For Hilary's life and influences, see 'Hilary of Poitiers, St.' *ODCC* (2005), n.p. Cited 10 December 2012. Online: http://www.oxfordreference.com/view/10.1093/acref/9780192802903.001.0001/acref-9780192802903-e-3265; M. Weedman, *The Trinitarian Theology of Hilary of Poitiers* (Leiden: Brill, 2007), pp. 25–7, 32, 42; Hanson, *Search*, pp. 459–72; P. C. Burns, *The Christology in Hilary of Poitiers' Commentary on Matthew* (Rome: Institutum Patristicum 'Augustinianum', 1981), pp. 9–33, 37, 44–5, 119; J. W. Jacobs, 'The Western Roots of the Christology of St. Hilary of Poitiers. A Heritage of Textual Interpretation', StPatr 13 (1975): 198–203 (198); G. Morrel, 'Hilary of Poitiers: A Theological Bridge Between Christian East and Christian West', *Anglican Theological Review* 44.3 (July 1962), pp. 313–16.

dating back to the fifth century concerning his seeming semi-Docetism);[28] and Torrance finds him ambiguous.[29]

4.2.1 Defence of Christ's human impassibility

For his own part, Hilary directly rejects Docetism, insisting that Christ had a true fleshly body which shed its blood.[30] The bishop's primary opponents, however, are anti-Nicene heretics who argue that Christ's creaturely infirmities of birth, ignorance, hunger, thirst, sorrow, and suffering demonstrate him to be a lesser being than the perfect, impassible God.[31] Hilary seeks to defend Christ's identity as one person who is simultaneously truly God and truly human,[32] but the bishop depicts the divine attributes of omniscience and impassibility as nearly reducing Christ's human limitations to epiphenomena: his hunger, thirst, and tears, his confession of ignorance and cries from Gethsemane and Golgotha – all are adaptations to human custom, not expressions of genuine weakness. They are performed for his disciples' benefit, not his own.[33] Hilary does concede two points regarding the Passion. First, in Gethsemane, Christ indeed was distressed, but it was lest his followers fail; his death brought no foreboding for his own sake.[34] Secondly, Christ's body really suffered pain; his human soul, however, did not feel that pain.[35]

---

[28] C. Beckwith, 'Suffering without Pain: The Scandal of Hilary of Poitiers' Christology', *Shadow*, pp. 71–96 (71–3); K. Madigan, 'Ancient and High-Medieval Interpretations of Jesus in Gethsemane: Some Reflections on Tradition and Continuity in Christian Thought', *HTR* 88.1 (1995), pp. 157–73; Weedman, *Trinitarian Theology*, p. 157; Jacobs, 'Western Roots', pp. 202–3, n. 3; J. Mercer, 'Suffering for Our Sake: Christ and Human Destiny in Hilary of Poitiers's *De Trinitate*', *JECS* 22.4 (Winter 2014), pp. 541–68 (543). DOI: 10.1353/earl.2014.0048. Cited 15 May 2015. Online: Academia.edu.

[29] Irving: 'On the Human Nature of Christ', p. 93; Dods: *Incarnation*, pp. 519–21; Bruce: *Humiliation*, pp. 238–43; Weinandy: *Likeness*, pp. 23–5; Torrance: *Trinitarian Faith*, p. 162, n. 54.

[30] *Trin.* 10.41. Unless otherwise noted, all citations of *Trin.* are taken from Saint Hilary of Poitiers, *The Trinity* (trans. S. McKenna; FC 25; Washington, DC: Catholic University of America Press, 1954).

[31] For example, *Trin.* 2.26; 10.9; Weedman, *Trinitarian Theology*, p. 167; Mercer, 'Suffering', p. 544; but cf. FC 25, p. xi.

[32] For example, *Trin.* 9.3, 5, 14.

[33] *Trin.* 9.59–75; 10.8, 24, 27–71. Cf. Hanson, *Search*, pp. 496–502; Jacobs, 'Western Roots', p. 202; Mercer, 'Suffering', pp. 559–62.

[34] *Trin.* 10.36-37; cf. 10.55–56; Weedman, *Trinitarian Theology*, pp. 167–9.

[35] *Trin.* 10.14, 23, 46-7; cf. 10.33, 67. Does Hilary moderate his position in his later writing? L. Casula, *La Cristologia di San Leone Magno: Il Fondamento Dottrinale e Soteriologico* (Milan: Glossa, 2000), pp. 66–7, says yes. L. F. Ladaria, *La Cristología de Hilario de Poitiers* (Rome: Editrice Pontificia Università Gregoriana, 1989), pp. 176–7, says no, as does P. C. Burns, *Model for the Christian Life: Hilary of Poitiers' Commentary on the Psalms* (Washington, DC: Catholic University of America Press, 2012), pp. 149, 159–64, 231. Cf. the nuanced discussions in P. Limongi, 'La trasmissione del peccato originale in S. Ilario di Poitiers', *La Scuola Cattolica* 69 (1941), pp. 260–73 (270, n. 38) and

Here Hilary relies upon Stoic psychology,[36] which taught that 'the wise and good man would be εὐδαίμων [*sic*] on the rack or while being roasted alive in the brazen bull of Phalaris'.[37] This philosophical ideal of a soul rendered impassible by virtue allegedly characterized Old Testament saints, the apostles, and Jewish and Christian martyrs; how much more Christ himself, who once rebuked Peter for attributing fear of death to his Lord![38] As Carl Beckwith explains, 'Christ's humanity, then, is not less human because he suffers without pain; rather, according to Hilary's anthropology and moral psychology, he is more truly human because his soul is properly and perfectly ordered towards that which is true and good.'[39]

He is more truly human because he is more than truly human: his deity has assured his humanity's perfection from the first. In fallen Adam, humanity is stained by original sin in body and soul, but Christ did not derive such a defective human nature from his mother, for he was not conceived in the ordinary manner. Rather, he himself sanctified her womb, generated a body for himself from her substance, and created to animate that body a soul not enfeebled by sin and thus not capable of pain.[40] His body itself was so full of

J. J. McMahon, *De Christo Mediatore Doctrina Sancti Hilarii Pictavensis* (Mundelein, IL: Seminarii Sanctae Mariae ad Lacum, 1947), pp. 44–8. Limongi sees a distinction in Hilary between the sin-free and so suffering-free human nature which Christ assumed at conception and the sufferings which he willingly accepted as part of his redemptive work. Limongi likewise distinguishes between the sort or measure of *passio* which Christ accepted and that which he did not. McMahon concludes that for Hilary, Christ's infirmities differ from ours in that they are voluntarily assumed, unmerited by personal sin, subject to his will, and effective over only part of his being (his humanity).

[36] Beckwith, 'Suffering without Pain', pp. 82–5. Burns, *Christology in Hilary*, pp. 88–91, 133–4, claims that Hilary draws from his education in Seneca's *De constantia sapientis*; Mercer, 'Suffering', pp. 544–6, sees an indirect influence as more likely.

[37] A. N. M. Rich, 'Body and Soul in the Philosophy of Plotinus', *Journal of the History of Philosophy* I (1963), p. 623, quoted in M. R. Miles, *Augustine on the Body* (n.p.: The American Academy of Religion, 1979; repr., Eugene, OR: Wipf & Stock, 2009), p. 47.

[38] *Trin.* 10.27, 45–6; Beckwith, 'Suffering without Pain', pp. 86–8, 96, n. 74.

[39] Beckwith, 'Suffering without Pain', p. 86. Cf. Weedman, *Trinitarian Theology*, p. 157; Ladaria, *Cristología*, p. 169. For a strongly sympathetic explanation of Hilary's position in its polemical and intellectual context, see Mercer, 'Suffering', pp. 541–68.

[40] *Trin.* 2.24 (here 'Holy Spirit' refers to the second, not the third, person of the Trinity: cf. 2.30; 9.3, 14, and FC 25, p. 54 n. 55), 26; 3.19; 9.7; 10.14-26. Cf. Ladaria, *Cristología*, pp. 94, 169–70; McMahon, *De Christo Mediatore*, pp. 41–4, 72–4; Weedman, *Trinitarian Theology*, 159–61; P. Limongi, 'Esistenza e universalità del peccato originale nella mente di S. Ilario di Poitiers' and *idem*, 'La trasmissione', *La Scuola Cattolica* 69 (1941), pp. 127–47 and 260–73, respectively. In 'La trasmissione', pp. 271–3, Limongi argues from silence and by special pleading on the basis of a single text (Hilary's *Tractate* on Ps. 118 [= Ps. 119] gimel 12) that Hilary also excludes the Virgin Mary from infection by original sin, despite Limongi's insistence throughout 'Esistenza' that Hilary teaches the universality of original sin (Christ alone excepted) and, throughout the rest of 'La trasmissione', that Hilary sees natural propagation as the mode of its transmission, so that the absence of male seed from Christ's conception was essential to preserving him from original sin.

divine power that it could walk on water and cure others' infirmities, yet so accommodated to weakness that it could be pierced and slain.[41]

4.2.2 Pauline exegesis

The paradoxical status of Christ's body appears in Hilary's treatment of Rom. 8.3. Occasionally, the bishop states that Christ took our flesh or body of sin;[42] at other times, he insists that Christ had not the flesh of sin but only its likeness.[43] In one place, he does both:

> Although He bears our sins, that is, while He assumes the body of our sin [Rom. 6.6], He Himself does not sin. He was sent in the likeness of our sinful flesh [Rom. 8.3]; while He indeed bears sins in the flesh, they are our sins. … 'For our sake he made him to be sin who knew nothing of sin.' [2 Cor. 5.21] He will condemn sin in the flesh through sin; although He is exempt from sin, He Himself was made sin, that is, through the flesh He condemns sin in the flesh [Rom. 8.3] who indeed does not know the flesh but was made flesh for us, and therefore was wounded because of our iniquities [Isa. 53.5].[44]

Recalling Stephen McKenna's observation that Hilary can use the same words with different meanings,[45] we shall assume that the bishop is not being self-contradictory. As previously indicated, Hilary excludes inherited Adamic sin from Christ's humanity. In the quotation above, 'flesh' and 'sin' seem virtually interchangeable,[46] so that Hilary equates the bearing of our sins with the bearing of our body and can rephrase 2 Cor. 5.21 to say that Christ 'does not know the flesh but was made flesh for us'. The context is a defence of Christ's freedom from the experience of pain even though his body is susceptible to suffering. Hilary's meaning, then, seems to be as follows: Christ knows (experiences) no sin and so knows (experiences) no pain, for only a sinful soul is weak enough to feel pain. But he is 'made sin' in the sense of freely submitting to bear a body which suffers due not to its own sins but to others'. His fleshly passibility is from and for our fleshly peccability. Insofar as it suffered, which is the consequence

---

[41]   *Trin.* 9.7, 13; 10.7, 23, 35, 46–7.
[42]   *Trin.* 1.13; 9.13.
[43]   *Trin.* 10.25-6; cf. 10.35; Ladaria, *Cristología*, pp. 61, 169–70.
[44]   *Trin.* 10.47; ET FC 25, p. 435.
[45]   FC 25, p. xiv.
[46]   Cf. *Trin.* 9.13's line that Rom. 6.10-11 'attributed death to sin, that is, to our body' (FC 25, p. 334).

of sin, his is the 'flesh of sin'; insofar as it suffered for others' sins rather than its own, his is the mere 'likeness of the flesh of sin'.[47]

Following Hilary, the Christological pendulum swung back from the extreme to which he had taken it. To insulate Christ from inward distress would seem to estrange him from sympathy with human need. In Italy, a theologian arose who spoke eloquently of the mystery of Christ's kenosis to bear others' woe in his soul, not only in his body.[48]

4.3 The passions of the Christ: Ambrose

Ambrose, bishop of Milan (ca. 339–397), built on the Latin foundations of Tertullian and Hilary, while his fluency in Greek permitted him to import to the Occident the theology of the Greek fathers. His own teaching found reception in the East through his volume *De Fide*, which was cited at the final five ecumenical councils. His legacy in the West is especially linked with the thought of his most famous convert, Augustine. Our examination concerns Ambrose's works cited in the fallenness debate: *De fide* (380) and three successor works, *De Spiritu Sancto* (381), *De incarnationis dominicae sacramento* (381/2) and *De paenitentia* (written between 384 and 394).[49]

4.3.1 Incarnation as identification with our injured state

Ambrose follows the Athanasian exegetical tradition by seeing biblical passages which speak of Christ's infirmities and inferiority to the Father as

---

[47] Hilary also speaks of Christ's baptism as the sanctifying of our humanity in him (*Trin.* 11.17-20). As Ladaria, *Cristología*, notes, the bishop closely links Christ's birth and baptism (107), and the sanctification involved in the latter is a matter of anointing for service, not cleansing from sin (114–15).
[48] Madigan, 'Ancient and High-Medieval Interpretations', pp. 162–3, contrasts Hilary's and Ambrose's views on Christ's passibility.
[49] For perspectives on Ambrose's life, sources, influence, and bibliography, cf. 'Ambrose, St.', ODCC (2005), n.p. Cited 11 December 2012. Online: http://www.oxfordreference.com/view/10.1093/acref/9780192802903. 001.0001/acref-9780192802903-e-240; J. Moorhead, *Ambrose: Church and Society in the Late Roman World* (London: Longman, 1999); K. E. Power, 'Ambrose of Milan: Keeper of the Boundaries', *Theology Today* 55.1 (1998), pp. 15–34 (16–20); B. Ramsey, *Ambrose* (London: Routledge, 1997), pp. 1–54, 59, 62–3; N. B. McLynn, *Ambrose of Milan: Church and Court in a Christian Capital* (Berkeley: University of California Press, 1994). Moorhead, *Ambrose*, p. 6, claims that 'Ambrose's thought was largely static and displays no marked evolution'. Unless otherwise noted, all citations of *Incarn.* are from Saint Ambrose, *Saint Ambrose: Theological and Dogmatic Works* (trans. R. J. Deferrari; FC 44; Washington, DC: Catholic University of America, 1963) and all citations of *Fid.*, *Spir.*, and *Paen.* are from NPNF² 10.

references to the Son's humanity and passages which ascribe divine attributes to him as markers of his deity. The bishop also insists on the unity of the theanthropic Christ and the depth of his self-humbling in assuming human soul and flesh,[50] even to the point that he 'fell' in death: 'For the same one suffered and did not suffer; died and did not die; was buried and was not buried; rose again and did not rise again; for the body proper took on life again; for what fell, this rose again [*quod cecidit, hoc resurgit*]; what did not fall, did not rise again.'[51]

In stark contrast with Hilary, Ambrose believes that Christ's Gethsemane prayers and cry of dereliction reveal fear of death, doubt (of his human ability, not of God), friction between his natural human will to live and the divine will that he die, and the creaturely perception of godforsakenness.[52] His suffering demonstrates that his flesh bears 'the injury of earthly corruption.'[53] Ambrose underscores the profound salvific solidarity in substance and situation between Christ and ourselves: it is 'my will' which he assumed, suffering and grieving with me and for me,[54] and 'my disposition of mind' which he took 'to emend it.'[55]

Does this solidarity include sinfulness and accursedness? In *De Spiritu Sancto's* typology of the bronze serpent, the bishop notes that 'not a real but a brazen serpent was hanged ... because the Lord took on Him the likeness of a sinner [Rom. 8.3], in the truth, indeed, of His Body, but without the truth of sin, ... imitating a serpent through the deceitful appearance of human weakness.'[56]

Like sinners, then, Christ had a weak human body, but unlike them he was sinless. Echoing Tertullian's exegesis of Rom. 8.3, Ambrose explains in *De paenitentia* that Paul 'does not say "in the likeness of flesh," for Christ took on Himself the reality not the likeness of flesh; nor does [Paul] say in the

---

[50] For example, *Fid.* 2.1, 8, 11; 3.2, 7-11; 5.16-17; *Spir.* 2.11.114-9; 3.17.124; *Incarn.* 35-37, 41, 72-75. On the theanthropic union, see especially *Fid.* 2.9.77; *Incarn.* 35, 75.

[51] *Incarn.* 36; ET FC 44, p. 232; Lat.: J.-P. Migne (ed.), Patrologia latina (217 vols; repr., Turnholti, Belgium: Typographi Brepols Editores Pontificii, 1966) 16, p. 827d. *Fid.* 2.8.59 contains the same line (PL 16, p. 572a).

[52] *Fid.* 2.5.41-46; 2.7.52, 56; *Incarn.* 37-38, 41, 63. Cf. Madigan, 'Ancient and High-Medieval Interpretations', pp. 162–3, 171.

[53] *Incarn.* 58; ET FC 44, p. 241.

[54] *Fid.* 2.7.53-56; 2.11.91-93.

[55] *Incarn.* 67; ET FC 44, p. 245.

[56] *Spir.* 3.8.50 (NPNF² 10, pp. 310–12); cf. *De officiis ministrorum* 3.15.94-95 (NPNF² 10, p. 197).

likeness of sin, for He did no sin [1 Pet. 2.22], but was made sin for us [2 Cor. 5.21]. … He has our flesh, but has not the failings of this flesh.'[57]

Nor was Christ's impeccability limited to actual sin, but extended to original sin. Citing Ps. 51.5 and Rom. 7.24, Ambrose goes on to describe how sin enfolds the births of all those naturally begotten, and implies that the agent is the concupiscence which attends conception. In the Virgin Birth, however, Christ 'received a stainless body, which not only no sins polluted, but which neither the generation nor the conception had been stained by any admixture of defilement. … But the flesh of Christ condemned sin [Rom. 8.3], which He felt not at His birth and crucified by His death.'[58]

In *De fide*, Ambrose twice interprets Christ's becoming a curse as meaning that he 'bore our curses'. This phrase could mean that he was the object of either our cursing or God's. Context suggests the former: following the phrase's first occurrence, Ambrose speaks of Christ's enduring insult – clearly not from God but from people.[59] Just before the phrase's second instance, the bishop parallels Christ's being made sin and a curse with his being imprisoned in the incarceration of 'the least of these my brethren' in the Matthean parable of the sheep and the goats. Again, the implication is that humanity rather than God is the source of the mistreatment, whether it takes the form of an unjust gaoling or undeserved verbal abuse.[60]

Thus far, Ambrose has excluded Christ's humanity from sinfulness and divine anathema. In *De incarnationis dominicae sacramento* 60, however, the bishop adjudges Gal. 3.13 to mean that Christ 'himself took on our curse' (note the singular) and continues:

> Do you wonder, then, that it is written: 'The Word was made flesh,' since flesh was assumed by the Word of God, when of the sin which He did not have, it is written that He was made sin, that is, not by the nature and operation

[57] *Paen.* 1.3.12 (*NPNF*[2] 10, p. 659). Cf. *Incarn.* 50 (on a Gnostic view of the 'likeness of flesh'), 76; *Spir.* 1.9.111 (both on 2 Cor. 5.21); 1.10.114 (on 1 Pet. 2.22).
[58] *Paen.* 1.3.13; ET *NPNF*[2] 10, pp. 659–60. Cf. *Spir.* 1.9.107, 109; J. L. Bastero, 'La virginidad de María en San Ambrosio y en San Gregorio de Nisa', *Studien zu Gregor von Nyssa und der Christlichen Spätantike* (ed. H. R. Drobner and C. Klock; Leiden: Brill, 1990), pp. 255–71 (261). On Ambrose's doctrine of original sin, cf. Tennant, *Sources*, pp. 338–43; Williams, *Ideas*, pp. 299–307; Rondet, *Original Sin*, pp. 109–13; Power, 'Ambrose of Milan', pp. 29–30; Bray, 'Original Sin', pp. 37, 41–3; J. W. Smith, *Christian Grace and Pagan Virtue: The Theological Foundation of Ambrose's Ethics* (Oxford: Oxford University Press, 2011), ch. 3.
[59] *Fid.* 2.11.94. The phrase *'nostra maledicta suscepit'* appears both here and at 5.14.178 (PL 16, pp. 580b and 684c, respectively). ET mine.
[60] *Fid.* 5.14.177-8.

of sin, inasmuch as He was made in the likeness of sinful flesh; but that He might crucify our sin in His flesh, He assumed for us the burden of the infirmities of a body already guilty of fleshly sin.[61]

One commentator has called these lines 'troubling' because they appear to describe Christ's body as being, in Ambrose's words, 'already guilty of fleshly sin'.[62] We first should note the continuities with *De paenitentia*: Christ did not sin, nor was he conceived through sinful concupiscence ('not by the nature and operation of sin') and by virtue of their absence, his was merely the likeness of sinful flesh. But 'sinful flesh' is equivalent to 'a body already guilty of fleshly sin'; therefore Ambrose's meaning is that Christ assumed the same infirmities that burden sinful flesh, not the same sinfulness of flesh: 'a body already guilty of fleshly sin' is what Christ's body was like, not what his body was.[63] He was made sin and a curse by bearing flesh laden with the infirmities consequent upon our sin and accursedness.

4.3.2 Incarnation as rectification of our fleshly state

Through his continuity with human nature yet discontinuity with human sin, Christ rendered salvation in a fitting manner. It is fitting that, since flesh had sinned and become Satan's spoil, the very flesh which had sinned in Adam should be sacrificed in Christ for its redemption.[64] It is apt that the flesh in which we are tempted, in which concupiscence wars against the law of our mind, should overcome temptation in Christ, thereby setting us an example. For just as in the Triumphal Entry he sat upon and directed a previously untrained donkey, so too in him the law of the mind ruled over the impulses of the flesh without any danger of peccability.[65] These and other

---

[61] FC 44, p. 242; translation altered in light of my own judgements and those of Smith, *Christian Grace*, pp. 274–5, n. 46. On FC 44's translation deficits, see J. C. M. van Winden, review of Saint Ambrose, *Theological and Dogmatic Works*, VC 17.4, pp. 241–3.

[62] Smith, *Christian Grace*, p. 266, n. 50 (slightly altered).

[63] My conclusion supports Smith's suggestion, 'Perhaps Ambrose simply means that Christ, though sinless, bore our physical infirmities that are the consequence of sin' (*Christian Grace*, p. 266, n. 50).

[64] *Incarn.* 54, 56.

[65] *Fid.* 2.11.90-92; 5.14.175; *Incarn.* 64-69. According to *Spir.* 1.9.109, Christ crucified our passions in his body. In his survey of Ambrose's *De Paradiso*, J. P. Burns, 'Creation and Fall according to Ambrose of Milan', in *Augustine: Biblical Exegete* (ed. J. Schnaubelt and F. Van Fleteren; New York: Peter Lang, 2001), describes the Ambrosian view of humanity's prelapsarian condition in a manner reminiscent of Nazianzen: human nature was created with a tension between mind and flesh. The rational mind (symbolized by Adam) was intended to govern the flesh's passions (typified by the

teachings of Ambrose reappear in the writings of his one-time disciple, Augustine of Hippo.

4.4 Settler of the West's opinion: Augustine

On Holy Saturday, 387, Ambrose baptized a 32-year-old African rhetoric teacher and ex-Manichaean whom his sermons had helped to convince of the truth of Catholic Christianity. Within a handful of years this convert had returned to Africa (389), taken holy orders (391), and become a bishop himself (395), an office he held until his death in 430. Over his long life, Augustine of Hippo produced a vast corpus which has exercised unequalled influence upon Western Christianity.[66] We will limit our consideration to those works which are referenced in the modern fallenness debate. We look first at Augustine's description of the Fall's relation to humanity generally, then to Christology specifically.

4.4.1 Humanity: Perfection, defection, infection

In his early postbaptismal works, Augustine refutes the Manichaean doctrine, which once had beguiled him, of evil as a nature coequal with goodness and as inherent in the human body. Evil, he insists, is the corruption of God's good creation; its root lies not in any nature but in rational beings' abuse of their volitional powers. It was Adam's soul which first led his body into sin rather than the reverse. Adam turned against God, the source of life and goodness, and so became for all his offspring the source of death as well as concupiscence (*concupiscentia*), a term which Augustine often (though not exclusively)

---

beasts over which he was to rule) so that humanity might move from mere innocence to final perfection. The Fall resulted in the mind–flesh tension becoming outright warfare in which the passions had the upper hand (76–92). Christ's sitting on a donkey, then, restores the prelapsarian order of man over beast, reason over passion.

[66] For biographies, see J. J. O'Donnell, 'Augustine the African', n.p. Cited 11 January 2013. Online: http://www9.georgetown.edu/faculty/jod/augustine/; B. G. Green, 'Augustine', *Shapers of Christian Orthodoxy: Engaging with Early and Medieval Theologians* (ed. B. G. Green; Downers Grove, IL: InterVarsity, 2010), pp. 235–92 (235–9); P. Brown, *Augustine of Hippo: A Biography* (Berkeley: University of California Press, rev. edn, 2000); G. Bonner, *St. Augustine: Life and Controversies* (repr.; Norwich, UK: Canterbury Press, rev. edn, 1997). Regarding Augustine's influence, Green emends Alfred North Whitehead's quip about Western philosophy's debt to Plato: 'At one level all of Western theology has been – in a sense – a long series of footnotes to Augustine' (287).

uses negatively to speak of lust for power, possessions, revenge, and sexual activity.[67] Sexual reproduction is a related result of the Fall, necessitated to counter mortality.[68]

Ironically, Augustine spent the last two decades of his life fighting against charges of residual Manichaeism. His accusers were the Pelagians. If Manichaeans exaggerated the world's evil, Pelagians minimized it. They held that mortality and sexual concupiscence were natural to humanity even in Eden, not penalties for sin; Adam transmitted to his line no fallen nature, no impediment to freely willed sinlessness.[69]

Augustine offered the Pelagians nuanced responses. Regarding death, he granted that, in Eden, Adam's body had been naturally mortal, but that continual feeding upon the tree of life had preserved it immortal. If Adam had retained his original innocence, eventually God would have translated him alive into a state of inherent bodily immortality.[70] The death, discomforts, and other imperfections plaguing the present world had no place in paradise.[71] Regarding sexuality, the bishop had reversed his earlier opinion that procreation

---

[67] *Ver. rel.* 1.11.21–1.12.15; 1.45.83; *Fid. symb.*4.10; 10.23; *Agon.* 10.11; *Fund.* 33; *Nat. bon.* On inherited mortality and concupiscence, cf. *Tract. Ev. Jo.* 3.12.1; 4.10.2. Unless otherwise noted, all citations of these works are from the following sources: for *Ver. rel.* and *Fid. symb.*, *On Christian Belief* (ed. B. Ramsey; WSA I/8; Hyde Park, NY: New City, 2005); for *Agon.*, *The Christian Combat* (trans. R. P. Russell; FC 2; New York: Fathers of the Church, 2nd edn, 1950); for *Fund.* and *Nat. bon.*, NPNF¹ 4; for *Tract. Ev. Jo.*, *Tractates on the Gospel of John* (trans. J. W. Rettig; FC 78 [*Tract.* 1–10], 79 [*Tract.* 11–27], 88 [*Tract.* 28–54]; Washington, DC: Catholic University of America Press, 1988, 1988, 1993, respectively). For discussions of Augustine's concept of *concupiscentia*, see M. Lamberigts, 'A Critical Evaluation of Critiques of Augustine's View of Sexuality', *Augustine and His Critics* (ed. R. Dodaro and G. Lawless; London: Routledge, 2002), pp. 176–97 (180, 185); S. J. Duffy, 'Anthropology', P. Burnell, 'Concupiscence', and K. A. Rogers, 'Fall', all in *Augustine through the Ages: An Encyclopedia* (A. D. Fitzgerald [gen. ed.]; Grand Rapids: Eerdmans, 2009), pp. 24–31, 224–7, 351–2, respectively; Miles, *Augustine on the Body*, pp. 67–75; U. Bianchi, 'Augustine on Concupiscence' and J. van Oort, 'Augustine on Sexual Concupiscence and Original Sin', StPatr 22 (1989), pp. 202–12, 382–6, respectively.

[68] *Ver. rel.* 1.46.88. For discussions of the content and ancient context of Augustine's view of sexuality by scholars sympathetic to him, see Lamberigts, 'Critical Evaluation', pp. 176–97; Miles, *Augustine on the Body*, pp. 50, 53, 67–75.

[69] G. Bonner, 'Anti-Pelagian Works', E. TeSelle, 'Pelagius, Pelagianism', and J. Wetzel, 'Sin', in *Augustine through the Ages*, 41–7, 633–40, 800–2, respectively.

[70] *Pecc. merit.*1.2–5; 2.21.35; *C. Jul. op. imp.* 6.12, 30. Unless otherwise noted, all citations of these works are from the following sources: for *Pecc. merit*, *Selected Writings on Grace and Pelagianism* (ed. B. Ramsey; trans. R. Teske; WSA [unnumbered]; Hyde Park, NY: New City, 2011); for *C. Jul. op. imp.*, *Answer to the Pelagians, III: Unfinished Work in Answer to Julian* (ed. J. E. Rotelle; trans. R. J. Testke; WSA I/25; Hyde Park, NY: New City, 1999). According to TeSelle, 'Pelagius, Pelagianism', pp. 635–8, in the decade prior to the Council of Carthage in 411, Augustine himself had hypothesized that death was natural even in Eden.

[71] *C. Jul. op. imp.* 3.154, 187; 4.114; 6.31.

would not have occurred without the Fall.[72] Paradisiacal procreation, however, would have happened without evil concupiscence[73] and would have produced instantly articulate, able, and perhaps even adult-bodied newborns.[74] The general sense of shame at nudity;[75] the unruliness of the genitals, which move by concupiscence rather than rationality;[76] the unreasoning ignorance, wordlessness, and helplessness of infants[77] – all are effects of what Augustine calls 'original sin' (*peccatum originale*), the sin bequeathed by Adam to all his naturally begotten descendants.[78]

Against the Pelagian denial that we inherit original sin from Adam, Augustine summons the testimonies of fathers both Latin and Greek, among them Irenaeus, Hilary of Poitiers, Ambrose, and Gregory Nazianzen.[79] Building upon hints from his old mentor Ambrose,[80] Augustine also develops an explanation as to how original sin has passed from generation to generation: the sexual concupiscence inseparable from postlapsarian procreation infects every child thereby conceived with concupiscence of its own, hence with original sin. Thus even neonates lie guilty before God and require baptism for the remission of Adam's sin.[81] Even after baptism and even in the holiest of mortals, concupiscence remains for a lifetime, goading us towards sin:

[72] E. A. Clark, 'Generation, Degeneration, Regeneration: Original Sin and the Conception of Jesus in the Polemic between Augustine and Julian of Eclanum', in *Generation and Degeneration: Tropes of Reproduction in Literature and History from Antiquity through Early Modern Europe* (ed. V. Finucci and K. Brownlee; Durham: Duke University Press, 2001), pp. 17–40 (31); R. A. Markus, 'Augustine's *Confessions* and the Controversy with Julian of Eclanum: Manicheism Revisited', in *Collectanea Augustiniana Mélanges T. J. van Bavel* (ed. B. Bruning, M. Lamberigts and J. van Houtem; 2 vols; Leuven: Leuven University Press, 1990) 2, pp. 913–25 (921–2); van Oort, 'Augustine on Sexual Concupiscence', p. 385.

[73] *C. Jul.* 3.25.57; 5.16.63; *C. Jul. op. imp.* 2.39, 42, 45, 122; 5.14-17, 20; cf. Brown, *Augustine of Hippo*, pp. 500–2. Unless otherwise noted, all citations of *C. Jul.* are from *Against Julian* (trans. M. A. Schumacher; FC 35; New York: Fathers of the Church, 1957).

[74] *Pecc. merit.*1.37.68–1.38.69.

[75] *Pecc. merit.*1.16.21; 2.22.36; *C. Jul. op. imp.* 1.48; 4.37, 41, 44; 5.5, 8.

[76] *Trin.* 13.18.23; *C. Jul.* 2.3.5; 3.26.61-62; 6.23.70-73; cf. *C. Jul. op. imp.* 4.39. Unless otherwise noted, all citations of *Trin.* are from *The Trinity* (trans. S. McKenna; FC 45; Washington, DC: Catholic University of America Press, 1963).

[77] *Pecc. merit.*1.35.65-1.36.69; 2.29.48; cf. *C. Jul. op. imp.* 3.154, 187; 4.114; 6.9.

[78] *Pecc. merit.*1.9.9–1.15.20; *Trin.* 13.12.16; *C. Jul. op. imp.* 2.76-77; 5.9. Cf. P. Rigby, 'Original Sin', *Augustine through the Ages*, pp. 607–14; *Selected Writings*, pp. 78, 97, n. 12; Bray, 'Original Sin', pp. 43–6.

[79] For example, *C. Jul.* 1.5.15; 1.7.32; *C. Jul. op. imp.*4.71-73. In his appeal to earlier fathers to establish doctrine, Augustine resembles Cyril of Alexandria, with whom he corresponded regarding the fortunes of Pelagianism in the East (Keating, *Appropriation*, p. 229).

[80] Rigby, 'Original Sin', p. 607; Bianchi, 'Augustine on Concupiscence', p. 211.

[81] *Pecc. merit.* 1.9.9-1.15.20; 1.28.55; 2.16.24-25; 2.20.34; 2.23.37; 2.29.47; *Ep.* 187.31; *C. Jul.* 1.2.4; *Enchir.* 26. Unless otherwise noted, citations of *Enchir.* are from both FC 2 and WSA I/8. For the fifth-century scientific context of Augustine's explanation, see Clark, 'Generation, Degeneration, Regeneration', pp. 17–40. For studies of the antecedents and components of Augustine's doctrine

the confessions of the Lord's Prayer and of Rom. 7.7-24 are those of every Christian.[82] No sinless human ever has been, is, or will be, save Christ.[83]

4.4.2 Christ: Originally sinless, actually sinless, vicariously sinful

Augustine's Christology fits easily within the Latin tradition, pioneered by Tertullian,[84] which affirmed two distinct natures, a divine and a human, united in one person for the world's salvation.[85] Christ is the one Mediator (1 Tim. 2.5) 'who both as God assists [*subvenit*] men by His divinity, and as man agrees [*convenit*] with men by His weakness'.[86] Early on, Augustine portrays Christ's saving work in exemplarist terms: Adam's proud lunge after Godhead wrought his downfall, but the divine Son's kenosis to assume humanity models the humility which we must imitate to return to God;[87] his victory over temptation sets us a sinless example to follow.[88] As bishop, however, Augustine teaches a deeper view of grace.[89] Christ's condescension to bear our weak nature provides not merely a moral pattern but a medicine which heals our pride by his humility, our grasping by his resignation, and our fear by his resurrection. Only through remaining in him do we share his victory over Satan.[90] In *De Trinitate*, the bishop details the dynamics of that victory: Satan had deceived humanity and gained the right to enslave it. Christ

---

of original sin, see Tennant, *Sources*; Williams, *Ideas*, chs 1–5; Rondet, *Original Sin*, chs 1–10; G. A. Riggan, *Original Sin in the Thought of Augustine* (Ann Arbor, MI: University Microfilms, 1970).

[82] *Pecc. merit.* 2.4.4; *C. Jul.* 2.3.5; 3.26.61-62; 6.23.70-73; *C. Jul. op. imp.* 4.89.

[83] *Pecc. merit.* 1.39.70; 2.4.4; 2.16.24-25; 2.20.34; 2.29.47; *Ep.* 187.28; cf. *Tract. Ev. Jo.* 41.5.1; 41.9.2. Before the Council of Carthage (418) ruled that all humans but Christ were sinful, Augustine had allowed that some may have lived sinlessly (*Selected Writings*, p. 218, n. 3). Unless otherwise noted, all citations of *Ep.* 187 are from *Letters Vol. IV [165–203]* (trans. W. Parsons; FC 30; New York: Fathers of the Church, 1955).

[84] On Augustine's relationship to Tertullian, see F. Chapot, 'Tertullian', *Augustine through the Ages*, pp. 822–4.

[85] B. E. Daley, 'Christology', *Augustine through the Ages*, pp. 164–9. Cf. Keating, *Appropriation*, pp. 230–51, who finds significant parallels between Augustine and Cyril of Alexandria on the Incarnation and deification.

[86] *Trin.* 13.17.22; ET FC 45, p. 343; Lat.: PL 42, p. 1032. Cf. *Agon.* 18.20–22.24; *Pecc. merit.* 1.31.60; *Serm.* 174.1-2; *Ep.* 137.8-9, 11-12; *Ep.* 187.7-10. Unless otherwise noted, all citations of *Serm.* 174 are from *Sermons III/5 [151–183]* (trans. E. Hill; WSA III/5; Hyde Park, NY: New City Press, 1992) and all citations of *Ep.* 137 are from *Letters Vol. III [131–164]* (trans. W. Parsons; FC 20; New York: Fathers of the Church, 1953).

[87] *Fid. symb.* 4.6.

[88] *Ver. rel.* 1.16.30-32; 1.24.45; 1.38.69-71.

[89] F. G. Clancy, 'Redemption', *Augustine through the Ages*, 702–4 (702); cf. the comment by M. Fiedrowicz and E. Hill in *On Christian Belief*, p. 49, n. 67.

[90] *Agon.* 1.1; 10.11–11.12; *Trin.* 13.17.22.

could have been made man without human parentage, as Adam was, but he submitted to enter Adam's line of descent in order to conquer Satan in the very nature conquered by Satan. Though the devil's temptations failed and he found nothing of sin in Christ (Jn 14.30), he still inflicted death, sin's punishment, upon Jesus. Satan's unjust penalizing of Christ resulted in the loss of Satan's right over the rest of humankind.[91]

Augustine accounts for Christ's sinlessness, so crucial to his exemplary and emancipative roles, in various complementary ways. First, his mother conceived virginally, by faith and not by conjugal concupiscence, and so broke the chain of contamination of the flesh by original sin. Although she herself had sinful flesh, from her he took flesh but not sin.[92] Secondly, at the moment of conception, Christ's human soul also was free or freed from original sin, either by being created pure and then remaining undefiled through union with a sinless body (if creationism be correct) or else by being purified by God immediately upon its derivation from Mary (if traducianism be true).[93] Finally, Christ's divine nature imparted such grace to the human nature united to it that the human nature became impeccable, thereby securing him against actual sin.[94] As Augustine never tires of repeating, Christ came in the *likeness* of sinful flesh, not in sinful flesh itself.[95] The story of the bronze serpent typifies this truth: 'The Lord did not take into his flesh sin, which is like the venom of the snake, but he did take death. Thus the punishment of sin was present in the likeness of sinful flesh without guilt so that he might destroy in sinful flesh both the guilt and the punishment.'[96]

---

[91] *Trin.* 4.13.17; 13.13-18. Cf. *Tract. Ev. Jo.* 3.13.1; *Pecc. merit.*2.30.49; *Serm.* 265D.4-5. Unless otherwise noted, all citations of *Serm.* 265D are from *Sermons* III/7 [230–272B] (trans. E. Hill; WSA III/7; Hyde Park, NY: New City Press, 1993).

[92] *Tract. Ev. Jo.* 4.10.2-3; 10.11-12; *Pecc. merit.*1.28-29; 2.24.38; *C. Jul.* 2.4.8; 5.15.52, 54, 57; *Enchir.* 34, 41; *C. Jul. op. imp.* 4.78-84, 134. On Mary's own birth as concupiscent, see D. E. Doyle, 'Mary, Mother of God', *Augustine through the Ages*, pp. 542–5 (544), but cf. *Selected Writings*, p. 218, n. 3.

[93] *Ep.* 164.19; cf. *Pecc. merit.* 2.11.16. Unless otherwise noted, all citations of *Ep.* 164 are from FC 20. For a fascinating, if speculative, argument that Augustine secretly held to a pre-existent, sinless human soul of Christ in the tradition of Origen, see D. Keech, *The Anti-Pelagian Christology of Augustine of Hippo, 396–430* (Oxford: Oxford University Press, 2012).

[94] *Enchir.* 36, 40-1. On the origins of Christ's sinlessness, see Daley, 'Christology', pp. 167–8.

[95] *Serms.* 184; 185.1; *Ep.* 164.19; *Pecc. merit.*1.27.44; 1.28.55; 1.39.70; 2.23.37; 2.36.58; 3.12.21; *Ep.* 187.31; *Tract. Ev. Jo.* 42.1.1 (which links Rom. 8.3 with Phil. 2.7; just as Christ is *like* sinful flesh but is *not* sinful flesh, so also he takes the *form* of a servant but is *not* a servant); *C. Jul.* 5.4.17; 5.15.52; 6.19.62; *Enchir.* 41–42; *C. Jul. op. imp.* 2.17, 225; 4.58, 63, 78-84; 6.33-34. Unless otherwise noted, all citations of *Serm.* 184 and 185 are from *Sermons* III/6 [184–229] (trans. E. Hill; WSA III/6; New Rochelle, NY: New City Press, 1993). For the significance of Rom. 8.3 to Augustine in the Pelagian controversy and his dependence on Origen's exegesis, see Keech, *Anti-Pelagian Christology*, chs 3–4.

[96] *Pecc. merit.*1.32.61; ET *Selected Writings*, p. 138.

Augustine's interpretation of 'the likeness of sinful flesh' permits him to ascribe some and deny others of the common characteristics of fallen humanity to Christ. As Dominic Keech notes, 'In order for it to be salvific, Christ has to assume a post-Adamic humanity, which is neither the pristine nature enjoyed by Adam at his first creation, nor fully conformed to sinful nature, as in the case of the rest of postlapsarian humanity.'[97] Thus the Saviour endured the imperfections of fallen infant physique and the need to grow up, but without the weak-mindedness of small children in their ignorance and irrational emotionalism.[98] Inasmuch as he lacked concupiscence, he was baptized not for his own sake but for ours, that by imitating him we might receive the regeneration which he did not require.[99] He suffered weariness in his flesh[100] and grief in his soul[101] but never godforsakenness: his cry of dereliction on the Cross expresses a counterfactual of identification with sinners, a placing of our complaint upon his lips.[102] He took mortal flesh from Mary,[103] yet could not die but by his choice.[104] Nor was it possible for his human soul to die, for soul-death is deadness in sin; rather, he died only bodily.[105] This death serves as a prefiguration of our death to sin, not a prototype of it – else Christ would have needed to have had personal sin to which to die.[106] The Pauline claim that for us the Sinless One 'became sin' (2 Cor. 5.21) means that Christ 'became a sin offering', for the *Septuagint* uses 'sin' to mean 'sin offering'.[107] Augustine

---

[97] Keech, *Anti-Pelagian Christology*, p. 101.

[98] *Pecc. merit.*1.37.68; 2.29.48. As Keech, *Anti-Pelagian Christology*, p. 186, comments, 'To account for the infancy of Christ, Augustine resorts to a formula which is difficult not to interpret as a subtle form of docetism.'

[99] *Tract. Ev. Jo.* 4.13-14; *Pecc. merit.*2.24.38; *Ep.* 187.30; *Enchir.* 49; *C. Jul. op. imp.* 4.45-54, 58-64.

[100] *Tract. Ev. Jo.* 15.6; *Ep.* 137.9.

[101] *Serm.* 265D.3.

[102] *Trin.* 4.3.6; 4.13.16; R. D. Williams, 'Augustine's Christology: Its Spirituality and Rhetoric', *Shadow*, pp. 176–89 (183–6). Based on this exegesis and on Augustine's denial of concupiscence to Christ, Teske argues that while the bishop may claim that Christ modelled for us successful resistance to temptation, this claim is undermined by Christ's being sheltered from any temptation by doubt or lust: see R. J. Teske, *Augustine of Hippo: Philosopher, Exegete, and Theologian: A Second Collection of Essays* (Milwaukee: Marquette University Press, 2009), pp. 215–33.

[103] *Tract. Ev. Jo.* 3.12.1-2; 4.2.3–4.3.1; *C. Jul.* 5.15.54-55.

[104] *Pecc. merit.* 2.29.48; cf. 2.31.51; *Trin.* 4.13.16; *C. Jul. op. imp.* 6.34; cf. *Tract. Ev. Jo.* 47.7. Augustine uses Jn 10.18; 14.31; and Phil. 2.8 as proof texts.

[105] *Serm.* 265D.3, 5; *Eps.* 137.12; 164.19; *Trin.* 4.2.4–4.3.6; cf. *Coll. Max.* 14. Unless otherwise noted, all citations of *Coll. Max.* are from *Arianism and Other Heresies* (trans. R. J. Teske; WSA I/18; Hyde Park, NY: New City Press, 1995).

[106] *Pecc. merit.* 2.23.37; *Tract. Ev. Jo.* 41.6; cf. *Ep.* 187.30; *C. Jul.* 6.3.7; *Enchir.* 42.

[107] *Tract. Ev. Jo.* 41.5-6; *Enchir.* 41. For the evolution of Augustine's exegesis of 2 Cor 5:21, see A. Bastiaensen, 'Augustine's Pauline Exegesis and Ambrosiaster', *Augustine: Biblical Exegete*, pp. 33–54 (47–50).

summarizes the whole interplay between Christ and sin: 'There is only one person who has been born without sin in the likeness of sinful flesh, who lived without sin in the midst of others' sins, and who died without sin on account of our sins.'[108] The bishop bequeathed this perspective to the West generally and to our last father particularly.

4.5 Chalcedon and context: Leo the Great

The final theologian whose view of Christ's humanity we shall analyse is Pope Leo the Great (reigned 440–61), who synthesized the thoughts of Latin and Greek authors alike, especially Augustine and Cyril of Alexandria.[109] Leo's *Epistola* 28, widely known as his *Tome* (449), received ecumenical approval at the Council of Chalcedon (451)[110] and is a key source in the fallenness debate. Yet that *Tome* – actually the first of two – must not be interpreted in isolation. In composing it, Leo drew upon Christmas sermons preached early in his papacy, sermons which themselves must be interpreted in relation to the whole of his systematic exposition of Christian doctrine through annual homiletic cycles. Furthermore, Leo's thought (or at least its expression) developed beyond the First *Tome*, and his most mature statement of Christology comes in his Second *Tome* (458).[111]

[108] *Pecc. merit.*2.35.57; ET *Selected Writings*, p. 193. Cf. *Trin.* 4.14.19; *Enchir.* 41–2.

[109] Leo, however, apparently knew no Greek. On Leo's life and patristic influences upon him, see A. Saenz, *San Leon Magno y los Misterios de Cristo* (Paraná, Argentina: Mikael, 1984), p. 24; P. L. Barclift, 'The Shifting Tones of Pope Leo the Great's Christological Vocabulary', *Church History* 66.2 (1997), pp. 221–39 (224); B. Green, *The Soteriology of Leo the Great* (Oxford: Oxford University Press, 2008), pp. vii, 13–17, 22, 25–8, 45–60, 104–16, 249; B. Neil, *Leo the Great* (London: Routledge, 2009), pp. 1–50, 95; 'Leo I, St.' ODCC (2005), n.p. Cited 14 December 2012. Online: http://www.oxfordreference.com/view/10.1093/acref/9780192802903.001.0001/acref-9780192802903-e-4020. For the consistency (though with different foci) between Leo and Cyril on Incarnation and deification, see Keating, *Appropriation*, pp. 251–88. Leo repeatedly claims unanimity in doctrine with Athanasius and Cyril, as well as with Theophilus of Alexandria (*Ep.* 117, 129). In the list of corroborative testimonies attached to his Second *Tome* (*Ep.* 165), Leo quotes them alongside Hilary of Poitiers, Ambrose, Augustine, Chrysostom, and Nazianzen. Unless otherwise noted, all citations of Leo's letters are from *Letters* (trans. E. Hunt; FC 34; New York: Fathers of the Church, 1957).

[110] 'Tome of Leo' in ODCC (2005), n.p. Cited 14 December 2012. Online: http://www.oxfordreference.com/view/10.1093/acref/9780192802903.001.0001/acref-9780192802903-e-6907. This source and Lampe, 'Christian Theology', pp. 140–1, claim Tertullian's influence on the First *Tome*, a claim questioned by J. A. McGuckin, 'Mystery or Conundrum? The Apprehension of Christ in the Chalcedonian Definition', *Shadow*, pp. 246–59 (252–3).

[111] Saenz synchronically surveys Leo's sermons in their specific liturgical contexts. Casula, *Cristologia*; Barclift, 'Shifting Tones'; and Green, *Soteriology*; and J. M. Armitage, *A Twofold Solidarity: Leo the Great's Theology of Redemption* (Strathfield, Australia: St Pauls, 2005) all seek to place the First

4.5.1 The Christmas sermons

In Leo's Christmas sermons, certain themes recur. Christ took from Mary a human nature consubstantial with ours, a lowly nature capable of death and physical corruption.[112] Yet in sharing these infirmities, Christ did not share the contagion of our sin. The homily for 442 is especially explicit on this point:

> In the whole and perfect nature of true man, therefore, true God was born, complete in divine attributes, complete in human ones. In speaking about 'human ones,' we mean those which the Creator put into us from the beginning, the same ones that he took on to be restored. Whatever the deceiver introduced and humanity in being deceived allowed, these things do not have even a trace in the Savior. Simply because he submitted to a share in human infirmities, he did not on that account become party to our sins. He assumed the 'form of a servant' without the stain of sin.[113]

Leo regularly employs an Augustinian explanation: no sinful concupiscence attended Christ's conception; rather, the undefiled virginity of his mother produced a child uniquely undefiled by original sin.[114] His nativity is thus the pattern for the new birth which we may share: the Holy Spirit who filled Mary's womb to exclude original sin from Christ's humanity is the same Spirit who fills the baptismal water to grant us the regeneration which frees our humanity from original sin.[115]

4.5.2 The Paschal sermons

Leo's Christmas sermons lay the dogmatic foundations for interpreting Christ's earthly life. For the full implications of the theanthropic Saviour's sinless participation in the human experience, we must turn to the pontiff's Holy Week sermons. Here he specifies that the human weaknesses endured

---

Tome in the wider context of Leo's corpus. Green's exceptional study discusses both diachronically and synchronically the interconnectedness of the pope's sermons (viii, 87–9) and the First *Tome*'s relation to Leo's *Ep*. 124 to Palestinian monks (453), later rewritten as the Second *Tome* (viii–ix, 188, 236–8, 247, 252). Unless otherwise noted, all citations of Leo's sermons are from *Sermons* (trans. J. P. Freeland and A. J. Conway; FC 93; Washington, DC: Catholic University of America Press, 1996).

[112] *Tr.* 21.1-2; 22.2; 24.3; 25.1-2.
[113] *Tr.* 23.2; ET FC 93, p. 89.
[114] *Tr.* 21.1-2; 22.1-3; 23.1, 3; 24.3; 25.4-5; 26.3; 28.2-4. Cf. Casula, pp. 201–6. *Pace* Armitage, pp. 67, 70, *Tr.* 22.2 teaches that God preserved Mary as *virgo en partu*, not that Christ's whole career was a preservation of 'Marian purity'.
[115] *Tr.* 21.3; 24.3; 25.5; 26.2; 27.2; cf. 63.6.

by Christ – fatigue, hunger, grief, fear, pain, mortality – were brought upon the human race by sin.[116] Echoing Nazianzen's *non-assumptus*, Leo preaches that Christ 'took the reality of our weakness and excluded nothing of human infirmity from himself except participation in our sin. That way, he might bring his own [divine] nature to us and heal ours in himself.'[117] For example, his confession of sorrow and prayer for the cup to pass while in Gethsemane and later his cry of dereliction on Calvary prove that he had taken not merely human flesh with its sensations but likewise a human mind with its feelings, even the feeling of fear. Christ's Gethsemane prayers reveal him overcoming a sincere yet sinless unwillingness to die – a victory which he confers to the cowardly Peter and to us. Leo is careful to note that even in Gethsemane, Christ retained his omnipotence, and even on the Cross, he remained undivided from the Father. The human weakness which his words express is ever voluntary, nonetheless genuine. He heals our weakness by persevering through the Passion to the Resurrection and communicating to us his sacramental power and ethical pattern.[118]

Throughout the homilies, Leo often links together the phrases 'the form of a slave' (Phil. 2.7) and 'the likeness of sinful flesh' (Rom. 8.3) to describe Christ's assumed human nature.[119] Due to the Fall, all humankind was enslaved to Satan, but God's Son took the *form*, yet not the *state*, of a slave.[120] He bore the *likeness* of sinful flesh but was sinless in the flesh. By these distinctions, Leo intends that Christ bore all the weaknesses associated with sin yet was without sin. This understanding remains constant even when the pope preaches that Christ 'took on not only the substance but even the conditions [*conditionem*] of sinful nature', for Leo straightaway clarifies, 'Divine impassibility allowed those things to be brought upon him which human mortality suffers in its misery.'[121] Thus Christ took both the true human substance and the condition of weakness

---

[116] *Tr.* 63.4.
[117] *Tr.* 67.5; ET FC 93, p. 294. Cf. Grillmeier, *Christ in Christian Tradition* 1, p. 531.
[118] *Tr.* 54.2, 4-5; 58.4-5; 59.1; 63.4; 67.5, 7; 68.1-2. On Christ's double provision of *sacramentum* and *exemplum* (terms derived from Hilary), see Green, *Soteriology*, pp. 59, 114, 177.
[119] *Tr.* 25.2; 63.4; 67.6; 77.2; cf. 62.2, which blends Augustine's interpretation of 2 Cor. 5.21 with Rom. 8.3 ('both "knowing no sin" and yet sacrificed "in the likeness of sinful flesh" for sinners' [FC 93, p. 270]).
[120] *Tr.* 22.3.
[121] *Tr.* 71.2; ET FC 93, p. 312; Lat.: PL 54, p. 387c. Barclift, 'Shifting Tones', p. 225, sees the first line as 'hyperbole'. H. Arens, *Die christologische Sprache Leos des Grossen: Analyse des Tomus an den Patriarchen Flavian* (Freiburg: Herder, 1982), p. 351, identifies this *conditionem* as susceptibility to death.

(misery and mortality), which in all other humans are characteristics of sin's slaves, but in him that substance and that weakened condition exist absent the state of enslavement to sin.[122]

The pope has good reason for such careful nuancing of Christ's appearing: it is crucial to Leonine interpretation of the Atonement. On this view, Satan did not enslave humanity by force, but by manipulating Adam into freely ceding authority to him. God's response was in keeping with principles of fair play: rather than liberate humanity by force and by mere divinity, God acted from within the very human nature which Satan had ensnared and manipulated Satan into freely overreaching himself. Because Jesus possessed a human nature in its condition of weakness consequent upon sin, Satan presumed that this Nazarene also must be afflicted by original sin and so be by right his prey. Since, however, Christ was entirely sinless, in killing him Satan overstepped his jurisdiction and so forfeited his claim to the rest of humanity.[123]

4.5.3 From the First to the Second *Tome*

Turning from Leo's sermons to his First *Tome*, we find much continuity.[124] Here the pope affirms that Christ was born of Mary without loss of divinity 'so that by his virtue he both conquered death and destroyed the devil, who used to have power over death [Heb. 2.14]. For we could not overcome the originator of sin and death, if he (sc. Christ) had not assumed our nature and made it his own, he whom sin could not stain nor death detain.'[125] Implicit in these lines is Leo's view of the Atonement.[126]

---

[122] Cf. Casula, *Cristologia*, p. 104. Armitage, *Twofold Solidarity*, pp. 75-6, compounds errors: 1. His own parenthetical Latin calls into question his claim that, for Leo, 'Christ deals with sin by inheriting "sinful flesh" (*factus in similitudinem carnis peccati*)': for an Augustinian like Leo, the *similitudinem* significantly qualifies the *carnis peccati*. 2. Neither Leo nor Tertullian taught that Christ possessed 'sin in the flesh' – quite the contrary, as this study demonstrates. 3. Inasmuch as, for Leo, Christ never took a slave's state, it is false to speak of 'his own liberation from slavery to the devil'. Cf. the careful distinction in D. Mozeris, *Doctrina Sancti Leonis Magni de Christo Restitutore et Sacerdote* (Mundelein, IL: Seminarii Sanctae Mariae ad Lacum, 1940), p. 11, between sin's penalties (infirmities and mortality), which Christ bore, and sin's guilt and captivity, from which he was free.
[123] *Tr.* 21.1; 22.3-4; 28.3; 69.3-4. For a 'modern version' of Leo's sermons on Christ's defeat of the devil, see A. Field, *Delivered from Evil: Jesus' Victory over Satan* (Cincinnati: Servant, 2005).
[124] For a thorough treatment of the First *Tome*, including its sources, see Arens, *Die christologische Sprache*. On a smaller scale, see Grillmeier, *Christ in Christian Tradition* 1, pp. 530-9.
[125] *Ep.* 28.2; ET Neil, *Leo the Great*, p. 97 (parenthetical remark hers). On the background of this passage in *Tr.* 21 and Heb. 2.14, see Arens, *Die christologische Sprache*, pp. 178, 180.
[126] Casula, *Cristologia*, pp. 240-1; Neil, *Leo the Great*, pp. 29, 68; cf. Green, *Soteriology*, p. 212.

Leo then quotes a series of passages from his first four Christmas sermons. The first passage describes the union of humble, weak, mortal, and passible human nature with majestic, mighty, eternal, and impassible divine nature in Christ for the sake of our healing.[127] The second passage is the affirmation, quoted in 4.5.1 above, that Christ assumed what the Creator originally had formed, not the sinful attributes which the devil had introduced into human nature. Christ's simultaneous existence in the form of God (the divine nature) and the form of a slave (the human nature) is the thrust of the third passage.[128] The fourth passage explains that because of the absence of lust from the virginal conception, Christ shares our passible, mortal substance but not our guilt.[129]

The pontiff proceeds to cite a series of events in the Gospels. In some, Christ displays human weakness (e.g. birth, hunger, temptation, suffering). In others, he reveals divine greatness (e.g. receiving worship, performing miracles, granting eternal life). Leo's point in citing these events – many of which had featured in his sermons – is to underscore the presence and integrity of both natures, human and divine, in Christ, over against Nestorius' alleged undervaluing of Christ's divinity[130] and Eutyches' apparent compromising of Christ's humanity.

Following the First *Tome*'s approval by the Council of Chalcedon, Leo continued to articulate these themes. His anti-Eutychian letter to Bishop Juvenal of Jerusalem reminds the hierarch that Christ's real humanity required food and sleep and felt sadness and fear even as his real divinity wrought miracles and raised his body from the grave.[131] Leo also makes his usual careful distinction between human weakness and sinfulness in Christ,

> who is crucified in our flesh … which, admitting of no sin, could not have been mortal had it not been of our species. In order to restore life to all, He took up the cause of all …. Thus, just as all were made sinners through the

---

[127] *Ep.* 28.3, quoting *Tr.* 21.2 (Green, *Soteriology*, pp. 108, 213–14; Arens, *Die christologische Sprache*, p. 314).

[128] *Ep.* 28.3; both passages are quotes from *Tr.* 23.2 (Green, *Soteriology*, p. 214; Arens, *Die christologische Sprache*, pp. 354–5); cf. *Tr.* 22.1. I find unconvincing the claim of Armitage, *Twofold Solidarity*, pp. 87–9, that for the ancients Christ's double consubstantiality was a matter of epistemology and sociology but not metaphysics. The lattermost is the ultimate ground of the former two, as a civilization soaked in classical philosophy would have known well.

[129] *Ep.* 28.4, quoting *Tr.* 22.1-3, with phrases from *Tr.* 24.3 (Green, *Soteriology*, p. 216; Arens, *Die christologische Sprache*, pp. 396, 399–403).

[130] Green, *Soteriology*, p. 53; but cf. 60, 229. Green argues that Leo wrote his First *Tome* under the illusion that Nestorius taught adoptionism.

[131] *Ep.* 139.2.

guilt of one man, so also all might become guiltless through the guiltlessness of one, with justification flowing upon all men from Him who took on man's nature. By no consideration is He lacking in the reality of our body.[132]

As in the past, the pope wishes to preserve the integrity of Christ's humanity against encroachment by either divinity or depravity – the former would render his flesh unable, the latter unfit, to die as a sacrifice.

Lastly, Leo's Second *Tome*, his definitive Christological statement sent to the Roman emperor, sounds the same notes. Christ took from Mary 'real flesh containing our weakness'.[133] As Mediator, he both is equal to his Father and shares the servile status of humanity.[134] We who are born bound by original sin were released by 'a man of our species and our nature ... who was not bound by any previous conviction for sin and who by His stainless blood would blot out the decree of death against us'.[135]

In light of the extensive context canvassed above, it is clear that when Leo's First *Tome* asserts that Christ assumed our nature as created, without 'whatever the deceiver introduced and humanity in being deceived allowed', the pope means only to exclude sin, not the amoral effects of the Fall.[136] His very next line speaks of how Christ 'submitted to a share in human infirmities ... [and] assumed the "form of a servant"'.[137] The rest of his corpus concurs. Leo thus depicts Christ's humanity as restored to a prelapsarian state of sinlessness while partaking thoroughly of postlapsarian infirmities.

Conclusion

Complementing the previous chapter's study of the Greek fathers, this chapter has queried the Latin fathers for their understanding of the relationship of the Fall to Christ's humanity. Terminologically, we found no exact parallels to the Greeks' occasional claims that Christ assumed a 'fallen' or 'sinful' humanity. The closest approximation appeared in Ambrose's statement that Christ 'fell'

[132] *Ep.* 139.3; ET FC 34, p. 229.
[133] *Ep.* 165.3; ET FC 34, p. 265.
[134] *Ep.* 165.4.
[135] *Ep.* 165.9; ET FC 34, p. 272.
[136] This is also Arends' contention in his careful discussion, *Die christologische Sprache*, pp. 371–5.
[137] *Ep.* 28.3; ET FC 93, p. 89; cf. *Tr.* 23.2.

in death, but here it is questionable whether the bishop, in employing a generic Latin circumlocution for dying, also means to allude to Genesis 3.[138] On the other hand, Tertullian and Leo echo Irenaeus and *Contra Apollinarium* in applying prelapsarian language to Christ's assumption of human nature.

Conceptually, the Latin fathers, like their Greek brethren, teach that in the virginal conception, God's Son breaks the hold of sin upon human nature so that his own humanity, like unfallen Adam's, is unblemished by sin, uncontrolled by Satan, and under no debt to die. Yet in salvific solidarity with guilty humanity, he suffers from various effects of the Fall, including bodily torment and death (and, for Augustine, the fallen state which is infancy). Hilary, however, reduces much of this solidarity in suffering to pretence. All the Latin fathers see Christ as keeping his inner human desires under discipline so that they never exist in a state of sin (i.e. concupiscence in Augustine's usual negative sense). Hilary so emphasizes this point as to make Christ's human soul insensible to pain, but the rest of the fathers do not follow the bishop of Poitiers to such an extreme. Rather, they allow for Christ to experience anger and strong desire (Tertullian), grief (Augustine, Leo), and even self-doubt and fear of death (Ambrose).

We have reached the end of our examination of the patristic sources most widely cited by our selected modern debaters. It remains for us to evaluate the debate in light of our findings, draw conclusions, and recommend avenues for further research. We will take up these tasks in our final chapter.

---

[138] Cf. the term 'the departed' in common English; generally the use of this term would not intend a biblical allusion to Israelites' departure from Egypt in the Exodus. On the generic Latin meaning of *cado*, see the entry in D. P. Simpson, *Cassell's Latin and English Dictionary* (Hoboken, NJ: Wiley, 2002), p. 29. According to Williams, *Ideas*, the noun *casus* is used for the Fall of Adam in 4 Esd. 7.118 (252, n. 4); later the term *lapsus* became the standard Latin designation for the Fall (302–3).

5

The Fleshing Out of the Findings

In relation to the modern fallenness debate, where do the fathers stand and what contribution might they make towards its resolution? This twofold question has guided our study. Chapters 1 and 2 summarized the views of, respectively, five modern fallenness proponents and five modern unfallenness proponents, including their appeals to or against the church fathers. In Chapter 3, we examined the positions of five Greek fathers, and in Chapter 4, those of five Latin fathers. This chapter uses our patristic findings to evaluate the modern debaters' historical and theological claims and then offers recommendations for advancing the conversation.

5.1 Righting history: The modern debaters on the fathers

In examining the patristic sources cited by the modern debaters, we found that there is some precedent in the Greek fathers for referring to the humanity which Christ bore as 'fallen', even 'sinful'. For their part, the Latin fathers do not follow this practice, except in Ambrose's use of 'fell' as a circumlocution for 'died' in relation to Christ's body. Despite this variation in terminology, the Greek and Latin fathers concur that, in the virginal conception, God acted to purify the postlapsarian human nature which Christ assumed so that it was free from sinful passions and from mastery by Satan and death. Some fathers, both Greek and Latin, describe this purified condition in prelapsarian terms. Yet all agree that Christ suffered all the ills of a physically corruptible human nature in a world traumatized by sin: hunger, fear, grief, temptation, pain, and mortality. For Hilary, much of this suffering is considerably enervated. For Nyssen and Augustine, however, even Christ's being born a helpless baby requiring growth indicates his sharing our fallen condition. Those

Greek fathers who call Christ's humanity 'fallen' or 'sinful' mean by these terms that it was afflicted with sin's results, not that it was genuinely sinful after conception. In light of these findings, the modern debaters' patristic interpretations require evaluation.

5.1.1 Edward Irving

Irving's teaching that Christ's humanity bears constitutional sin, including guilty concupiscence, has no patristic grounding, whether in the (mostly Latin) fathers whom he cites or in the (mostly Greek) fathers whom his contemporary defenders have adduced in his support.[1] Irving culls patristic proof texts which speak of Christ's humanity's reality and completeness and of his sharing our infirmities, including suffering and death.[2] Irving then interprets these texts under the belief that the attributes of fallenness are indivisible and so infirmities imply sinful concupiscence even in Christ's case. The fathers believe otherwise. Irenaeus and Tertullian both reject the Gnostic equation of flesh with sinfulness and its implication that Christ either shared our sin by sharing our nature or else did not share our nature lest he share our sin. Augustine later does likewise with Manichaeism; *Contra Apollinarium*'s author and the Gregories oppose Apollinarianism for the same reason; and Cyril anathematizes Nestorius for teaching (according to Cyril) that Christ sacrificed himself for his own sinfulness. All the fathers assert Christ's assumption of a real humanity like ours and, with it, sinless infirmities, but exclude every manifestation of sin – whether sinful impulse or sinful action.

Additionally, Irving makes a more thorough division between Christ's divine person and human nature than is the fathers' tendency. While they distinguish between the two, they still allow for the attributes of Christ's humanity to be predicated of his person. Irving, however, refuses to predicate of Christ's person the sinfulness which he graphically predicates of Christ's humanity. Although less than full-bodied Nestorianism, such refusal raises that heresy's spectre, however strenuously Irving and his defenders may insist that he confesses but one person in Christ.[3] In the end, Irving seems guilty

---

[1] See the reviews of Nantomah's and Dorries' works in this study's Introduction, 0.3.
[2] See the appendix for Irving's quotations from the fathers selected for this study.
[3] As in Lee, 'Humanity of Christ', p. 44.

of a hybrid heresy – 'Gnostorianism', if one wishes to summarize it – which combines Gnostic substantialization of the flesh's sinfulness with Nestorian predication of sin to Christ's humanity and non-predication of human attributes to Christ's person.[4]

Irving himself accuses his contemporaries of Gnosticism, Manichaeism, Eutychianism, and Monothelitism for presenting a Christ whose humanity is better than ours.[5] This study has considered only one of those contemporaries, the elder Marcus Dods, against whom twentieth-century defenders of Irving also have levelled charges of Monophysitism and Eutychianism.[6] Yet the fathers themselves present a Christ whose earthly humanity was 'better' than ours in the specific sense that it was free from sinful passions. Leo's *Tome* teaches this point simultaneously with condemning Eutychianism. The Council of Chalcedon authorized the *Tome* and issued a Definition which excludes both Eutychianism and sin in its account of the constitution of Christ. These formative documents of orthodoxy cannot reasonably be construed as Gnostic or Manichaean, and Monothelitism eventually was ruled to be incompatible with their doctrine.

As for Dods, he distances himself directly from Manichaeism (and indirectly from Gnosticism) by asserting the essential goodness of human nature, whether in Christ or in us.[7] Regarding Eutychianism and Monophysitism (and, by extension, Monothelitism), the evidence is less clear. Dods allows that Christ experienced various infirmities but insists that his flesh was free from the necessity of death and corruption; rather, he voluntarily surrendered his life.[8] It may be that Dods means that Christ's humanity was naturally prone to death and decay but that his divine power regulated these natural

---

[4] Nestorianism, it bears recalling, is a set of doctrines condemned by ecumenical councils and may not reflect accurately Nestorius' own views. Lee, 'Humanity of Christ', p. 50, claims that Irving is orthodox because he affirms Chalcedon's two-nature Christology. But the Definition of Chalcedon also states that Christ is 'like us in all respects, apart from sin' and speaks of 'the characteristics of each nature … coming together to form one person and subsistence' (H. Bettenson [ed.], *Documents of the Christian Church* [New York: Oxford University Press, 1947], p. 73). Our study shows that the fathers understood Christ's sinlessness to exclude already-sinful passions. Furthermore, Irving counts constitutional sin as a characteristic of Christ's human nature, yet one which does not contribute to the formation of his person. Irving, then, fails the test of Chalcedon. Cf. Bathrellos, 'Sinlessness', pp. 115–17; Crisp, *Divinity and Humanity*, p. 113.
[5] *CW* 5, pp. 215–16.
[6] Nantomah, 'Jesus the God-Man', p. 217 (Monophysitism); Dorries, *Incarnational Christology*, pp. 364–70 (Eutychianism).
[7] See ch. 2.1.1.
[8] *Incarnation*, pp. 215–27.

effects in keeping with his will. In this case, Dods would be of one mind with the fathers.[9] If, though, Dods means that Christ's humanity was inherently immortal and incorruptible, so that his death required a miracle,[10] then Dods does subscribe to Monophysitism – specifically, to the extreme form known as Aphthartodocetism.[11] Should this be the case, the clash between Dods and Irving would prove to be a contest of equal and opposite heresies.

5.1.2 Karl Barth

Barth's *CD* I/2 criticizes the early church for failing to teach that Christ assumed human nature in the fullness of its fallen, sinful state. It is ironic that Barth cites Nyssen as one of two examples of this failing, for Nyssen strikingly describes God's Son as assuming our 'filth', our 'sinful human soul', our thorn-cursed, straying, serpentine, 'sinful nature'. Barth's second example comes from Pope Honorius I's pronouncement that Christ assumed human nature as created by God, not as vitiated by sin. Although this study has not investigated Honorius, we note that his pronouncement echoes Pope Leo I's First *Tome*, which uses similar language to teach that the Son overcame original sin by the virginal conception while condescending to bear sin's consequences. Barth's own position has terminological similarities to that of Nyssen (and Irenaeus and Cyril) and conceptual similarities to that of Honorius (and of all the fathers surveyed in this study).[12] The Swiss divine does differ from his patristic forebears in denying a causal connection from Adam's sin to our own and in affirming an actualistic metaphysics.[13]

---

[9] According to J. S. Romanides, response to V. C. Samuel, 'One Incarnate Nature of God the Word', *Greek Orthodox Theological Review* 10.2 (Winter 1964–5), pp. 52–3 (52),

> Most Fathers would rather say that the human nature of Christ was by nature mortal but not by nature under the power or sentence of death and corruption which are the wages of sin. In this sense even angels are by nature mortal. Only God is by nature immortal. It is for this reason that the death of the Lord of Glory in the flesh was voluntary and not the wages of personal or inherited sin.

[10] Bruce, *Humiliation*, p. 261, warns against interpreting Dods in this latter sense.
[11] On which heresy, see Bruce, *Humiliation*, pp. 58, 268; Weinandy, *Likeness*, p. 35, n. 39. Cf. McFarland, *In Adam's Fall*, p. 136, n. 30: 'Insofar as [the Aphthartodocetists] denied that Christ's human nature had any natural susceptibility to suffering, while also maintaining that he willingly subjected himself to it, their position is arguably not as discontinuous with standard defenses of Christ's "unfallen" human nature as it may first appear.'
[12] Bromiley, 'Reformers', pp. 84–5, suggests that by *CD* III/2 Barth had moved closer to the traditional view that he criticizes in *CD* I/2.
[13] McCormack, *Orthodox and Modern*, pp. 206–13, 219–29. Cf. Jones, *Humanity of Christ*, p. 38.

5.1.3 T. F. Torrance and Colin Gunton

Unlike their continental mentor, Torrance and Gunton recognize antecedents in the early church for the doctrine of Christ's fallen flesh. They correctly interpret Nazianzen and the other Greek fathers as claiming that, in the act of assumption, God's Son healed and sanctified the fallen humanity which he assumed. While Gunton merely nods to the fathers, Torrance extensively documents their support. His accusation of Tertullian, Augustine, Leo's *Tome*, and the Chalcedonian Definition as fomenters of the 'Latin heresy' of an unfallen humanity in Christ, however, is problematic. True, the Latin fathers do not use the language of fallenness or sinfulness as the Greeks sometimes do, but conceptually both Latins and Greeks concur that Christ's humanity was fallen in his mother and regained in the Incarnation a sinlessness which is prelapsarian in the sense of reflecting Edenic innocence, yet still postlapsarian in the sense of suffering from many of the Fall's effects.

Torrance's historical reconstruction suffers from various inconsistencies. For instance, he enlists support from *Contra Apollinarium* and Hilary of Poitiers, despite the latter's buffering of Christ's soul from affliction and the former's insistence on Christ's prelapsarian sinlessness in language as strong as Leo's *Tome*'s, if not more so. Likewise, Torrance critiques the Chalcedonian Definition for not stating that Christ's humanity was fallen. The Council of Chalcedon asserted the normative authority of the original Creed of Nicaea, the Nicene-Constantinopolitan Creed, and, as mentioned above, Leo's *Tome*.[14] Neither of these earlier creeds speaks of Christ's humanity as fallen, yet Torrance does not critique them, while Leo's *Tome* does ascribe to Christ the infirmities inflicted by the Fall, yet suffers Torrance's censure. Such inconsistencies undermine the reliability of the 'Latin heresy' as a patristic paradigm, at least through Chalcedon and as regards the status of Christ's humanity vis-à-vis the Fall. On this doctrine Torrance, like Gunton and other twentieth-century theologians on various matters, presents Christian intellectual history in terms of (good, non-Augustinian) Greek East versus (bad, Augustinian) Latin West.[15] These dualistic accounts have come under serious scrutiny recently, not

---

[14] Cyril, *Select Letters*, p. xxxix.
[15] Williams, *Ideas* (see my critique in ch 3 n. 3); Aulén, *Christus Victor*; G. E. Demacopoulos and A. Papanikolaou, 'Augustine and the Orthodox: "The West" in the East', in *Orthodox Readings of Augustine* (ed. G. E. Demacopoulos and A. Papanikolaou; Crestwood, NY: St Vladimir's Seminary

least as employed by Torrance and Gunton.[16] Although our own examination
has partitioned the fathers into Greek (Chapter 3) and Latin (Chapter 4),
repeatedly we have noted the interchange between the two wings of the church
so as to avoid portraying them as hermetically (or hermeneutically) sealed off
from one another.

5.1.4 Thomas Weinandy

Weinandy corrects Torrance's patristic perspective both by demonstrating
consensus between the Christian East and Westerners like Tertullian,
Augustine, and Leo on Christ's participation in Fall-consequent infirmities and
by acknowledging Hilary of Poitiers' shortcoming in this regard. Yet Weinandy
is so intent on underscoring the fathers' attributions of postlapsarian elements
to the Incarnation that, like Torrance, he fails to do justice to patristic use
of prelapsarian language for Christ's sinlessness. Whereas Torrance reacts
against such language in Leo's *Tome*, Weinandy successfully contextualizes
Leo's statements but disagrees with Honorius' pronouncement that, insofar as
it lacked the law of sin in the flesh, Christ's humanity was unfallen.[17] Weinandy
ignores similar ideas in Irenaeus, Tertullian, and *Contra Apollinarium*, thus
imitating Irving's and Torrance's lapsarian lopsidedness.

Press, 2008), pp. 11–40 (20–1, 27–8, 31–2, 37); Gunton, *Promise*, ch. 3; Gunton, *The One, the Three and the Many*. Torrance's narrative of doctrinal history as a whole is more nuanced: see J. Radcliff, 'T.F. Torrance in the light of Stephen Holmes' Critique of Contemporary Trinitarian Thought', *Evangelical Quarterly* 86.1 (2014), pp. 21–38.

[16] On Eastern 'physicalist-Incarnationist' versus Western 'juridical-redemption' soteriologies: Keating, *Appropriation*, pp. 289–93 (quotes from 290). On various East-versus-West political and theological explanations of the Nestorian controversy: Fairbairn, *Grace and Christology*, pp. 6–11. On Torrance's 'Latin heresy' and other dualisms: D. Farrow, 'T. F. Torrance and the Latin Heresy', *First Things* (December 2013), n.p. Cited 22 September 2016. Online: https://www.firstthings.com/article/2013/12/t-f-torrance-and-the-latin-heresy; Radcliff, *Thomas F. Torrance and the Church Fathers*, pp. 120–3, 138–48, 187–97. On Cappadocian 'social trinitarianism' versus Augustinian 'monism' (as claimed by Gunton, among others): M. R. Barnes, 'Augustine in Contemporary Trinitarian Theology', *TS* 56.2 (1995), pp. 237–50; the whole of *HTR* 100.2 (April 2007), including L. Ayres, '*Nicaea and Its Legacy*: An Introduction', pp. 141–4; J. Behr, 'Response to Ayres: The Legacies of Nicaea, East and West', pp. 145–52; K. Anatolios, 'Yes and No: Reflections on Lewis Ayres, Nicaea and Its Legacy', pp. 153–8; B. Nausner, 'The Failure of a Laudable Project: Gunton, the Trinity, and Self-Understanding', *SJT* 62.4 (2009), pp. 403–20; J. McNall, *A Free Corrector: Colin Gunton and the Legacy of Augustine* (Minneapolis: Fortress, 2015).

[17] Weinandy, *Likeness*, pp. 35–7, incl. n. 41. McFarland, *In Adam's Fall*, pp. 121, 134, n. 14, finds fault with Weinandy's interpretation of Aquinas. Weinandy's view of a distancing of Christ's humanity from ours by medieval theologians seems generally accurate; cf. Adams, *What Sort of Human Nature?*. Yet here Sturch's observation is apt: many theologians of the past whose Christologies seem overly rarefied still showed 'a passionate (some might even say excessive) devotion, not to God the Word, but to the human figure of Jesus' (*The Word and the Christ*, p. 182).

5.1.5 The unfallenness theologians

Unlike the diversity of historical reconstructions among the modern fallenness advocates, their unfallenness counterparts maintain a single narrative, which seconds Barth's: they claim that the orthodox view ever has been that God's Son assumed an unfallen humanity. Dods, Bruce, Mackintosh, and Macleod all note a patristic tendency 'to downplay Christ's historical humanity and infirmities, a tendency which they see as evidence that the fathers were far from ascribing a fallen, sinful humanity to him. Bruce and Mackintosh, influenced as they are by modern kenoticism, are particularly critical of the waxing eclipse of the humanity of Jesus of Nazareth throughout the patristic and medieval periods in both the East and the West.

The unfallenness theologians are right to affirm the fathers' consensus that, from the womb, Christ's humanity existed in a condition of sinlessness, which some of them describe in prelapsarian terms. Yet, as this study has shown, some Greek fathers allow the terms 'fallen' and 'sinful' to be used of his flesh, and fathers both Greek and Latin (albeit haltingly for Hilary) attribute to him not only outward but also inward infirmities, such as fear and grief. Here the extensive patristic research of Torrance and Weinandy provides a valuable corrective to the unfallenness representatives' one-sided historical account. For example, Weinandy's contextualization of Leo's prelapsarian statement in his *Tome*, coupled with the Council of Chalcedon's sanction of it as an authoritative source, defeats Bruce's objection that Leo and Chalcedon do not address Christ's human infirmities and their relationship to his deity and so inaugurate an era of abstract Christologizing.[18] Likewise, Torrance's location of the *non-assumptus* within the broader sweep of Greek fallenness teaching counters the contention by all five unfallenness champions that Nazianzen had in mind simply a morally neutral assumption of human mind by the Logos.

Dods, followed by Macleod, accuses Irving of Gnostic and Nestorian proclivities. As noted in 5.1.1 above, this study concurs. Macleod also extends the charge of Nestorianism to Torrance.[19] There it sticks less well, for, as 1.3.2

---

[18] *Humiliation*, pp. 65–8.

[19] Dods, *Incarnation*, pp. viii–xi, 234–6, 285–8, 316–17, 326, 420–45, 452–9, 569–70, 73 (on Irving); Macleod, *Person of Christ*, p. 228; *Jesus is Lord*, pp. 128–9 (on Irving and Torrance). Chiarot, *Unassumed*, p. 164, also suggests 'a latent Nestorianism' in Torrance (cf. 209). By contrast (and perhaps as a testament to the difficulty of Torrance's thought), B. L. McCormack, 'The Ontological Presuppositions of Barth's Doctrine of the Atonement', in *The Glory of the Atonement: Biblical,*

of this study has discussed, Torrance envisages Christ as engaged in lifelong combat with 'our self-will' and 'our carnal mind' as present in the rest of us, not our purified mind and will as present in himself.[20] Torrance's designation of Christ's sinless humanity as 'fallen' reflects that term's use by Nestorianism's arch-antagonist, Cyril of Alexandria. Besides Irving, none of the fallenness proponents here studied depict schizophrenic friction within Christ; none dichotomize the predicates of his personhood and human nature;[21] and, when speaking of Christ's humanity, none use the term 'sinful' to refer to sin per se, but only to its associates (e.g. temptation and the suffering of divine judgement). Thus none of them share Irving's condemnation as 'Gnostorian'.[22]

5.1.6 Summary of findings concerning historical claims

In summary, the various versions of the early history of Christology here canvassed are mutually corrective. Barth and the unfallenness advocates rightly see Christ's prelapsarian sinlessness affirmed across the early church but miss the accompanying affirmation of his salvific solidarity with our postlapsarian state. Weinandy (and, less accurately, Irving) do the opposite, seeing what the aforementioned theologians miss and missing what they see. Torrance combines the strengths and weaknesses of both the above versions by postulating a pro-fallenness East versus an increasingly anti-fallenness West. Based on the East–West polarity in his own historical reconstruction, Gunton may be grouped with Torrance's version; or, based on his endorsement of *In the Likeness of Sinful Flesh*, he may be associated with Weinandy's version.

We also found mixed results concerning the heresies condemned by the early church and, according to Torrance, the one countenanced in its Latin half. Irving's Gnostic and Nestorian tendencies are plausible; Dods's

---

Historical, & Practical Perspectives: Essays in Honor of Roger Nicole (ed. C. E. Hill and F. A. James III; Downers Grove, IL: InterVarsity, 2004), pp. 346–66 (352, n. 9), sees a rarefied Apollinarianism in Torrance.

[20] Quotations from *Incarnation*, p. 118; *Atonement*, p. 440, respectively.

[21] Gunton does call attention to Irving's person–nature distinction in 'Two Dogmas', p. 369, and *Christ and Creation*, p. 53, n. 13, but Gunton's own practice does not follow Irving's thoroughgoing compartmentalization of the two with regard to sinfulness.

[22] Kapic, 'Assumption', pp. 155–9, 164, and Davidson, 'Pondering', pp. 378–9, n. 16, 397, both raise the question of Nestorianism in relation to fallenness advocates, including Irving, Barth, Torrance, and Weinandy.

Aphthartodocetism is possible; the Nestorianism of the other fallenness thinkers and the 'Latin heresy' of the fathers here surveyed are improbable.[23] Having addressed the modern debaters' historical claims, we turn to proposals regarding theological taxonomy and terminology arising from our study.

5.2 Righting theology: Taxonomy

Just as the adequacy of the East-versus-West taxonomy used by Torrance and Gunton has come under fire, so also has the fallenness-versus-unfallenness taxonomy.[24] We have seen the spectrum of thought of twenty theologians, ancient and modern. We now evaluate and build upon two of the proposed new taxonomies for the fallenness debate.

5.2.1 Sykes' taxonomy

In a 1972 essay, Stephen W. Sykes presented a fourfold classification of views of Christ's humanity along with a representative of each view:

1. Christ assumed a humanity transformed at conception into a new sort of humanity (Nyssen, as interpreted by Srawley's 1906 *JTS* article)
2. Christ assumed humanity weakened by the Fall but not corrupted in nature by it (R. L. Ottley, *The Doctrine of the Incarnation*)
3. Christ assumed a humanity vitiated by all the effects of the Fall (Barth, *CD* I/2:151–52; cf., though, IV/2:27–28)
4. Christ assumed original unfallen humanity (Leo's *Tome*).[25]

The imprecision of Sykes' taxonomy appears when we compare his placement of Nyssen, Barth, and Leo with our study's findings. Chapter 3.4 showed that Nyssen holds that the sinful humanity assumed by the Logos was cleansed

---

[23] Note that this judgement against Torrance's 'Latin heresy' construct applies strictly to the fallenness debate and the patristic era through Chalcedon. Cf. Radcliff, *Thomas F. Torrance and the Church Fathers*, p. 193, who finds the whole construct too simplistic.

[24] Kapic, 'Assumption', pp. 163–4; Hastings, 'Pneumatological Christology', pp. 287–90; Davidson, 'Pondering', p. 397; cf. Allen, *The Christ's Faith*, p. 128.

[25] S. W. Sykes, 'The Theology of the Humanity of Christ', in *Christ Faith and History* (ed. S. W. Sykes and J. P. Clayton; Cambridge: Cambridge University Press, 1972), pp. 53–72 (58–9; the wording of the above taxonomy is mine).

at conception, so that Christ suffered no sinful passions, yet it remained ἁμαρτικήν in that it was a Fall-affected humanity until its full deification in the Resurrection. Likewise, Chapter 1.2 revealed that, for Barth, original sin is unrepeated in the Incarnation; rather, as Sykes' citation of *CD* IV/2 reflects, Christ ever actualizes himself as our substitute under God's judgement, hence simultaneously 'sinful' (in accepting a sinner's punishment) and sinless (in doing so by God's will). Lastly, Leo's *Tome* teaches *both* Christ's prelapsarian sinlessness *and* his sharing our postlapsarian weaknesses. If treated as mutually exclusive, totalizing explications, Sykes' categories turn out to be too static to capture the fullness of these theologians' views of the Christ-event. These categories may be rehabilitated, however, as potentially overlapping markers of the 'temporally indexed qualities of the humanity he assumed'[26] at different times within the entirety of that event.

5.2.2 Hastings' taxonomy

Precisely by focusing on such 'temporally indexed qualities' and the temporal transitions accompanying them, scholars lately have used John Calvin's Christology to pursue a way forward in the fallenness debate.[27] Hastings explains that, for Calvin, 'the humanity which the Son received, was, in its derivation from Mary, fallen'; by the Holy Spirit's intervention, however, that nature 'was purified … as he was conceived' so as to be free from inherited guilt and sinful proclivities.[28] Calvin understood such a humanity to be morally unfallen – as 'pure and undefiled as *would have been true before Adam's fall*', according to the *Institutes* – while still suffering the amoral infirmities brought by the Fall.[29] In terms of Sykes' categories, the humanity which God's Son made his own was in Category Three up to the moment of conception, at which point it was transformed (as in Category One) so that, as regards

---

[26] McFarland, *In Adam's Fall*, pp. 124–5 (quote from latter page).

[27] Hastings, 'Pneumatological Christology', pp. 287–90; Allen, 'Calvin's Christ', pp. 394–5; Ahn, 'Humanity of Christ', p. 147.

[28] Hastings, 'Pneumatological Christology', p. 287; but cf. Allen, 'Calvin's Christ', pp. 388–400; *idem*, *The Christ's Faith*, pp. 132–5, who denies that Calvin teaches inherited guilt.

[29] Kapic, 'Assumption', pp. 160–1, on the latter page quoting J. Calvin, *The Institutes of the Christian Religion* (ed. J. T. McNeill; trans. F. L. Battles; Philadelphia: Westminster, 1960), 2.13.4 (italics Kapic's). Cf. Ahn, 'Humanity of Christ', pp. 145–7, 151–4; Allen, 'Calvin's Christ', pp. 394–5; Hastings, 'Pneumatological Christology', pp. 286–7. Both Ahn and Hastings (or their editors) incorrectly cite *Institutes* 2.13.4: Ahn, p. 151, gives it as 3.13.1; Hastings, p. 287, n. 35, gives it as 2.8.4.

the Fall's moral effects, it became Category Four humanity, but as regards the Fall's amoral effects, Category Two. Hastings contrasts Calvin's view with two others: the view that Christ's humanity was created *ex nihilo* and therefore unfallen, as held by Menno Simons and Jonathan Edwards;[30] and Irving's, Barth's, and Torrance's alleged view of 'a gradual process, by which the person of Christ (viewed as a whole person) is able to be obedient always, but by overcoming a human nature which is not itself purified until the experience of the sufferings of the Cross'.[31] Hastings fairly describes Irving's view (which fits under Sykes' Category Three)[32] but incorrectly identifies it with Barth's and Torrance's positions, which do depict Christ's own human nature as purified from conception onward.

5.2.3 A Sykes-Hastings taxonomy

A corrected and combined Sykes-Hastings taxonomy, when applied to the twenty theologians covered in this study, yields the following results:

1. All but Weinandy concur that, prior to Christ's conception, the human nature which he was to assume existed in Mary in a state of original sin, broadly defined, and of subjection to all the effects of the Fall (Sykes' Category Three). Due to Weinandy's faith in the Immaculate Conception, for him Mary's humanity inhabits Sykes' Category Two, although her parents and the rest of Jesus' family line populate Category Three. For Irving, as noted above, Christ's humanity remains in Category Three until death.

2. All but Irving and Weinandy hold that at the time of Christ's conception, his humanity was transformed (Sykes' Category One). Of these, seventeen would accept Hastings' language of purification; Macleod prefers the language of creation (*ex virgine*, not *ex nihilo*). Weinandy would relocate the transformation to the time of Mary's conception.

[30] Other variations of this 'heavenly flesh' view have been held by some Gnostics and Marcionites (Irenaeus, *Haer.* 1.6.1; Tertullian, *Carn. Chr.* 1.16-17); Apollinaris, allegedly (see ch 3.2.2 and 3.3); and some Pietists (McFarland, 'Fallen or Unfallen?', p. 404, n. 18).
[31] Hastings, 'Pneumatological Christology', pp. 288–9 (quote from former page); he adds another category, involving pneumatology, which does not concern us here.
[32] McFarlane, *Christ and the Spirit*, pp. 138–47, cited in D. Rainey, 'Edward Irving and the Doctrine of the Humanity of Christ: "The Method Is By Taking Up the Fallen Humanity"' (paper presented at the annual meeting of the Wesleyan Theological Society, Anderson, Ind., 6 March 2009), p. 10.

3. All but Irving hold that, throughout Christ's earthly life, his humanity suffered the Fall's amoral weaknesses but not its moral corruption (Sykes' Category Two). In Hilary's case, and possibly in Dods's, this belief in Christ's infirmities is attenuated – severely so, for Hilary.

4. All but Irving teach that Christ's humanity was free from original sin and guilty propensities from at least the moment of his conception (or from the moment of his mother's conception, in Weinandy's case).[33] This is what Calvin, the modern unfallenness advocates, and the ancient fathers mean when they employ prelapsarian language with respect to Christ's flesh, and it is in this sense that Sykes' Category Four must be applied. Modern fallenness advocates may resist the terminology of unfallenness, but at the level of its intention, their doctrine harmonizes with it. As pro-fallenness theologian R. Michael Allen has observed, 'To some degree, then, the *fallenness* position simply insists on a logical distinction between Christ's assumption of flesh and the Spirit's sanctification of such flesh, whereas the *unfallenness* position insists that assumption and sanctification are cotemporaneous and, furthermore, logically synonymous.'[34]

The usage above of a fresh taxonomy provides insight into the underlying consensus among the Greek and Latin fathers, modern unfallenness proponents, and most of the fallenness thinkers surveyed in this study. The two most consistent outliers are Weinandy and Irving. Weinandy stands close to the consensus but defers some of its elements from Christ's to Mary's conception. Irving, though, deviates radically from the consensus. The association of his name with other fallenness theologians, whether done by themselves or their opponents, serves as a red herring regarding the fundamental differences between him and them. Another distraction from the consensus is the language of fallenness and unfallenness itself. To a consideration of these and related terms we now turn.

---

[33] Thus when K. Sonderegger, *Systematic Theology Volume 1, The Doctrine of God* (Minneapolis: Fortress, 2015), p. 217, comments that 'Barth and Irving do not persuade … in their rejection of Christ's absolute sinlessness', she misreads Barth but not Irving.

[34] *The Christ's Faith*, p. 130, n. 105 (italics his). He continues, 'Yet cotemporaneous action fails to sustain the ontological relation between Mary's fallen humanity and Christ's inherited human nature, a concern which seems to require a logical (if not temporal) ordering.' Cf. Baillie, *God Was in Christ*, p. 17, who suggests that the fallenness debate involves 'an unnecessary and unreal theological dilemma'.

5.3 Righting theology: Terminology

The problem of definitions underlies the whole fallenness debate.[35] What is meant when theologians assert that God's Son 'assumed' a humanity that was 'fallen', 'sinful', or their antonyms, and might clearer terminology bring the debate closer to resolution? In what follows, we assess each of these terms.

5.3.1 'Assumed'

In the mid-twentieth century, Donald Baillie surveyed the terrain of the fallenness debate and found it beset by a terminological fog. He singled out the phrases 'fallen human nature' and 'assumption of human nature' as problematic.[36] We shall address the latter phrase first before dealing with the former phrase below. The term 'assumed' and similar words, such as 'took' and 'received', describe the action of the Logos in initiating the hypostatic union with human nature. Ambiguity arises from the fact that these terms may be applied to Christ's human nature in either of two conditions: the condition *out of which* he assumed it or the condition *into which* he assumed it. Thus Athanasius, for instance, can write without contradiction both that the Logos took enslaved, errant flesh and that he received his body from his mother as a pure temple and sacerdotal robe,[37] for the Alexandrian is considering two different aspects of the same compound event of the assumption. Fallenness advocates may wish to seize on the former of Athanasius' statements and unfallenness champions on the latter, but both are gripping opposite halves of the same whole. Given the consensual taxonomy established above, a claim like, 'The Son assumed depraved human nature,' ought to be acceptable to the most ardent Protestant unfallenness proponent – so long as it is understood that this is the condition whence, not whither, the Son took it. (For Catholic theologians, Marian dogma would complicate acceptance of such a claim.) Likewise, fallenness supporters must recognize that when their unfallenness counterparts speak of the Word's taking unfallen flesh, this does not require belief in the Immaculate Conception, a new act of *ex nihilo* creation, a

---

[35] Kapic, 'Assumption', p. 164.
[36] Baillie, *God Was in Christ*, p. 17.
[37] See ch. 3.2.1.

pre-existent humanity of Christ, or any similar device.[38] It only need mean that humanity which in Mary exists as fallen into sin has been relieved of that condition in her Son's act of Incarnation.

5.3.2 'Unfallen'

Before discussing the attribution of unfallenness specifically to Christ's humanity, two preliminary objections to prelapsarian language in general call for comment. First, those who deny that humanity ever existed in an unfallen state may protest that there was no 'pre-' before the *lapsus*; the Incarnation presents us with a new, not a renewed, humanity. In response, one may note that the biblical metanarrative certainly depicts a prelapsarian state, however briefly, and its logical and theological priority to the Fall, if not chronological priority, is crucial to avoiding metaphysical monism or dualism.[39] Even if there were no historical time during which humanity was unfallen, the term 'prelapsarian' could still be permissible either as a metaphor or as a (theo) logical abstraction.[40] Nonetheless, belief in a historical Fall best fits with an anti-Gnostic faith which affirms history as the pre-eminent arena of divine revelation.[41] Nor is such belief incompatible with current scientific theory regarding early human history, so long as one eschews an overly literalistic or perfectionistic reading of the opening chapters of Genesis.[42] In the dialogue with science, the model put forward by Irenaeus, the Cappadocians, and Bruce of the Fall as a deviation from the divinely intended developmental trajectory is more fruitful than Athanasius' and Augustine's model of the Fall as a plummet from an original human perfection (or near-perfection).

Secondly, it has been claimed that the discourse of prelapsarianism presumes a theological method which moves from Adam to Christ, Creation (and Fall) to

---

[38] For example, 'a Platonic *real* perfect human nature different from the *actual* fallen human nature that we now have', as suggested in the critique of the unfallenness view in Eugenio, *Communion with God*, p. 43.

[39] But T. A. Noble, 'Original sin and the Fall: definitions and a proposal', pp. 113–16, follows Williams, *Ideas*, in arguing that a historical Fall is necessary to skirt those two metaphysical conclusions. Cf. M. Shuster, *The Fall and Sin: What We Have Become as Sinners* (Grand Rapids: Eerdmans, 2004), pp. 5, 6, 8–12.

[40] See for example, M. F. Wiles, 'Does Christology Rest on a Mistake?', *Christ Faith and History*, pp. 3–12.

[41] See J. N. Oswalt, *The Bible among the Myths: Unique Revelation or Just Ancient Literature?* (Grand Rapids: Zondervan, 2009).

[42] Cf. P. R. Baelz, 'A Deliberate Mistake?', in *Christ Faith and History*, pp. 13–34; Shuster, *The Fall and Sin*, chs 1–4; R. J. Berry and T. A. Noble (eds), *Darwin, Creation and the Fall*; Johnson, *Humanity*, pp. 12–13; and ch. 2.2.4 of this volume.

Redemption, rather than the reverse, as in Torrance (and Barth).[43] The concern here is that such theologizing starts elsewhere than with Christ and so forces him into a presuppositional Procrustean bed instead of respecting him as the unconstrained Lord and sole revelatory Word of God and so beginning with him. There is much merit in this Barthian concern. Again, though, the biblical metanarrative must be respected, including the progress of revelation which it records. In structuring its scriptural canon, the early church did not place the Gospels before Genesis. On the other hand, neither did patristic exegetes simply move from Adam to Christ, from a Unitarian account of Creation and Fall to a tardily Trinitarian Redemption story. As sampled in this study,[44] they moved from the pre-incarnate Christ to Adam to the incarnate Christ, from the Son's presence to humanity in Genesis to his union with humanity in the Gospels. Likewise, it is possible for our notions of a prelapsarian state to be refined rather than replaced by the Incarnation.

Having defended the use of unfallen or prelapsarian terminology generally, we now address its application to Christ. Such talk, as noted previously, may make it sound as if his is a human nature utterly unaffected by the Fall or unconnected with the fallen human race (such as in Simons' and Edwards' view as discussed by Hastings). The 'pre-' in 'prelapsarian' may even give the impression that his humanity existed before the Fall. None of these views, however, is standard in unfallenness tradition, which asserts that Christ drew his humanity from his mother and endured the infirmities which beset postlapsarian life.[45] Considering the potential for unfallenness language to be misunderstood, Bruce McCormack has proffered 'restored' as the adjective of choice over 'unfallen' with reference to Calvin's view of Christ's humanity.[46] To speak of Christ's human nature as becoming in its assumption a 'restored', 'redeemed', 'sanctified', or 'uprighted' human nature communicates something

---

[43] Eugenio, *Communion*, pp. 43–4.

[44] Chapter 3.1.1 and 3.2 (introduction).

[45] Kapic, 'Assumption', p. 164. According to Crisp, *Divinity and Humanity*, pp. 115–16, and McFarland *In Adam's Fall*, pp. 121–2, 135–6, n. 27, the unfallenness tradition typically has taught that Christ freely bore the effects of fallenness (i.e. infirmities) but not their cause, fallenness itself (construed in terms of original sin). See also ch. 2 of this study.

[46] B. L. McCormack, *For Us and Our Salvation: Incarnation and Atonement in the Reformed Tradition* (n.p.: Princeton Theological Seminary, 1993), p. 18, quoted in Allen, 'Calvin's Christ', p. 395. Cf. Kapic, *Communion with God*, p. 101. McCormack is responding to the potential misreading of unfallenness as creation *ex nihilo*; Kapic, to the caricature of a prelapsarian Christ 'completely alien and oblivious to the painful realities of a fallen world'.

of the dynamism of the Sykes-Hastings taxonomy in ways that the static- and perfectionistic-sounding terms 'unfallen' and 'prelapsarian' do not.

5.3.3 'Fallen'

Like its privative, the term 'fallen' cries out for careful delineation. For instance, Kevin Chiarot has bemoaned Torrance's 'lack of a crisp definition of "fallen human nature"'.[47] One such 'crisp definition' comes, appropriately, from Oliver Crisp: fallenness means sinfulness – specifically, possession of original sin. Crisp's definition relies on the traditional Western view, which, he claims, reduces to unorthodox nonsense any attempt to distinguish fallenness from sinfulness.[48] For Christ to have a fallen humanity would be to have a humanity inclined towards sin, which itself would be sinful because it would be deviant from God's norm for human nature. In this case, Christ would be 'loathsome to God'.[49] Crisp grants that 'Christ's sinless nature was affected by the Fall without actually being fallen' in that he 'possessed the symptoms and effects of being sinful in terms of moral and physical weakness, without himself possessing the sinful human nature that gives rise to these effects'.[50] Crisp represents the general stance of this study's unfallenness theologians, as demonstrated in Chapter 2.[51]

Irving would disagree with Crisp on the definition of original sin but would concur that fallenness entails sinfulness, including inclinations towards sin, which are themselves already sinful. He would challenge Crisp's separation of the effects of the Fall from their cause, sin. Instead, both the effects and the cause are bound up in the indivisible reality of fallenness. It is precisely by bearing and overcoming the 'moral and physical weaknesses' which he has in common with the rest of us, along with the sin which underlies them, that Christ redeems us.[52]

---

[47] Chiarot, *Unassumed*, p. 199.
[48] Crisp, *Divinity and Humanity*, pp. 93, 106–8, 115, 117.
[49] Ibid., pp. 105–6, 108–14. Variations on the quote appear multiple times in these pages.
[50] Ibid., pp. 115–16. Ahn, 'Humanity of Christ', pp. 149, 151–3, falsely claims that Crisp and other unfallenness advocates (with the exception of Calvin) deny that Christ's humanity possessed infirmities, including mortality. Ahn's article suffers from severe disengagement from unfallenness literature.
[51] For a concise book-length rebuttal to Crisp using T. F. Torrance as a test case, see D. J. Cameron, *Flesh and Blood: A Dogmatic Sketch Concerning the Fallen Nature View of Christ's Human Nature* (Eugene, OR: Wipf & Stock, 2016).
[52] Crisp, *Divinity and Humanity*, p. 114, claims that if Christ's humanity had original sin, it would contaminate his divinity. Irving argues the reverse: the divine Spirit ever enabled Christ to suppress his flesh's wickedness and convert its motions into God-pleasing ones. See ch. 1.1.1 of this study. Allen, *The Christ's Faith*, p. 127, n. 91, critiques Crisp's view as implying an incipient Monophysitism.

The other fallenness theologians here surveyed agree with Crisp that the cause (original sin) and its effects may be uncoupled but insist that the term 'fallenness' applies to the effects even absent their cause. Thus Barth and Torrance particularly relate being fallen to being treated as a sinner by God and humanity, whether or not one actually is a sinner. Gunton speaks of the biological and sociological conditioning of the world towards disorder, to which even a person in perfect relationship with God – as Christ was – may contribute. Weinandy stresses the full solidarity in human afflictions, which even a non-concupiscent Saviour experiences. For these scholars, original sin is a constituent of fallenness but not necessarily or exclusively so. They distinguish between '*metaphysical*' and '*moral* aspects of fallenness'.[53] This distinction recalls Irenaeus' affirmation of Christ's 'fallen' flesh in relation to death but denial that he ever 'fell' under the power of sin, as well as Cyril's testimony that the Lord took a 'fallen' body but purified its proclivities.

The fact that some Greek fathers did use the language of fallenness relativizes Crisp's and the other unfallenness proponents' appeal to historical usage. The definition of fallenness which equates it with (original) sinfulness is not the only one available from church tradition. Furthermore, the Sykes-Hastings taxonomy above has exposed that, Irving excepted, ancient and modern users of fallenness language are in harmony with those who do not use it regarding the issues of Christ's liberty from original sin and fraternity in human infirmities. One could argue, then, that the usage or non-usage of fallenness terminology is a matter of *adiaphora*, not anathemas.

Irving's exception, though, signals a concern: fallenness advocates themselves do not present a unified definition of the term. On its own, this leads to confusion. This confusion is deepened by Irving's fallenness comrades' promotion of him, although his definition differs from theirs. Exacerbating the situation is that the unfallenness tradition has a unified definition of fallenness – Crisp's – which can be applied to Christ only at the risk of heterodoxy. Worse yet, Irving's definition hews closely enough to the unfallenness tradition's as to overshadow him with suspicion of heterodoxy and render the rest of the fallenness camp guilty by (sometimes invited) association.[54]

---

[53] Hastings, 'Pneumatological Christology', p. 286 (italics his).
[54] See for example, Macleod, *Jesus is Lord*, ch. 5.

Regardless of exact definition, speech about Christ's 'fallen humanity' may evoke the opposite misunderstanding to talk of his 'unfallen humanity'. He may be viewed as so thoroughly enmeshed in sin's web as to be one of us indeed, but too much so to save. But the humanity of Christ is less prelapsarian or postlapsarian than *exlapsarian*.[55] Here again McCormack's language of Christ's 'restored' human nature and similar adjectives such as 'redeemed', 'sanctified', or 'uprighted' commend themselves as alternatives, ones whose implications for our own humanity will be explored subsequently.

5.3.4 'Sinful'

Modern unfallenness and fallenness theologians alike tend to use the term 'sinful' as interchangeable with 'fallen' and either deny or apply both terms to Christ's humanity. Bruce is the exception: in his later writings, he allows that Christ had 'sinful flesh' yet was unfallen. The other unfallenness advocates and Irving use 'sinful' in its most straightforward sense, 'possessing sin'. Barth, Torrance, and Weinandy use 'sinful' to mean 'suffering the effects of sin, whether possessing sin or not'. This usage has a precedent in Nyssen. Bruce and Gunton can use 'sinful' for 'being solicited by sin'.

Bruce, Gunton, and Dods agree that sinfulness and fallenness are, strictly speaking, properties of persons, not their physical natures. More recently, McFarland has distinguished between sinfulness as an attribute of persons and fallenness (in the fallenness advocates' sense of the suffering of the Fall's effects) as an attribute of their natures. He sees this distinction as disabling us from blaming our nature for our personal sinfulness while also enabling the second person of the Trinity to assume a fallen nature in common with ours without thereby becoming sinful.[56]

Setting aside these four thinkers' differences on the term 'fallen', their consensus concerning the term 'sinful' commends itself as promoting accurate, responsible discourse. To describe as 'sinful' the suffering of infirmities such as hunger, weariness, illness, loneliness, or sorrow and the temptations which

---

[55] Cf. Allen, *The Christ's Faith*: 'In fact, the occurrence [of the constant hallowing of Christ's flesh] may best be described as the Word's sanctification of a human nature *from* sinful flesh, albeit without morphing the humanity of Christ (post-conception) into a *tertium quid*' (131); Christ's humanity was '*sanctified from fallenness*' (132; all italics his).

[56] McFarland, *In Adam's Fall*, pp. 126–31. Sumner, 'Fallenness', seconds McFarland's distinction.

accompany these infirmities,[57] as well as the fleshly body in which we experience all the above, is to muddle cause and effect, means and ends, and risk fostering doctrines closer to those of Job's friends, Gnosticism, or Buddhism[58] than to orthodox Christianity. Granted, there is apostolic warrant for the phrase 'sinful flesh' (Rom. 8.3), but such an expression must be used carefully: Paul had a reputation for occasionally confusing his readers (2 Pet. 3.15-16), as the contentious exegetical history of Rom. 8.3 indicates.[59] Responsible theological discourse seeks to explicate biblical phraseology rather than simply repeating it when there is a strong likelihood that simple repetition will engender serious misunderstanding.[60] Thus the 1984 edition of the New International Version rendered Rom. 8.3's 'likeness of sinful flesh' as 'likeness of sinful man', while the New Living Translation interprets it as 'a body like the bodies we sinners have'.[61]

5.3.5 'Sinless'

The Sykes-Hastings taxonomy has revealed agreement among the fathers and modern debaters, except for Irving, that Christ's sinlessness must not be restricted to his divine nature or to the non-committal of actual sin; the roots of his humanity must be free from sin. This fact should allay the fears of those like Crisp who believe that fallenness proponents necessarily compromise Christ's sinlessness.[62] If, as urged above, the usage of 'sinful' is narrowed, then the usage of 'sinless' is widened. Yet scripture itself limits Christ's sinlessness: the Sinless One was 'made ... to be sin' (2 Cor. 5.21) and 'bore our sins in his body on the tree' (1 Pet. 2.24), coming 'in the likeness of sinful flesh and for

---

[57] For example, Weinandy, *Likeness*, p. 18.
[58] Cf. Machida, 'Jesus, Man of Sin'.
[59] Cf. chs 1.1.2, 1.2.1, 1.3.3, 1.5.2; 2.1.2, 2.2.4, 2.3.1, 2.5.1; 3.1.3, 3.2.1-2, 3.4, 3.5; 4.1.2, 4.2, 4.3, 4.4.2, 4.5.2.
[60] For example, the Nicene use of *homoousios* to clarify the New Testament's sonship language for Christ; the use of gender-inclusive language in various contemporary Bible translations (or, in the ESV's case, gender-inclusive footnotes).
[61] Cf. Noble, *Holy Trinity: Holy People*, p. 176, who equates Rom. 8.3's 'sinful flesh' with 'our sinful human race'.
[62] The inconsistency of Johnson, *Humanity*, on this point bears noting. He describes two definitions of sin, one which sees it as one's volitional rebellion against God and one which sees it as anything contrary to God's will. In order to retain the term 'original sin', Johnson chooses the second definition (11, 23). He depicts the state of fallenness as a state of original sin (22-5). When he asserts that Christ had a fallen human nature, however, Johnson claims that this does not compromise Christ's sinlessness because he never volitionally rebelled against God (25-7, 33-5; cf. 207). Here Johnson has switched hamartiologies in midstream. Shortly later he admits that, on his view, Christ had original sin (43; cf. 119), but then denies that Christ needed purification from it (49).

sin' (Rom. 8.3). These are the very passages upon which Irving established his position, but they can be incorporated into various views which avoid his extremes and which align with the consensus revealed by the Sykes-Hastings taxonomy. Particularly broad-based is the interpretation that Christ was counted counterfactually as sinful through identification with sinners. This interpretation certainly is not simply 'forensic', as though an angel or asteroid randomly were selected to stand in for sinful humanity. Instead, the consensual teaching sees an ontological foundation for Christ's forensic (or, more biblically, cultic) identification with sinners: God's Son takes our common nature, restoring it from sin upon assumption so that he can stand as the Sinless One for the sinful many, the Sinless One treated as sinful so that the sinful may be treated as sinless, the Sinless One actively overcoming sin so that the sinful may be delivered from its sway.[63]

5.3.6 A case study as a summary

Harry Johnson records a debate at a World Council of Churches committee meeting, which underscores the need for consensual definitions of the above terms or at least recognition of diversity in their usage. At the meeting, Torrance proposed, 'We need to take more seriously that the Word of God assumed our *sarx*, i.e. our fallen humanity (not one immaculately conceived) and in so doing hallowed it.' In response, Methodist theologian Albert Outler 'pointed out that Jesus Christ was "yet without sin." Was humanity therefore fallen on purpose? Is humanity sinful in itself?' Russian Orthodox patristic scholar Georges Florovsky likewise protested, 'If the divine assumes human nature, how can this nature be anything but sinless?'[64] Here communication broke down because of lack of clarity concerning the meanings of 'assumed' and 'fallen' and their relationships to 'sinful' and 'sinless' (and, implicitly, 'unfallen'). If the above discussion of these terms were taken into account, it would move the fallenness debate past the communicative impasse exemplified in the WCC meeting.

---

[63] This interpretation features in Barth, Torrance, the unfallenness theologians, Nazianzen, Cyril, Augustine, and Leo.

[64] Faith and Order Commission Paper, No. 23, in *Minutes of the Working Committee, July 1956, Herrenalb, Germany, Commission on Faith and Order, World Council of Churches*, quoted in Johnson, *Humanity*, pp. 172–3.

5.4 Further implications

If both fallenness and unfallenness theologians were to acknowledge their common ground and clarify their terminology, what would remain for them to discuss? Much, in point of fact. The following is a sampling of areas in which the implications of Christ's purifying assumption of fallen human nature require to be further explored.

5.4.1 Mariology

Any development in Christology carries special implications for Mariology. Torrance raised the issue of the Immaculate Conception in the WCC meeting described above. Historically, Protestant fallenness proponents from Irving forward have viewed this dogma as a misguided attempt to shield the all-holy Son of God from contact with original sin. Such quarantining runs counter to Jesus' modus operandi in the Gospels: he touches the unclean, eats with sinners, traverses impure territories (e.g. Samaria), and is baptized and crucified in solidarity with the wicked, but rather than being contaminated by these contacts, he brings healing, hallowing power to bear in each case. As we have seen, this is precisely what the patristic and contemporary consensus envisages as happening in the Virgin's womb when the Logos assumed defiled human nature. Yet the impulse towards affirming the Immaculate Conception has at least as much to do with promoting Mary's purity as Christ's.[65] Weinandy has demonstrated that it is possible to confess both the Immaculate Conception and Christ's assumption of 'sinful flesh'. Whether it is theologically responsible to confess both, however, or whether the former interferes with the soterio-logic of the latter by buffering Christ from sanctifying contact with original sin, is a matter for further discussion.

Another implication of the fallenness debate for Mariology touches on the delicate topic of Mary's virginity *in partu* and the alleged impassibility of her

---

[65] 'It is important to remember that the immaculate conception is formulated not to preserve Mary (and therefore Christ as the inheritor of her humanity) from original sin. Rather, it is founded on an argument from "fittingness" (i.e. it is fitting that a sinless Son should have a sinless mother).' – T. Perry, *Mary for Evangelicals: Toward an Understanding of the Mother of Our Lord* (Downers Grove, IL: InterVarsity, 2006), p. 280, n. 8; cf. 187–203; S. J. Boss, 'The Development of the Doctrine of Mary's Immaculate Conception', in *Mary: The Complete Resource* (ed. S. J. Boss; London: Continuum, 2007), pp. 207–35; Farrow, 'T. F. Torrance and the Latin Heresy'.

delivery of the Christ-child. Attempting to reclaim this ancient teaching for Protestant evangelicals, Tim Perry suggests, 'If Jesus stands alongside rather than beneath Adam, then it seems reasonable to assume that he stands outside the curse that has fallen on all Adam's sons and daughters, including pain in childbirth' (Gen 3:16).[66] Perry's logic clashes with the consensual evangel of a Saviour who assumes Adamic flesh and suffers its curse in order to re-create humanity. If his earthly life ended with sweat, thorns, and death reminiscent of the Edenic curse on Adam, it would be strange if that life began without the birth pangs inflicted on Eve.

5.4.2 Hamartiology

In various volumes on hamartiology over the past thirty years, the details of Christ's earthly experience (e.g. his emotions, the acts which he commits and those which he omits) play no normative role in shaping the doctrine of sin. Rather, various biblical teachings are woven together with strands of theological, philosophical, political, sociological, psychological, and literary discourse to produce a mesh so fine that no human being or act may slip through the net of depravity. If these hamartiologies were to be applied to the Jesus of the Gospels, it is unclear how he himself could escape the charge of sin, but instead he is presumed innocent and exempted from examination. The result is that orthodoxy is upheld – we are convicted as sinners, Christ is presented as the sinless, sin-loosing Saviour – but at the price of special pleading.[67] What follows are some general aspects of Christ's earthly experience which have a bearing on hamartiology.

Hebrews 4.15-16 teaches that Christ 'in every respect has been tempted as we are, yet without sin' and so can both sympathize with and support us in our trials. Much of the friction underlying the fallenness debate comes from

---

[66] Perry, *Mary for Evangelicals*, pp. 281–2. This belief first appears in the second-century *Ascension of Isaiah* 11.2-16; *Odes of Solomon* 19.6-9; and *Protevangelium of James* 19–20 (Perry, *Mary for Evangelicals*, pp. 123–8).

[67] McFarland, *In Adam's Fall*; Shuster, *The Fall and Sin*; C. Gestrich, *The Return of Splendor in the World: The Christian Doctrine of Sin and Forgiveness* (trans. D. W. Bloesch; Grand Rapids: Eerdmans, 1997); C. Plantinga, Jr., *Not the Way It's Supposed to Be: A Breviary of Sin* (Grand Rapids: Eerdmans, 1995); D. L. Smith, *With Willful Intent: A Theology of Sin* (Wheaton, IL: Victor, 1994); B. Ramm, *Offense to Reason: The Theology of Sin* (San Francisco: Harper & Row, 1985); and, to a somewhat lesser degree, M. E. Biddle, *Missing the Mark: Sin and Its Consequences in Biblical Theology* (Nashville: Abingdon, 2005). For a step in the right direction, see H. Connolly, *Sin* (London: Continuum, 2002).

the perceived tension between Christ's sympathy and his sinlessness. How can he truly sympathize if he never sinned even in thought or desire? What can he know, for instance, of the alcoholic's struggle to resist the lure of the bottle? On the other hand, how can he truly be sinless if he felt any attraction at all towards that with which he was tempted? Were his agonized pleas in Gethsemane mere playacting? Or again: How can he truly sympathize with me if he did not experience the temptations peculiar to my precise social, economic, political, historical, ethnic, genderal, or temperamental situation? To adapt Rosemary Ruether's famous query, can a male Saviour sympathize with Mary Magdalene, or even Theresa May?[68] On the other hand, how can he truly be sinless if he existed as one enmeshed within the systemic evils endemic to his own particular social, economic, political, and historical situations? In advising the paying of taxes to Rome, in filling his followers' nets with fish, was he not complicit in cruelty to the people and animals of Palestine?[69]

A perfectionism of sympathy would require that Christ become a sinner – indeed, that he assume into union with himself every last sinner in history.[70] A perfectionism of sinlessness would demand that no Incarnation occur, but that the Logos, like the Supreme Being of Gnosticism, maintain a distance from the world in order to remain untainted by it. The Christological consensus which we have identified steers between both these extremes, but its implications for hamartiology require to be worked out satisfactorily. These include an analysis of the qualities common to all encounters with temptation – the 'transcendentals of temptation', so to speak[71] – such that the experience of a particular range of temptations by a unique individual (in this case, Jesus) grants that individual a measure of insight sufficient for sympathizing with all others' temptations.

Another line of inquiry concerns the distinction between sinful and sinless (i.e. guilty and innocent) passions and their relation to Christ's humanity. The

---

[68] Cf. Sykes, 'Theology of the Humanity of Christ', p. 61.

[69] As Davidson, 'Pondering', p. 372, asks, if Christ 'belonged in a specific web of social relations and a particular context of political and economic realities, was he not implicated in the structural defects and injustices of that environment?'

[70] Such a polyhypostatic union would be hypothetically possible on a Nestorian model of the Incarnation. Adams, *What Sort of Human Nature?*, pp. 38–9, notes that Bonaventure entertains, then refutes, the notion that the Logos should have assumed fallen Adam himself. She gives additional reasons for rejecting the notion (39) while herself proposing an 'Incarnation into a human nature that not only suffers but perpetrates horrors' (!) (98) – a proposal further developed in her *Christ and Horrors: The Coherence of Christology* (Cambridge: Cambridge University Press, 2006).

[71] Cf. 1 Cor. 10.13.

common qualities of temptation correspond to certain common qualities of human nature, such as the needs for and related cravings for sustenance, rest, shelter, companionship, and meaning. Traditional hamartiology has taught that the Fall precipitated a disordering of these cravings, as well as, perhaps, the introduction of new cravings (such as libido in Augustine's view). Yet theologians such as Nazianzen and Bruce have ascribed a degree of disorderliness even to prelapsarian passions. Even if it is allowed that Christ suffered no sinful passions, exactly what is being excluded needs to be clearly identified: certain objects of desire (e.g. Peter's wife)? Certain degrees of desire (e.g. feeling not just sorrow but overwhelming sorrow)? Certain sorts of desire (e.g. longing for recognition or revenge)?[72] Certain durations of desire (e.g. deliberating whether to turn stones into bread and deciding against it rather than spontaneously dismissing the temptation)? Various combinations of the above? Would any degree of Fall-consequent disorder in Christ's passions render him sinful, or would culpability depend on what he did with them? Whatever the answers, care must be taken to ground them in careful exegesis of the biblical record.[73]

Much the same may be said regarding Christ's absence of guilt in relation to the sin-stained systems in which his earthly life was embedded. Where are the boundaries between sinless and sinful participation in such systems? How does the particularity of Christ's mission affect which sinful structures he explicitly condemns (the Temple establishment) and which he does not (Rome)? What of, for example, his shocking lack of honour towards the family system, including his own (e.g. Mt. 8.21-22; 12.46-50; 19.29)? Christ's sinless life in a human nature conditioned by the Fall provides a model for understanding his sinless life in a world of systems conditioned by the Fall.

5.4.3 Sanctification

The value of a thoroughly Christologically informed hamartiology lies not merely nor even primarily in providing a greater consistency between doctrines within one's overarching theological system. Calibrating one's understanding of sin to Christ's earthly life has significant relevance for one's doctrine of Christian sanctification. It bears underscoring that the biblical

---

[72] Recall how Dods (ch. 2.1.1) and Bruce (2.2.3) differentiate holy desires from sinful desires.
[73] Kapic, 'Assumption', p. 165 (Point 5); Davidson, 'Pondering', pp. 378–82 (including his cautionary note on the lattermost page that such a line of inquiry may ultimately prove futile), 398.

texts which most emphatically assert Christ's sinlessness do so in the context of summoning his followers to sinlessness.[74]

Thus 2 Cor. 5.21 describes the 'wondrous exchange' in which God 'made him to be sin who knew no sin so that in him we might become the righteousness of God'. To be God's righteousness, though, has definite lifestyle implications both for the apostles, whose integrity appears in their 'purity, … patience, kindness, … genuine love … [and] truthful speech' (6.6-7) while ministering amid hardships (6.1-13), as well as for the Corinthian church, which must avoid any contaminating compromise of its loyalty to God (6.14-16) but instead must pursue entire sanctification (6.17–7.1). The Letter to the Hebrews presents Christ as the high priest who remained sinless under testing (4.15) and whose purity perfectly reconciles us to God (7.26-28) precisely in order to motivate its original recipients to remain faithful under testing and avoid re-alienating themselves from God by apostasy (2.1-3; 3.6–4.2; 5.11–6.8; 10.26-31; 12.25).[75] They are to cast aside sin and follow the example of Jesus' fidelity (12.1-3). Similar is 1 Peter's defence of Christ's innocence in the midst of elevating him both as the spotless lamb whose death has redeemed his people (1.18-19) and as an example of non-retaliatory, righteous suffering for beleaguered believers to imitate (2.19-23; cf. 4.1, 12-19). Finally, the Johannine writings depict Christ as the guiltless Son who frees sin's slaves (Jn 8.34-36, 46); as the teacher who instructs his disciples to reflect his obedient love for his Father, which excludes any hold on his life by Satan (Jn 14.15-31); as the blameless one who atones and intercedes for the world (Jn 1.29, 36; 1 Jn 2.1-2); and as the sin-free pattern for our 'walk' (1 Jn 2.6), purification (1 Jn 3.3), and cessation from sin (1 Jn 3.5-10).

None of the above should be taken to imply that Christians may achieve a state of absolute sinlessness in the present age. Believers' freedom from sin will always be analogous to, not equal to, Christ's own.[76] Nor may Christian sanctification be reduced to Pelagian self-effort or Pharisaical focus on externals and casuistry, forgetting that 'it is God who works in you, both to will and to work for his good pleasure' (Phil. 2.13; cf. Rom 9.16). Sanctification as ethics is always only the outworking of believers' union through the Spirit with

---

[74] As recognized in the survey of the following texts (except for those from John's Gospel) by Davidson, 'Pondering', pp. 383–5.
[75] For a concise presentations of various possible interpretations of these passages, see H. W. Bateman IV (ed.), *Four Views on the Warning Passages in Hebrews* (Grand Rapids: Kregel, 2007).
[76] E. J. Van Kuiken, 'Edward Irving on Christ's Sinful Flesh and Sanctifying Spirit: A Wesleyan Appraisal', *Wesleyan Theological Journal* 49.1 (2014), pp. 175–85.

the Christ who assumed and healed our fallen nature.[77] Nevertheless, scripture plainly sets forth the expectation that Christian character and conduct increasingly will approximate Christ's. This expectation is hamstrung by any hamartiology which de facto equates life in a fallen world with unmitigated sinfulness.[78] Close attention to the earthly Christ's sinless character and conduct amid Fall-affected internal and external conditions can prove heuristic for Christian living amid the same conditions.[79] Proper methodology, however, is vital: starting with general theories of sin or holiness and imposing them upon the New Testament data regarding Christ's life may produce distortion, an ignoring or misconstruing of the particulars of his unique identity and mission.[80] Something similar may happen with Christians when the principles of general ethics are applied to them. It bears recalling that early believers were seen as profoundly *immoral* – atheists, disloyal citizens, and haters of humankind – by their pagan neighbours in the Roman Empire when measured against the prevailing ethics of the day. N. T. Wright articulates well the distinctiveness of a truly Christ-shaped Christian ethic of sanctification:

> Jesus came, in fact, to launch God's new creation, and with it a new way of being human, a way which picked up the glimpses of 'right behavior' afforded by ancient Judaism and paganism and, transcending both, set the truest insights of both on quite a new foundation. And, with that, he launched also a project for rehumanizing human beings, a project in which they would find their hearts cleansed and softened, find themselves turned upside down and inside out, and discover a new [moral] language to learn and every incentive to learn it.[81]

---

[77] See Noble, *Holy Trinity: Holy People*, chs 7–8, for a good general account of the implications of the fallenness debate for Christian sanctification. Cf. D. Sumner, 'Jesus Christ's Fallen and Gifted Nature As The Pattern For Christian Sanctification' (paper presented at the Edinburgh Dogmatics Conference, University of Edinburgh, 2011).

[78] For a brief history of the development of a hyperactive hamartiology in Western Christianity and the related misreading of the Apostle Paul's self-understanding, see K. Stendahl's classic essay, 'The Apostle Paul and the Introspective Conscience of the West', in his *Paul Among Jews and Gentiles* (Philadelphia: Fortress, 1976), pp. 78–96.

[79] Thus I find approaches to Christian ethics which affirm the necessity of sinning in cases of conflicts of moral duties (i.e. 'tragic morality') to be problematic on Christological grounds. On this point I concur with N. L. Geisler, *Christian Ethics: Options and Issues* (Grand Rapids: Baker, 1989), ch. 6, especially pp. 106–10, although not with his own ethical system. For critiques of both 'tragic morality' and Geisler's 'graded absolutism', see D. C. Jones, *Biblical Christian Ethics* (Grand Rapids: Baker, 1994), pp. 130–6.

[80] Davidson, 'Pondering', pp. 379–82.

[81] N. T. Wright, *After You Believe: Why Christian Character Matters* (New York: HarperOne, 2010), p. 133. Cf. Wright's entire discussion of Christian sanctification (118–25) and whether and to what extent Jesus himself may serve as a moral exemplar (125–33).

5.4.4 Bibliology

Wright's reference to 'a new language' points towards a final theological locus to which the fallenness debate may contribute: the doctrine of scripture. As in the Incarnation, the Word has assumed fallen flesh and rendered it sinlessly suitable to reveal God's grace and truth (Jn 1.14); so in the inspiration of scripture, God has 'commandeered' fallen language[82] and has renewed, redeemed, and 'uprighted' it so that it bears truthful, gracious witness to the ways of God and pre-eminently to the incarnate Word. Like its Lord, scripture too has a chequered genealogy and carries the stigmata of the clash between God's holy purpose and humanity's wickedness. Thus, for instance, majorities of both the Psalms and the Epistles are ascribed to a pair of sometime murderers – one from Bethlehem, the other from Tarsus. Yet the salvific providence of God which peaks in Christ's dying and rising again judges, justifies, and sanctifies both the material of scripture and those who produced it.[83] Granted all this, the debate persists as to whether fallibility, error, or their opposites may be predicated of scripture, as well as the exact meaning of such labels if they are affirmed or denied.[84] To the degree to which this debate is analogous to the fallenness debate, gains made in the latter may shed light on the former.

---

[82] I borrow this arresting verb from Sonderegger, *Systematic Theology Volume 1*, p. 96. She discusses her doctrine of scripture in §9 of her book.

[83] Here lie the seeds of a response to W. H. Katerberg, 'Redemptive Horizons, Redemptive Violence, and Hopeful History', *Fides et Historia* 36.1 (2004), pp. 1–14. Katerberg urges that scripture itself both constructs a metanarrative (Creation-Fall-Redemption) and deconstructs it (through contradictions, 'texts of terror', and the like, which he describes on p. 10 as 'open wounds' which render scripture 'full of holes') and that we should embrace and further this paradox, simultaneously affirming and denying redemptive metanarrative. Where Katerberg promotes simultaneity, I would preach sequence: the deconstructive elements in scripture reach their acme and receive their atonement in the Cross, and the reconstruction of the world issues forth from an emptied tomb. The 'open wounds' of a Saviour 'full of holes' paradoxically become the signs of our redemption by Christ, as do the 'wounds' and 'holes' in scripture as a whole. Cf. W. Brueggemann, *Theology of the Old Testament: Testimony, Dispute, Advocacy* (Minneapolis: Fortress, 1997), ch. 12.

[84] For a sampling of the debate, cf. Pontifical Biblical Commission, *The Inspiration and Truth of Sacred Scripture: The Word That Comes from God and Speaks of God for the Salvation of the World* (Collegeville, MN: Liturgical Press, 2014); M. Graves, *The Inspiration and Interpretation of Scripture: What the Early Church Can Teach Us* (Grand Rapids: Eerdmans, 2014); N. T. Wright, *Scripture and the Authority of God: How to Read the Bible Today* (New York: HarperOne, rev. and expanded edn, 2013); J. Merrick and S. M. Garrett (eds), *Five Views on Biblical Inerrancy* (Grand Rapids: Zondervan, 2013); and P. Enns' tellingly titled *Inspiration and Incarnation: Evangelicals and the Problem of the Old Testament* (Grand Rapids: Baker, 2nd edn, 2015).

5.5 A final word

This study has described the fallenness debate and the hidden consensus of the majority of ancient and modern theologians implicated in it. It has also prescribed terminological adjustments for the sake of ameliorating the debate and has surveyed further implications of the position here put forward. Funding these descriptions, prescriptions, and implications is the conviction that the truth of God and humanity stands disclosed in Jesus Christ in such a way that theological language and concepts may be assessed in light of that disclosure for their fidelity to it.[85] The penultimate goal of theological inquiry, then, is right belief. The final goal, though, is right worship: orthodoxy ends in doxology. Thus it is fitting to conclude our study of the relationship of the Fall to Christ's humanity with lines from two of Charles Wesley's hymns:[86]

> He deigns in flesh t'appear,
> Widest extremes to join;
> To bring our vileness near,
> And make us all divine:
> And we the life of God shall know,
> For God is manifest below.

> Now display Thy saving power,
> Ruined nature now restore;
> Now in mystic union join
> Thine to ours, and ours to Thine.

> Adam's likeness, Lord, efface,
> Stamp Thine image in its place:
> Second Adam from above,
> Reinstate us in Thy love.

---

[85] Cf. A. J. Torrance, 'Can the Truth Be Learned? Redressing the "Theologistic Fallacy" in Modern Biblical Scholarship', in *Scripture's Doctrine and Theology's Bible: How the New Testament Shapes Christian Dogmatics* (ed. M. Bockmuehl and A. J. Torrance; Grand Rapids: Baker, 2008), pp. 143–63.

[86] So as not to detract from the intended effect of these lines, I here cite them before quoting them: stanza 1 is from C. Wesley, 'Let Earth and Heaven Combine', and stanzas 2–3 from his 'Hark! The Herald Angels Sing', *The Cyber Hymnal* #3632 and #2384, respectively, n.p. Cited 22 September 2016. Online: www.hymnary.org.

Appendix: Edward Irving's Patristic Sources

Edward Irving's article 'On the Human Nature of Christ', *Morning Watch* 1 (March 1829), is the one place in which he compiles quotations from individual church fathers in support of his fallenness Christology. In this compilation, two obscurantist practices appear. First, Irving's citations are imprecise: his only consistent citation is of the name of a particular author. Occasionally, he cites the title of the work from which he quotes, but no more, except in Tertullian's case. By contrast, his nemesis Marcus Dods's patristic survey in *The Incarnation of the Eternal Word* is much more carefully documented. Secondly, several of Irving's quotations are literary montages: he presents them in paragraph format, but in fact these paragraphs consist of sentences or parts of sentences pulled from their originally disparate locations and assembled into artificial unities. When reading such paragraphs, one must bear in mind that they do not represent seamless progressions of thought on the part of their authors.

This appendix presents the fruit of efforts at more exact identification of Irving's patristic sources, specifically those associated with the fathers who appear in Chapters 3 and 4 of this study. In some cases, attempts at identification were unsuccessful, thus leaving room for further research. The ordering of the material below is as follows: citations and quotations from Irving's article are presented in block quote format. My own more exact citations appear in brackets within the block quotes, inserted at appropriate 'seams' in Irving's quotations. Inasmuch as all of Irving's quotations presented here are in Latin, I have supplied English translations in the footnotes following each quotation.

> *Tertullian de Carne Christi*, p. 555. – 'Ita utriusque substantiae census hominem et Deum exhibuit: hinc natum, inde non natum; hinc carneum inde spiritualem; hinc infirmum, inde praefortem; hinc morientem, inde viventem. [*Carn. Chr.* 5] Nihil passus est, qui non vere passus est. [*Carn. Chr.* 5 (garbled)] .... Christus salus hominis fuit, causa scilicet ad

restituendum quod perierat. Homo perierat, hominem restitui oportuerat.' p. 559. [*Carn. Chr.* 14][1]

'Defendimus autem non carnem peccati evacuatam esse in Christo, sed peccatum carnis: Secundum Apostoli auctoritatem dicentis: Evacuavit peccatum in carne. Nam et alibi, In similitundinem, inquit, carnis peccati fuisse Christum: non quod similitudinem carnis acceperit, quasi imaginem corporis, et non veritatem, sed similitudinem peccatricis carnis vult intelligi. Quod ipsa non peccatrix caro Christi ejus fuit par, cujus erat peccatum, genere, non vitio Adae, quando hinc etiam confirmamus eam fuisse carnem in Christo, cujus natura est in homine peccatrix. Etsi in illa peccatum evacuatum, quod in Christo sine peccato habeatur, quae in homine sine peccato non habebatur. Nam neque ad propositum Christi faceret evacuantis peccatum carnis, non in ea carne evacuare illud, in qua erat natura peccati. Neque ad gloriam: quid enim magnum, si in carne meliore et alterius, id est, non peccatricis naturae, naevum peccati redemit? Ergo, inquit, si nostram induit, peccatrix fuit caro Christi? Noli constringere explicabilem sensum: nostram enim induendo suam fecit: suam faciens, non peccatricem eam fecit. [*Carn. Chr.* 16]. ... In hac carne, peccatrici nostrae simili, salutem perfecit. [*Marc.* 5.14 (paraphrased)?] Nam et haec erit Dei virtus, in substantia pari perficere salutem. Non enim magnum, si Spiritus Dei carnem remediaret, sed si caro consimilis peccatrici, dum caro est, sed non peccati.' p. 796 [*Marc.* 5.14][2]

---

[1] 'On the Human Nature of Christ', 90. 'Thus the official record of both substances represents him as both man and God: on the one hand born, on the other not born: on the one hand fleshly, on the other spiritual: on the one hand weak, on the other exceeding strong: on the one hand dying, on the other living' (*Tertullian's Treatise*, p. 19.). 'He suffered nothing, who did not in reality suffer.' (Trans. mine; cf. '[N]ihil enim ab eis passus est Christus, si nihil vere est passus.' – 'For of them Christ suffered nothing, if he in reality suffered nothing' [*Tertullian's Treatise*, pp. 16–19]). '[That] Christ [assumed human nature], man's salvation was the reason, the restitution of that which had perished. Man had perished: it was man that must be restored' [*Tertullian's Treatise*, p. 49.]).

[2] 'On the Human Nature of Christ', pp. 90–1.

> Our contention, however, is not that the flesh of sin, but that the sin of the flesh, was brought to nought in Christ, ... according to the apostle's authority when he says, *He brought to nought sin in the flesh* [Rom. 8.3]. For in another place also he says that Christ was in the likeness of the flesh of sin: not that he took upon him the likeness of flesh, as it were a phantasm of a body and not its reality: but the apostle will have us understand by 'the likeness of sinful flesh' that the flesh of Christ, itself not sinful, was the like of that to which sin did belong, ... with Adam in species but not in defect. From this text [then] we also prove that in Christ there was that flesh whose nature is in man sinful, and [yet] that it is by virtue of this that sin has been brought to nought, [because] in Christ that same flesh exists without sin which in man did not exist without sin. [For] it would not suit Christ's purpose, when bringing to nought the sin of the flesh, not to bring it to nought in that flesh in which was the nature of sin: neither would it be to his glory. For what would it amount to if it was in a better kind of flesh, of a different (that is, non-sinful) nature, that he [redeemed] the birthmark of sin? 'In that case,' you will reply, 'if it was our flesh Christ clothed himself with, Christ's flesh was sinful.' Forbear to tie up tight a conception which admits of unravelling. By clothing himself with our flesh he made it his own, and by making it his own he made it non-sinful (*Tertullian's Treatise*, p. 57).

'Christus dilexit hominem illum in immundicitiis [*sic*]. Propter eum descendit: propter eum praedicavit: propter eum omni se humilitate dejecit usque ad mortem, et mortem crucis: amavit utique quem magno pretio redemit. Si Christus creator ejus est, suum merito amavit. Amavit ergo cum homine etiam nativitatem, etiam carnem ejus. Nihil amari potest sine eo per quod, est id quod est. Aut aufer nativitatem, et exhibe hominem; adime carnem, et praesta quem Deus redemit. Si haec sunt homo, quem Deus redemit, tu haec erubescenda illi facis, quae redemit; et indigna, quae nisi dilexisset, non redemisset.' [*Carn. Chr.* 4][3]

'Cur dubitemus dicere quod Scriptura non dubitat exprimere? Cur haesitabit fidei veritas, in quo Scripturae nunquam haesitavit auctoritas?' [Novatian, *Trin.* 12.1] …. 'Oportebat Deum carnem fieri ut in semet ipso concordiam consibularet [*sic*] terrenorum pariter atque coelestium, dum utriusque partis in se connectens pignora, et Deum pariter homini, et hominem Deo copularet.' [Novatian, *Trin.* 23.7][4]

….

Athanasius contra Arrian [*sic*]. – Quum Filius verus Deus esset, proprium corpus cepit, eoque utens ut organo, homo factus est propter nos: ideoque

---

'In this flesh, which was like our sinful flesh, he accomplished salvation.' (ET mine; cf. the following translation from Evans.) 'For in this will consist the power of God, in using a similar substance to accomplish salvation. For it would be no great matter if the Spirit of God were to give healing to flesh, though it is so when this is done by flesh exactly like sinful flesh, which is flesh, though not flesh of sin' (*AMOECT* 2, p. 599).

[3] 'On the Human Nature of Christ', p. 91. (Regarding 'immundicitiis', it seems that Irving's, the editor's, or the printer's eye slipped and added the extra 'ci' to 'immunditiis' either from 'peccatrici' above it or 'dejecit' or 'crucis' below it.) 'Christ … did care for the sort of man … in uncleannessnesses. … For his sake he came down, for his sake he preached the gospel, for his sake he cast himself down in all humility even unto death, yea, the death of the cross. Evidently he loved him: for he redeemed him at a great price. If Christ [is] the Creator, with good reason he loved his own …. In any case, along with man he loved also his nativity, and his flesh besides: nothing can be loved apart from that by which it is what it is. Else you must remove nativity and show me man, you must take away flesh and present to me him whom God has redeemed. If these are the constituents of man whom God has redeemed, who are you to make them a cause of shame to him [, which] he redeemed …, or to make them beneath his dignity, when he would not have redeemed them unless he had loved them?' (*Tertullian's Treatise*, p. 15.)

[4] 'On the Human Nature of Christ', p. 91. 'Why should we hesitate to say what Scripture does not hesitate to express? Why will the truth of faith be undecided in that which the authority of Scripture has never been undecided?' (J. L. Papandrea, 'The Rule of Truth: A New Translation of the *De Trinitate* of Novatian', in *idem, The Trinitarian Theology of Novatian of Rome: A Study in Third Century Orthodoxy* [n.p.: Edwin Mellen Press, 2008], [p. 245]. Cited 18 November 2013. Online: http://novatianus.info. Regarding 'consibularet', the correct word is 'confibularet', as attested by Papandrea, 'Rule of Truth', [p. 300] n. 482; Novatian, *De trinitate* 28. Cited 18 November 2013. Online: http://www.documentacatholicaomnia.eu/04z/z_0251-0258__Novatianus__De_ Trinitate__LT. doc.html. Perhaps the printer mistook the 'f' in the original for the marking known as a 'long s'.) 'God had to be made flesh, so that He might unite in Himself the harmony of earthly things together with the heavenly, while connecting tokens of both parts in Himself, so that He might join together both God to humanity and humanity to God' (Papandrea, 'Rule of Truth', [p. 300]; trans. alt.).

quae propria sunt carnis, de illo referuntur: erat enim caro ipsius. [*C. Ar.* 3.31] Necesse est passiones quoque carnis ejus dici cujus est ista caro: [*C. Ar.* 3.32] et recte passiones Domini appellantur. [*C. Ar.* 3.32] Quia et illa propria sunt carnis et caro illa proprium est corpus Dei salvatoris. [*C. Ar.* 3.34] Verum corpus ex Maria genitum, idem cum corporibus nostris. Verum corpus ex Maria secundum Scripturas, genitum est: verum inquam, quia idem est cum corporibus nostris. [*C. Ar.* 3.56 or 4.35-36 (summarized)?]⁵

....

Ambrose. – Pater si possibile est, transfer a me calicem hunc. [*Fid.* 2.5.41] In qua forma loquatur adverte. Hominis substantiam gessit, hominis assumpsit affectum. [*Fid.* 2.5.42] Non ergo quasi Deus, sed quasi homo loquitur. [*Fid.* 2.5.42] Alia voluntas hominis, alia Dei, [*Fid.* 2.7.52] ut homo suscepit tristitiam meam, ut homo locutus est. [*Fid.* 2.7.53] Mihi compatitur, mihi tristis est, mihi dolet. [*Fid.* 2.7.53] Sicut mors ejus, mortem abstulit: [*Fid.* 2.7.55] ita maerorem nostrum, maeror ejus abolet. [*Fid.* 2.7.55] Turbatur secundum humanae fragilitatis assumptionem. Et ideo quia suscepit animam, suscepit et animae passiones. [*Fid.* 2.7.56] Ut homo turbatur, ut homo flet, ut homo crucifigitur. [*Fid.* 2.7.56] Quasi homo dicit quae sunt humana: quia in mea substantia loquebatur. [*Fid.* 2.9.77] Propter me Christus suscepit meas infirmitates. [*Fid.* 2.11.93] Timuerunt in Deo carnem credere, et ideo redemptionis gratiam perdiderunt, quia causam salutis abjurant. [*Fid.* 3.5.38]⁶

---

⁵ 'On the Human Nature of Christ', p. 91. 'Together with being the Son of the true God, He took His own body, and using this as an instrument, He became man for our sakes. And on account of this, the properties of the flesh are said to be His ... for His was the flesh' (*NPNF*² 4, p. 410, alt.). 'Of necessity ... the affections also of the flesh are ascribed to Him, whose the flesh is' (*NPNF*² 4, p. 411). 'And fittingly such affections are ascribed ... to the Lord' (*NPNF*² 4, p. 411). 'Since they are proper to the flesh, and the body itself is proper to the Saviour ...' (*NPNF*² 4, p. 412; 'corpus Dei' seems to be an insertion from *C. Ar.* 3.31, in which the phrase 'the body was God's' appears. [*NPNF*² 4, p. 410]). 'A true body [was] born of Mary, the same as our bodies. According to the Scriptures, a true body was born of Mary: true, I say, because it is the same as our bodies' (ET mine; the phrase, 'a true body' appears in *C. Ar.* 3.42 [*NPNF*² 4, p. 416], but the rest of the content more closely aligns with *C. Ar.* 3.56 or 4.35-36).

⁶ 'On the Human Nature of Christ', 92. '"Father, if it be possible, take away this cup from Me." ... In what character He speaks. He hath taken upon Him the substance of man, and therewith his affections. ... Not as God, then, but as man, speaketh He.' (*NPNF*² 10, p. 464). 'The will of God is one, and the human will another' (*NPNF*² 10, p. 467; Irving's order is reversed). 'As man He bore my grief, as man He spake .... With me and for me He suffers, for me He is sad, for me He is heavy' (*NPNF*² 10, p. 467). ' Even as His death made an end of death ... so also His sorrow took away our sorrow' (*NPNF*² 10, p. 468). 'He is amazed by consequence of having taken human infirmity upon Him. Seeing, then, that He took upon Himself a soul He also took the affections of a soul .... As man, therefore, He is distressed, as man He weeps, as man He is crucified' (*NPNF*² 10, p. 468). 'As man He speaks the things of man, because He speaks in my nature' (*NPNF*² 10, p. 474). 'For my sake Christ bore my infirmities.' (*NPNF*² 10, p. 478). '[They] feared to believe in [flesh] taken up into God, and therefore have lost the grace of redemption, because they reject that on which salvation depends' (*NPNF*² 10, p. 501).

'Caro ipsius et anima, ejusdem cujus anima nostra caroque; substaniae est. [*Incarn.* 76] Quid est formam servi accipiens? Sine dubio perfectionem naturae et conditionis humanae.' [*Ep.* 23 (46)][7]

Ambrose on Heb. ii. 14, says, Quare dixit apprehendit? quia nos quasi recedentes ab eo, et longe fugientes insecutus apprehendit, et in unam personam nostrae fragilitatis naturam sibi contemperavit. In eo, id est, homine quo passus est, potens est vinctos liberare; tentatosque adjuvare ne vincantur: quia tentationes nostras non solum sicut Deus, sed etiam sicut homo in seipso per experimentum cognovit. [?][8]

....

Augustin. – Deus Verbum, animam et carnem totius hominis suscepit. [*Serm.* 174.2] Ipsa natura suscipienda erat quae liberanda. [*Ver. rel.* 1.16.30] Quidam haeretici perverse mirando laudandoque Chrisi virtutem, naturam humanam in eo prorsus noluerunt agnoscere, ubi est omnis gratiae commendatio, qua facit salvos, credentes in se. Inter Deum et homines apparuit Mediator in unitate personae copulans utranque naturam. [*Ep.* 137.3.9] Quod ad hominem creatura est Christus: [?] secundum animam tristis fuit; secundum carnem passus est mortem. [*Serm.* 265D.3 (paraphrased)?] Caro in illo mortua est, non ipse mortuus est. [*Coll. Max.* 14] –Idem et aeternus in suo, moriturus in nostro, dum utrumque continet ex seipso, et neutrum perdit ex altero. [?] In illo divinitas est unigeniti facta particeps mortalitatis nostrae, ut et nos participes ejus immortalitatis essemus. [*Ep.* 187.6.20][9]

---

[7] 'On the Human Nature of Christ', p. 92. 'His body and soul are of the same substance as are our soul and body' (FC 44, p. 248). 'What is the meaning of "taking the nature of a slave" [Phil. 2.7]? Without doubt, it means the perfection of nature and the human condition' (*Letters 1–91* [trans. M. M. Beyenka; FC 26; repr., Washington, DC: Catholic University of America, 1967], p. 140; this source numbers this epistle as 23; the Benedictine numbering followed in PL 16 is 46; see FC 26, p. xv).

[8] 'On the Human Nature of Christ', p. 92.

Why did it say 'he takes hold of' [Heb. 2.16]? Because having pursued us as those who had left him and fled far away, he takes hold of us, and in one person has adjusted our weak nature to himself. In his case, that is, in the case of this man, the one who has suffered has been able to free the captives and to help the tempted lest they be conquered, because he has known our temptations not only as God, but also as a man, by his own experience. (ET mine)

[9] 'On the Human Nature of Christ', pp. 92–3. 'The Word of God ... assumed the soul and flesh of a man' (WSA III/5, p. 258). 'The same nature had to be taken on as needed to be set free' (WSA I/8, p. 48). 'Certain heretics, by excessive admiration and praise of [Christ's] power, refuse to acknowledge the human nature which is undoubtedly His. Herein is all the worth of grace, by which He saves those who believe .... He has appeared as Mediator between God and men, in such wise as to join both natures in the unity of one Person' (FC 20, pp. 24–5). 'What belongs to a human creature to be, Christ is' (ET mine). 'In terms of his being soul, he was sorrowful; in terms of his being flesh, he suffered death' (ET mine, but following WSA III/7, p. 256). 'The flesh died in him; he himself did not die' (WSA I/18, p. 198). 'In his own nature, he is eternal; in our nature, he is going to die, while each of the two natures stays the same on its own, and neither loses anything due to the other' (ET mine, taking the first 'et' as a typographical error for 'est'). 'In Him the divinity of the only-begotten Son shared in our mortality, that we might be made sharers in His immortality' (FC 30, p. 237).

....

Hilary [of Poitiers]. 'Ejusdem periculi res est, Christum Jesum vel Spiritum Deum, vel carnem corporis nostri denegare.' [*Trin.* 9.3][10]

....

Leo Primus. – 'Corpus Christi nulla ratione est extra corporis nostri vertatem.' [*Ep.* 139.3][11]

It bears noting that Irving's most carefully documented, most sustained quotations come from Tertullian. The similarities between the two men are intriguing: both defend the sameness of Christ's flesh to ours against opponents who advocate a 'better' flesh for him; both contribute to Trinitarian theology; both are critics of the churches to which they belong; both become associated with premillennial and charismatic renewal movements; and both leave behind a mixed reputation for heresy and schism on the one hand and zeal and pioneering insight on the other. These similarities, as well as the question of the full extent of Tertullian's influence on Irving, cry out for further investigation.

Additional research also remains to be done into the patristic sources in 'On the Human Nature of Christ'. First, the sources of the quotations left unidentified or identified only tentatively above must be located. Secondly, the quotations given above include only those from church fathers cited by Irving who are subjects of this study. Irving, however, quotes from other authorities who are not of interest to this study. The sources of those quotations, too, require more exact identification.

---

[10] 'On the Human Nature of Christ', 93. 'It is an equally dangerous matter to deny either that Christ Jesus is the Spirit of God or that He is the flesh of our body' (FC 34, p. 276).

[11] 'On the Human Nature of Christ', 93. 'In no way is [the body of Christ] outside our true bodily nature' (*NPNF*[2] 12, p. 221).

Bibliography

'1911 Encyclopædia Britannica/Bruce, Alexander Balmain', *Wikisource, The Free Library*; n.d.; n.p. Cited 28 September 2011. Online: //en.wikisource.org/w/index. php?title=1911_Encyclop%C3%A6dia_Britannica/Bruce,_ Alexander_Balmain& oldid=662873.

Adams, M. M., *Christ and Horrors: The Coherence of Christology* (Cambridge: Cambridge University Press, 2006).

Adams, M. M., *What Sort of Human Nature?Medieval Philosophy and the Systematics of Christology* (Milwaukee: Marquette University Press, 1999).

Ahn, H.-J., 'The Humanity of Christ: John Calvin's Understanding of Christ's Vicarious Humanity', *SJT* 65.2 (2012), pp. 145–58.

Allen, R. M., 'Calvin's Christ: A Dogmatic Matrix for Discussion of Christ's Human Nature', *IJST* 9.4 (2007), pp. 382–97.

Allen, R. M., *The Christ's Faith: A Dogmatic Account* (London: T&T Clark, 2009).

'Ambrose, St', *ODCC* (2005), n.p. Cited 11 December 2012. Online: http://www. oxfordreference.com/view/10.1093/acref/9780192802903. 001.0001/acref-9780192802903-e-240.

Ambrose, St., *Saint Ambrose: Theological and Dogmatic Works* (trans. R. J. Deferrari; FC 44; Washington, DC: Catholic University of America, 1963).

Ambrose, St., *Letters 1–91* (trans. M. M. Beyenka; FC 26; repr., Washington, DC: Catholic University of America, 1967).

Anatolios, K., *Athanasius* (London: Routledge, 2004).

Anatolios, K., *Athanasius: The Coherence of His Thought* (New York: Routledge, 2002).

Anatolios, K., 'The Influence of Irenaeus on Athanasius', *StPatr* 36, pp. 463–76.

Anatolios, K., 'Yes and No: Reflections on Lewis Ayres, Nicaea and Its Legacy', *HTR* 100.2 (April 2007), pp. 153–8.

Arens, H., *Die christologische Sprache Leos des Grossen: Analyse des Tomus an den Patriarchen Flavian* (Freiburg: Herder, 1982).

Armitage, J. M., *A Twofold Solidarity: Leo the Great's Theology of Redemption* (Strathfield, Australia: St Pauls, 2005).

Athanasius, Contra Gentes *and* De Incarnatione (ed. and trans. R. W. Thomson; Oxford: Clarendon, 1971).

Athanasius, *Later Treatises of S. Athanasius, Archbishop of Alexandria, with Notes; and an Appendix on S. Cyril of Alexandria and Theodoret* (trans. members of the English Church; Oxford: James Parker & Co., and London: Rivingtons, 1881).

Augustine, St., *Against Julian* (trans. M. A. Schumacher; FC 35; New York: Fathers of the Church, 1957).

Augustine, St., *Answer to the Pelagians, III: Unfinished Work in Answer to Julian* (ed. J. E. Rotelle; trans. R. J. Testke; WSA I/25; Hyde Park, NY: New City, 1999).

Augustine, St., *Arianism and Other Heresies* (trans. R. J. Testke; WSA I/18; Hyde Park, N.Y.: New City Press, 1995).

Augustine, St., *The Christian Combat* (trans. R. P. Russell; FC 2; New York: Fathers of the Church, 2nd edn, 1950).

Augustine, St., *Letters Vol. III [131–164]* (trans. W. Parsons; FC 20; New York: Fathers of the Church, 1953).

Augustine, St., *Letters Vol. IV [165–203]* (trans. W. Parsons; FC 30; New York: Fathers of the Church, 1955).

Augustine, St., *On Christian Belief* (ed. B. Ramsey; WSA I/8; Hyde Park, NY: New City, 2005).

Augustine, St., *Selected Writings on Grace and Pelagianism* (ed. B. Ramsey; trans. R. Teske; WSA [unnumbered]; Hyde Park, NY: New City, 2011).

Augustine, St., *Sermons* III/5 [151–183] (trans. E. Hill; WSA III/5; Hyde Park, NY: New City Press, 1992).

Augustine, St., *Sermons* III/6 [184–229] (trans. E. Hill; WSA III/6; New Rochelle, NY: New City Press, 1993).

Augustine, St., *Sermons* III/7 [230–272B] (trans. E. Hill; WSA III/7; Hyde Park, NY: New City Press, 1993).

Augustine, St., *Tractates on the Gospel of John 1–10* (trans. J. W. Rettig; FC 78; Washington, DC: Catholic University of America Press, 1988).

Augustine, St., *Tractates on the Gospel of John 11–27* (trans. J. W. Rettig; FC 79; Washington, DC: Catholic University of America Press, 1988).

Augustine, St., *Tractates on the Gospel of John 28–54* (trans. J. W. Rettig; FC 88; Washington, DC: Catholic University of America Press, 1993).

Augustine, St., *The Trinity* (trans. S. McKenna; FC 45; Washington, DC: Catholic University of America Press, 1963).

Aulén, G., *Christus Victor: An Historical Study of the Three Main Types of the Idea of the Atonement* (trans. A. G. Hebert; New York: Macmillan, 1960).

Ayres, L., 'Nicaea and Its Legacy: An Introduction', *HTR* 100.2 (April 2007), pp. 141–4.

Baelz, P. R., 'A Deliberate Mistake?', in *Christ Faith and History* (eds S. W. Sykes and J. P. Clayton; Cambridge: Cambridge University Press, 1972), pp. 13–34.

Baillie, D. M., *God Was in Christ* (New York: Charles Scribner's Sons, 1948).

Baker, E. W., *A Herald of the Evangelical Revival: A Critical Inquiry into the Relation of William Law to John Wesley and the Beginnings of Methodism* (New-World Library; London: Epworth, 1948).

Baker, M., 'The Place of St. Irenaeus of Lyons in Historical and Dogmatic Theology According to Thomas F. Torrance', *Participatio* 2 (2010), pp. 23–4. Cited 21 January 2011. Online: http://www.tftorrance.org/journal/participatio_ vol_2_2010.pdf.

Balthasar, H. U. von, *Mysterium Paschale: The Mystery of Easter* (trans. with an introduction by A. Nichols; Edinburgh: T&T Clark, 1990; 1st American edn. San Francisco: Ignatius, 2000).

Barclift, P. L., 'The Shifting Tones of Pope Leo the Great's Christological Vocabulary', *Church History* 66.2 (1997), pp. 221–39.

Barnes, M. R., 'Augustine in Contemporary Trinitarian Theology', *TS* 56.2 (1995), pp. 237–50.

Barnes, T. D., *Tertullian: A Historical and Literary Study* (Oxford: Clarendon Press, 1971).

Barth, K., *Christ and Adam: Man and Humanity in Romans 5* (trans. T. A. Smail; New York: Harper Bros., 1956, 1957).

Barth, K., *Church Dogmatics* (eds G. W. Bromiley and T. F. Torrance; 5 vols in 14 parts; Edinburgh: T&T Clark, 1956–77; repr., Peabody, MA: Hendrickson, 2010).

Barth, K., *Church Dogmatics Study Edition* vol 3 (London: T&T Clark, 2010).

Barth, K., *Credo* (trans. J. S. McNab; London: Hodder & Stoughton, 1936, 1964).

Barth, K., *Epistle to the Philippians* (trans. J. W. Leitch; Louisville: Westminster John Knox, 40th anniversary edn, 2002).

Barth, K., *The Epistle to the Romans* (trans. E. C. Hoskyns; London: Oxford University Press, 1933).

Barth, K., *The Humanity of God* (trans. J. N. Thomas; Richmond, VA: John Knox, 1960).

Barth, K., *Die Kirchliche Dogmatik* (5 vols in 14 parts; Zollikon, Switzerland: Verlag der Evangelischen Buchhandlun, 1932–70). Cited 10 September 2013. Online: *The Digital Karl Barth Library*.

Bastero, J. L., 'La virginidad de María en San Ambrosio y en San Gregorio de Nisa', in *Studien zu Gregor von Nyssa und der Christlichen Spätantike* (ed. H. R. Drobner and C. Klock; Leiden: Brill, 1990), pp. 255–71.

Bastiaensen, A., 'Augustine's Pauline Exegesis and Ambrosiaster', in *Augustine: Biblical Exegete* (eds J. Schnaubelt and F. Van Fleteren; New York: Peter Lang, 2001), pp. 33–54.

Bateman IV, H. (ed.), *Four Views on the Warning Passages in Hebrews* (Grand Rapids: Kregel, 2007).

Bathrellos, D., 'The Sinlessness of Jesus: A Theological Exploration in the Light of Trinitarian Theology', in *Trinitarian Soundings in Systematic Theology* (ed. P. L. Metzger; London: T&T Clark, 2005), pp. 113–26.

Beckwith, C., 'Suffering without Pain: The Scandal of Hilary of Poitiers' Christology', in *In the Shadow of the Incarnation: Essays on Jesus Christ in the Early Church in Honor of Brian E. Daley, S.J.* (ed. P. W. Martens; Notre Dame: University of Notre Dame Press, 2008), pp. 71–96.

Beeley, C. A., *Gregory of Nazianzus on the Trinity and the Knowledge of God: In Your Light We Shall See Light* (Oxford: Oxford University Press, 2008).

Beeley, C. A. *The Unity of Christ: Continuity and Conflict in Patristic Tradition* (New Haven, CT: Yale University Press, 2012).

Behr, J., 'Response to Ayres: The Legacies of Nicaea, East and West', *HTR* 100.2 (April 2007), pp. 145–52.

Berry, R. J., and T. A. Noble (eds), *Darwin, Creation and the Fall: Theological challenges* (Nottingham, UK: Apollos, 2009).

Bettenson, H. (ed.), *Documents of the Christian Church* (New York: Oxford University Press, 1947).

Bianchi, U., 'Augustine on Concupiscence' and J. van Oort, 'Augustine on Sexual Concupiscence and Original Sin', *StPatr* 22 (1989), pp. 202–12.

Biddle, M. E., *Missing the Mark: Sin and Its Consequences in Biblical Theology* (Nashville: Abingdon, 2005).

Bingham, 'The Apocalypse, Christ, and the Martyrs of Gaul', in *In the Shadow of the Incarnation: Essays on Jesus Christ in the Early Church in Honor of Brian E. Daley, S.J.* (ed. P. W. Martens; Notre Dame: University of Notre Dame Press, 2008), pp. 11–28.

'Biography', n.p. Cited 27 May 2013. Online: http://www.donaldmacleod.org/?page_id=7.

Blaikie, W. G., 'Dods, Marcus', in *Dictionary of National Biography, 1885–900*, 15; n.p. (cited 28 September 2011). Online: http://en.wikisource.org/wiki/Dods,_Marcus_(DNB00).

Boersma, H., *Embodiment and Virtue in Gregory of Nyssa: An Anagogical Approach* (Oxford: Oxford University Press, 2013).

Bonner, G., 'Anti-Pelagian Works', in *Augustine through the Ages: An Encyclopedia* (gen. ed. A. D. Fitzgerald; Grand Rapids: Eerdmans, 2009), pp. 41–7.

Bonner, G., *St. Augustine: Life and Controversies* (repr.; Norwich, UK: Canterbury Press, rev. edn, 1997).

Boss, S. J., 'The Development of the Doctrine of Mary's Immaculate Conception', in *Mary: The Complete Resource* (ed. S. J. Boss; London: Continuum, 2007), pp. 207–35.

Bounds, C. T., 'Competing Doctrines of Perfection: The Primary Issue in Irenaeus' Refutation of Gnosticism', *StPatr* 45 (2010), pp. 403–8.

Bouteneff, P. C., 'Essential or Existential: The Problem of the Body in the Anthropology of St Gregory of Nyssa', in Gregory of Nyssa, *Homilies on the Beatitudes: An English Version with Commentary and Supporting Studies. Proceedings of the Eighth*

International Colloquium on Gregory of Nyssa (Paderborn, 14–18 September 1998) (eds H. R. Drobner and A. Viciano; Leiden: Brill, 2000), pp. 409–19.

Bray, G. L., *Holiness and the Will of God: Perspectives on the Theology of Tertullian* (Atlanta: John Knox, 1979).

Bray, G. L., 'Original Sin in Patristic Thought', *Churchman* 108.1 (1994), pp. 37–47.

Briggman, A., *Irenaeus of Lyons and the Theology of the Holy Spirit* (Oxford: Oxford University Press, 2012).

Bright, W., *The Orations of St. Athanasius Against the Arians* (Ann Arbor, MI: University Microfilms International, 1978).

Bromiley, G. W., 'The Reformers and the Humanity of Christ', in *Perspectives on Christology: Essays in Honor of Paul K. Jewett* (eds M. Shuster and R. Muller; Grand Rapids: Zondervan, 1991), pp. 79–104.

Brown, P., *Augustine of Hippo: A Biography* (Berkeley: University of California Press, rev. edn, 2000).

Brown, R. F., 'On the Necessary Imperfection of Creation: Irenaeus's *Adversus Haereses* IV, 38', *SJT* 28 (1975), pp. 17–25.

Bruce, A. B., *Apologetics; or, Christianity Defensively Stated* (Edinburgh: T&T Clark, 2nd edn, 1893).

Bruce, A. B., *The Epistle to the Hebrews: The First Apology for Christianity. An Exegetical Study* (Edinburgh: T&T Clark, 1899).

Bruce, A. B., *The Humiliation of Christ in its Physical, Ethical,* and *Official Aspects* (New York: A. C. Armstrong & Son, 2nd edn, 1889; repr., n.p.: Forgotten Books AG, 2010).

Bruce, A. B., *The Kingdom of God* (Edinburgh: T&T Clark, 2nd edn, 1890).

Bruce, A. B., *St. Paul's Conception of Christianity* (Edinburgh: T&T Clark, 1894).

'Bruce, Alexander Balmain', in *ODCC* (2005), n.p. Cited 28 September 2011. *Online:* http://www.oxford-christianchurch.com/entry?entry=t257.e1019.

Brueggemann, W., *Theology of the Old Testament: Testimony, Dispute, Advocacy* (Minneapolis: Fortress, 1997).

Burghardt, W. J., *The Image of God in Man according to Cyril of Alexandria* (Washington, DC: Catholic University of America Press, 1957).

Burnell, P., 'Concupiscence', in *Augustine through the Ages: An Encyclopedia* (gen. ed. A. D. Fitzgerald; Grand Rapids:Eerdmans, 2009), pp. 224–7.

Burns, J. P., 'Creation and Fall according to Ambrose of Milan', in *Augustine: Biblical Exegete* (ed. J. Schnaubelt and F. Van Fleteren; New York: Peter Lang, 2001).

Burns, P. C., *The Christology in Hilary of Poitiers' Commentary on Matthew* (Rome: Institutum Patristicum 'Augustinianum', 1981).

Burns, P. C. *Model for the Christian Life: Hilary of Poitiers' Commentary on the Psalms* ([Washington, DC]: Catholic University of America Press, 2012).

Calvin, J., *The Institutes of the Christian Religion* (ed. J. T. McNeill; trans. F. L. Battles; Philadelphia: Westminster, 1960).

Cameron, D. J., *Flesh and Blood: A Dogmatic Sketch Concerning the Fallen Nature View of Christ's Human Nature* (Eugene, OR: Wipf & Stock, 2016).

Cantalamessa, R., *La Cristologia di Tertulliano* ([Fribourg, Switzerland]: Edizioni Universitarie Friburgo Svizzera, 1962).

Carson, D. A., *Exegetical Fallacies* (Grand Rapids: Baker, 2nd edn, 1996).

Cass, P., *Christ Condemned Sin in the Flesh: Thomas F. Torrance's Doctrine of Soteriology and Its Ecumenical Significance* (Saarbrücken, Germany: Dr. Müller, 2009).

Casula, L., *La Cristologia di San Leone Magno: Il Fondamento Dottrinale e Soteriologico* (Milan: Glossa, 2000).

Chapot, F., 'Tertullian,' in *Augustine through the Ages: An Encyclopedia* (gen. ed. A. D. Fitzgerald; Grand Rapids: Eerdmans, 2009), pp. 822–4.

Chiarot, K., 'The Non-Assumptus and the Virgin Birth in T. F. Torrance', *Scottish Bulletin of Evangelical Theology* 29.2 (2011), pp. 229–44.

Chiarot, K., *The Unassumed is the Unhealed: The Humanity of Christ in the Theology of T. F. Torrance* (Cascade, OR: Pickwick, 2013).

Clancy, F. G., 'Redemption', in *Augustine through the Ages: An Encyclopedia* (gen. ed. A. D. Fitzgerald; Grand Rapids: Eerdmans, 2009), pp. 702–4.

Clark, E. A., 'Generation, Degeneration, Regeneration: Original Sin and the Conception of Jesus in the Polemic between Augustine and Julian of Eclanum', in *Generation and Degeneration: Tropes of Reproduction in Literature and History from Antiquity through Early Modern Europe* (eds V. Finucci and K. Brownlee; Durham: Duke University Press, 2001), pp. 17–40.

Clark, J. C., and M. P. Johnson, *The Incarnation of God: The Mystery of the Gospel as the Foundation of Evangelical Theology* (Wheaton: Crossway, 2015).

Colyer, E. M., *How to Read T. F. Torrance: Understanding His Trinitarian & Scientific Theology* (Downers Grove, IL: InterVarsity, 2001).

Connolly H., *Body in the 4th Century* (Farnham, UK: Ashgate, 2009).

Crisp, O., 'Did Christ Have a *Fallen* Human Nature?', *IJST* 6.3 (2004), pp. 270–88; repr. in *idem, Divinity and Humanity: The Incarnation Reconsidered* (Cambridge: Cambridge University Press, 2007), pp. 90–117.

Cumin, P., 'The Taste of Cake: Relation and Otherness with Colin Gunton and the Strong Second Hand of God', in *The Theology of Colin Gunton* (ed. L. Harvey; London: T&T Clark, 2010), pp. 69–72.

'Curriculum Vitae: Revd. Dr. Thomas G. Weinandy, O.F.M. Cap', n.p. Cited 22 March 2011. Online: http://thomasweinandy.com/cv.html.

Cyril of Alexandria, *Five Tomes Against Nestorius* (trans. P. E. Pusey; LFC 47; Oxford: James Parker & Co., 1881). Cited 2 September 2012. Online: http://www.elpenor.org/cyril-alexandria/against-nestorius.asp.

Cyril of Alexandria, *Scholia on the Incarnation of the Only-Begotten* (trans. P. E. Pusey; LFC 47). Cited 1 September 2012. Online: http://www.elpenor.org/cyril-alexandria/incarnation-only-begotten.asp.

Cyril of Alexandria, *Select Letters* (ed. and trans. L. R. Wickham; Oxford: Clarendon, 1983).

St Cyril of Alexandria, *On the Unity of Christ* (trans. J. A. McGuckin; Crestwood, NY: St Vladimir's Seminary Press, 2000).

Daley, B. E., 'Christology', in *Augustine through the Ages: An Encyclopedia* (gen. ed. A. D. Fitzgerald; Grand Rapids: Eerdmans, 2009), pp. 164–9.

Daley, B. E., *Gregory of Nazianzus* (London: Routledge, 2006).

Daley, B. E., '"Heavenly Man" and "Eternal Christ": Apollinarius and Gregory of Nyssa on the Personal Identity of the Savior', *JECS* 10.4 (2002), pp. 469–88.

Dallimore, A., *The Life of Edward Irving: Fore-runner of the Charismatic Movement* (Edinburgh: Banner of Truth, 1983).

Daniélou, J., *Platonisme et Théologie mystique: doctrine spirituelle de Saint Grégoire de Nysse* (Paris: Aubier, 2nd edn, 1944).

Davidson, I. J., 'Pondering the Sinlessness of Jesus Christ: Moral Christologies and the Witness of Scripture', *IJST* 10.4 (2008), pp. 372–98.

Dawson, G. S., 'Far as the Curse is Found: The Significance of Christ's Assuming a *Fallen* Human Nature in the Torrance Theology', in *An Introduction to Torrance Theology: Discovering the Incarnate Saviour* (ed. G. S. Dawson; London: T&T Clark, 2007), pp. 55–74.

Demacopoulos, G. E., and A. Papanikolaou, 'Augustine and the Orthodox: "The West" in the East', in *Orthodox Readings of Augustine* (eds G. E. Demacopoulos and A. Papanikolaou; Crestwood, NY: St Vladimir's Seminary Press, 2008), pp. 11–40.

Dempsey, M. T. (ed.), *Trinity and Election in Contemporary Theology* (Grand Rapids: Eerdmans, 2011).

Diller, K., 'Is God *Necessarily* Who God Is? Alternatives for the Trinity and Election Debate', *SJT* 66.2 (2013), pp. 209–20.

Dods, M., *On the Incarnation of the Eternal Word* (London: R. B. Seeley & W. Burnside, 1831).

Dods, M., 'Review of New Publications', *Edinburgh Christian Instructor* (January 1830), pp. 1–96.

'Donald Macleod', n.p. Cited 13 September 2016. Online: http://www.ets.ac.uk/teaching-faculty/part-time-faculty.

Donovan, M. A., *One Right Reading?: A Guide to Irenaeus* (Collegeville, MN: The Liturgical Press, 1997).

Dorries, D. W., *Edward Irving's Incarnational Christology* (Fairfax, VA: Xulon, 2002).

Dorries, D. W., 'Nineteenth Century British Christological Controversy, Centring upon Edward Irving's Doctrine of Christ's Human Nature' (unpublished PhD thesis, University of Aberdeen, 1987).

Doyle, D. E., 'Mary, Mother of God', in *Augustine through the Ages: An Encyclopedia* (gen. ed. A. D. Fitzgerald; Grand Rapids: Eerdmans, 2009), pp. 542–5.

Dragas, G. D., '*Athanasius Contra Apollinarem* (The Questions of authorship and Christology)', *Church and Theology* 6 (1985), pp. 5–609.

Dragas, G. D., *Saint Athanasius of Alexandria: Original Research and New Perspectives* (Rollinsford, NH: Orthodox Research Institute, 2005).

Dragas, G. D., 'T.F. Torrance as a Theologian For Our Times: An Eastern Orthodox Assessment' (lecture presented at the annual meeting of the Thomas F. Torrance Theological Society, Chicago, 16 November 2012. Cited 3 August 2015. Online: http://www.youtube.com/watch?v=Frhvk-MY3dg).

Drummond, A. L., *Edward Irving and His Circle* ([London]: James Clarke, [1936]).

Duffy, S. J., 'Anthropology', in *Augustine through the Ages: An Encyclopedia* (gen. ed. A. D. Fitzgerald; Grand Rapids: Eerdmans, 2009), pp. 24–31.

Dunn, G. D., *Tertullian* (London: Routledge, 2004).

Elliott, P., 'Edward Irving: Romantic Theology in Crisis' (unpublished Ph.D. thesis, Murdoch University, 2010), p. 233. Cited 23 September 2011. Online: http://researchrepository.murdoch.edu.au/2996/.

Enns, P., *Inspiration and Incarnation: Evangelicals and the Problem of the Old Testament* (Grand Rapids: Baker, 2nd edn, 2015).

Eugenio, D. O., *Communion with God: The Trinitarian Soteriology of T. F. Torrance* (Eugene, OR: Pickwick, 2014).

Fairbairn, D., *Grace and Christology in the Early Church* (Oxford: Oxford University Press, 2003).

Farrow, D., 'T. F. Torrance and the Latin Heresy', *First Things* (December 2013), n.p. Cited 22 September 2016. Online: https://www.firstthings.com/article/2013/12/t-f-torrance-and-the-latin-heresy.

Ferguson, E., 'Tertullian', in *Early Christian Thinkers: The Lives and Legacies of Twelve Key Figures* (ed. P. Foster; Downers Grove, IL: InterVarsity, 2010), pp. 85–99.

Fergusson, D., 'Torrance as a Scottish Theologian', Participatio 2 (2010), pp. 86–7. Cited 21 January 2011. Online: http://www.tftorrance.org/journal/participatio_vol_2_2010.pdf.

Field, A., *Delivered from Evil: Jesus' Victory over Satan* (Cincinnati: Servant, 2005).

Geisler, N. L., *Christian Ethics: Options and Issues* (Grand Rapids: Baker, 1989).

Gestrich, C., *The Return of Splendor in the World: The Christian Doctrine of Sin and Forgiveness* (trans. D. W. Bloesch; Grand Rapids: Eerdmans, 1997).

Godfrey, W. R., and J. L. Boyd III (eds), *Through Christ's Word: A Festschrift for Dr. Philip E. Hughes* (Phillipsburg, NJ: Presbyterian & Reformed Publishing, 1985).

Grant, R. M., *Irenaeus of Lyons* (Florence, KY: Routledge, 1996).

Grass, T., *The Lord's Watchman* (Milton Keynes, UK: Paternoster, 2011).

Graves, D., 'Hugh Ross Mackintosh's Scottish Theology', n.p. Cited 25 March 2011. Online: http://www.christianity.com/ChurchHistory/11630761/.

Graves, M., *The Inspiration and Interpretation of Scripture: What the Early Church Can Teach Us* (Grand Rapids: Eerdmans, 2014).

Green, B., *The Soteriology of Leo the Great* (Oxford: Oxford University Press, 2008).

Green, B. G., 'Augustine', in *Shapers of Christian Orthodoxy: Engaging with Early and Medieval Theologians* (ed. B. G. Green; Downers Grove, IL: InterVarsity, 2010), pp. 235–92.

Greer, R., 'Sinned We All in Adam's Fall?', in *The Social World of the First Christians* (eds L. M. White and O. L. Yarbrough; Minneapolis: Fortress, 1995), pp. 382–94.

Grégoire de Nysse, *Discours Catéchétique* (trans. R. Winling; SC 453; Paris: Cerf, 2000).

Gregory of Nazianzus, St., *On God and Christ: The Five Theological Orations and Two Letters to Cledonius* (trans. F. Williams and L. Wickham; Crestwood, NY: St Vladimir's Seminary Press, 2002).

Gregory of Nazianzus, St., *Select Orations* (trans. M. Vinson; FC 107; Washington, DC: Catholic University of America Press, 2003).

Gregory of Nyssa, *The Letters: Introduction, Translation and Commentary* (trans. A. M. Silvas; Leiden: Brill, 2007).

Gregory of Nyssa, *The Life of Moses* (trans. A. J. Malherbe and E. Ferguson; New York: Paulist, 1978).

Grillmeier, A., *Christ in Christian Tradition* (trans. J. Bowden; 2 vols; Atlanta: John Knox, 2nd edn, 1975).

Gschwandtner, C., 'Threads of Fallenness according to the Fathers of the First Four Centuries', *European Explorations in Christian Holiness* 2 (2001), pp. 19–40.

Gunton, C., foreword to T. Weinandy, *In the Likeness of Sinful Flesh: An Essay on the Humanity of Christ* (Edinburgh: T&T Clark, 1993), pp. ix–xi.

Gunton, C., 'Two Dogmas Revisited: Edward Irving's Christology', *SJT* 41.3 (1988), pp. 359–76, repr. in C. E. Gunton, *Theology through the Theologians: Selected Essays 1972–1995* (Edinburgh: T&T Clark, 1996), pp. 151–68.

Gunton, C. E., *The Actuality of Atonement: A Study of Metaphor, Rationality and the Christian Tradition* (Grand Rapids: Eerdmans, 1989).

Gunton, C. E., *The Barth Lectures* (ed. P. H. Brazier; London: Continuum, 2007).

Gunton, C. E., *Christ and Creation* (Bletchley, UK: Paternoster, 2005).

Gunton, C. E., *The Christian Faith: An Introduction to Christian Doctrine* (Oxford: Blackwell, 2002).

Gunton, C. E., *Enlightenment and Alienation: An Essay towards a Trinitarian Theology* (Grand Rapids: Eerdmans, 1985).

Gunton, C. E., *Father, Son and Holy Spirit: Essays toward a Fully Trinitarian Theology* (London: T&T Clark, 2003).

Gunton, C. E., *The One, the Three and the Many: God, Creation and the Culture of Modernity* (Cambridge: Cambridge University Press, 1993).

Gunton, C. E., *The Promise of Trinitarian Theology* (Edinburgh: T&T Clark, 2nd edn, 1997).

Gunton, C. E., *Theology through Preaching: Sermons for Brentwood* (Edinburgh: T&T Clark, 2001).

Gunton, C. E., *Theology through the Theologians: Selected Essays 1972–1995* (Edinburgh: T&T Clark, 1996).

Gunton, C. E., *The Triune Creator: A Historical and Systematic Study* (Grand Rapids: Eerdmans, 1998).

Gunton, C. E., 'The triune God and the freedom of the creature', in *Karl Barth: Centenary Essays* (ed. S. W. Sykes; Cambridge: Cambridge University Press, 1989), pp. 46–68.

Gunton, C. E., *Yesterday and Today: A Study of Continuities in Christology* (Grand Rapids: Eerdmans, 1983).

Gwynn, D. M., *Athanasius of Alexandria: Bishop, Theologian, Ascetic, Father* (Oxford: Oxford University Press, 2012).

Habets, M., 'The Fallen Humanity of Christ: A Pneumatological Clarification of the Theology of Thomas F. Torrance', *Participatio* 5 (2015), pp. 18–44.

Habets, M., *Theology in Transposition: A Constructive Appraisal of T. F. Torrance* (Minneapolis: Fortress, 2013).

Habets, M., Theosis *in the Theology of Thomas Torrance* (Farnham, UK: Ashgate, 2009).

Hallman, J. M., 'The Seed of Fire: Divine Suffering in the Christology of Cyril of Alexandria and Nestorius of Constantinople', *JECS* 5 (1997), pp. 369–91.

Hanson, R. P. C., *The Search for the Christian Doctrine of God* (Edinburgh: T&T Clark, 1988).

Harrison, N. V., *God's Many-Splendored Image: Theological Anthropology for Christian Formation* (Grand Rapids: Baker, 2010).

Hart, T. A., 'Sinlessness and Moral Responsibility: A Problem in Christology', *SJT* 48.1 (1995), pp. 37–54.

Hardy, E. R., and C. C. Richardson (eds), *Christology of the Later Fathers* (London: SCM, 1954).

Harvey, L., 'Introduction', in *The Theology of Colin Gunton* (ed. L. Harvey; London: T&T Clark, 2010), pp. 1–7.

Hastings, W. R., '"Honouring the Spirit": Analysis and Evaluation of Jonathan Edwards' Pneumatological Doctrine of the Incarnation', *IJST* 7.3 (2005), pp. 279–99.

Hatzidakis, E., *Jesus: Fallen? The Human Nature of Christ Examined from an Eastern Orthodox Perspective* (Clearwater, FL: Orthodox Witness, 2013).

Hennessey, L. R., 'Gregory of Nyssa's Doctrine of the Resurrected Body', *StPatr* 22, pp. 28–34.

'Hilary of Poitiers, St.' *ODCC* (2005), n.p. Cited 10 December 2012. Online: http://www.oxfordreference.com/view/10.1093/acref/9780192802903.001.0001/acref-9780192802903-e-3265.

Hilary of Poitiers, St., *The Trinity* (trans. S. McKenna; FC 25; Washington, DC: Catholic University of America Press, 1954).

'History – Secretaries – Philip Edgcumbe Hughes', n.p. Cited 3 December 2011. Online: www.churchsociety.org/aboutus/History/Secretaries-Hughes.asp.

Hofer, A., *Christ in the Life and Teaching of Gregory of Nazianzus* (Oxford: Oxford University Press, 2013).

Höhne, D. A., *Spirit and Sonship: Colin Gunton's Theology of Particularity and the Holy Spirit* (Farnham, UK: Ashgate, 2010).

Holmes, M. W. (ed. and trans.), *The Apostolic Fathers: Greek Texts and English Translations* (Grand Rapids: Baker, 3rd edn, 2007).

Holmes, S. R., introduction to C. E. Gunton, *The Barth Lectures* (ed. P. H. Brazier; London: Continuum, 2007), p. 1.

Holmes, S. R., 'Obituary: The Rev Prof Colin Gunton', *The Guardian* (3 June 2003), n.p. Cited 13 September 2010. Online: www.guardian.co.uk/news/2003/jun/03/guardianobituaries.highereducation.

Holmes, S. R., 'Towards the *Analogia Personae et Relationis*', in *The Theology of Colin Gunton* (ed. L. Harvey; London: T&T Clark, 2010), pp. 32–48.

Holsinger-Friesen, T., *Irenaeus and Genesis: A Study of Competition in Early Christian Hermeneutics* (Winona Lake, IN: Eisenbrauns, 2009).

Horrocks, D., *Laws of the Spiritual Order: Innovation and Reconstruction in the Soteriology of Thomas Erskine of Linlathen* (Bletchley, UK: Paternoster, 2004).

Horton, M. S., 'Covenant, Election, and Incarnation: Evaluating Barth's Actualist Christology', in *Karl Barth and American Evangelicalism* (eds B. L. McCormack and C. B. Anderson; Grand Rapids: Eerdmans, 2011), pp. 112–47.

Houssiau, A., *La Christologie de saint Irénée* (Louvain: Publications Universitaires de Louvain & Gembloux, France: J. Duculot, 1955).

Hughes, P. E., *A Commentary on the Epistle to the Hebrews* (Grand Rapids: Eerdmans, 1977).

Hughes, P. E., 'The Creative Task of Theology', in *Creative Minds in Contemporary Theology: A Guidebook to the Principal Teachings of Karl Barth, G. C. Berkouwer, Emil Brunner, Rudolf Bultmann, Oscar Cullmann, James Denney, C. H. Dodd, Herman Dooyeweerd, P. T. Forsyth, Charles Gore, Reinhold Niebuhr, Pierre Teilhard de Chardin, and Paul Tillich* (ed. P. E. Hughes; Grand Rapids: Eerdmans, 1966), pp. 9–25.

Hughes, P. E., *Hope for a Despairing World: The Christian Answer to the Problem of Evil* (Grand Rapids: Baker, 1977).

Hughes, P. E., *Paul's Second Epistle to the Corinthians: The English Text with Introduction, Exposition and Notes* (NICNT; Grand Rapids: Eerdmans, 1962; repr. 1986).

Hughes, P. E., 'The Sovereignty of God – Has God Lost Control', n.p. Cited 3 December 2011. Online: www.the-highway.com/articleMay99.html.

Hughes, P. E., *The True Image: The Origin and Destiny of Man in Christ* (Grand Rapids: Eerdmans, 1989).

Hunsinger, G., *How to Read Karl Barth: The Shape of His Theology* (New York: Oxford University Press, 1991).

Hunsinger, G., *Reading Barth with Charity: A Hermeneutical Proposal* (Grand Rapids: Baker, 2015).

Hunsinger, G., 'Thomas F. Torrance: A Eulogy', *Participatio* 1 (2009), p. 11. Cited 18 January 2011. Online: http://www.tftorrance.org/journal/participatio_vol_1_2009.pdf.

'Irenaeus, St', *ODCC* (2005), n.p. Cited 13 March 2012. Online: http://www. oxford-christianchurch.com/entry?entry=t257.e3565.

Irenaeus, *Adversus Haereses* (ed. W. W. Harvey; 2 vols.; Cambridge: Cambridge University Press, 1857).

Irenaeus of Lyons, St., *Against the Heresies (Book 3)* (trans. and annotated by D. J. Unger, with an introduction and further revisions by I. M. C. Steenberg; New York: The Newman Press, 2012).

Irenaeus of Lyons, St., *On the Apostolic Preaching* (trans. J. Behr; Crestwood, NY: St Vladimir's Seminary Press, 1997).

Irénée de Lyon, *Contre les Hérésies Livre III Tome II: Texte et Traduction* (trans. A. Rousseau and L. Doutreleau; SC 211; Paris: Cerf, 1974).

Irénée de Lyon, *Contre les Hérésies Livre V Tome II: Texte et Traduction* (trans. A. Rousseau, L. Doutreleau, and C. Mercier; SC 153; Paris: Cerf, 1969).

Irénée de Lyon, *Démonstration de la Prédication apostolique* (trans. A. Rousseau; SC 406; Paris: Cerf, 1995).

Irving, E., *Christ's Holiness in Flesh, the Form, Fountain Head, and Assurance to Us of Holiness in Flesh* (Edinburgh: John Lindsay, 1831).

Irving, E., *The Collected Works of Edward Irving* (ed. G. Carlyle; 5 vols; London: Alexander Strahan, 1864).

Irving, E., *The Day of Pentecost, Or, The Baptism with the Holy Ghost* (London: Baldwin & Cradock, 1831).

Irving, E., 'On the Human Nature of Christ', *Morning Watch* 1 (1829), pp. 75–99.

Irving, E., 'On the True Humanity of Christ', *Morning Watch* 1 (1829), pp. 421–45.

Irving, E., *The Opinions Circulating Concerning Our Lord's Human Nature, Tried by the Westminster Confession of Faith* (Edinburgh: John Lindsay, 1830).

Irving, E., *The Orthodox and Catholic Doctrine of Our Lord's Human Nature* (London: Baldwin & Cradock, 1830).

Irving, E., with T. Carlyle, *The Doctrine Held by the Church of Scotland Concerning the Human Nature of Our Lord, As Stated in Her Standards* (Edinburgh: John Lindsay, 1830).

Jenson, R. W., *Alpha and Omega: A Study in the Theology of Karl Barth* (New York: Thomas Nelson & Sons, 1963).

Jenson, R. W., 'Colin Gunton (1940–2003)', *Theology Today* 61.1 (April 2004), p. 85.

Isbell, S., 'Dods, Marcus', in *DSCHT*, (eds D. F. Wright, N. M. de S. Cameron and D. C. Lachman; Edinburgh: T&T Clark, 1993), pp. 249–50.

Jacobs, J. W., 'The Western Roots of the Christology of St. Hilary of Poitiers. A Heritage of Textual Interpretation', *StPatr* 13 (1975), pp. 198–203.

Jennings, W. J., 'Undoing Our Abandonment: Reading Scripture through the Sinlessness of Jesus. A Meditation on Cyril of Alexandria's *On the Unity of Christ*', *Ex Auditu* 14 (1998), pp. 85–96.

Johnson, H., *The Humanity of the Savior: A Biblical and Historical Study of the Human Nature of Christ in relation to Original Sin, with Special Reference to its Soteriological Significance* (London: Epworth, 1962).

Jones, D. C., *Biblical Christian Ethics* (Grand Rapids: Baker, 1994).

Jones, P., *The Humanity of Christ: Christology in Karl Barth's* Church Dogmatics (London: T&T Clark, 2008).

Jüngel, E., *Karl Barth, a Theological Legacy* (trans. G. E. Paul; Philadelphia: Westminster, 1986).

Kang, P. S., 'The Concept of the Vicarious Humanity of Christ in the Theology of Thomas Forsyth Torrance' (unpublished PhD thesis, University of Aberdeen, 1983).

Kannengiesser, C., 'Athanasius of Alexandria and the Foundation of Traditional Christology', *TS* 34 (1973), pp. 103–13.

Kantzer, K. S., 'The Christology of Karl Barth', *Bulletin of the Evangelical Theological Society* 1.20 (1958), pp. 25–7.

Kapic, K. M., *Communion with God: The Divine and the Human in the Theology of John Owen* (Grand Rapids: Baker, 2007).

Kapic, K. M., 'The Son's Assumption of a Human Nature: A Call for Clarity', *IJST* 3.2 (2001), pp. 154–66.

Katerberg, W. H., 'Redemptive Horizons, Redemptive Violence, and Hopeful History', *Fides et Historia* 36.1 (2004), pp. 1–14.

Kearsley, R., 'The Impact of Greek Concepts of God on the Christology of Cyril of Alexandria', *Tyndale Bulletin* 43.2 (1992), pp. 307–29.

Keating, D. A., *The Appropriation of Divine Life in Cyril of Alexandria* (Oxford: Oxford University Press, repr. 2005).

Keating, D. A., 'Divinization in Cyril: The Appropriation of Divine Life', *Theology of St. Cyril*, pp. 149–87.

Keech, D., *The Anti-Pelagian Christology of Augustine of Hippo, 396–430* (Oxford: Oxford University Press, 2012).

Kelly, J. N. D., *Early Christian Doctrines* (repr., Peabody, MA: Prince Press, rev. edn, 2004).

Kimel, A., 'The God-Man Who Could Not Die', *Eclectic Orthodoxy* (31 July 2016), n.p. Cited 11 October 2016. Online: https://afkimel.wordpress.com.

Kimel, A., 'The God-Man Who Freely Wills His Passions', *Eclectic Orthodoxy* (21 July 2016), n.p. Cited 11 October 2016. Online: https://afkimel.wordpress.com.

Kimel, A., 'The Prelapsarian Christ', *Eclectic Orthodoxy* (19 July 2016), n.p. Cited 11 October 2016. Online: https://afkimel.wordpress.com.

Kimel, A., 'When Did Jesus Decide to Die?', *Eclectic Orthodoxy* (15 August 2016), n.p. Cited 11 October 2016. Online: https://afkimel.wordpress.com.

Kimel, A., 'Would Christ have died of natural causes?', *Eclectic Orthodoxy* (25 July 2016), n.p. Cited 11 October 2016. Online: https://afkimel.wordpress.com.

'King's announces the 2003 Fellows'. Cited 13 September 2010. Online: www.kcl. ac.uk/news/wmprint.php?news_id=225&year=2003.

Knight, D., 'From Metaphor to Mediation: Colin Gunton and the Concept of Mediation', *Neue Zeitschrift für Systematische Theologie und Religionsphilosophie* 43.1 (2001), pp. 118–36.

Knox, J., *The Humanity and Divinity of Christ: A Study of Pattern in Christology* (Cambridge: Cambridge University Press, 1967).

Koen, L., *The Saving Passion: Incarnational and Soteriological Thought in Cyril of Alexandria's Commentary on the Gospel according to St. John* (Stockholm: Almqvist & Wiksell, 1991).

Krötke, W., 'The Humanity of the Human Person in Karl Barth's Anthropology', in *The Cambridge Companion to Karl Barth* (ed. J. Webster; trans. P. G. Ziegler; Cambridge: Cambridge University Press, 2000), pp. 159–76.

Kunze, W. P., *The German-English Dictionary of Religion and Theology*. Cited 19 April 2014. Online: http://dictionary-theologicalgerman.org.

Ladaria, L. F., *La Cristología de Hilario de Poitiers* (Rome: Editrice Pontificia Università Gregoriana, 1989).

Ladner, G. B., 'The Philosophical Anthropology of St. Gregory of Nyssa', *Dumbarton Oaks Papers* 12 (1958), pp. 59–94. Cited 7 June 2013. Online: http://www.jstor.org/stable/1291117.

Lamberigts, M., 'A Critical Evaluation of Critiques of Augustine's View of Sexuality', in *Augustine and His Critics* (eds R. Dodaro and G. Lawless; London: Routledge, 2002).

Lampe, G. W. H., 'Christian Theology in the Patristic Period', in *A History of Christian Doctrine* (ed. H. Cunliffe-Jones; London: T&T Clark, 1978; repr. 2006), pp. 21–180.

Lane, A. N. S., 'Irenaeus on the Fall and original sin', in *Darwin, Creation and the Fall: Theological Challenges* (eds R. J. Berry and T. A. Noble; Nottingham, UK: Apollos, 2009), pp. 130–49.

Law, W., *The Spirit of Love* (London: G. Robinson & J. Roberts, 1752/1754).

Law, W., *The Spirit of Prayer* (London: M. Richardson, 1749/1750).

Lawson, J., *The Biblical Theology of Saint Irenaeus* (London: Epworth, 1948).

Lee, B.-S., *'Christ's Sinful Flesh': Edward Irving's Christological Theology within the Context of his Life and Times* (Newcastle upon Tyne, UK: Cambridge Scholars Publishing, 2013).

Lee, D. Y. T., 'The Humanity of Christ and the Church in the Teaching of Edward Irving' (unpublished PhD thesis, Brunel University and London Bible College, 2002).

Lee, K. W., *Living in Union with Christ: The Practical Theology of Thomas F. Torrance* (New York: Peter Lang, 2003).

Leithart, P. J., *Athanasius* (Grand Rapids: Baker, 2011).

'Leo I, St.' *ODCC* (2005), n.p. Cited 14 December 2012. Online: http://www.oxfordreference.com/view/10.1093/acref/9780192802903.001.0001/acref-9780192802903-e-4020.

Leo the Great, St., *Letters* (trans. E. Hunt; FC 34; New York: Fathers of the Church, 1957).

Leo the Great, St., *Sermons* (trans. J. P. Freeland and A. J. Conway; FC 93; Washington, DC: Catholic University of America Press, 1996).

Limongi, P., 'Esistenza e universalità del peccato originale nella mente di S. Ilario di Poitiers', *La Scuola Cattolica* 69 (1941), pp. 127–47.

Limongi, P., 'La trasmissione del peccato originale in S. Ilario di Poitiers', *La Scuola Cattolica* 69 (1941), pp. 260–73.

Logan, A. H. B., review of M. Vinzent, Pseudo-Athanasius: Contra Arianos IV, *JTS* (NS) 49.1 (1998), pp. 382–5.

Machida, S., 'Jesus, Man of Sin: Toward a New Christology in the Global Era', *Buddhist-Christian Studies* 19 (1999), pp. 81–91.

Mackintosh, H. R., *The Christian Experience of Forgiveness* (New York: Harper & Bros., 1927).

Mackintosh, H. R., *The Doctrine of the Person of Jesus Christ* (Edinburgh: T&T Clark, 2nd edn, 1913, 1920).

Mackintosh, H. R., *The Person of Jesus Christ* (ed. T. F. Torrance; Edinburgh: T&T Clark, new edn, 2000).

Mackintosh, H. R., *Types of Modern Theology: From Schleiermacher to Barth* (New York: Charles Scribner's Sons, [1937]).

'Mackintosh, Hugh Ross', *ODCC* (2005), n.p. Cited 28 September 2011. Online: http://www.oxford-christianchurch.com/entry?entry=t257.e4242.

Mackenzie, I. M., *Irenaeus's* Demonstration of the Apostolic Preaching: *A Theological Commentary and Translation* (Aldershot, UK: Ashgate, 2002).

Macleod, D., 'Christology', in *DSCHT* (eds D. F. Wright, N. M. de S. Cameron and D. C. Lachman; Edinburgh: T&T Clark, 1993), pp. 172–7.

Macleod, D., 'The Christology of Chalcedon', in *The Only Hope: Jesus Yesterday Today Forever* (eds M. Elliott and J. L. McPake; Fearn, UK: Mentor, 2001), pp. 77–94.

Macleod, D., '"Church" Dogmatics: Karl Barth as Ecclesial Theologian', in *Engaging with Barth: Contemporary Evangelical Critiques* (eds D. Gibson and D. Strange; Nottingham, UK: Apollos, 2008), pp. 323–45.

Macleod, D., 'Did Christ Have a Fallen Human Nature?', *The Monthly Record of the Free Church of Scotland* (March 1984), pp. 51–3.

Macleod, D., *A Faith to Live By: Studies in Christian Doctrine* (Fearn, UK: Mentor, 1998).

Macleod, D., *From Glory to Golgotha: Controversial Issues in the Life of Christ* (Fearn, UK: Christian Focus, 2002).

Macleod, D., *Jesus is Lord: Christology Yesterday and Today* (Fearn, UK: Mentor, 2000).

Macleod, D., *The Person of Christ* (Downers Grove, IL: InterVarsity, 1998).

Madigan, K., 'Ancient and High-Medieval Interpretations of Jesus in Gethsemane: Some Reflections on Tradition and Continuity in Christian Thought', *HTR* 88.1 (1995), pp. 157–73.

'Marcus Dods – Definition', in *Encyclopædia Britannica* (1911); n.p. Cited 21 November 2011. Online: www.wordiq.com/definition/Marcus_Dods.

Markus, R. A., 'Augustine's *Confessions* and the Controversy with Julian of Eclanum: Manicheism Revisited', in *Collectanea Augustiniana Mélanges T. J. van Bavel* (eds B. Bruning, M. Lamberigts and J. van Houtem; 2 vols; Leuven: Leuven University Press, 1990) 2, pp. 913–25.

Martenson, H. J., *Jacob Boehme (1575–1624): Studies in His Life and Teaching by Hans J. Martenson (1808–1884) Primate Bishop of Denmark* (trans. T. Rhys Evans; Salisbury Square, UK: Rockliff, 1949).

Martindale, T. W., 'Edward Irving's Incarnational Christology: A Theological Examination of Irving's Notion of Christ's Sinful Flesh as it relates to the Fullness of the Incarnation', n.p. Cited 15 June 2010. Online: http://www.pneumafoundation. org/resources/articles/TMartindale-EdwardIrvingIncarnationalChristology.pdf.

Mateo-Seco, L. F., *Estudios Sobre La Cristologia de San Gregorio de Nisa* (Pamplona: Ediciones Universidad de Navarra, 1978).

Mateo-Seco, L. F., Ὁ εὔκαιρος θάνατος. Consideraciones en torno a la muerte en las *Homilias al Eclesiastes* de Gregorio de Nisa', in Gregory of Nyssa, *Homilies on Ecclesiastes: an English Version with Supporting Studies: Proceedings of the Seventh International Colloquium on Gregory of Nyssa (St. Andrews, 5-10 September 1990)* (ed .S. G. Hall; Berlin: Walter de Gruyter, 1993), pp. 277–97.

McClear, E. V., 'The Fall of Man and Original Sin in the Theology of Gregory of Nyssa', *TS* 9 (1948), pp. 175–212.

McCormack, B. L., *Karl Barth's Critically Realistic Dialectical Theology: Its Genesis and Development 1909–1936* (Oxford: Clarendon, 1995).

McCormack, B. L., 'The Ontological Presuppositions of Barth's Doctrine of the Atonement', in *The Glory of the Atonement: Biblical, Historical, & Practical Perspectives: Essays in Honor of Roger Nicole* (eds C. E. Hill and F. A. James III; Downers Grove, IL: InterVarsity, 2004), pp. 346–66.

McCormack, B. L., *Orthodox and Modern: Studies in the Theology of Karl Barth* (Grand Rapids: Baker Academic, 2008).

McFarland, I. A., 'Fallen or Unfallen? Christ's Human Nature and the Ontology of Human Sinfulness', *IJST* 10.4 (2008), pp. 399–415, repr. in *idem, In Adam's Fall: A Meditation on the Christian Doctrine of Original Sin* (Chichester: Wiley-Blackwell, 2010).

McFarlane, G., *Christ and the Spirit: The Doctrine of the Incarnation according to Edward Irving* (Carlisle: Paternoster, 1996).

McFarlane, G., *Edward Irving: The Trinitarian Face of God* (Edinburgh: St. Andrews Press, 1996).

McFarlane, G., 'Profile: Colin E. Gunton', *Catalyst* 27 (2001), p. 2. Cited 13 September 2010. Online: http://catalystresources.org/issues/272mcfarlane.html.

McGrath, A. E., *T. F. Torrance: An Intellectual Biography* (Edinburgh: T&T Clark, 1999).

McGuckin, J., 'Mystery or Conundrum? The Apprehension of Christ in the Chalcedonian Definition', in *In the Shadow of the Incarnation: Essays on Jesus Christ in the Early Church in Honor of Brian E. Daley, S.J.* (ed. P. W. Martens; Notre Dame: University of Notre Dame Press, 2008), pp. 246–59.

McGuckin, J., *Saint Gregory of Nazianzus: An Intellectual Biography* (Crestwood, NY: St Vladimir's Seminary Press, 2001).

McKinion, S. A., *Words, Imagery, and the Mystery of Christ: A Reconstruction of Cyril of Alexandria's Christology* (Leiden: Brill, 2000).

McLynn, N. B., *Ambrose of Milan: Church and Court in a Christian Capital* (Berkeley: University of California Press, 1994).

McMahon, J. J., *De Christo Mediatore Doctrina Sancti Hilarii Pictavensis* (Mundelein, IL: Seminarii Sanctae Mariae ad Lacum, 1947).

McNall, J., *A Free Corrector: Colin Gunton and the Legacy of Augustine* (Minneapolis: Fortress, 2015).

Meijering, E. P., *God Being History: Studies in Patristic Philosophy* (Amsterdam: North-Holland Publishing, 1975).

Meijering, E. P., *Orthodoxy and Platonism in Athanasius: Synthesis or Antithesis?* (Leiden: Brill, 1974).

Mercer, J., 'Suffering for Our Sake: Christ and Human Destiny in Hilary of Poitiers's *De Trinitate*', *JECS* 22.4 (Winter 2014), pp. 541–68 (543). DOI:10.1353/earl.2014.0048. Cited 15 May 2015. Online: Academia.edu.

Meredith, A., *The Cappadocians* (Crestwood, NY: St Vladimir's Seminary Press, 1995).

Meredith, A., *Gregory of Nyssa* (London: Routledge, 1999).

Merrick, J., and S. M. Garrett (eds), *Five Views on Biblical Inerrancy* (Grand Rapids: Zondervan, 2013).

Migne, J.-P. (ed.), Patrologia graeca (162 vols; repr., Turnholti, Belgium: Typographi Brepols Editores Pontificii, 1966).

Migne, J.-P. (ed.), Patrologia latina (217 vols; repr., Turnholti, Belgium: Typographi Brepols Editores Pontificii, 1966).

Miles, M. R., *Augustine on the Body* (n.p.: The American Academy of Religion, 1979; repr., Eugene, OR: Wipf & Stock, 2009).

Minns, D., 'Irenaeus', in *Early Christian Thinkers: The Lives and Legacies of Twelve Key Figures* (ed. P. Foster; Downers Grove, IL: InterVarsity, 2010), pp. 36–51.

Minns, D., *Irenaeus: An Introduction* (London: T&T Clark, 2010).

Molnar, P. D., *Faith, Freedom and the Spirit: The Economic Trinity in Barth, Torrance and Contemporary Theology* (Downers Grove, IL: InterVarsity, 2015).

Moorhead, J., *Ambrose: Church and Society in the Late Roman World* (London: Longman, 1999).

Morgan, D. D., *Barth Reception in Britain* (London: T&T Clark, 2010).

Morrel, G., 'Hilary of Poitiers: A Theological Bridge Between Christian East and Christian West', *Anglican Theological Review* 44.3 (July 1962), pp. 313–16.

Mozeris, D., *Doctrina Sancti Leonis Magni de Christo Restitutore et Sacerdote* (Mundelein, IL: Seminarii Sanctae Mariae ad Lacum, 1940).

Nagasawa, M. A., 'Penal Substitution vs. Medical-Ontological Substitution: A Historical Comparison', *Nagasawa Family News Pages* (26 August 2016), pp. 1–90. Cited 27 September 2016. Online: http://nagasawafamily.org/article-penal-substitution-vs-ontological-substitution-historical-comparison.pdf.

Nantomah, J. J., 'Jesus the God-Man: The Doctrine of the Incarnation in Edward Irving in the Light of the Teaching of the Church Fathers and Its Relevance for a Twentieth Century African Context' (unpublished PhD thesis, University of Aberdeen, 1982).

Nausner, B., 'The Failure of a Laudable Project: Gunton, the Trinity, and Self-Understanding', *SJT* 62.4 (2009), pp. 403–20.

Neder, A., 'History in Harmony: Karl Barth on the Hypostatic Union', in *Karl Barth and American Evangelicalism* (eds B. L. McCormack and C. B. Anderson; Grand Rapids: Eerdmans, 2011), pp. 148–76.

Needham, N. R., 'Erskine, Thomas', in *DSCHT* (eds D. F. Wright, N. M. de S. Cameron and D. C. Lachman; Edinburgh: T&T Clark, 1993), pp. 302–3.

Needham, N. R., 'Irving, Edward', in *DSCHT* (eds D. F. Wright, N. M. de S. Cameron and D. C. Lachman; Edinburgh: T&T Clark, 1993), pp. 436–7.

Needham, N. R., *Thomas Erskine of Linlathen: His Life and Theology 1788–1837* (Edinburgh: Rutherford House, 1990).

Neil, B., *Leo the Great* (London: Routledge, 2009).

Nestorius, *The Bazaar of Heracleides* (ed. and trans. G. R. Driver and L. Hodgson; repr. New York: AMS Press, 1978).

Noble, T. A., *Holy Trinity: Holy People. The Theology of Christian Perfecting* (Eugene, OR: Cascade, 2013).

Noble, T. A., Personal communication (12 April 2013).

Noble, T. A., '*Prolegomena* for a Conference on Original Sin', *European Explorations in Christian Holiness* 2 (2001), pp. 10–17.

Norris, F. W., *Gregory Nazianzen's Doctrine of Jesus Christ* (New Haven, CT: Yale, 1971).

Norris, F. W., L. Wickham and F. Williams, *Faith Gives Fullness to Reasoning: The Five Theological Orations of Gregory of Nazianzen* (Leiden: Brill, 1991).

Norris Jr., R. A., *Manhood and Christ: A Study in the Christology of Theodore of Mopsuestia* (Oxford: Clarendon, 1963).

Novatian, *De trinitate* 28. Cited 18 November 2013. Online: http://www.documentacatholicaomnia.eu/04z/z_0251-0258__Novatianus__De_Trinitate__LT.doc.html.

O'Donnell, J. J., 'Augustine the African', n.p. Cited 11 January 2013. Online: http://www9.georgetown.edu/faculty/jod/augustine/.

O'Keefe, J. J., 'Impassible Suffering? Divine Passion and Fifth-Century Christology', *TS* 58 (1997), pp. 39–60.

O'Keefe, J. J., 'The Persistence of Decay: Bodily Disintegration and Cyrillian Christology', in *In the Shadow of the Incarnation: Essays on Jesus Christ in the Early*

Church in Honor of Brian E. Daley, S.J. (ed. P. W. Martens; Notre Dame: University of Notre Dame Press, 2008), pp. 228–45.

Oliphant, M., *The Life of Edward Irving* (2 vols; London: Hurst & Blackett, 2nd edn., rev., 1862).

Orbe, A., *Espiritualidad de San Ireneo* (Rome: Editrice Pontificia Università Gregoriana, 1989).

Orbe, A., *Teología de san Ireneo* (4 vols.; Madrid: Biblioteca de Autores Cristianos, 1985, 1987, 1988, 1996).

'Original Sin', *ODCC* (2005), n.p. Cited 18 May 2012. Online: http://www.oxford-christianchurch.com/entry?entry=t257.e5017.

Osborn, E., *Irenaeus of Lyons* (Cambridge: Cambridge University Press, 2001).

Osborn, E., 'Irenaeus: Rocks in the Road', *The Expository Times* 114.8 (2003), pp. 255–8.

Osborn, E., *Tertullian, First Theologian of the West* (Cambridge: Cambridge University Press, 1997, 2001).

Oswalt, J. N., *The Bible among the Myths: Unique Revelation or Just Ancient Literature?* (Grand Rapids: Zondervan, 2009).

Paget, M., 'Christology and Original Sin: Charles Hodge and Edward Irving Compared', *Churchman* 121.3 (2007), pp. 229–48.

Pannenberg, W., *Jesus – God and Man* (London: SCM, 1968, 2002).

Papandrea, J. L., 'The Rule of Truth: A New Translation of the *De Trinitate* of Novatian', in *idem*, *The Trinitarian Theology of Novatian of Rome: A Study in Third Century Orthodoxy* [n.p.: Edwin Mellen Press, 2008], [p. 245]. Cited 18 November 2013. Online: http://novatianus.info.

Parvis, P., 'Who Was Irenaeus? An Introduction to the Man and His Work', in *Irenaeus: Life, Scripture, Legacy* (eds S. Parvis and P. Foster; Minneapolis: Fortress, 2012), pp. 13–24.

Paton, J., 'Human Nature in the Light of the Incarnation', *European Explorations in Christian Holiness* 2 (2001), pp. 151–65.

Pelikan, J., *Christianity and Classical Culture: The Metamorphosis of Natural Theology in the Christian Encounter with Hellenism* (New Haven, CT: Yale University Press, 1993).

Perry, T., *Mary for Evangelicals: Toward an Understanding of the Mother of Our Lord* (Downers Grove, IL: InterVarsity, 2006).

Pettersen, A., *Athanasius* (Harrisburg, PA: Morehouse, 1995).

Plantinga, Jr., C., *Not the Way It's Supposed to Be: A Breviary of Sin* (Grand Rapids: Eerdmans, 1995).

Pontifical Biblical Commission, The Inspiration and Truth of Sacred Scripture: The Word That Comes from God and Speaks of God for the Salvation of the World (Collegeville, MN: Liturgical Press, 2014).

Power, K. E., 'Ambrose of Milan: Keeper of the Boundaries', *Theology Today* 55.1 (1998), pp. 15–34 (16–20).

Pratz, G., 'The Relationship between Incarnation and Atonement in the Theology of Thomas F. Torrance', *Journal for Christian Theological Research* 3.2 (1998), n.p. Cited 15 March 2011. Online: http://www2.luthersem.edu/ctrf/jctr/Vol03/Pratz.htm.

Purves, A., *Exploring Christology and Atonement: Conversations with John McLeod Campbell, H. R. Mackintosh and T. F. Torrance* (Downers Grove, IL: InterVarsity, 2015).

Purves, J., 'The Interaction of Christology and Pneumatology in the Soteriology of Edward Irving', *Pneuma* 14.1 (1992), pp. 81–90.

Radcliff, J., 'T.F. Torrance in the light of Stephen Holmes' Critique of Contemporary Trinitarian Thought', *Evangelical Quarterly* 86.1 (2014), pp. 21–38.

Radcliff, J. R., *Thomas F. Torrance and the Church Fathers: A Reformed, Evangelical, and Ecumenical Reconstruction of the Patristic Tradition* (Eugene, OR: Pickwick, 2014).

Rainey, D., 'Edward Irving and the Doctrine of the Humanity of Christ: "The Method Is By Taking Up the Fallen Humanity"' (paper presented at the annual meeting of the Wesleyan Theological Society, Anderson, Ind., 6 March 2009).

Ramm, B., *Offense to Reason: The Theology of Sin* (San Francisco: Harper & Row, 1985).

Ramsey, B., *Ambrose* (London: Routledge, 1997).

Rankin, W. D., 'Carnal Union with Christ in the Theology of T.F. Torrance' (unpublished PhD thesis, University of Edinburgh, 1997).

Raven, C. E., *Apollinarianism: An Essay on the Christology of the Early Church* (Cambridge: Cambridge University Press, 1923).

Redman Jr., R. R., 'H. R. Mackintosh's Contribution to Christology and Soteriology in the Twentieth Century', *SJT* 41.4 (1988), pp. 517–34.

Redman Jr., R. R., *Reformulating Reformed Theology: Jesus Christ in the Theology of Hugh Ross Mackintosh* (Lanham, MD: University Press of America, 1997).

Redman, R., 'Mackintosh, Torrance and Reformulation of Reformed Theology in Scotland', Participatio 2 (2010), pp. 64–76. Cited 9 December 2011. Online: www.tftorrance.org/journal/participatio_vol_2_2010.pdf.

Rigby, P., 'Original Sin', in *Augustine through the Ages: An Encyclopedia* (gen. ed. A. D. Fitzgerald; Grand Rapids: Eerdmans, 2009), pp. 607–14.

Riggan, G. A., *Original Sin in the Thought of Augustine* (Ann Arbor, MI: University Microfilms, 1970).

Roberts, A., and J. Donaldson (eds), *The Ante-Nicene Fathers* (10 vols; repr., Peabody, MA: Hendrickson, 1994; electronic version: *AGES Digital Library* version 8, 2000).

Rogers, K. A., 'Fall', in *Augustine through the Ages: An Encyclopedia* (gen. ed. A. D. Fitzgerald; Grand Rapids: Eerdmans, 2009), pp. 351–2.

Roldanus, J., *Le Christ et l'Homme dans la Théologie d'Athanase d'Alexandrie: Étude de la Conjonction de sa Conception de l'Homme avec sa Christologie* (Leiden: Brill, corrected edn, 1977).

Romanides, J. S., response to V. C. Samuel, 'One Incarnate Nature of God the Word', *Greek Orthodox Theological Review* 10.2 (Winter 1964–5), pp. 52–3.

Rondet, H., *Original Sin: The Patristic and Theological Background* (trans. C. Finegan; Staten Island, NY: Alba House, 1972).

Ruether, R. R., *Gregory of Nazianzus: Rhetor and Philosopher* (Oxford: Clarendon, 1969).

Russell, N., *Cyril of Alexandria* (London: Routledge, 2000).

Russell, N., *The Doctrine of Deification in the Greek Patristic Tradition* (Oxford: Oxford University Press, 2004).

Saenz, A., *San Leon Magno y los Misterios de Cristo* (Paraná, Argentina: Mikael, 1984).

Schaff, P., and H. Wace (eds), *The Nicene and Post-Nicene Fathers* (2 series; 28 vols; repr., Peabody, MA: Hendrickson, 1994; electronic version: *AGES Digital Library* version 8, 2000).

Scharlemann, M. H., '"In the Likeness of Sinful Flesh"', *Concordia Theological Monthly* 32.3 (March 1961), pp. 133–8.

Schwöbel, C., foreword to C. E. Gunton, *The Barth Lectures* (ed. P. H. Brazier; London: Continuum, 2007), pp. xx–xxi.

Schwöbel, C., 'The Shape of Colin Gunton's Theology. On the Way towards a Fully Trinitarian Theology', in *The Theology of Colin Gunton* (ed. L. Harvey; London: T&T Clark, 2010), pp. 182–208.

Secord, J., 'The Cultural Geography of a Greek Christian: Irenaeus from Smyrna to Lyons', in *Irenaeus: Life, Scripture, Legacy* (eds S. Parvis and P. Foster; Minneapolis: Fortress, 2012), pp. 25–33.

Shuster, M., *The Fall and Sin: What We Have Become as Sinners* (Grand Rapids: Eerdmans, 2004).

Shuster, M., 'The Temptation, Sinlessness, and Sympathy of Jesus: Another Look at the Dilemma of Hebrews 4:15', in *Perspectives on Christology: Essays in Honor of Paul K. Jewett* (eds M. Shuster and R. Muller; Grand Rapids: Zondervan, 1991), pp. 197–209.

Simpson, D. P., *Cassell's Latin and English Dictionary* (Hoboken, NJ: Wiley, 2002).

Smith, D. A., 'Irenaeus and the Baptism of Jesus', *TS* 58 (1997), pp. 618–42.

Smith, D. L., *With Willful Intent: A Theology of Sin* (Wheaton, IL: Victor, 1994).

Smith, J. W., *Christian Grace and Pagan Virtue: The Theological Foundation of Ambrose's Ethics* (Oxford: Oxford University Press, 2011).

Smith, J. W., *Passion and Paradise: Human and Divine Emotion in the Thought of Gregory of Nyssa* (New York: Crossroad, 2004).

Sonderegger, K., *Systematic Theology Volume 1, The Doctrine of God* (Minneapolis: Fortress, 2015).

Spence, A., 'The Person as Willing Agent: Classifying Gunton's Christology', in *The Theology of Colin Gunton* (ed. L. Harvey; London: T&T Clark, 2010), pp. 49–64.

Srawley, J. H., 'St Gregory of Nyssa on the Sinlessness of Christ', *JTS* 7.27 (1906), pp. 434–41.

Stead, C., review of C. Kannengiesser, Athanase d'Alexandrie évêque et écrivain, *JTS* (NS) 36.1 (1985), pp. 220–9.

Steenberg, I. M. C., *Of God and Man: Theology as Anthropology from Irenaeus to Athanasius* (London: T&T Clark, 2009).

Steenberg, I. M. C., 'Tracing the Irenaean Legacy', in *Irenaeus: Life, Scripture, Legacy* (eds S. Parvis and P. Foster; Minneapolis: Fortress, 2012), pp. 199–211.

Stendahl, K., 'The Apostle Paul and the Introspective Conscience of the West', in *idem, Paul Among Jews and Gentiles* (Philadelphia: Fortress, 1976), pp. 78–96.

Stevenson, P. K., *God in Our Nature: The Incarnational Theology of John McLeod Campbell* (Bletchley, UK: Paternoster, 2004).

Strachan, C. G., *The Pentecostal Theology of Edward Irving* (London: Darton, Longman & Todd, 1973).

Stramara Jr., D. F., 'The Sinlessness and Moral Integrity of Jesus according to Gregory of Nyssa', *Patristic and Byzantine Review* 24.1–3 (2006), pp. 67–83.

Sturch, R. L., *The Word and the Christ: An Essay in Analytic Christology* (Oxford: Clarendon, 1991).

Sumner, D., 'Fallenness and *anhypostasis*: A Way Forward in the Debate over Christ's Humanity', *SJT* 67 (2014), pp. 195–212. Cited 19 June 2014. Online: http://dx.doi.org/10.1017/S0036930614000064.

Sumner, D., 'Jesus Christ's Fallen and Gifted Nature As The Pattern For Christian Sanctification' (paper presented at the Edinburgh Dogmatics Conference, University of Edinburgh, 2011).

Sykes, S. W., 'The Theology of the Humanity of Christ', in *Christ Faith and History* (eds S. W. Sykes and J. P. Clayton; Cambridge: Cambridge University Press, 1972), pp. 53–72.

Tennant, F. R., *The Sources of the Doctrines of the Fall and Original Sin* (Cambridge: Cambridge University Press, 1903).

Tertullian, *Adversus Marcionem* (ed. and trans. E. Evans; 2 vols.; Oxford Early Christian Texts; London: Clarendon, 1972).

Tertullian, *Tertullian's Treatise on the Incarnation* (ed. and trans. E. Evans; London: SPCK, 1956).

TeSelle, E., 'Pelagius, Pelagianism', in *Augustine through the Ages: An Encyclopedia* (gen. ed. A. D. Fitzgerald; Grand Rapids: Eerdmans, 2009), pp. 633–40.

Teske, R. J., *Augustine of Hippo: Philosopher, Exegete, and Theologian: A Second Collection of Essays* (Milwaukee: Marquette University Press, 2009).

Thompson, T. R., 'Nineteenth-Century Kenotic Christology: The Waxing, Waning, and Weighing of a Quest for a Coherent Orthodoxy', in *Exploring Kenotic Christology: The Self-Emptying of God* (ed. C. S. Evans; Oxford: Oxford University Press, 2006), pp. 74–111.

'Tome of Leo', in *ODCC* (2005), n.p. Cited 14 December 2012. Online: http://www.oxfordreference. com/view/10.1093/acref/9780192802903.001.0001/acref-9780192802903-e-6907.

Torrance, A. J., 'Can the Truth Be Learned? Redressing the "Theologistic Fallacy" in Modern Biblical Scholarship', in *Scripture's Doctrine and Theology's Bible: How the New Testament Shapes Christian Dogmatics* (eds M. Bockmuehl and A. J. Torrance; Grand Rapids: Baker, 2008), pp. 143–63.

Torrance, J. B., 'The Vicarious Humanity of Christ', in *The Incarnation: Ecumenical Studies in the Nicene-Constantinopolitan Creed A.D. 381* (ed. T. F. Torrance; Edinburgh: Handsel, 1981), pp. 127–47.

Torrance, T. F., 'Appreciation: Hugh Ross Mackintosh Theologian of the Cross', in H. R. Mackintosh, *The Person of Jesus Christ* (ed. T. F. Torrance; Edinburgh: T&T Clark, new edn, 2000), pp. 71–94.

Torrance, T. F., *Atonement: The Person and Work of Christ* (ed. R. T. Walker; Downers Grove, IL: InterVarsity, 2009).

Torrance, T. F., 'The Atonement. The Singularity of Christ and the Finality of the Cross: The Atonement and the Moral Order', in *Universalism and the Doctrine of Hell* (ed. N. M. de S. Cameron; Carlisle: Paternoster, 1992), pp. 223–56.

Torrance, T. F., *The Christian Doctrine of God: One Being Three Persons* (Edinburgh: T&T Clark, 1996).

Torrance, T. F., *The Christian Frame of Mind* (Edinburgh: Handsel, 1985).

Torrance, T. F., foreword to H. R. Mackintosh, *The Person of Jesus Christ* (ed. T. F. Torrance; Edinburgh: T&T Clark, new edn, 2000), pp. vii–ix.

Torrance, T. F., 'Christ's human nature', *The Monthly Record of the Free Church of Scotland* (May 1984), p. 114.

Torrance, T. F., *Divine Meaning: Studies in Patristic Hermeneutics* (Edinburgh: T&T Clark, 1995).

Torrance, T. F., *The Doctrine of Jesus Christ* (Eugene, OR: Wipf & Stock, 2002).

Torrance, T. F., *Incarnation: The Person and Life of Christ* (ed. R. T. Walker; Downers Grove, IL: InterVarsity, 2008).

Torrance, T. F., *Karl Barth, Biblical and Evangelical Theologian* (Edinburgh: T&T Clark, 1990).

Torrance, T. F., *The Mediation of Christ* (Colorado Springs, CO: Helmers & Howard, 2nd edn, 1992).

Torrance, T. F., *Preaching Christ Today: The Gospel and Scientific Thinking* (Grand Rapids: Eerdmans, 1994).

Torrance, T. F., *The School of Faith: The Catechisms of the Reformed Church* (New York: Harper & Bros., 1959).

Torrance, T. F., *Scottish Theology: From John Knox to John McLeod Campbell* (Edinburgh: T&T Clark, 1996).

Torrance, T. F., *Theology in Reconciliation: Essays towards Evangelical and Catholic Unity in East and West* (London: Geoffrey Chapman, 1975).

Torrance, T. F., *Theology in Reconstruction* (Grand Rapids: Eerdmans, 1965).

Torrance, T. F., *The Trinitarian Faith: The Evangelical Theology of the Ancient Catholic Church* (Edinburgh: T&T Clark, 1988).

Tuttle, G. M., *John McLeod Campbell on Christian Atonement: So Rich a Soil* (Edinburgh: Handsel, 1986).

Van Kuiken, E. J., 'Edward Irving on Christ's Sinful Flesh and Sanctifying Spirit: A Wesleyan Appraisal', *Wesleyan Theological Journal* 49.1 (2014), pp. 175–85.

Van Oort, J., 'Augustine on Sexual Concupiscence and Original Sin', *StPatr* 22 (1989), pp. 382–6.

Van Winden, J. C. M., review of Saint Ambrose, *Theological and Dogmatic Works*, *VC* 17.4, pp. 241–3.

Viciano, A., *Cristo Salvador y Liberador del Hombre: Estudio sobre la Soteriología de Tertuliano* (Pamplona: Ediciones Universidad de Navarra, 1986).

Vogel, J., 'The Haste of Sin, the Slowness of Salvation: An Interpretation of Irenaeus on the Fall and Redemption', *Anglican Theological Review* 89.3 (2007), pp. 443–59.

Ward, W. R., *Early Evangelicalism: A Global Intellectual History, 1670–1789* (Cambridge: Cambridge University Press, 2006).

Webster, J., *Barth* (London: Continuum, 2000).

Webster, J., *Barth's Moral Theology: Human Action in Barth's Thought* (Grand Rapids: Eerdmans, 1998).

Webster, J., 'Gunton and Barth', *The Theology of Colin Gunton* (ed. L. Harvey; London: T&T Clark, 2010), pp. 17–31.

Weedman, M., *The Trinitarian Theology of Hilary of Poitiers* (Leiden: Brill, 2007).

Weinandy, T. G., *Athanasius: A Theological Introduction* (Farnham, UK: Ashgate, 2007).

Weinandy, T. G., 'Cyril and the Mystery of the Incarnation', in *The Theology of St. Cyril of Alexandria: A Critical Appreciation* (ed. T. G. Weinandy and D. A. Keating; London: T&T Clark, 2003), pp. 23–54.

Weinandy, T. G., *In the Likeness of Sinful Flesh: An Essay on the Humanity of Christ* (Edinburgh: T&T Clark, 1993).

Welch, L. J., *Christology and Eucharist in the Early Thought of Cyril of Alexandria* (San Francisco: Catholic Scholars Press, 1994).

Wesley, C., 'Hark! The Herald Angels Sing', *The Cyber Hymnal* #2384, n.p. Cited 22 September 2016. Online: www.hymnary.org.

Wesley, C., 'Let Earth and Heaven Combine', *The Cyber Hymnal* #3632, n.p. Cited 22 September 2016. Online: www.hymnary.org.

Wetzel, J., 'Sin', in *Augustine through the Ages: An Encyclopedia* (gen. ed. A. D. Fitzgerald; Grand Rapids: Eerdmans, 2009), pp. 800–2.

Wiles, M. F., 'Does Christology Rest on a Mistake?', in *Christ Faith and History* (eds S. W. Sykes and J. P. Clayton; Cambridge: Cambridge University Press, 1972), pp. 3–12.

Wiles, M. F., 'Soteriological Arguments in the Fathers', *StPatr* 9 (1966), pp. 321–5.

Wilken, R. L., *Judaism and the Early Christian Mind: A Study of Cyril of Alexandria's Exegesis and Theology* (New Haven, CT: Yale University Press, 1971).

Wilks, W., *Edward Irving: An Ecclesiastical and Literary Biography* (London: William Freeman, 1854).

Williams, N. P., *The Ideas of the Fall and of Original Sin: A Historical and Critical Study* (London: Longmans, Green & Co., 1927).

Williams, R., '"Tempted as we are": Christology and the Analysis of the Passions', *StPatr* 44 (2010), pp. 391–404.

Williams, R. D., 'Augustine's Christology: Its Spirituality and Rhetoric', in *In the Shadow of the Incarnation: Essays on Jesus Christ in the Early Church in Honor of Brian E. Daley, S.J.* (ed. P. W. Martens; Notre Dame: University of Notre Dame Press, 2008), pp. 176–89.

Wingren, G., *Man and the Incarnation: A Study in the Biblical Theology of Irenaeus* (trans. R. Mackenzie; Philadelphia: Muhlenberg Press, 1959).

Winslow, D. F., *The Dynamics of Salvation: A Study in Gregory of Nazianzus* (Cambridge, MA: Philadelphia Patristic Foundation, 1979).

Wright, N. T., *After You Believe: Why Christian Character Matters* (New York: HarperOne, 2010).

Wright, N. T., *Scripture and the Authority of God: How to Read the Bible Today* (New York: HarperOne, rev. and expanded edn, 2013).

Wynne, J., 'The Livingness of God; or, the Place of Substance and Dynamism in a Theology of the Divine Perfections', *IJST* 13.2 (2011), pp. 190–203.

Young, F., '*Theotokos*: Mary and the Pattern of Fall and Redemption in the Theology of Cyril of Alexandria', *Theology of St. Cyril*, pp. 55–74.

Young, F. M., *From Nicaea to Chalcedon: A Guide to the Literature and its Background* (Philadelphia: Fortress, 1983).

Zachhuber, J., *Human Nature in Gregory of Nyssa: Philosophical Background and Theological Significance* (Leiden: Brill, 2000).

Zathureczky, K., 'Jesus' Impeccability: Beyond Ontological Sinlessness', *Science et Esprit* 60/1 (2008), pp. 55–71.

'ἀνεπίδεκτος', *A Patristic Greek Lexicon* (ed. G. W. H. Lampe; Oxford: Clarendon, 1961), pp. 135–6.

'πάθος', *PGL*, pp. 992–5.

'προσπίπτω', *A Greek-English Lexicon* (eds H. G. Liddell and R. Scott; Oxford: Clarendon, 9th edn, repr. 1976), p. 1523.

'προσπίπτω', *PGL*, p. 1181.

'φθορά', *PGL*, pp. 1474–5.

Index

Made in United States
Orlando, FL
12 October 2022

23289103R00128